INTERNATIONAL FINANCE

INTERNATIONAL FINANCE
Theory and Policy

Sarah Cox
Albert Allen

Kruger Brentt
Publishers
2023

Kruger Brentt Publishers UK. LTD.
Company Number 9728962

Regd. Office: 68 St Margarets Road, Edgware, Middlesex HA8 9UU

ISBN: 978-1-78715-151-2

For information on all our publications visit our website at http://krugerbrentt.com/

PREFACE

Most countries of the world which raced to the path of economic and industrial development had to depend on foreign capital to some extent. Under developed countries like India have to depend on foreign capital for financing their development programmes as they suffer from low level of income and low level of capital accumulation. The degree of dependence, however, varies from country to country depending upon its level of mobilization of domestic capital, technology development, attitude of the government, etc. But the fact cannot be denied that foreign capital contributes in many ways to the process of rapid economic growth and industrialization. Like international trade and business, international finance exists due to the fact that economic activities of businesses, governments, and organizations get affected by the existence of nations. It is a known fact that countries often borrow and lend from each other. In such trades, many countries use their own currencies. Therefore, we must understand how the currencies compare with each other.

We live in a globalized world. Every country is dependent on another country in some other means. Developed countries look for the cheap workforce from developing countries and developing countries look for services and products from developing countries. When a trade happened between two countries as in this case, there are many factors that come into the picture and have to be considered while the execution of the trade so that no violation of regulation happens. For any economy international finance is a significant critical factor, the local government should accordingly execute the policies so that the local players are not facing severe competition from the non-local players. International trade is one of the most important factors of growth and prosperity of participating economies. Its importance has got magnified many times due to globalization. Moreover, the resurgence of the US from being the biggest international creditor to become the largest international debtor is an important issue. These issues are a part of international macroeconomics, which is popularly known as international finance.

The present book contains 13 -chapters namely Introductory finance issues: current patterns, past history, and international institutions, national income and the balance of payments accounts, the whole truth about trade imbalances, foreign exchange markets and rates of return, interest rate parity, purchasing power parity, interest rate determination, national output determination, the aa-dd model, policy effects with floating exchange rates, fixed exchange rates, policy effects with fixed exchange rates, fixed versus floating exchange rates. It provides engaging, balanced coverage of the key concepts and practical applications of the discipline. An intuitive introduction to international finance theory is followed by detailed coverage of policy applications. The text presents a balance of theoretical and practical coverage of international finance. The book will be of interest to students, teachers and professional engaged in the field of economics, finance, management, commerce and marketing.

We are grateful to all those persons as well as various books, manuals, periodicals, magazines, journals etc. that helped in the preparation of this book. In spite of the best efforts, it is possible that some errors may have occurred into the compilation and editing of the book. Further queries, constructive suggestions and criticisms for the improvement of the book are always welcomed and shall be thankfully acknowledged.

Sarah Cox

Albert Allen

CONTENTS

CHAPTER

1 FINANCE ISSUES: AN INTRODUCTION

INTRODUCTION: AN OVERVIEW

Economics is a social science whose purpose is to understand the workings of the real-world economy. An economy is something that no one person can observe in its entirety. We are all a part of the economy, we all buy and sell things daily, but we cannot observe all parts and aspects of an economy at any one time.

For this reason, economists build mathematical models, or theories, meant to describe different aspects of the real world. For some students, economics seems to be all about these models and theories, these abstract equations and diagrams. However, in actuality, economics is about the real world, the world we all live in.

For this reason, it is important in any economics course to describe the conditions in the real world before diving into the theory intended to explain them. In this case, in a textbook about international finance, it is very useful for a student to know some of the values of important macroeconomic variables, the trends in these variables over time, and the policy issues and controversies surrounding them.

This first chapter provides an overview of the real world with respect to international finance. It explains not only how things look now but also where we have been and why things changed along the way. It describes current economic conditions and past trends with respect to the most critical international macroeconomic indicators. In particular, it compares the most recent worldwide economic recession with past business cycle activity to put our current situation into perspective. The chapter also discusses important institutions and explains why they have been created.

With this overview about international finance in the real world in mind, a student can better understand why the theories and models in the later chapters are being developed. This chapter lays the groundwork for everything else that follows.

1.1 INTERNATIONAL ECONOMICS AND THE GLOBAL ECONOMY

International economics is growing in importance as a field of study because of the rapid integration of international economic markets. Increasingly, businesses, consumers, and governments realize that their lives are affected not only by what goes on in their own town, state, or country but also by what is happening around the world. Consumers can walk into their local shops today and buy goods and services from all over the world. Local businesses must compete with these foreign products. However, many of these same businesses also have new opportunities to expand their markets by selling to a multitude of consumers in other countries. The advance of telecommunications is also rapidly reducing the cost of providing services internationally, while the Internet will assuredly change the nature of many products and services as it expands markets even further.

One simple way to see the rising importance of international economics is to look at the growth of exports in the world during the past fifty or more years. Figure 1.1 "World Exports, 1948–2008 (in Billions of U.S. Dollars)" shows the overall annual exports measured in billions of U.S. dollars from 1948 to 2008. Recognizing that one country's exports are another country's imports, one can see the exponential growth in outflows and inflows during the past fifty years.

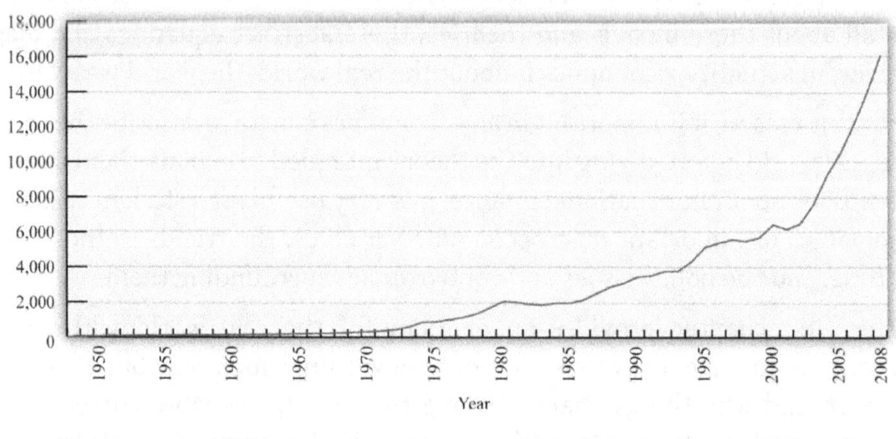

Figure 1.1 World Exports, 1948–2008 (in Billions of U.S. Dollars)

Source: World Trade Organization, International trade and tariff data, http://www.wto.org/english/res_e/statis_e/statis_e.htm.

However, rapid growth in the value of exports does not necessarily indicate that trade is becoming more important. A better method is to look at the share of traded goods in relation to the size of the world economy. Figure 1.2 "World Exports, 1970–2008 (Percentage of World GDP)" shows world exports as a percentage of the world gross domestic product (GDP) for the years 1970 to 2008. It shows a steady increase in trade as a share of the size of the world economy. World exports grew from just over

10 percent of the GDP in 1970 to over 30 percent by 2008. Thus trade is not only rising rapidly in absolute terms; it is becoming relatively more important too.

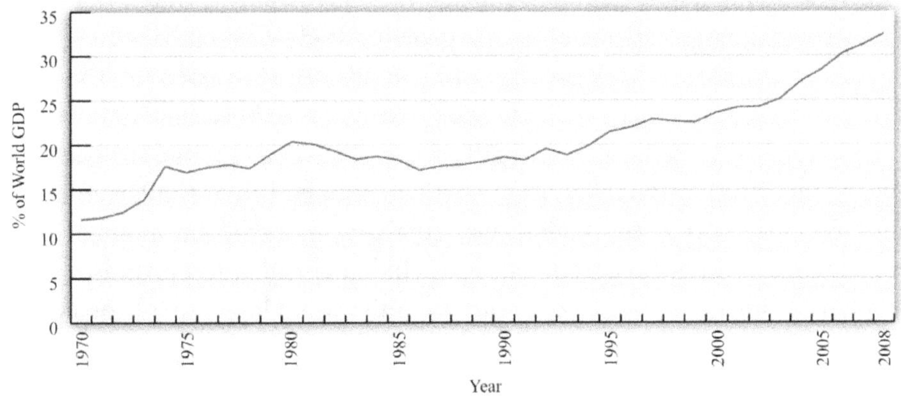

Figure 1.2 World Exports, 1970–2008 (Percentage of World GDP)

Source: IMF World Economic Outlook Database, http://www.imf.org/external/pubs/ft/weo/2009/02/weodata/index.aspx.

One other indicator of world interconnectedness can be seen in changes in the amount of foreign direct investment (FDI). FDI is foreign ownership of productive activities and thus is another way in which foreign economic influence can affect a country. Figure 1.3 "World Inward FDI Stocks, 1980–2007 (Percentage of World GDP)" shows the stock, or the sum total value, of FDI around the world taken as a percentage of the world GDP between 1980 and 2007. It gives an indication of the importance of foreign ownership and influence around the world. As can be seen, the share of FDI has grown dramatically from around 5 percent of the world GDP in 1980 to over 25 percent of the GDP just twenty-five years later.

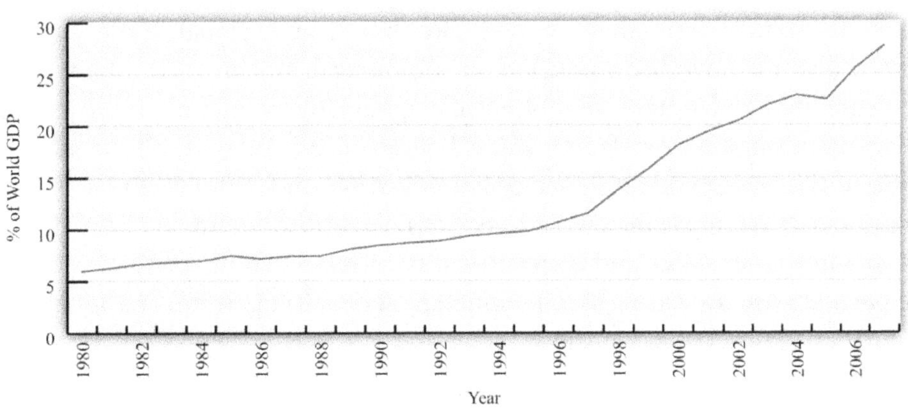

Figure 1.3 World Inward FDI Stocks, 1980–2007 (Percentage of World GDP)

Source: IMF World Economic Outlook Database, http://www.imf.org/external/pubs/ft/weo/2009/02/weodata/index.aspx; UNCTAD, FDI Statistics: Division on Investment and Enterprise, http://www.unctad.org/Templates/Page.asp?intItemID=4979&lang=1.

The growth of international trade and investment has been stimulated partly by the steady decline of trade barriers since the Great Depression of the 1930s. In the post-World War II era, the General Agreement on Tariffs and Trade, or GATT, prompted regular negotiations among a growing body of members to reciprocally reduce tariffs (import taxes) on imported goods. During each of these regular negotiations (eight of these rounds were completed between 1948 and 1994), countries promised to reduce their tariffs on imports in exchange for concessions—that means tariff reductions—by other GATT members. When the Uruguay Round, the most recently completed round, was finalized in 1994, the member countries succeeded in extending the agreement to include liberalization promises in a much larger sphere of influence. Now countries not only would lower tariffs on goods trade but also would begin to liberalize the agriculture and services markets. They would eliminate the many quota systems—like the multifiber agreement in clothing—that had sprouted up in previous decades. And they would agree to adhere to certain minimum standards to protect intellectual property rights such as patents, trademarks, and copyrights. The World Trade Organization (WTO) was created to manage this system of new agreements, to provide a forum for regular discussion of trade matters, and to implement a well-defined process for settling trade disputes that might arise among countries.

As of 2009, 153 countries were members of the WTO "trade liberalization club," and many more countries were still negotiating entry. As the club grows to include more members—and if the latest round of trade liberalization talks, called the Doha Round, concludes with an agreement—world markets will become increasingly open to trade and investment.Note that the Doha Round of discussions was begun in 2001 and remains uncompleted as of 2009.

Another international push for trade liberalization has come in the form of regional free trade agreements. Over two hundred regional trade agreements around the world have been notified, or announced, to the WTO. Many countries have negotiated these agreements with neighboring countries or major trading partners to promote even faster trade liberalization. In part, these have arisen because of the slow, plodding pace of liberalization under the GATT/WTO. In part, the regional trade agreements have occurred because countries have wished to promote interdependence and connectedness with important economic or strategic trade partners. In any case, the phenomenon serves to open international markets even further than achieved in the WTO.

These changes in economic patterns and the trend toward ever-increasing openness are an important aspect of the more exhaustive phenomenon known as globalization. Globalization more formally refers to the economic, social, cultural, or environmental changes that tend to interconnect peoples around the world. Since the economic aspects of globalization are certainly the most pervasive of these changes, it is increasingly important to understand the implications of a global marketplace on consumers, businesses, and governments. That is where the study of international economics begins.

International Economics

International economics is a field of study that assesses the implications of international trade, international investment, and international borrowing and lending. There are two broad subfields within the discipline: international trade and international finance.

International trade is a field in economics that applies microeconomic models to help understand the international economy. Its content includes basic supply-and-demand analysis of international markets; firm and consumer behavior; perfectly competitive, oligopolistic, and monopolistic market structures; and the effects of market distortions. The typical course describes economic relationships among consumers, firms, factory owners, and the government.

The objective of an international trade course is to understand the effects of international trade on individuals and businesses and the effects of changes in trade policies and other economic conditions. The course develops arguments that support a free trade policy as well as arguments that support various types of protectionist policies. By the end of the course, students should better understand the centuries-old controversy between free trade and protectionism.

International finance applies macroeconomic models to help understand the international economy. Its focus is on the interrelationships among aggregate economic variables such as GDP, unemployment rates, inflation rates, trade balances, exchange rates, interest rates, and so on. This field expands basic macroeconomics to include international exchanges. Its focus is on the significance of trade imbalances, the determinants of exchange rates, and the aggregate effects of government monetary and fiscal policies. The pros and cons of fixed versus floating exchange rate systems are among the important issues addressed.

This international trade textbook begins in this chapter by discussing current and past issues and controversies relating to microeconomic trends and policies. We will highlight past trends both in implementing policies that restrict trade and in forging agreements to reduce trade barriers. It is these real-world issues that make the theory of international trade worth studying.

- International trade and investment flows have grown dramatically and consistently during the past half century.
- International trade is a field in economics that applies microeconomic models to help understand the international economy.

- International finance focuses on the interrelationships among aggregate economic variables such as GDP, unemployment, inflation, trade balances, exchange rates, and so on.

1.2 GDP, UNEMPLOYMENT, INFLATION, AND GOVERNMENT BUDGET BALANCES

One way to make judgments is to compare these numbers with other countries. To this end, the next few sections will present some recent data for a selected set of countries. Although memorizing these numbers is not so important, especially since they will all soon change, it is helpful to have an idea about what the values are for a few countries; or if not that, to know the approximate normal average for a particular variable. Thus it is useful to know that GDP per person ranges from about $500 per year at the low end to about $50,000 to $75,000 per person at the high end. It is also useful to know that unemployment rates are normally less than 10 percent. So when you read that Zimbabwe recently had unemployment of 75 percent, a reader will know how unusually large that is. Once you also recognize that inflation rates are normally less than 10 percent, a rate of 10,000 percent will strike you as extraordinary.

Thus the values for some of these numbers will be helpful to make comparisons across countries today and to make comparisons over time for a particular country. Therefore, it can be very helpful to know the numbers for at least a few countries, or what may be deemed a set of reference countries. The countries in Table 1.1 "GDP and GDP per Capita (PPP in Billions of Dollars), 2009" were selected to provide a cross section of countries at different levels of economic development. Thus the United States, the European Union, and Japan represent the largest economies in the world today. Meanwhile, countries like Brazil, Russia, India, and China are watched so closely today that they have acquired their own acronym: the BRIC countries. Finally, countries like Indonesia, Kenya, Ghana, and Burundi are among the poorest nations of the world. Note that in later tables other countries were substituted for the African countries because data are less difficult to obtain.

Gross Domestic Product around the World

Macroeconomics is the study of the interrelationships of aggregate economic variables. The most important of these, without question, is a country's gross domestic product (GDP). GDP measures the total value of all goods and services produced by a country during a year. As such, it is a measure of the extent of economic activity in a country or the economic size of a country.

And because the consumption of goods and services is one way to measure an individual's economic well-being, it is easy to calculate the GDP per capita (i.e., per person) to indicate the average well-being of individuals in a country.

Details about how to measure and interpret GDP follow in subsequent chapters, but before doing so, it makes some sense to know a little about how economy size and GDP per person vary across countries around the world. Which are the biggest countries, and which are the smallest? Which countries provide more goods and services, on average, and which produce less? And how wide are the differences between countries? Table 1.1 "GDP and GDP per Capita (PPP in Billions of Dollars), 2009" provides recent information for a selected group of countries. Note that reported numbers are based on purchasing power parity (PPP), which is a better way to make cross-country comparisons and is explained later. A convenient source of the most recent comprehensive data from three sources (the International Monetary Fund [IMF], the World Bank, and the U.S. CIA) of GDP (http://en.wikipedia.org/wiki/List_of_countries_by_GDP_%28PPP%29) and GDP per person (http://en.wikipedia.org/wiki/List_of_countries_by_GDP_%28PPP%29_per_capita) is available at Wikipedia.

Table 1.1 GDP and GDP per Capita (PPP in Billions of Dollars), 2009

Country/Region (Rank)	GDP (Percentage in the World)	GDP per Capita (Rank)
World	68,997 (100)	10,433
European Union (1)	15,247 (22.1)	—
United States (2)	14,265 (20.7)	47,440 (6)
China (3)	7,916 (11.5)	5,970 (100)
Japan (4)	4,354 (6.3)	34,116 (24)
India (5)	3,288 (4.8)	2,780 (130)
Russia (7)	2,260 (3.3)	15,948 (52)
Brazil (10)	1,981 (2.9)	10,466 (77)
South Korea (14)	1,342 (1.9)	27,692 (33)
Indonesia (17)	908 (1.3)	3,980 (121)
Kenya (82)	60 (nil)	1,712 (148)
Ghana (96)	34 (nil)	1,518 (152)
Burundi (158)	3 (nil)	390 (178)

Table 1.1 "GDP and GDP per Capita (PPP in Billions of Dollars), 2009" displays several things that are worth knowing. First, note that the United States and European Union each make up about one-fifth of the world economy; together the two are 42 percent. Throw Japan into the mix with the European Union and the United States and together they make up less than one-sixth of the world's population. However, these three developed nations produce almost one-half of the total world production. This is a testament to the high productivity in the developed regions of the world. It is also a testament to the low productivity in much of the rest of the world, where it takes another five billion people to produce the remaining half of the GDP.

The second thing worth recognizing is the wide dispersion of GDPs per capita across countries. The United States ranks sixth in the world at $47,440 and is surpassed by several small countries like Singapore and Luxembourg and/or those with substantial oil and gas resources such as Brunei, Norway, and Qatar (not shown in Table 1.1 "GDP and GDP per Capita (PPP in Billions of Dollars), 2009"). Average GDP per capita in the world is just over $10,000, and it is just as remarkable how far above the average some countries like the United States, Japan, and South Korea are as it is how far below the average other countries like China, India, Indonesia, and Kenya are. Perhaps most distressing is the situation of some countries like Burundi that has a GDP of only $370 per person. (Other countries in a similar situation include Zimbabwe, Congo, Liberia, Sierra Leone, Niger, and Afghanistan.)

Unemployment and Inflation around the World

Two other key macroeconomic variables that are used as an indicator of the health of a national economy are the unemployment rate and the inflation rate. The unemployment rate measures the percentage of the working population in a country who would like to be working but are currently unemployed. The lower the rate, the healthier the economy and vice versa. The inflation rate measures the annual rate of increase of the consumer price index (CPI). The CPI is a ratio that measures how much a set of goods costs this period relative to the cost of the same set of goods in some initial year. Thus if the CPI registers 107, it would cost $107 (euros or whatever is the national currency) to buy the goods today, while it would have cost just $100 to purchase the same goods in the initial period. This represents a 7 percent increase in average prices over the period, and if that period were a year, it would correspond to the annual inflation rate. In general, a relatively moderate inflation rate (about 0–4 percent) is deemed acceptable; however, if inflation is too high it usually contributes to a less effective functioning of an economy. Also, if inflation is negative, it is called deflation, and that can also contribute to an economic slowdown.

Table 1.2 Unemployment and Inflation Rates

Country/Region	Unemployment Rate (%)	Inflation Rate (%)
European Union	9.8 (Oct. 2009)	+0.5 (Nov. 2009)
United States	10.0 (Nov. 2009)	+1.8 (Nov. 2009)
China	9.2 (2008)	+0.6 (Nov. 2009)
Japan	5.1 (Oct. 2009)	-2.5 (Oct. 2009)
India	9.1 (2008)	+11.5 (Oct. 2009)
Russia	7.7 (Oct. 2009)	+9.1 (Nov. 2009)
Brazil	7.5 (Oct. 2009)	+4.2 (Nov. 2009)
South Korea	3.5 (Nov. 2009)	+2.4 (Nov. 2009)
Indonesia	8.1 (Feb. 2009)	+2.4 (Oct. 2009)

Country/Region	Unemployment Rate (%)	Inflation Rate (%)
Spain	19.3 (Oct. 2009)	+0.3 (Nov. 2009)
South Africa	24.5 (Sep. 2009)	+5.8 (Nov. 2009)
Estonia	15.2 (Jul. 2009)	-2.1 (Nov. 2009)

Source: Economist, Weekly Indicators, December 17, 2009.

The unemployment rates and inflation rates in most countries are unusual in the reported period because of the economic crisis that hit the world in 2008. The immediate effect of the crisis was a drop in demand for many goods and services, a contraction in GDP, and the loss of jobs for workers in many industries. In addition, prices were either stable or fell in many instances. When most economies of the world were booming several years earlier, a normal unemployment rate would have been 3 to 5 percent, while a normal inflation rate would stand at about 3 to 6 percent.

As Table 1.2 "Unemployment and Inflation Rates" shows, though, unemployment rates in most countries in 2009 are much higher than that, while inflation rates tend to be lower with several exceptions. In the United States, the unemployment rate has more than doubled, but in the European Union, unemployment was at a higher rate than the United States before the crisis hit, and so it has not risen quite as much. Several standouts in unemployment are Spain and South Africa. These are exceedingly high rates coming very close to the United States unemployment rate of 25 percent reached during the Great Depression in 1933.

India's inflation rate is the highest of the group listed but is not much different from inflation in India the year before of 10.4 percent. Russia's inflation this year has actually fallen from its rate last year of 13.2 percent. Japan and Estonia, two countries in the list, are reporting deflation this year. Japan had inflation of 1.7 percent in the previous year, whereas Estonia's rate had been 8 percent.

Government Budget Balances around the World

Another factor that is often considered in assessing the health of an economy is the state of the country's government budget. Governments collect tax revenue from individuals and businesses and use that money to finance the purchase of government provided goods and services. Some of the spending is on public goods such as national defense, health care, and police and fire protection. The government also transfers money from those better able to pay to others who are disadvantaged, such as welfare recipients or the elderly under social insurance programs.

Generally, if government were to collect more in tax revenue than it spent on programs and transfers, then it would be running a government budget surplus and there would be little cause for concern. However, many governments oftentimes tend to spend and transfer more than they collect in tax revenue. In this case, they run a government budget deficit that needs to be paid for or financed in some manner. There are two ways to cover a budget deficit. First, the government can issue Treasury bills and bonds and thus borrow money from the private market; second, the government can sometimes print additional money. If borrowing occurs, the funds become unavailable to finance private investment or consumption, and thus the situation represents a substitution of public spending for private spending. Borrowed funds must also be paid back with accrued interest, which implies that larger future taxes will have to be collected assuming that budget balance or a surplus is eventually achieved.

When governments borrow, they will issue Treasury bonds with varying maturities. Thus some will be paid back in one of two years, but others perhaps not for thirty years. In the meantime, the total outstanding balance of IOUs (i.e., I owe you) that the government must pay back in the future is called the national debt. This debt is owed to whoever has purchased the Treasury bonds; for many countries, a substantial amount is purchased by domestic citizens, meaning that the country borrows from itself and thus must pay back its own citizens in the future. The national debt is often confused with a nation's international indebtedness to the rest of the world, which is known as its international investment position (defined in the next section).

Excessive borrowing by a government can cause economic difficulties. Sometimes private lenders worry that the government may become insolvent (i.e., unable to repay its debts) in the future. In this case, creditors may demand a higher interest rate to compensate for the higher perceived risk. To prevent that risk, governments sometimes revert to the printing of money to reduce borrowing needs. However, excessive money expansion is invariably inflationary and can cause long-term damage to the economy.

In Table 1.3 "Budget Balance and National Debt (Percentage of GDP), 2009", we present budget balances for a selected set of countries. Each is shown as a percentage of GDP, which gives a more accurate portrayal of the relative size. Although there is no absolute number above which a budget deficit or a national debt is unsustainable, budget deficits greater than 5 percent per year, those that are persistent over a long period, or a national debt greater than 50 percent of GDP tends to raise concerns among investors.

Table 1.3 Budget Balance and National Debt (Percentage of GDP), 2009

Country/Region	Budget Balance (%)	National Debt (%)
European Union	-6.5	—
United States	-11.9	37.5
China	-3.4	15.6
Japan	-7.7	172.1

Country/Region	Budget Balance (%)	National Debt (%)
India	-8.0	56.4
Russia	-8.0	6.5
Brazil	-3.2	38.8
South Korea	-4.5	24.4
Indonesia	-2.6	29.3
Spain	-10.8	40.7
South Africa	-5.0	31.6
Estonia	-4.0	4.8

Source: Economist, Weekly Indicators, December 17, 2009, and the CIA World Factbook.

Note that all the budget balances for this selected set of countries are in deficit. For many countries, the deficits are very large, exceeding 10 percent in the U.S. and Spain. Although deficits for most countries are common, usually they are below 5 percent of the GDP. The reason for the higher deficits now is because most countries have increased their government spending to counteract the economic recession, while at the same time suffering a reduction in tax revenues also because of the recession. Thus budget deficits have ballooned around the world, though to differing degrees.

As budget deficits rise and as GDP falls due to the recession, national debts as a percent of GDP are also on the rise in most countries. In the United States, the national debt is still at a modest 37.5 percent, but recent projections suggest that in a few years it may quickly rise to 60 percent or 70 percent of the GDP. Note also that these figures subtract any debt issued by the government and purchased by another branch of the government. For example, in the United States for the past decade or more, the Social Security system has collected more in payroll taxes than it pays out in benefits. The surplus, known as the Social Security "trust fund," is good because in the next few decades as the baby boom generation retires, the numbers of Social Security recipients is expected to balloon. But for now the surplus is used to purchase government Treasury bonds. In other words, the Social Security administration lends money to the rest of the government. Those loans currently sum to about 30 percent of GDP or somewhat over $4 trillion. If we include these loans as a part of the national debt, the United States debt is now, according to the online national debt clock, more than $12 trillion or about 85 percent of GDP. (This is larger than 37.5 + 30 percent because the debt clock is an estimate of more recent figures and reflects the extremely large government budget deficit run in the previous year.)

Most other countries' debts are on a par with that of the U.S. with two notable exceptions. First, China and Russia's debts are fairly modest at only 15.6 percent and 6.5 percent of GDP, respectively. Second, Japan's national debt is an astounding 172 percent of GDP. It has arisen because the Japanese government has tried to extricate its economy from an economic funk by spending and borrowing over the past two decades.

- GDP and GDP per capita are two of the most widely tracked indicators of both the size of national economies and an economy's capacity to provide for its citizens.
- In general, we consider an economy more successful if its GDP per capita is high, unemployment rate is low (3–5 percent), inflation rate is low and nonnegative (0–6 percent), government budget deficit is low (less than 5 percent of GDP) or in surplus, and its national debt is low (less than 25 percent).
- The United States, as the largest national economy in the world, is a good reference point for comparing macroeconomic data.
- The U.S. GDP in 2008 stood at just over $14 trillion while per capita GDP stood at $47,000. U.S. GDP made up just over 20 percent of world GDP in 2008.
- The U.S. unemployment rate was unusually high at 10 percent in November 2009 while its inflation rate was very low at 1.8 percent.
- The U.S. government budget deficit was at an unusually high level of 11.9 percent of GDP in 2009 while its international indebtedness made it a debtor nation in the amount of 37 percent of its GDP.
- Several noteworthy statistics are presented in this section:
- Average world GDP per person stands at around $10,000 per person.
- The GDP in the U.S. and most developed countries rises as high as $50,000 per person.
- The GDP in the poorest countries like Kenya, Ghana, and Burundi is less than $2,000 per person per year.
- U.S. unemployment has risen to a very high level of 10 percent; however, in Spain it sits over 19 percent, while in South Africa it is over 24 percent.
- Inflation is relatively low in most countries but stands at over 9 percent in Russia and over 11 percent in India. In several countries like Japan and Estonia, deflation is occurring.
- Due to the world recession, budget deficits have grown larger in most countries, reaching almost 12 percent of GDP in the United States.
- The national debts of countries are also growing larger, and Japan's has grown to over 170 percent of GDP.

Jeopardy Questions: As in the popular television game show, you are given an answer to a question and you must respond with the question. For example, if the answer is "a tax on imports," then the correct question is "What is a tariff?"

- The approximate value of world GDP in 2008.
- The approximate value of EU GDP in 2008.
- The approximate value of U.S. GDP in 2008.
- The approximate value of world GDP per capita in 2008.
- The approximate value of EU GDP per capita in 2008.
- The approximate value of U.S. GDP per capita in 2008.
- The approximate value of South Africa's unemployment rate in 2009.
- The approximate value of India's inflation rate in 2009.
- The approximate value of the U.S. budget balance as a percentage of its GDP in 2009.
- The approximate value of Japan's national debt as a percentage of its GDP in 2009.

Use the information in Table 1.1 "GDP and GDP per Capita (PPP in Billions of Dollars), 2009" and Table 1.3 «Budget Balance and National Debt (Percentage of GDP), 2009» to calculate the dollar values of the government budget balance and the national debt for Japan, China, Russia, South Korea, and Indonesia.

1.3 TRADE BALANCES, EXCHANGE RATE REGIMES, AND INVESTMENT POSITIONS

Exchange Rate Regimes

Because countries use different national currencies, international trade and investment requires an exchange of currency. To buy something in another country, one must first exchange one's national currency for another. Governments must decide not only how to issue its currency but how international transactions will be conducted. For example, under a traditional gold standard, a country sets a price for gold (say $20 per ounce) and then issues currency such that the amount in circulation is equivalent to the value of gold held in reserve. In this way, money is "backed" by gold because individuals are allowed to convert currency to gold on demand.

Today's currencies are not backed by gold; instead most countries have a central bank that issues an amount of currency that will be adequate to maintain a vibrant growing economy with low inflation and low unemployment. A central bank's ability to achieve these goals is often limited, especially in turbulent economic times, and this makes monetary policy contentious in most countries.

One of the decisions a country must make with respect to its currency is whether to fix its exchange value and try to maintain it for an extended period, or whether to allow its value to float or fluctuate according to market conditions. Throughout history, fixed exchange rates have been the norm, especially because of the long period that countries maintained a gold standard (with currency fixed to gold) and because of the fixed exchange rate system (called the Bretton Woods system) after World War II. However, since 1973, when the Bretton Woods system collapsed, countries have pursued a variety of different exchange rate mechanisms.

The International Monetary Fund (IMF), created to monitor and assist countries with international payments problems, maintains a list of country currency regimes. The list displays a wide variety of systems currently being used. The continuing existence of so much variety demonstrates that the key question, "Which is the most suitable currency system?" remains largely unanswered. Different countries have chosen differently. Later, this course will explain what is necessary to maintain a fixed exchange rate or floating exchange rate system and what are some of the pros and cons of each regime. For now, though, it is useful to recognize the varieties of regimes around the world.

Table 1.4 Exchange Rate Regimes

Country/Region	Regime
Euro Area	Single currency within: floating externally
United States	Float
China	Crawling peg
Japan	Float
India	Managed float
Russia	Fixed to composite
Brazil	Float
South Korea	Float
Indonesia	Managed float
Spain	Euro zone; fixed in the European Union; float externally
South Africa	Float
Estonia	Currency board

Source: International Monetary Fund, De Facto Classification of Exchange Rate Regimes and Monetary Policy Framework, 2008.

Table 1.4 "Exchange Rate Regimes" shows the selected set of countries followed by a currency regime. Notice that many currencies—including the U.S. dollar, the Japanese yen, the Brazilian real, the South Korean won, and the South African rand—are independently floating, meaning that their exchange values are determined in the private market on the basis of supply and demand. Because supply and demand for currencies fluctuate over time, so do the exchange values, which is why the system is called floating.

Note that India and Indonesia are classified as "managed floating." This means that the countries' central banks will sometimes allow the currency to float freely, but at other times will nudge the exchange rate in one direction or another.

China is listed and maintaining a crawling peg, which means that the currency is essentially fixed except that the Chinese central bank is allowing its currency to appreciate slowly with respect to the U.S. dollar. In other words, the fixed rate itself is gradually but unpredictably adjusted.

Estonia is listed as having a currency board. This is a method of maintaining a fixed exchange rate by essentially eliminating the central bank in favor of a currency board that is mandated by law to follow procedures that will automatically keep its currency fixed in value.

Russia is listed as fixing to a composite currency. This means that instead of fixing to one other currency, such as the U.S. dollar or the euro, Russia fixes to a basket of currencies, also called a composite currency. The most common currency basket to fix to is the Special Drawing Rights (SDR), a composite currency issued by the IMF used for central bank transactions.

Finally, sixteen countries in the European Union are currently members of the euro area. Within this area, the countries have retired their own national currencies in favor of using a single currency, the euro. When all countries circulate the same currency, it is the ultimate in fixity, meaning they have fixed exchange rates among themselves because there is no need to exchange. However, with respect to other external currencies, like the U.S. dollar or the Japanese yen, the euro is allowed to float freely.

Trade Balances and International Investment Positions

One of the most widely monitored international statistics is a country's trade balance. If the value of total exports from a country exceeds total imports, we say a country has a trade surplus. However, if total imports exceed total exports, then the country has a trade deficit. Of course, if exports equal imports, then the country has balanced trade.

The terminology is unfortunate because it conveys a negative connotation to trade deficits, a positive connotation to trade surpluses, and perhaps an ideal connotation to trade balance. Later in the text, we will explain if or when these connotations are accurate and when they are inaccurate. Suffice it to say, for now, that sometimes trade deficits can be positive, trade surpluses can be negative, and trade balance could be immaterial.

Regardless, it is popular to decry large deficits as being a sign of danger for an economy, to hail large surpluses as a sign of strength and dominance, and to long for the fairness and justice that would arise if only the country could achieve balanced trade. What could be helpful at an early stage, before delving into the arguments and explanations, is to know how large the countries' trade deficits and surpluses are. A list of trade balances as a percentage of GDP for a selected set of countries is provided in Table 1.5 "Trade Balances and International Investment Positions GDP, 2009".

It is important to recognize that when a country runs a trade deficit, residents of the country purchase a larger amount of foreign products than foreign residents purchase from them. Those extra purchases are financed by the sale of domestic assets to foreigners. The asset sales may consist of property or businesses (a.k.a. investment), or it may involve the sale of IOUs (borrowing). In the former case, foreign investments entitle foreign owners to a stream of profits in the future. In the latter case, foreign loans entitle foreigners to a future repayment of principal and interest. In this way, trade and international investment are linked.

Because of these future profit takings and loan repayments, we say that a country with a deficit is becoming a debtor country. On the other hand, anytime a country runs a trade surplus, it is the domestic country that receives future profit and is owed repayments. In this case, we say a country running trade surpluses is becoming a creditor country. Nonetheless, trade deficits or surpluses only represent the debts or credits extended over a one-year period. If trade deficits continue year after year, then the total external debt to foreigners continues to grow larger. Likewise, if trade surpluses are run continually, then credits build up. However, if a deficit is run one year followed by an equivalent surplus the second year, rather than extending new credit to foreigners, the surplus instead will represent a repayment of the previous year's debt. Similarly, if a surplus is followed by an equivalent deficit, rather than incurring debt to foreigners, the deficit instead will represent foreign repayment of the previous year's credits.

All of this background is necessary to describe a country's international investment position (IIP), which measures the total value of foreign assets held by domestic residents minus the total value of domestic assets held by foreigners. It corresponds roughly to the sum of a country's trade deficits and surpluses over its entire history. Thus if the value of a country's trade deficits over time exceeds the value of its trade surpluses, then its IIP will reflect a larger value of foreign ownership of domestic assets than domestic ownership of foreign assets and we would say the country is a net debtor. In contrast, if a country has greater trade surpluses than deficits over time, it will be a net creditor.

Note how this accounting is similar to that for the national debt. A country's national debt reflects the sum of the nation's government budget deficits and surpluses over time. If deficits exceed surpluses, as they often do, a country builds up a national debt. Once a debt is present, though, government surpluses act to retire some of that indebtedness.

The key differences between the two are that the national debt is public indebtedness to both domestic and foreign creditors whereas the international debt (i.e., the IIP) is both public and private indebtedness but only to foreign creditors. Thus repayment of the national debt sometimes represents a transfer between domestic citizens and so in the aggregate has no impact on the nation's wealth. However, repayment of international debt always represents a transfer of wealth from domestic to foreign citizens.

Table 1.5 Trade Balances and International Investment Positions GDP, 2009

Country/Region	Trade Balance (%)	Debtor (-)/Creditor (+) Position (%)
Euro Area	-0.9	-17.5
United States	-3.1	-24.4
China	+6.1	+35.1
Japan	+2.7	+50.4
India	-0.3	-6.8
Russia	+2.2	+15.1
Brazil	-0.8	-26.6
South Korea	+3.8	-57.9
Indonesia	+1.2	-31.4
Spain	-5.7	-83.6
South Africa	-5.4	-4.1
Estonia	+5.8	-83.1

Sources: Economist, the IMF, and the China State Administration of Foreign Exchange. See Economist, Weekly Indicators, December 30, 2009; IMF Dissemination Standards Bulletin Board at http://dsbb.imf.org/Applications/web/dsbbhome; IMF GDP data from Wikipedia at http://en.wikipedia.org/wiki/List_of_countries_by_GDP_%28nominal%29; and China State Administration of Foreign Exchange at http://www.safe.gov.cn/model_safe_en/tjsj_en/tjsj_detail_en.jsp?ID=30303000000000000,18&id=4.

Table 1.5 "Trade Balances and International Investment Positions GDP, 2009" shows the most recent trade balances and international investment positions, both as a percentage of GDP, for a selected set of countries. One thing to note is that some of the selected countries are running trade deficits while others are running trade surpluses. Overall, the value of all exports in the world must equal the value of all imports, meaning that some countries' trade deficits must be matched with other countries' trade surpluses. Also, although there is no magic number dividing good from bad, most observers contend that a trade deficit over 5 percent of GDP is cause for concern and an international debt position over 50 percent is probably something to worry about. Any large international debt is likely to cause substantial declines in living standards for a country when it is paid back—or at least if it is paid back.

The fact that debts are sometimes defaulted on, meaning the borrower decides to walk away rather than repay, poses problems for large creditor nations. The more money one has lent to another, the more one relies on the good faith and effort of the borrower. There is an oft-quoted idiom used to describe this problem that goes, "If you owe me $100, you have a problem, but if you owe me a million dollars, then I have a problem." Consequently, international creditor countries may be in jeopardy if their credits exceed 40 ,30, or 50 percent of GDP.

Note from the data that the United States is running a trade deficit of 3.1 percent of GDP, which is down markedly from about 6 percent a few years prior. The United States has also been running a trade deficit for more than the past thirty years and as a result has amassed a debt to the rest of the world larger than any other country, totaling about $3.4 trillion or almost 25 percent of U.S. GDP. As such, the U.S. is referred to as the largest debtor nation in the world.

In stark contrast, during the past twenty-five or more years Japan has been running persistent trade surpluses. As a result, it has amassed over $2.4 trillion of credits to the rest of the world or just over 50 percent of its GDP. It is by far the largest creditor country in the world. Close behind Japan is China, running trade surpluses for more than the past ten years and amassing over $1.5 trillion of credits to other countries. That makes up 35 percent of its GDP and makes China a close second to Japan as a major creditor country. One other important creditor country is Russia, with over $250 billion in credits outstanding or about 15 percent of its GDP.

Note that all three creditor nations are also running trade surpluses, meaning they are expending their creditor position by becoming even bigger lenders.

Like the United States, many other countries have been running persistent deficits over time and have amassed large international debts. The most sizeable are3 for Spain and Estonia, both over 80 percent of their GDPs. Note that Spain continues to run a trade deficit that will add to it international debt whereas Estonia is now running a trade surplus that means it is in the process of repaying its debt. South Korea and Indonesia are following a similar path as Estonia. In contrast, the Euro area, South Africa, and to a lesser degree Brazil and India are following the same path as the United States—running trade deficits that will add to their international debt.

KEY TAKEAW

- Exchange rates and trade balances are two of the most widely tracked international macroeconomic indicators used to discern the health of an economy.
- Different countries pursue different exchange rate regimes, choosing variations of floating and fixed systems.
- The United States, as the largest national economy in the world, is a good reference point for comparing international macroeconomic data.
- The United States maintains an independently floating exchange rate, meaning that its value is determined on the private market.
- The United States trade deficit is currently at 3.1 percent of GDP. This is down from 6 percent recently but is one of a string of deficits spanning over thirty years.
- The U.S. international investment position stands at almost 25 percent of GDP, which by virtue of the U.S. economy size, makes the United States the largest debtor nation in the world.
- Several other noteworthy statistics are presented in this section:
- China maintains a crawling peg fixed exchange rate.
- Russia fixes its currency to a composite currency while Estonia uses a currency board to maintain a fixed exchange rate.
- Japan is the largest creditor country in the world, followed closely by China and more distantly by Russia.
- Spain and Estonia are examples of countries that have serious international debt concerns, with external debts greater than 80 percent of their GDPs.

Jeopardy Questions: As in the popular television game show, you are given an answer to a question and you must respond with the question. For example, if the answer is "a tax on imports," then the correct question is "What is a tariff?"

- The de facto exchange rate regime implemented in China in 2008.
- The de facto exchange rate regime implemented in the United States in 2008.
- The de facto exchange rate regime implemented in Indonesia in 2008.
- The de facto exchange rate regime implemented in Estonia in 2008.
- The name for the exchange rate regime in which a fixed exchange rate is adjusted gradually and unpredictably.
- The name for the exchange rate regime in which the exchange rate value is determined by supply and demand for currencies in the private marketplace.

- The term for the measure of the total value of foreign assets held by domestic residents minus the total value of domestic assets held by foreigners.
- This country was the largest creditor country in the world as of 2008.

Use the information in Table 1.1 "GDP and GDP per Capita (PPP in Billions of Dollars), 2009" and Table 1.5 «Trade Balances and International Investment Positions GDP, 2009» to calculate the dollar values of the trade balance and the international investment position for Japan, China, Russia, South Korea, and Indonesia.

1.4 BUSINESS CYCLES: UPS AND DOWNS IN THE ECONOMY

In 2009 the world was in the midst of the largest economic downturn since the early 1980s. Economic production was falling and unemployment rising. International trade fell substantially everywhere in the world, while investment both domestically and internationally dried up.

The source of these problems was the bursting of a real estate bubble. Bubbles are fairly common in both real estate and stock markets. A bubble is described as a steady and persistent increase in prices in a market, in this case, in the real estate markets in the United States and abroad. When bubbles are developing, many market observers argue that the prices are reflective of true values despite a sharp and unexpected increase. These justifications fool many people into buying the products in the hope that the prices will continue to rise and generate a profit.

When the bubble bursts, the demand driving the price increases ceases and a large number of participants begin to sell off their product to realize their profit. When these occur, prices quickly plummet. The dramatic drop in real estate prices in the United States in 2007 and 2008 left many financial institutions near bankruptcy. These financial market instabilities finally spilled over into the real sector (i.e., the sector where goods and services are produced), contributing to a world recession. As the current economic crisis unfolds, there have been many suggestions about similarities between this recession and the Great Depression in the 1930s. Indeed, it is common for people to say that this is the biggest economic downturn since the Great Depression. But is it?

To understand whether it is or not, it is useful to look at the kind of data used to measure recessions or depressions and to compare what has happened recently with what happened in the past. First, here are some definitions.

An economic recession refers to a decline in a country's measured real gross domestic product (GDP) over a period usually coupled with an increasing aggregate unemployment rate. In other words, it refers to a decline in economic productive activity. How much of a decline is necessary before observers will begin to call it a recession is almost always arguable, although there are a few guidelines one can follow.

In the United States, it is typical to define a recession as two successive quarters of negative real GDP growth. This definition dates to the 1970s and is little more than a rule of thumb, but it is one that has become widely applied. A more official way to define a recession is to accept the pronouncements of the National Bureau of Economic Research (NBER). This group of professional economists looks at more factors than just GDP growth rates and will also make judgments about when a recession has begun and when one has ended. According to the NBER, the current recession began in December 2007 in the United States. However, it did not proclaim that until December 2008. Although the U.S. economy contracted in the fourth quarter of 2007, it grew in the first two quarters of 2008, meaning that it did not fulfill the two successive quarters rule. That wasn't satisfied until the last two quarters of 2008 both recorded a GDP contraction. As of January 2010, the U.S. economy continues in a recession according to the NBER.See the National Bureau of Economic Research, http://www.nber.org/cycles.html.

A very severe recession is referred to as a depression. How severe a recession has to be to be called a depression is also a matter of judgment. In fact in this regard there are no common rules of thumb or NBER pronouncements. Some recent suggestions in the press are that a depression is when output contracts by more than 10 percent or the recession lasts for more than two years. Based on the second definition and using NBER records dating the length of recessions, the United States experienced depressions from 1865 to 1867, 1873 to 1879, 1882 to 1885, 1910 to 1912, and 1929 to 1933. Using this definition, the current recession could be judged a depression if NBER dates the end of the contraction to a month after December 2009.

The opposite of a recession is an economic expansion or economic boom. Indeed, the NBER measures not only the contractions but the expansions as well because its primary purpose is to identify the U.S. economy's peaks and troughs (i.e., high points and low points). When moving from a peak to a trough the economy is in a recession, but when moving from a trough to a peak it is in an expansion or boom. The term used to describe all of these ups and downs over time is the business cycle.

The business cycle has been a feature of economies since economic activity has been measured. The NBER identifies recessions going back to the 1800s with the earliest listed in 1854. Overall, the NBER has classified thirty-four recessions since 1854 with an average duration of seventeen months. The longest recession was sixty-five months from 1873 to 1879, a contraction notable enough to be called the Great Depression until another one came along to usurp it in the 1930s. On the upside, the average economic expansion in the United States during this period lasted thirty-eight months, with the longest being 120 months from 1991 to 2001. Interestingly, since 1982 the United States has experienced three of its longest expansions segmented only by relatively mild recessions in 1991 and 2001. This had led some observers to proclaim, "The business cycle is dead." Of course, that was until we headed into the current crisis. (See here for a complete listing of NBER recessions: http://www.nber.org/cycles/cyclesmain.html.)

The Recession of 2008–2009

Next, let's take a look at how the GDP growth figures look recently and see how they compare with previous periods. First, growth rates refer to the percentage change in real GDP, which means that the effects of inflation have been eliminated. The rates are almost always reported in annual terms (meaning the growth rate over a year) even when the period is defined as one quarter. In the United States and most other countries, GDP growth rates are reported every quarter, and that rate represents how much GDP would grow during a year if the rate of increase proceeded at the same pace as the growth during that quarter. Alternatively, annual growth rates can be reported as the percentage change in real GDP from the beginning to the end of the calendar year (January 1 to December 31).

Table 1.6 "U.S. Real GDP Growth and Unemployment Rate, 2007–2009" presents the quarterly real GDP growth rates from the beginning of 2007 to the end of 2009 and the corresponding unemployment rate that existed during the middle month of each quarter. Note first that in 2007, GDP growth was a respectable 2 to 3 percent and unemployment was below 5 percent, signs of a healthy economy. However, by the first quarter in 2008, GDP became negative although unemployment remained low. Growth rebounded to positive territory in the second quarter of 2008 while at the same time unemployment began to rise rapidly. At this time, there was great confusion about whether the U.S. economy was stalling or whether it was experiencing a temporary slowdown. By late 2008, though, speculation about an impending recession came to an end. Three successive quarters of significant GDP decline occurred between the second quarter of 2008 and the end of the first quarter in 2009, while the unemployment rate began to skyrocket. By the middle of 2009, the decline of GDP subsided and reversed to positive territory by the third quarter. However, the unemployment rate continued to rise, though at a slower pace. What happens next is anyone's guess, but to get a sense of the severity of this recession it is worth analyzing at least two past recessions: that of 1981 to 1982 and the two that occurred in the 1930s, which together are known as the Great Depression.

Table 1.6 U.S. Real GDP Growth and Unemployment Rate, 2007–2009

Year Quarter	Growth Rate (%)	Unemployment Rate (%)
2007.1	1.2	4.5
2007.2	3.2	4.5
2007.3	3.6	4.7
2007.4	2.1	4.7

Year Quarter	Growth Rate (%)	Unemployment Rate (%)
2008.1	-0.7	4.8
2008.2	1.5	5.6
2008.3	-2.7	6.2
2008.4	-5.4	6.8
2009.1	-6.4	8.1
2009.2	-0.7	9.4
2009.3	2.2	9.7
2009.4	—	10.0

Sources: U.S. Bureau of Economic and Analysis and U.S. Department of Labor.

The Recession of 1980–1982

At a glance the current recession most resembles the recessionary period from 1980 to 1982. The NBER declared two recessions during that period; the first lasting from January to July 1980 and the second lasting from July 1981 to November 1982. As can be seen in Table 1.7 "U.S. Real GDP Growth and Unemployment Rate, 1980–1983", GDP growth moved like a roller coaster ride. Coming off a sluggish period of stagflation in the mid-1970s, unemployment began somewhat higher at around 6 percent, while growth in 1979 (not shown) was less than 1 percent in several quarters. Then in the second quarter of 1980, GDP plummeted by almost 8 percent, which is much more severe than anything in the current recession. Note that the largest quarterly decrease in the U.S. GDP in the post–World War II era was -10.4 percent in the first quarter of 1958. In the same quarter, unemployment soared, rising over a percentage point in just three months. However, this contraction was short-lived since the GDP fell only another 0.7 percent in the third quarter and then rebounded with substantial growth in the fourth quarter of 1980 and the first quarter of 1981. Notice that despite the very rapid increase in the GDP, unemployment hardly budged downward, remaining stubbornly fixed around 7.5 percent. The rapid expansion was short-lived, as the GDP tumbled again by over 3 percent in the second quarter of 1981 only to rise again by a healthy 5 percent in the third quarter. But once again, the economy plunged back into recession with substantial declines of 5 percent and over 6 percent for two successive quarters in the GDP in late 1981 and early 1982. Meanwhile, from mid-1981 until after the real rebound began in 1983, the unemployment rate continued to rise, reaching a peak of 10.8 percent in late 1982, the highest unemployment rate in the post–World War II period.

Table 1.7 U.S. Real GDP Growth and Unemployment Rate, 1980–1983

Year. Quarter	Growth Rate (%)	Unemployment Rate (%)
1980.1	+1.3	6.3
1980.2	-7.9	7.5

Year. Quarter	Growth Rate (%)	Unemployment Rate (%)
1980.3	-0.7	7.7
1980.4	+7.6	7.5
1981.1	+8.6	7.4
1981.2	-3.2	7.5
1981.3	+4.9	7.4
1981.4	-4.9	8.3
1982.1	-6.4	8.9
1982.2	+2.2	9.4
1982.3	-1.5	9.8
1982.4	+0.3	10.8
1983.1	+5.1	10.4
1983.2	+9.3	10.1
1983.3	+8.1	9.5
1983.4	+8.5	8.5

Sources: U.S. Bureau of Economics and Analysis (http://www.bea.gov) and U.S. Department of Labor (http://www.dol.gov).

If indeed the current recession turns out like the 1980 to 1983 episode, we might expect to see substantial swings in the GDP growth rates in future quarters in the United States. The ups and downs are analogous to a bicycle smoothly traversing along a smooth road when the rider suddenly hits a large obstruction. The obstruction jolts the bike to one side while the rider compensates to pull the bike upright. However, the compensation is often too much, and the bike swings rapidly to the opposite side. This too inspires an exaggerated response that pushes the bike again too quickly to the original side. In time, the rider regains his balance and directs the bike along a smooth trajectory. That is what we see in Table 1.7 "U.S. Real GDP Growth and Unemployment Rate, 1980–1983" of the last quarters in 1983, when rapid growth becomes persistent and unemployment finally begins to fall.

The other lesson from this comparison is to note how sluggishly unemployment seems to respond to a growing economy. In late 1980 and early 1981, unemployment didn't budge despite the rapid revival of economic growth. In 1983, it took almost a full year of very rapid GDP growth before the unemployment rate began to fall substantially. This slow response is why the unemployment rate is often called a lagging indicator of a recession; it responds only after the recession has already abated.

THE GREAT DEPRESSION

During the current recession there have been many references to the Great Depression of the 1930s. One remark often heard is that this is the worst recession since the Great Depression. As we can see in Table 1.7 "U.S. Real GDP Growth and Unemployment Rate, 1980–1983", this is not quite accurate since the recession of the early 1980s can easily be said to have been worse than the current one...at least so far.

It is worth comparing numbers between the current period and the Depression years if only to learn how bad things really were during the 1930s. The Great Depression was a time that transformed attitudes and opinions around the world and can surely be credited with having established the necessary preconditions for the Second World War.

So let's take a look at how bad it really was. Once again, we'll consider the U.S. experience largely because the data are more readily available. However, it is worth remembering that all three of the economic downturns described here are notable in that they were worldwide in scope.

First of all, there is no quarterly data available for the 1930s as quarterly data in the United States first appeared in 1947. Indeed, there was no formal organized collection of data in the 1930s for a variable such as GDP. Thus the numbers presented by the U.S. Bureau of Economic and Analysis (BEA) were constructed by piecing together available data.

A second thing to realize is that annual GDP growth rates tend to have much less variance than quarterly data. In other words, the highs are not as high and the lows not as low. This is because the annual data are averaging the growth rates over the four quarters. Also, sometimes economic downturns occur at the end of one year and the beginning of the next so that the calendar year growth may still be positive in both years. For example in 2008, even though GDP growth was negative in three of four quarters, the annual GDP growth that year somehow registered a +0.4 percent. Also in 1980, despite an almost 8 percent GDP drop in the second quarter, the annual GDP growth that year was -0.3 percent. The same is true for 1982, which registered two quarters of negative GDP growth at -6.4 percent and -1.5 percent but still the GDP fell annually at only -1.9 percent.

With this caveat in mind, the U.S. GDP growth rates for the 1930s are astounding. From 1930 to 1933, the United States registered annual growth rates of -8.6 percent, -6.5 percent, -13.1 percent, and -1.3 percent. The unemployment rate, which is estimated to have been around 3 percent in the 1920s, rose quickly in 1930 to 8.9 percent and continued to rise rapidly to a height of almost 25 percent in 1933. Although growth returned with vigor in 1934 and for another four years, the unemployment rate remained high and only slowly fell to 14.3 percent by 1937.

Table 1.8 U.S. Real GDP Growth and Unemployment Rate, 1930–1940

Year	Growth Rate (%)	Unemployment Rate (%)
1930	-8.6	8.9
1931	-6.5	15.9
1932	-13.1	23.6
1933	-1.3	24.9
1934	+10.9	21.7
1935	+8.9	20.1
1936	+13.0	17.0
1937	+5.1	14.3
1938	-3.4	19.0
1939	+8.1	17.2
1940	+8.8	14.6

Sources: U.S. Bureau of Economics and Analysis and U.S. Department of Labor.

The NBER dated the first part of the Depression as having started in August 1929 and ending in March 1933. But a second wave came, another recession beginning in May 1937 and ending in June 1938. This caused GDP to fall by another 3.4 percent in 1938 while unemployment rose back above 15 percent for another two years.

The Great Depression is commonly used to refer to the economic crisis (or crises) that persisted for the entire decade of the 1930s, only truly coming to an end at the start of World War II. Even then it is worth mentioning that although GDP began to grow rapidly during World War II, with GDP growth from 1941 to 1943 at 17.1 percent, 18.5 percent, and 16.4 percent, respectively, and with U.S. unemployment falling to 1.2 percent in 1944, these data mask the fact that most of the extra production was for bullets and bombs and much of the most able part of the workforce was engaged in battle in the Atlantic and Pacific war theaters. In other words, the movement out of the Great Depression was associated with a national emergency rather than a more secure and rising standard of living.

Although the data presented only cover the United States, the Great Depression was a worldwide phenomenon. Without digging too deeply into the data or just by taking a quick look at Wikipedia's article on the Great Depression, it reveals the following: unemployment in 1932 peaked at 29 percent in Australia, 27 percent in Canada, and 30 percent in Germany. In some towns with specialized production in the United Kingdom, unemployment rose as high as 70 percent.

Needless to say, the Great Depression was indeed "great" in the sense that it was the worst economic downturn the world experienced in the twentieth century. In comparison, the current recession, which is coming to be known as the Great Recession, comes nowhere close to the severity of the Great Depression...at least for the moment (as of January 2010). A more accurate description of the current recession is that it is the worst since the 1980s in the United States. However, we should always be mindful of a second downturn as was seen in the late 1930s. Even after things begin to improve, economies can suffer secondary collapses. Hopefully, demands will soon rebound, production will sluggishly increase, and unemployment rates will begin to fall around the world. We will soon see.

- The business cycle refers to the cyclical pattern of economic expansions and contractions. Business cycles have been a persistent occurrence in all modern economies.
- The current recession, sometimes called the Great Recession, is comparable in GDP decline and unemployment increases in the United States to the recessions in the early 1980s.
- The Great Depression of the 1930s displayed much greater decreases in GDP, showed much larger increases in unemployment, and lasted for a longer period than any economic downturn in the United States since then.
- The largest annual decrease in the U.S. GDP during the Great Depression was -13.1 percent while the highest unemployment rate was 24.9 percent.
- The largest quarterly decrease in the U.S. GDP during the current recession was -6.4 percent while the highest unemployment rate was 10.1 percent.
- The largest quarterly decrease in the U.S. GDP since World War II was -10.4 percent in the first quarter of 1958, while the highest unemployment rate was 10.8 percent in 1982.
- Of the thirty-four U.S. recessions since 1854 classified by the NBER, the longest was sixty-five months in the 1870s, whereas the average length was seventeen months.
- Of all the U.S. expansions since 1854 classified by the NBER, the longest was 120 months in the 1990s whereas the average length was thirty-eight months.

EXERCISE

Jeopardy Questions: As in the popular television game show, you are given an answer to a question and you must respond with the question. For example, if the answer is "a tax on imports," then the correct question is "What is a tariff?"

- Approximately the worst U.S. quarterly economic growth performance between 2007 and 2009.
- Approximately the worst U.S. quarterly economic growth performance between 1980 and 1983.
- Approximately the worst U.S. annual economic growth performance between 1930 and 1940.

- Approximately the best U.S. annual economic growth performance between 1930 and 1940.
- Approximately the period of time generally known as the Great Depression.
- Approximately the highest unemployment rate in the U.S. during the Great Depression.
- Approximately the highest unemployment rate in Germany during the Great Depression.
- Approximately the best U.S. annual economic growth performance in the midst of World War II.
- The longest economic recession (in months) in the United States since 1854 as classified by the NBER.
- The longest economic expansion (in months) in the United States since 1854 as classified by the NBER.
- The term used to describe the cyclical pattern of economic expansions followed by economic contractions.

1.5 INTERNATIONAL MACROECONOMIC ORGANISATIONS INCLUDE THE WORLD BANK AND THE IMF.

After the Great Depression, one of the things policymakers thought was important was to return the international economy to a system of fixed exchange rates. Before the Depression (i.e., in the 1920s and before), the world mostly maintained a gold standard. Under such a system, a country establishes two rules: first, it fixes its currency value to a weight of gold; second, it establishes convertibility between the currency and gold. This means that any individual holding the national currency is allowed to cash in the currency for its equivalent in gold upon demand.

In essence, the gold standard derives from a system in which gold itself was used as a currency in exchange. Since gold was sufficiently rare and because it was inherently valuable to people, it was an ideal substance to use as a store of value and a medium of exchange (as was silver). However, once trucking gold around became more difficult, it became easier for governments to issue paper currency but to back up that currency with gold on reserve. Thus currency in circulation was just a representation of actual gold in the government's vault, and if a person ever wished to see that actual gold, he or she could simply demand conversion.

There is much that can be said about how a gold standard operates, but that discussion is reserved for a later chapter. For our purposes here, it is sufficient to explain that the gold standard was a system of fixed exchange rates. For example, before the 1930s the United States fixed the dollar at $20.67 per ounce of gold. During the same period, the United Kingdom fixed its currency at £4.24 per ounce. As a result of the gold-currency convertibility in both countries, this meant the dollar and pound were fixed to each other at a rate of $4.875/£.

During the Depression years, most countries dropped off the gold standard because the loss of confidence threatened a complete conversion of currency to gold and the depletion of national gold reserves. But, as World War II drew to a close, experts were assembled in Bretton Woods, New Hampshire, in the United States in 1944 to design a set of institutions that would help establish an effective international monetary system and to prevent some of the adjustment catastrophes that occurred after World War I. One such catastrophe occurred in Germany in 1922 to 1923 when a floating German currency resulted in one of the worst hyperinflations in modern history. Photos from that period show people with wheelbarrows full of money being used to make basic purchases. One way to prevent a reoccurrence was to establish a system of fixed exchange rates. As will be shown later, an important benefit of fixed exchange rates is the potential for such a system to prevent excessive inflation.

The Bretton Woods Conference, more formally called the United Nations Monetary and Financial Conference, was held in July 1944. The purpose of the conference was to establish a set of institutions that would support international trade and investment and prevent some of the monetary instabilities that had plagued the world after World War I. The conference proposed three institutions, only two of which finally came into being.

The unsuccessful institution was the International Trade Organization (ITO), which was intended to promote the reduction of tariff barriers and to coordinate domestic policies so as to encourage a freer flow of goods between countries. Although a charter was drawn up for the ITO, the United States refused to sign onto it, fearing that it would subordinate too many of its domestic policies to international scrutiny. A subagreement of the ITO, the General Agreement on Tariffs and Trade (GATT), designed to promote multilateral tariff reductions, was established independently though.

The two successfully chartered institutions from the Bretton Woods Conference were the International Bank for Reconstruction and Development (IBRD) and the International Monetary Fund (IMF).

The IBRD is one component of a larger organization called the World Bank. Its purpose was to provide loans to countries to aid their reconstruction after World War II and to promote economic development. Much of its early efforts focused on reconstruction of the war-torn economies, but by the 1960s, its efforts were redirected to developing countries. The intent was to get countries back on their feet, economically speaking, as quickly as possible.

The second successfully chartered organization was the IMF. Its purpose was to monitor and maintain the stability of the fixed exchange rate system that was established. The system was not the revival of a gold standard but rather what is known as a gold-exchange standard. Under this system, the U.S. dollar was singled out as the international reserve currency. Forty-four of the forty-five ratifying countries agreed to have their currency fixed to the dollar. The dollar in turn was fixed to gold at $35 per ounce. The countries also agreed not to exchange officially held gold deposits for currency as had been the practice under the gold standard. However, countries agreed that officially held gold could be exchanged between central banks.

Another important requirement designed to facilitate the expansion of international trade was that countries agreed not to put any restrictions or controls on the exchange of currencies when that exchange was intended for transactions on the current account. In other words, individuals would be free to exchange one currency for another if they wanted to import goods from another country. However, currency controls or restrictions were allowed for transactions recorded on the financial accounts. This allowed countries to prevent foreign purchases of businesses and companies or to prevent foreign banks from lending or borrowing money. These types of restrictions are commonly known as capital controls (also, currency controls and/or exchange restrictions). These controls were allowed largely because it was believed they were needed to help maintain the stability of the fixed exchange rate system.

The way a fixed exchange system operates in general, and the way the Bretton Woods gold exchange standard operated in particular, is covered in detail in Chapter 11 "Fixed Exchange Rates". For now I will simply state without explanation that to maintain a credible fixed exchange rate system requires regular intervention in the foreign exchange markets by country central banks. Sometimes to maintain the fixed rate a country might need to sell a substantial amount of U.S. dollars that it is holding on reserve. These reserves are U.S. dollar holdings that had been purchased earlier, but sometimes a country can run what is called a balance of payments deficit—that is, run out of dollar reserves and threaten the stability of the fixed exchange rate system.

At the Bretton Woods Conference, participants anticipated that this scenario would be a common occurrence and decided that a "fund" be established to essentially "bail out" countries that suffered from balance of payments problems. That fund was the IMF.

The IMF was created to help stabilize exchange rates in the fixed exchange rate system. In particular, member countries contribute reserves to the IMF, which is then enabled to lend money to countries suffering balance of payments problems. With these temporary loans, countries can avoid devaluations of their currencies or other adjustments that can affect the confidence in the monetary system. Because the monies used by the IMF are contributions given by other countries in the group, it is expected that once a balance of payments problem subsides that the money will be repaid. To assure repayment the IMF typically establishes conditions, known as conditionality, for the recipients of the loans. These conditions generally involve changes in monetary and fiscal policies intended to eliminate the original problems with the balance of payments in the first place.

The role of the IMF has changed more recently though. The fixed exchange rate system, under which the IMF is designed to operate, collapsed in 1973. Since that time, most of the major currencies in the world—including the U.S. dollar, the British pound, the Japanese yen, and many others—are floating. When a currency is allowed to float, its value is determined by supply and demand in the private market and there is no longer any need for a country's central bank to intervene. This in turn means that a country can no longer get into a balance of payments problem since that balance is automatically achieved with the adjustment in the exchange rate value. In essence the raison d'être of the IMF disappeared with the collapse of the Bretton Woods system.

Curiously, the IMF did not fall out of existence. Instead, it reinvented itself as a kind of lender of last resort to national governments. After 1973, the IMF used its "fund" to assist national governments that had international debt problems. For example, a major debt crisis developed in the early 1980s when national governments of Mexico, Brazil, Venezuela, Argentina, and eventually many other nations were unable to pay the interest on their external debt, or the money they borrowed from other countries. Many of these loans were either taken by the national governments or were guaranteed by the national governments. This crisis, known as the Third World debt crisis, threatened to bring down the international financial system as a number of major banks had significant exposure of foreign loans that were ultimately defaulted on. The IMF stepped in to provide "structural adjustment programs" in this instance. So the IMF not only loaned money for countries experiencing balance of payments crises but also now provided loans to countries that could not pay back their foreign creditors. And also, because the IMF wanted to get its money back (meaning the money contributed by the member nations), the structural adjustment loans came with strings attached: IMF conditionality.

Since that time, the IMF has lent money to many countries suffering from external debt repayment problems. It stepped in to help Brazil and Argentina several times in the 1980s and later. It helped Mexico during the peso crisis in 1994. It assisted countries during the Asian currency crisis of 1997 and helped Russia one year later when the Asian contagion swept through.

Although the IMF has come under much criticism, especially because conditionality is viewed by some as excessively onerous, it is worth remembering that the IMF makes loans, not grants. Thus it has the motivation to demand changes in policies that raise the chances of being repaid. These conditions have generally involved things like fiscal and monetary responsibility. That means reducing one's government budget deficit and curtailing the growth of the money supply. It also prescribed privatization that involves the sale or divestiture of state-owned enterprises. The free market orientation of these conditions came to be known as the Washington Consensus.

Also mitigating the criticisms is the fact that the countries that participate in IMF programs are free to accept the loans, or not. To illustrate the alternative, Malaysia was one country that refused to participate in an IMF structural adjustment program during the Asian currency crisis and as a result did not have to succumb to any conditions. Thus it is harder to criticize the IMF's conditions when the countries themselves have volunteered to participate. In exchange for what were often tens of billions of dollars in loans, these countries were able to maintain their good standing in the international financial community.

Although controversial, the IMF has played a significant role in maintaining the international financial system even after the collapse of fixed exchange rates. One last issue worth discussing in this introduction is the issue of moral hazard. In the past thirty years or so, almost every time a country has run into difficulty repaying its external debt, the IMF has stepped in to assure continued repayment. That behavior sends a signal to international investors that the risk of lending abroad is reduced. After all, if the country gets into trouble the IMF will lend the country money and the foreign creditors will still get their money back. The moral hazard refers to the fact that lending institutions in the developed countries may view the IMF like an insurance policy and thus make much riskier loans than they would have otherwise. In this way, the IMF could be contributing to the problem of international financial crisis rather than merely being the institution that helps clean up the mess.

- The World Bank and the IMF were proposed during the Bretton Woods Conference in 1944.
- The main purpose of the World Bank is to provide loans for postwar reconstruction and economic development for developing countries.
- The main purpose of the IMF was to monitor the international fixed exchange rate system and to provide temporary loans to countries suffering balance of payments problems.
- Since the breakup of the Bretton Woods fixed exchange rate system in 1973, the IMF has mostly assisted countries by making structural adjustment loans to those that have difficulty repaying international debts.

- The IMF conditionalities are the often-criticized conditions that the IMF places on foreign governments accepting their loans. The free-market orientation of these conditions is known as the Washington Consensus.

EXERCISE

Jeopardy Questions: As in the popular television game show, you are given an answer to a question and you must respond with the question. For example, if the answer is "a tax on imports," then the correct question is "What is a tariff?"

- The name for the original division of the World Bank that describes its original purpose.
- The name for the international institution that was designed to assist countries suffering from balance of payments problems.
- The common name for the international institution whose primary function today is to make loans to countries to assist their economic development.
- In the Bretton Woods system, these types of regulations were allowed for transactions recorded on the financial account.
- This type of currency regime was implemented immediately after the collapse of the Bretton Woods system.
- The term used for the conditions the IMF places on loans it makes to countries.

The term used for the type of loans made by the IMF to assist countries having difficulty making international debt repayments.

The term used to describe the standard free market package of conditions typically invoked by the IMF on loans it makes to countries.

CHAPTER

NATIONAL INCOME AND THE BALANCE OF PAYMENTS ACCOUNTS 2

INTRODUCTION

The most important macroeconomic variable tracked by economists and the media is the gross domestic product (GDP). Whether it ought to be so important is another matter that is discussed in this chapter. But before that evaluation can occur, the GDP must be defined and interpreted. This chapter presents the national income identity, which defines the GDP. It also presents several other important national accounts, including the balance of payments, the twin-deficit identity, and the international investment position. These are the variables of prime concern in an international finance course.

2.1 ACCOUNTS OF NATIONAL INCOME AND PRODUCT

Many of the key aggregate variables used to describe an economy are presented in a country's National Income and Product Accounts (NIPA). National income represents the total amount of money that factors of production earn during the course of a year. This mainly includes payments of wages, rents, profits, and interest to workers and owners of capital and property. The national product refers to the value of output produced by an economy during the course of a year. National product, also called national output, represents the market value of all goods and services produced by firms in a country.

Because of the circular flow of money in exchange for goods and services in an economy, the value of aggregate output (the national product) should equal the value of aggregate income (national income). Consider the adjoining circular flow diagram, Figure 2.1 "A Circular Flow Diagram", describing a very simple economy. The economy is composed of two distinct groups: households and firms. Firms produce all the final goods and services in the economy using factor services (labor and capital) supplied by the households. The households, in turn, purchase the goods and services supplied by the firms. Thus goods and services move between the two groups in the counterclockwise direction. Exchanges are facilitated with the use of money for payments. Thus when firms sell goods and services, the households give the money to the firms in exchange. When the households supply labor and capital to firms, the firms give money to the households in exchange. Thus money flows between the two groups in a clockwise direction.

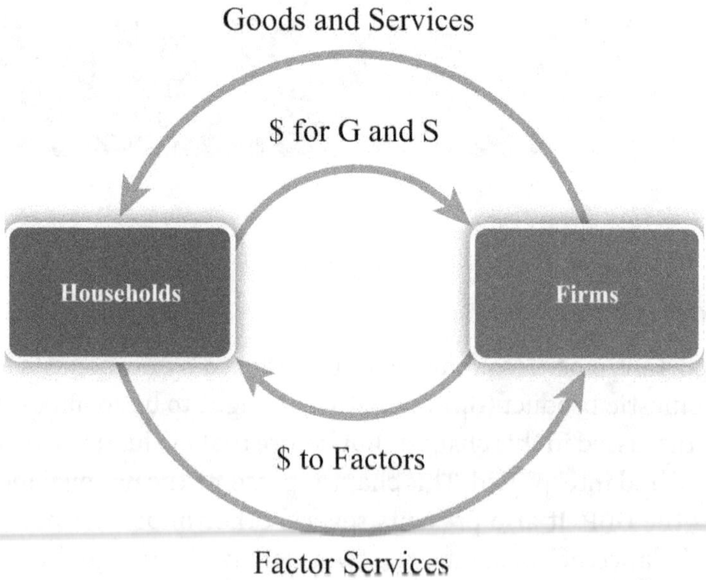

Figure 2.1 A Circular Flow Diagram

National product measures the monetary flow along the top part of the diagram—that is, the monetary value of goods and services produced by firms in the economy. National income measures the monetary flow along the bottom part of the diagram—that is, the monetary value of all factor services used in the production process. As long as there are no monetary leakages from the system, national income will equal national product.

The national product is commonly referred to as gross domestic product (GDP). GDP is defined as the value of all final goods and services produced within the borders of a country during some period of time, usually a year. A few things are worth emphasizing about this definition.

First, GDP is measured in terms of the monetary (or dollar) value at which the items exchange in the market. Second, it measures only final goods and services as opposed to intermediate goods. Thus wheat sold by a farmer to a flour mill will not be directly included as part of GDP since the value of the wheat will be included in the value of the flour that the mill sells to the bakery. The value of the flour will in turn be included in the value of the bread sold to the grocery store. Finally, the value of the bread will be included in the price charged by the grocery when the product is finally purchased by the consumer. Only the final bread sale should be included in GDP or else the intermediate values would overstate total production in the economy. Finally, GDP must be distinguished from another common measure of national output, gross national product (GNP).

Briefly, GDP measures all production within the borders of the country regardless of who owns the factors used in the production process. GNP measures all production achieved by domestic factors of production regardless of where that production takes place. For example, if a U.S. resident owns a factory in Malaysia and earns profits on the operation of that factory, then those profits would be counted as production by a U.S. factory owner and thus would be included in the U.S. GNP. However, since that production took place beyond U.S. borders, it would not be counted as the U.S. GDP. Alternatively, if a Dutch resident owns a factory in the United States, then the fraction of that production that accrues to the Dutch owner would be counted as part of the U.S. GDP since the production took place in the United States. It would not be counted as part of the U.S. GNP, however, since the production was done by a foreign factor owner.

GDP is probably the most widely reported and closely monitored aggregate statistic. GDP is a measure of the size of an economy. It tells us the total amount of "stuff" the economy produces. Since most of us, as individuals, prefer to have more stuff rather than less, it is straightforward to extend this to the national economy to argue that the higher the GDP, the better off the nation. For this simple reason, statisticians track the growth rate of GDP. Rapid GDP growth is a sign of growing prosperity and economic strength. Falling GDP indicates a recession, and if GDP falls significantly, we call it an economic depression.

For a variety of reasons, GDP should be used only as a rough indicator of the prosperity or welfare of a nation. Indeed, many people contend that GDP is an inadequate measure of national prosperity. Below is a list of some of the reasons why GDP falls short as an indicator of national welfare.

GDP only measures the amount of goods and services produced during the year. It does not measure the value of goods and services left over from previous years. For example, used cars, two-year-old computers, old furniture, old houses, and so on are all useful and provide welfare to individuals for years after they are produced. Yet the value of these items is only included in GDP in the year in which they are produced. National wealth, on the other hand, measures the value of all goods, services, and assets available in an economy at a point in time and is perhaps a better measure of national economic well-being than GDP.

GDP, by itself, fails to recognize the size of the population that it must support. If we want to use GDP to provide a rough estimate of the average standard of living among individuals in the economy, then we ought to divide GDP by the population to get per capita GDP. This is often the way in which cross-country comparisons are made.

GDP gives no account of how the goods and services produced by the economy are distributed among members of the economy. One might prefer a lower GDP with a more equitable distribution to a higher GDP in which a small percentage of the population receives most of the product.

Measured GDP growth may overstate the growth of the standard of living since price level increases (inflation) would raise measured GDP. Thus even if the economy produces exactly the same amount of goods and services as the year before and prices of those goods rise, then GDP will rise as well. For this reason, real GDP is typically used to measure the growth rate of GDP. Real GDP divides nominal (or measured) GDP by the price level and is designed to eliminate some of the inflationary effects.

Sometimes, economies with high GDPs may also produce a large amount of negative production externalities. Pollution is one such negative externality. Thus one might prefer to have a lower GDP and less pollution than a higher GDP with more pollution. Some groups also argue that rapid GDP growth may involve severe depletion of natural resources, which may be unsustainable in the long run.

GDP often rises in the aftermath of natural disasters. Shortly after the Kobe earthquake in Japan in the 1990s, economists predicted th1at Japan's GDP would probably rise more rapidly. This is mostly because of the surge of construction activities required to rebuild the damaged buildings. This illustrates why GDP growth may not be indicative of a healthy economy in some circumstances.

GDP measures the value of production in the economy rather than consumption, which is more important for economic well-being. As will be shown later, national production and consumption are equal when a country's trade balance is zero; however, if a country has a trade deficit, then its national consumption will exceed its production. Ideally, because consumption is pleasurable while production often is not, we should use the measure of national consumption to measure economic well-being rather than GDP.

KEY TAKEAWAYS

- GDP is defined as the value of all final goods and services produced within the borders of a country during some period of time, usually a year.
- The following are several important weaknesses of GDP as a measure of economic well-being:
- GDP measures income, not wealth, and wealth is a better measure of economic well-being.
- GDP does not account for income distribution effects that may be important to economic well-being.
- GDP measures "bads" like pollution as well as "goods."

- GDP measures production, not consumption, and consumption is more important to economic well-being.

EXERCISES

Jeopardy Questions: As in the popular television game show, you are given an answer to a question and you must respond with the question. For example, if the answer is "a tax on imports," then the correct question is "What is a tariff?"

- The term for the measure of national output occurring within the nation's borders.
- The term for the measure of national output that includes all production by domestic factors regardless of location.
- Of income or wealth, this term better describes the gross domestic product (GDP).
- Of income or wealth, this term better describes the gross national product (GNP).
- The term used to describe the measure of GDP that takes account of price level changes or inflationary effects over time.
- The term used to describe the measure of GDP that allows better income comparisons between countries that have different population sizes.
- Many people argue that GDP is an inadequate measure of a nation's economic well-being. List five reasons why this may be so.
- GDP is used widely as an indicator of the success and economic well being of the people of a nation. However, for many reasons it is not the perfect indicator. Briefly comment on the following statements related to this issue:
- Domestic spending is a better indicator of standard of living than GDP.
- National wealth is a better indicator of standard of living than GDP.

2.2 IDENTITY OF THE NATIONAL INCOME OR PRODUCT

The national income or product identity describes the way in which the gross domestic product (GDP) is measured, as the sum of expenditures in various broad spending categories. The identity, shown below, says that GDP is the sum of personal consumption expenditures (C), private investment expenditures (I), government consumption expenditures (G), and expenditures on exports (EX) minus expenditures on imports (IM):

$$GDP = C + I + G + EX - IM.$$

Personal consumption expenditures (C), or "consumption" for short, include goods and services purchased by domestic residents. These are further subdivided into durable goods, commodities that can be stored and that have an average life of at least three years; nondurable goods, all other commodities that can be stored; and services, commodities that cannot be stored and are consumed at the place and time of purchase. Consumption also includes foreign goods and services purchased by domestic households.

Private domestic investment (I), or "investment" for short, includes expenditures by businesses on fixed investment and any changes in business inventories. Fixed investment, both residential and nonresidential, consists of expenditures on commodities that will be used in a production process for more than one year. It covers all investment by private businesses and by nonprofit institutions, regardless of whether the investment is owned by domestic residents or not. Nonresidential investment includes new construction, business purchases of new machinery, equipment, furniture, and vehicles from other domestic firms and from the rest of the world. Residential investment consists of private structures, improvements to existing units, and mobile homes. Note that this term does not include financial investments made by individuals or businesses. For example, one purchase of stock as an "investment" is not counted here.

Government expenditures include purchases of goods, services, and structures from domestic firms and from the rest of the world by federal, state, and local government. This category includes compensation paid to government employees, tuition payments for higher education, and charges for medical care. Transfer payments, such as social insurance payments, government medical insurance payments, subsidies, and government aid are not included as a part of government expenditures.

- Exports consist of goods and services that are sold to nonresidents.
- Imports include goods and services purchased from the rest of the world.

The difference between exports and imports (EX - IM) is often referred to as net exports. Receipts and payments of factor income and transfer payments to the rest of the world (net) are excluded from net exports. Including these terms changes the trade balance definition and reclassifies national output as growth national product (GNP).

The Role of Imports in the National Income Identity

It is important to emphasize why imports are subtracted in the national income identity because it can lead to serious misinterpretations. First, one might infer (incorrectly) from the identity that imports are subtracted because they represent a cost to the economy. This argument often arises because of the typical political emphasis on jobs or employment. Thus higher imports imply that goods that might have been produced at home are now being produced abroad. This could represent an opportunity cost to the economy and justify subtracting imports in the identity. However, this argument is wrong.

The second misinterpretation that sometimes arises is to use the identity to suggest a relationship between imports and GDP growth. Thus it is common for economists to report that GDP grew at a slower than expected rate last quarter because imports rose faster than expected. The identity suggests this relationship because, obviously, if imports rise, GDP falls. However, this interpretation is also wrong.

The actual reason why imports are subtracted in the national income identity is because imports appear in the identity as hidden elements in consumption, investment, government, and exports. Thus imports must be subtracted to assure that only domestically produced goods are being counted. Consider the following details.

When consumption expenditures, investment expenditures, government expenditures, and exports are measured, they are measured without accounting for where the purchased goods were actually made. Thus consumption expenditures (C) measures domestic expenditures on both domestically produced and foreign-produced goods. For example, if a U.S. resident buys a television imported from Korea, that purchase would be included in domestic consumption expenditures. Likewise, if a business purchases a microscope made in Germany, that purchase would be included in domestic investment. When the government buys foreign goods abroad to provide supplies for its foreign embassies, those purchases are included in government expenditures. Finally, if an intermediate product is imported, used to produce another good, and then exported, the value of the original imports will be included in the value of domestic exports.

This suggests that we could rewrite the national income identity in the following way:

$$GDP = (C_{D + CF) + (ID + IF) + (GD + GF) + (EXD + EXF) - IM,}$$

where C_D represents consumption expenditures on domestically produced goods, C_F represents consumption expenditures on foreign-produced goods, I_D represents investment expenditures on domestically produced goods, I_F represents investment expenditures on foreign-produced goods, G_D represents government expenditures on domestically produced goods, G_F represents government expenditures on foreign-produced goods, EX_D represents export expenditures on domestically produced goods, and EX_F represents export expenditures on previously imported intermediate goods. Finally, we note that all imported goods are used in consumption, investment, or government or are ultimately exported, thus

$$IM = C_{F + IF + GF + EXF.}$$

Plugging this expression into the identity above yields

$$GDP = C_{D + ID + GD + EXD}$$

and indicates that GDP does not depend on imports at all.

The reason imports are subtracted in the standard national income identity is because they have already been included as part of consumption, investment, government spending, and exports. If imports were not subtracted, GDP would be overstated. Because of the way the variables are measured, the national income identity is written such that imports are added and then subtracted again.

This exercise should also clarify why the previously described misinterpretations were indeed wrong. Since imports do not affect the value of GDP in the first place, they cannot represent an opportunity cost, nor do they directly or necessarily influence the size of GDP growth.

KEY TAKEAWAYS

- GDP can be decomposed into consumption expenditures, investment expenditures, government expenditures, and exports of goods and services minus imports of goods and services.
- Investment in GDP identity measures physical investment, not financial investment.
- Government includes all levels of government and only expenditures on goods and services. Transfer payments are not included in the government term in the national income identity.
- Imports are subtracted in the national income identity because imported items are already measured as a part of consumption, investment and government expenditures, and as a component of exports. This means that imports have no direct impact on the level of GDP. The national income identity does not imply that rising imports cause falling GDP.

EXERCISES

Jeopardy Questions: As in the popular television game show, you are given an answer to a question and you must respond with the question. For example, if the answer is "a tax on imports," then the correct question is "What is a tariff?"

- A measure of the value of all capital equipment and services purchased during a year.
- The term for the goods and services sold to residents of foreign countries.
- The component of GDP that includes household purchases of durable goods, nondurable goods, and services.
- The component of GDP that includes purchases by businesses for physical capital equipment used in the production process.
- The government spending in the GDP identity does not count these types of government expenditures.

- Of true or false, imported goods and services are counted once in the C, I, G, or EX terms of the GDP identity.
- The national income identity says that gross domestic product is given by consumption expenditures, plus investment expenditures, plus government expenditures, plus exports, minus imports. In short, this is written as GDP = C+I+G+EX–IM.
- Consider each of the following expenditures below. Indicate in which category or categories (C, I, G, EX, or IM) the item would be accounted for in the United States.

Product	Category
a. German resident purchase of a U.S.-made tennis racket	
b. U.S. firm purchase of a U.S.-made office copy machine	
c. Salaries to U.S. troops in Iraq	
d. School spending by county government	
e. U.S. household purchase of imported clothing	

What is the gross domestic product in a country whose goods and services balance is a $300 billion deficit, consumption is $900 billion, investment is $300 billion, and government spending is $500 billion?

Below are the economic data for the fictional country of Sandia. Write out the national income identity. Verify whether Sandia's data satisfy the identity.

TABLE 2.1 SANDIA'S ECONOMIC DATA (BILLIONS OF DOLLARS)

Gross Domestic Product	400
Imports of Goods and Services	140
Investment Spending	20
Private Saving	30
Exports of Goods and Services	100
Government Transfers	40
Government Tax Revenues	140
Government Spending	140
Consumption Spending	280

2.3 STATISTICS ON US NATIONAL INCOME (2007–2008)

To have a solid understanding of the international economy, it is useful to know the absolute and relative sizes of some key macroeconomic variables like the gross domestic product (GDP). For example, it is worthwhile to know that the U.S. economy is the largest in the world because its annual GDP is about $14 trillion, not $14 million or $14 billion. It can also be useful to know about how much of an economy's output each year is consumed, invested, or purchased by the government. Although knowing that the U.S. government expenditures in 2008 were about $2.9 trillion is not so important, knowing that government expenditures made up about 20 percent of GDP can be useful to know.

Table 2.2 "U.S. Gross Domestic Product (in Billions of Dollars)" contains U.S. statistics for the national income and product accounts for the years 2007 and 2008. The table provides the numerical breakdown of GDP not only into its broad components (C, I, G, etc.) but also into their major subcategories. For example, consumption expenditures are broken into three main subcategories: durable goods, nondurable goods, and services. The left-hand column indicates which value corresponds to the variables used in the identity.

Table 2.2 U.S. Gross Domestic Product (in Billions of Dollars)

		2007	2008	2008 (Percentage of GDP)
GDP	Gross domestic product	13,807.5	14,280.7	100.0
C	Personal consumption expenditures	9,710.2	10,058.5	70.4
	Durable goods	1,082.8	1,022.8	7.2
	Nondurable goods	2,833.0	2,966.9	20.8
	Services	5,794.4	6,068.9	42.5
I	Gross private domestic investment	2,134.0	2,004.1	14.0
	Nonresidential	1,503.8	1,556.2	10.9
	Structures	480.3	556.3	3.9
	Equipment and software	1,023.5	999.9	7.0
	Residential	630.2	487.8	3.4
	Change in business inventories	-3.6	-39.9	-0.0
G	Government consumption expenditures and gross investment	2,674.8	2,883.2	20.2
	Federal	979.3	1,071.2	7.5
	National defense	662.2	734.3	5.1
	Nondefense	317.1	336.9	2.4
	State and local	1,695.5	1,812.1	12.6
EX	Exports	1,662.4	1,867.8	13.1
	Goods	1,149.2	1,289.6	9.0
	Services	513.2	578.2	4.0

		2007	2008	2008 (Percentage of GDP)
IM	Imports	2,370.2	2,533.0	17.7
	Goods	1,985.2	2,117.0	14.8
	Services	385.1	415.9	2.9

Source: Bureau of Economic Analysis, National Economic Accounts, Gross Domestic Product (GDP), at http://www.bea.gov/national/nipaweb/Index.asp.

There are a number of important things to recognize and remember about these numbers.

First, it is useful to know that U.S. GDP in 2008 was just over $14 trillion (or $14,000 billion). This is measured in 2008 prices and is referred to as nominal GDP. This number is useful to recall, first because it can be used in to judge relative country sizes if you happen to come across another country's GDP figure. The number will also be useful in comparison with U.S. GDP in the future. Thus if in 2020 you read that U.S. GDP is $20 trillion, you'll be able to recall that back in 2008 it was just $14 trillion. Also, note that between 2007 and 2008, the United States added over $600 billion to GDP.

The next thing to note about the numbers is that consumption expenditures are the largest component of U.S. GDP, making up about 70 percent of output in 2008. That percentage is relatively constant over time, even as the economy moves between recessions and boom times (although it is up slightly from 68 percent in 1997). Notice also that services is the largest subcategory in consumption. This category includes health care, insurance, transportation, entertainment, and so on.

Gross private domestic investment, "investment" for short, accounted for just 14 percent of GDP in 2008. This figure is down from almost 17 percent just two years before and is reflective of the slide into the economic recession. As GDP began to fall at the end of 2008, prospects for future business opportunities also turned sour, and so investment spending also fell. As the recession continued into 2009, we can expect that number to fall even further the next year.

The investment component of GDP is often the target of considerable concern in the United States. Investment represents how much the country is adding to the capital stock. Since capital is an input into production, in general the more capital equipment available, the greater will be the national output. Thus investment spending is viewed as an indicator of future GDP growth. Perhaps the higher is investment, the faster the economy will grow in the future.

One concern about the U.S. investment level is that, as a percentage of GDP, it is lower than in many countries in Europe, especially in China and other Asian economies. In many European countries, it is above 20 percent of GDP. The investment figure is closer to 30 percent in Japan and over 35 percent in China. There was a fear among some observers, especially in the 1980s and early 1990s, that lower U.S. investment relative to the rest of the world would ultimately lead to slower growth. That this projection has not been borne out should indicate that higher investment is not sufficient by itself to assure higher growth.

Government expenditures on goods and services in the United States amounted to 20 percent of GDP in 2008. Due to the recession and the large government stimulus package in 2009, we can expect this number will rise considerably next year. Recall that this figure includes state, local, and federal spending but excludes transfer payments. When transfer payments are included, government spending plus transfers as a percentage of GDP exceeds 30 percent in the United States.

Two things are worth noting. First, the state and local spending is almost twice the level of federal spending. Second, most of the federal spending is on defense-related goods and services.

Exports in the United States accounted for 13 percent of GDP in 2008 (up from 10 percent in 2003) and are closing in on the $2 trillion level. Imports into the United States are at $2.5 trillion, amounting to almost 18 percent of GDP. In terms of the dollar value of trade, the United States is the largest importer and exporter of goods and services in the world. However, relative to many other countries, the United States trades less as a percentage of GDP.

KEY TAKEAWAYS

- U.S. GDP stands at just over $14 trillion per year in 2008.
- U.S. consumption is about 70 percent of GDP; investment, 14 percent; government expenditures, 20 percent; exports, 13 percent; and imports, about 18 percent.

EXERCISE

Jeopardy Question: As in the popular television game show, you are given an answer to a question and you must respond with the question. For example, if the answer is "a tax on imports," then the correct question is "What is a tariff?"

- The approximate share of U.S. consumption as a share of U.S. GDP in 2008.
- The approximate share of U.S. investment as a share of U.S. GDP in 2008.
- The approximate share of U.S. government spending as a share of U.S. GDP in 2008.
- The approximate share of U.S. exports of goods and services as a share of U.S. GDP in 2008.
- The approximate share of U.S. imports of goods and services as a share of U.S. GDP in 2008.

- This main category represents the largest share of GDP spending in the U.S. economy.

2.4 PAYMENT ACCOUNT BALANCE: DEFINITIONS

The balance of payments accounts is a record of all international transactions that are undertaken between residents of one country and residents of other countries during the year. The accounts are divided into several subaccounts, the most important being the current account and the financial account. The current account is often further subdivided into the merchandise trade account and the service account. These are each briefly defined in Table 2.3 “Balance of Payments Accounts Summary”.

Table 2.3 Balance of Payments Accounts Summary

Current Account	Record of all international transactions for **goods and services**, **income payments and receipts**, **and unilateral transfers.** The current account is used in the national income identity for GNP.
Merchandise Trade Account	Record of all international transactions for **goods only.** Goods include physical items like autos, steel, food, clothes, appliances, furniture, etc.
Services Account	Record of all international transactions for **services only**. Services include transportation, insurance, hotel, restaurant, legal, consulting, etc.
Goods and Services Account	Record of all international transactions for **goods and services only.** The goods and services account is used in the national income identity for GDP.
Financial Account	Record of all international transactions for **assets.** Assets include bonds, Treasury bills, bank deposits, stocks, currency, real estate, etc.

The balance on each of these accounts is found by taking the difference between exports and imports.

Current Account

The current account (CA) balance is defined as $CA = EX^{G,S,IPR,UT} - IM^{G,S,IPR,UT}$ where the G,S,IPR,UT superscript is meant to include exports and imports of goods (G), services (S), income payments and receipts (IPR), and unilateral transfers (UT). If $CA > 0$, then exports of goods and services exceed imports and the country has a current account surplus. If $CA < 0$, then imports exceed exports and the country has a current account deficit.

Income payments represent the money earned (i.e., income) by foreign residents on their investments in the United States. For example, if a British company owns an office building in the United States and brings back to the United Kingdom a share of the profit earned there as a part of its income, then this is classified as an income payment on the current account of the balance of payments.

Income receipts represent the money earned by domestic residents on their investments abroad. For example, if a U.S. company owns an assembly plant in Costa Rica and brings back to the United States a share of the profit earned there as a part of its income, then this is classified as an income receipt on the current account of the balance of payments.

It may be helpful to think of income payments and receipts as payments for entrepreneurial services. For example, a British company running an office building is providing the management services and taking the risks associated with operating the property. In exchange for these services, the company is entitled to a stream of the profit that is earned. Thus income payments are classified as an import, the import of a service. Similarly, the U.S. company operating the assembly plant in Costa Rica is also providing entrepreneurial services for which it receives income. Since in this case the United States is exporting a service, income receipts are classified as a U.S. export.

Unilateral transfers represent payments that are made or received that do not have an offsetting product flow in the opposite direction. Normally, when a good is exported, for example, the good is exchanged for currency such that the value of the good and the value of the currency are equal. Thus there is an outflow and an inflow of equal value. An accountant would record both sides of this transaction, as will be seen in the next section. However, with a unilateral transfer, money flows out, but nothing comes back in exchange or vice versa. The primary examples of unilateral transfers are remittances and foreign aid. Remittances occur when a person in one country transfers money to a relative in another country and receives nothing in return. Foreign aid also involves a transfer, expecting nothing in return.

Merchandise Trade Balance

The merchandise trade balance (or goods balance) can be defined as $GB=EX^G-IM^G$, where we record only the export and import of merchandise goods. If $GB > 0$, the country would have a (merchandise) trade surplus. If $GB < 0$, the country has a trade deficit.

Services Balance

The service balance can be defined as $SB = EX^S - IM^S$, where we record only the export and import of services. If $SB > 0$, the country has a service surplus. If $SB < 0$, the country has a service deficit.

Goods and Services Balance

The goods and services balance (or goods balance) can be defined as $GSB=EX^{G\&S}-IM^{G\&S}$, where we record the export and import of both merchandise goods and services. If $GSB > 0$, the country would have a goods and services (G&S) surplus. If $GB < 0$, the country has a G&S deficit. Note that sometimes people will refer to the difference $EX^{G\&S}-IM^{G\&S}$as net exports. Often when this term is used the person is referencing the goods and services balance.

Here it is important to point out that when you hear a reference to a country's trade balance, it could mean the merchandise trade balance, or it could mean the goods and services balance, or it could even mean the current account balance.

Occasionally, one will hear trade deficit figures reported in the U.S. press followed by a comment that the deficit figures refer to the "broad" measure of trade between countries. In this case, the numbers reported refer to the current account deficit rather than the merchandise trade deficit. This usage is developing for a couple of reasons. First of all, at one time, around thirty years ago or more, there was very little international trade in services. At that time, it was common to report the merchandise trade balance since that accounted for most of the international trade. In the past decade or so, service trade has been growing much more rapidly than goods trade and it is now becoming a significant component of international trade. In the United States, service trade exceeds 30 percent of total trade. Thus a more complete record of a country's international trade is found in its current account balance rather than its merchandise trade account.

But there is a problem with reporting and calling it the current account deficit because most people don't know what the current account is. There is a greater chance that people will recognize the trade deficit (although most could probably not define it either) than will recognize the current account deficit. Thus the alternative of choice among commentators is to call the current account deficit a trade deficit and then define it briefly as a "broad" measure of trade.

A simple solution would be to call the current account balance the "trade balance" since it is a record of all trade in goods and services and to call th3e merchandise trade balance the "merchandise goods balance," or the "goods balance" for short. I will ascribe to this convention throughout this text in the hope that it might catch on.

GDP versus GNP

There are two well-known measures of the national income of a country: GDP and GNP. Both represent the total value of output in a country during a year, only measured in slightly different ways. It is worthwhile to understand the distinction between the two and what adjustments must be made to measure one or the other.

Conceptually, the gross domestic product (GDP) represents the value of all goods and services produced within the borders of the country. The gross national product (GNP) represents the value of all goods and services produced by domestic factors of production.

Thus production in the United States by a foreign-owned company is counted as a part of U.S. GDP since the productive activity took place within the U.S. borders, even though the income earned from that activity does not go to a U.S. citizen. Similarly, production by a U.S. company abroad will generate income for U.S. citizens, but that production does not count as a part of GDP since the productive activity generating that income occurred abroad. This production will count as a part of GNP though since the income goes to a U.S. citizen.

The way GDP versus GNP is measured is by including different items in the export and import terms. As noted above, GDP includes only exports and imports of goods and services, implying also that GDP excludes income payments and receipts and unilateral transfers. When these latter items are included in the national income identity and the current account balance is used for EX - IM, the national income variable becomes the GNP. Thus the GNP measure includes income payments and receipts and unilateral transfers. In so doing, GNP counts as additions to national income the profit made by U.S. citizens on its foreign operations (income receipts are added to GNP) and subtracts the profit made by foreign companies earning money on operations in the U.S. (income payments are subtracted).

To clarify, the national income identities for GDP and GNP are as follows:

$$GDP = C + I + G + EXG\&S - IMG\&S$$

and

$$GNP = C + I + G + EXG,S,IPR,UT - IMG,S,IPR,UT.$$

Financial Account Balance

Finally, the financial account balance can be defined as KA = EXA - IMA, where EXA and IMA refer to the export and import of assets, respectively. If KA > 0, then the country is exporting more assets than it is importing and it has a financial account surplus. If KA < 0, then the country has a financial account deficit.

The financial account records all international trade in assets. Assets represent all forms of ownership claims in things that have value. They include bonds, Treasury bills, stocks, mutual funds, bank deposits, real estate, currency, and other types of financial instruments. Perhaps a clearer way to describe exports of assets is to say that domestic assets are sold to foreigners, whereas imports of assets mean foreign assets that are purchased by domestic residents.

It is useful to differentiate between two different types of assets. First, some assets represent IOUs (i.e., I owe you). In the case of bonds, savings accounts, Treasury bills, and so on, the purchaser of the asset agrees to give money to the seller of the asset in return for an interest payment plus the return of the principal at some time in the future. These asset purchases represent borrowing and lending. When the U.S. government sells a Treasury bill (T-bill), for example, it is borrowing money from the purchaser of the T-bill and agrees to pay back the principal and interest in the future. The Treasury bill certificate, held by the purchaser of the asset, is an IOU, a promissory note to repay principal plus interest at a predetermined time in the future.

The second type of asset represents ownership shares in a business or property, which is held in the expectation that it will realize a positive rate of return in the future. Assets, such as common stock, give the purchaser an ownership share in a corporation and entitle the owner to a stream of dividend payments in the future if the company is profitable. The future sale of the stock may also generate a capital gain if the future sales price is higher than the purchase price. Similarly, real estate purchases—say, of an office building—entitle the owner to the future stream of rental payments by the tenants in the building. Owner-occupied real estate, although it does not generate a stream of rental payments, does generate a stream of housing services for the occupant-owners. In either case, if real estate is sold later at a higher price, a capital gain on the investment will accrue.

An important distinction exists between assets classified as IOUs and assets consisting of ownership shares in a business or property. First of all, IOUs involve a contractual obligation to repay principal plus interest according to the terms of the contract or agreement. Failure to do so is referred to as a default on the part of the borrower and is likely to result in legal action to force repayment. Thus international asset purchases categorized as IOUs represent international borrowing and lending.

Ownership shares, on the other hand, carry no such obligation for repayment of the original investment and no guarantee that the asset will generate a positive rate of return. The risk is borne entirely by the purchaser of the asset. If the business is profitable, if numerous tenants can be found, or if real estate values rise over time, then the purchaser of the asset will make money. If the business is unprofitable, office space cannot be leased, or real estate values fall, then the purchaser will lose money. In the case of international transactions for ownership shares, there is no resulting international obligation for repayment.

KEY TAKEAWAYS

- The trade balance may describe a variety of different ways to account for the difference between exports and imports.
- The current account is the broadest measure of trade flows between countries encompassing goods, services, income payments and receipts, and unilateral transfers.
- The merchandise trade balance is a more narrow measure of trade between countries encompassing only traded goods.
- Net exports often refer to the balance on goods and services alone.
- GDP is a measure of national income that includes all production that occurs within the borders of a country. It is measured by using the goods and services balance for exports and imports.

- GNP is a measure of national income that includes all production by U.S. citizens that occurs anywhere in the world. It is measured by using the current account balance for exports and imports.
- The financial account balance measures all exports and imports of assets, which means foreign purchases of domestic assets and domestic purchases of foreign assets.

EXERCISE

Jeopardy Questions: As in the popular television game show, you are given an answer to a question and you must respond with the question. For example, if the answer is "a tax on imports," then the correct question is "What is a tariff?"

- A record of all international transactions for goods and services.
- A record of all international transactions for assets.
- The name of the balance of payments account that records transactions for goods.
- The term used to describe the profit earned by domestic residents on their foreign business operations.
- The term used to describe the profit earned by foreign residents on their domestic business operations.
- The term used to describe remittances because they do not have a corresponding product flow to offset the money export or import.
- Of net importer or net exporter of services, this describes a country that has more income payments than income receipts.
- This measure of national output includes only the imports and exports of goods and services in its trade balance.
- This measure of national output includes income payments and receipts in its trade balance.

2.5 LOGGING TRANSACTIONS ON THE PAYMENT BALANCE

Almost every transaction involves an exchange between two individuals of two items believed to be of equal value.An exception is the case of unilateral transfers. These transfers include pension payments to domestic citizens living abroad, foreign aid, remittances, and other types of currency transfers that do not include an item on the reverse side being traded.Thus if one person exchanges $20 for a baseball bat with another person, then the two items of equal value are the $20 of currency and the baseball bat. The debit and credit columns in the ledger are used to record each side of every transaction. This means that every transaction must result in a credit and debit entry of equal value.

By convention, every credit entry has a "+" placed before it, while every debit entry has a "-" placed before it. The plus on the credit side generally means that money is being received in exchange for that item, while the minus on the debit side indicates a monetary payment for that item. This interpretation in the balance of payments accounts can be misleading, however, since in many international transactions, as when currencies are exchanged, money is involved on both sides of the transaction. There are two simple rules of thumb to help classify entries on the balance of payments:

Any time an item (good, service, or asset) is exported from a country, the value of that item is recorded as a credit entry on the balance of payments.

Any time an item is imported into a country, the value of that item is recorded as a debit entry on the balance of payments.

In the following examples, we will consider entries on the U.S. balance of payments accounts. Since it is a U.S. account, the values of all entries are denominated in U.S. dollars. Note that each transaction between a U.S. resident and a foreign resident would result in an entry on both the domestic and the foreign balance of payments accounts, but we will look at only one country's accounts.

Finally, we will classify entries in the balance of payments accounts into one of the two major subaccounts, the current account or the financial account. Any time an item in a transaction is a good or a service, the value of that item will be recorded in the current account. Any time an item in a transaction is an asset, the value of that item will be recorded in the financial account.

Note that in June 1999, what was previously called the "capital account" was renamed the "financial account" in the U.S. bal2ance of payments. A capital account stills exists but now includes only exchanges in nonproduced, nonfinancial assets. This category is very small, including such items as debt forgiveness and transfers by migrants. However, for some time, it will be common for individuals to use the term "capital account" to refer to the present "financial account." So be warned.

A Simple Exchange Story

Consider two individuals, one a resident of the United States, the other a resident of Japan. We will follow them through a series of hypothetical transactions and look at how each of these transactions would be recorded on the balance of payments. The exercise will provide insight into the relationship between the current account and the financial account and give us a mechanism for interpreting trade deficits and surpluses.

Step 1: We begin by assuming that each individual wishes to purchase something in the other country. The U.S. resident wants to buy something in Japan and thus needs Japanese currency (yen) to make the purchase. The Japanese resident wants to buy something in the United States and thus needs U.S. currency (dollars) to make the purchase. Therefore, the first step in the story must involve an exchange of currencies.

So let's suppose the U.S. resident exchanges $1,000 for ¥112,000 on the foreign exchange market at a spot exchange rate of 112 ¥/$. The transaction can be recorded by noting the following:

The transaction involves an exchange of currency for currency. Since currency is an asset, both sides of the transaction are recorded on the financial account.

The currency exported is $1,000 in U.S. currency. Hence, we have made a credit entry in the financial account in the table below. What matters is not whether the item leaves the country, but that the ownership changes from a U.S. resident to a foreign resident.

The currency imported into the country is the ¥112,000. We record this as a debit entry on the financial account and value it at the current exchange value, which is $1,000 as noted in the table.

Step 1	**U.S. Balance of Payments ($)**	
	Credits (+)	**Debits (-)**
	Current Account	0
Financial Account	+1,000 ($ currency)	-1,000 (¥ currency)

Step 2: Next, let's assume that the U.S. resident uses his ¥112,000 to purchase a camera from a store in Japan and then brings it back to the United States. Since the transaction is between the U.S. resident and the Japanese store owner, it is an international transaction and must be recorded on the balance of payments. The item exported in this case is the Japanese currency. We'll assume that there has been no change in the exchange rate and thus the currency is still valued at $1,000. This is recorded as a credit entry on the financial account and labeled "¥ currency" in the table below. The item being imported into the United States is a camera. Since a camera is a merchandise good and is valued at ¥112,000 = $1,000, the import is recorded as a debit entry on the current account in the table below.

Step 2	**U.S. Balance of Payments ($)**	
	Credits (+)	**Debits (-)**
	Current Account	0
Financial Account	+1,000 (¥ currency)	0

Step 3a: Next, let's assume that the Japanese resident uses his $1,000 to purchase a computer from a store in the United States and then brings it back to Japan. The computer, valued at $1,000, is being exported out of the United States and is considered

a merchandise good. Therefore, a credit entry of $1,000 is made in the following table on the current account and labeled as "computer." The other side of the transaction is the $1,000 of U.S. currency being given to the U.S. store owner by the Japanese resident. Since the currency, worth $1,000, is being imported and is an asset, a $1,000 debit entry is made in the table on the financial account and labeled "$ currency."

Step 3a	U.S. Balance of Payments ($)	
	Credits (+)	**Debits (-)**
	Current Account	+1,000 (computer)
Financial Account	0	-1,000 ($ currency)

Summary Statistics (after Steps 1, 2, and 3a)

We can construct summary statistics for the entries that have occurred so far by summing the debit and credit entries in each account and eliminating double entries. In the following table, we show all the transactions that have been recorded. The sum of credits in the current account is the $1,000 computer. The sum of debits in the current account is the $1,000 camera. On the financial account there are two credit entries of $1,000, one representing U.S. currency and the other representing Japanese currency. There are two identical entries on the debit side. Since there is a U.S. currency debit and credit entry of equal value, this means that the net flow of currency is zero. The dollars that left the country came back in subsequent transactions. The same is true for Japanese currency. When reporting the summary statistics, the dollar and yen currency financial account entries would cancel, leaving a net export of assets equal to zero and the net inflow of assets equal to zero as well.

Summary 1, 2, 3a	**U.S. Balance of Payments ($)**	
	Credits (+)	**Debits (-)**
	Current Account	+1,000 (computer)
Financial Account	+1,000 ($ currency), +1,000 (¥ currency)	-1,000 ($ currency), -1,000 (¥ currency)

After cancellations, then, the summary balance of payments statistics would look as in the following table.

Summary 1, 2, 3a	U.S. Balance of Payments ($)	
	Credits (+)	**Debits (-)**
	Current Account	+1,000 (computer)
Financial Account	0	0

The current account balance is found by summing the credit and debit entries representing exports and imports, respectively. This corresponds to the difference between exports and imports of goods and services. In this example, the current account (or trade) balance is CA = 0 = 1,000$ - 1,000$. This means the trade account is balanced—exports equal imports.

The financial account balance is also found by summing the credit and debit entries. Since both entries are zero, the financial account balance is also zero.

Step 3b: Step 3b is meant to substitute for step 3a. In this case, we imagine that the Japanese resident decided to do something other than purchase a computer with the previously acquired $1,000. Instead, let's suppose that the Japanese resident decides to save his money by investing in a U.S. savings bond. In this case, $1,000 is paid to the U.S. government in return for a U.S. savings bond certificate (an IOU) that specifies the terms of the agreement (i.e., the period of the loan, interest rate, etc.). The transaction is recorded on the financial account as a credit entry of $1,000 representing the savings bond that is exported from the country and a debit entry of $1,000 of U.S. currency that is imported back into the country.

Step 3b	U.S. Balance of Payments ($)	
	Credits (+)	Debits (-)
	Current Account	0
Financial Account	+1,000 (U.S. savings bond)	-1,000 ($ currency)

Summary Statistics (after Steps 1, 2, and 3b)

We can construct summary statistics assuming that steps 1, 2, and 3b have taken place. This is shown in the following table. The sum of credits in the current account in this case is zero since there are no exports of goods or services. The sum of debits in the current account is the $1,000 camera.

On the financial account, there are three credit entries of $1,000: one representing U.S. currency, the other representing Japanese currency, and the third representing the U.S. savings bond. There are two $1,000 entries on the debit side: one representing U.S. currency and the other representing Japanese currency. Again, the dollar and yen currency financial account entries would cancel, leaving only a net export of assets equal to the $1,000 savings bond. The net inflow of assets is equal to zero.

Summary 1, 2, 3b	**U.S. Balance of Payments ($)**	
	Credits (+)	Debits (-)
	Current Account	0
Financial Account	+1,000 ($ currency), +1,000 (¥ currency), +1,000 (U.S. savings bond)	-1,000 ($ currency), -1,000 (¥ currency)

After cancellations, the summary balance of payments statistics would look like the following table.

Summary 1, 2, 3b	U.S. Balance of Payments ($)	
	Credits (+)	Debits (-)
	Current Account	0
Financial Account	+1,000 (U.S. savings bond)	0

The current account balance is found by summing the credit and debit entries representing exports and imports, respectively. This corresponds to the difference between exports and imports of goods and services. In this example, the current account (or trade) balance is CA = 1,000$- = 1,000$ - 0$. This means there is a trade deficit of 1,000$. Imports of goods and services exceed exports of goods and services.

The financial account balance is also found by summing the credit and debit entries. In this example, the financial account balance is KA = 1,000$+ = 0$ - 1,000$. This means the financial account has a surplus of 1,000$. Exports of assets exceed imports of assets.

Important Lessons from the Exchange Story

The exercise above teaches a number of important lessons. The first lesson follows from the summary statistics, suggesting that the following relationship must hold true:

current account balance + financial account balance = 0.

In the first set of summary statistics (1, 2, 3a), both the current account and the financial account had a balance of zero. In the second example (1, 2, 3b), the current account had a deficit of $1,000 while the financial account had a surplus of $1,000.

This implies that anytime a country has a current account deficit, it must have a financial account surplus of equal value. When a country has a current account surplus, it must have a financial account deficit of equal value. And when a country has balanced trade (a balanced current account), then it must have balance on its financial account.

It is worth emphasizing that this relationship is not an economic theory. An economic theory could be right or it could be wrong. This relationship is an accounting identity. (That's why an identity symbol rather than an equal sign is typically used in the formula above.) An accounting identity is true by definition.

Of course, the identity is valid only if we use the true (or actual) current account and financial account balances. What countries report as their trade statistics are only the measured values for these trade balances, not necessarily the true values.

Statisticians and accountants attempt to measure international transactions as accurately as possible. Their objective is to record the true values or to measure trade and financial flows as accurately as possible. However, a quick look at any country's balance of payments statistics reveals that the balance on the current account plus the balance on the financial account rarely, if ever, sums to zero. The reason is not that the identity is wrong but rather that not all the international transactions on the balance of payments are accounted for properly. Measurement errors are common.

These errors are reported in a line in the balance of payments labeled "statistical discrepancy." The statistical discrepancy represents the amount that must be added or subtracted to force the measured current account balance and the measured financial account balance to zero. In other words, in terms of the measured balances on the balance of payments accounts, the following relationship will hold:

current account balance + financial account balance + statistical discrepancy = 0.

The second lesson from this example is that imbalances (deficits and surpluses) on the balance of payments accounts arise as a result of a series of mutually voluntary transactions in which equally valued items are traded for each other. This is an important point because it is often incorrectly interpreted that a trade deficit implies that unfair trade is taking place. After all, the logic goes, when imports exceed exports, foreigners are not buying as many of our goods as we are buying of theirs. That's unequal exchange and that's unfair.

The story and logic are partially correct but incomplete. The logic of the argument focuses exclusively on trade in goods and services but ignores trade in assets. Thus it is true that when imports of goods exceed exports, we are buying more foreign goods and services than foreigners are buying of ours. However, at the same time, a current account deficit implies a financial account surplus. A financial account surplus, in turn, means that foreigners are buying more of our assets than we are buying of theirs. Thus when there is unequal exchange on the trade account, there must be equally opposite unequal exchange on the financial account. In the aggregate, imbalances on a current account, a trade account, or a financial account do not represent unequal exchanges between countries.

KEY TAKEAWAYS

- Every transaction between a domestic and foreign resident can be recorded as a debit and credit entry of equal value on the balance of payments accounts.
- All components of transactions that involve assets, including currency flows, are recorded on the financial account; all other items are recorded on the current account.
- All trade deficits on a country's current account implies an equally sized financial account surplus, while all trade surpluses implies an equally sized financial account deficit.
- In the aggregate, imbalances on a current account, a trade account, or a financial account do not represent unequal exchanges, or inequities, between countries.

EXERCISES

Jeopardy Questions:As in the popular television game show, you are given an answer to a question and you must respond with the question. For example, if the answer is "a tax on imports," then the correct question is "What is a tariff?"

- The balance on a country's financial account when its current account has a deficit of $80 billion.
- A country's financial account balance when its trade balance is -$60 billion, its service balance is +$25 billion, and its unilateral transfer and income account has a surplus of +$10 billion.
- The international transactions for shares of stock in corporations (in excess of 10 percent of the company's value) or for real estate.
- Of credit or debit, this is how exports are recorded on the balance of payments.
- Of current account or financial account, this is where an export of a clock will be recorded.
- Of current account or financial account, this is where an import of currency from your aunt in Paraguay will be recorded.

Use the information below from the 1997 U.S. national income accounts to calculate the following. (Assume the balance on income and unilateral transfers was zero.)

Current account balance: _________

Merchandise trade balance: _________

Service balance: _________

Net income payments and receipts: _________

Goods and services balance: _________

TABLE 2.4 U.S. NATIONAL INCOME STATISTICS, 1997 (BILLIONS OF DOLLARS)

Gross Domestic Product	8,080
Exports of Goods and Services	934
Merchandise Exports	678
Income Receipts	257
Imports of Goods and Services	1,043
Merchandise Imports	877
Income Payments	244
Net Unilateral Transfers	-45

2.6 STATISTICS FOR THE U.S. BALANCE OF PAYMENTS (2008)

The line numbers refer to the line item on the complete Bureau of Economic Analysis (BEA) report. All debit entries have a minus sign, and all credit entries have a plus sign. A brief description of each line item is provided below where all values are rounded downward for easy reference with the table. To see the entries for every line or for more recent statistics, see the U.S. Department of Commerce, Bureau of Economic Analysis Web site, located at http://www.bea.gov.

Table 2.5 U.S. Balance of Payments, 2008 (Millions of Dollars Seasonally Adjusted)

Line Number	Category	Value (credits [+], debits [-])
Current Account		
1	Exports of goods, services, and income receipts	+2,591,233
3	Goods	+1,276,994
4	Services	+549,602
13	Income receipts on U.S. assets abroad	+761,593
14	Direct investment receipts	+370,747
15	Other private receipts	+385,940
16	U.S. government receipts	+4,906
18	Imports of goods, services, and income	-3,168,938
20	Goods	-2,117,245
21	Services	-405,287
30	Income payments on foreign assets in the United States	-636,043
31	Direct investment payments	-120,862
32	Other private payments	-349,871
33	U.S. government payments	-165,310
35	Unilateral transfers, net	-128,363
Capital Account		
39	Capital account transactions, net	+953
Financial Account		
40	U.S. assets abroad (increase/financial outflow [-])	-106
41	U.S. official reserve assets	-4,848
46	U.S. government assets	-529,615
50	U.S. private assets	+534,357
51	Direct investment	-332,012
52	Foreign securities	+60,761
53	U.S. claims reported by U.S. nonbanks	+372,229

Line Number	Category	Value (credits [+], debits [-])
54	U.S. claims reported by U.S. banks	+433,379
55	Foreign assets in the United States (increase/financial inflow [+])	+534,071
56	Foreign official assets in the United States	+487,021
63	Other foreign assets in the United States, net	+47,050
64	Direct investment	+319,737
65	U.S. Treasury securities	+196,619
66	U.S. securities other than T-bills	-126,737
67	U.S. currency	+29,187
68	U.S. liabilities reported by U.S. nonbanks	-45,167
69	U.S. liabilities reported by U.S. banks	-326,589
71	Statistical discrepancy (sum of above with sign reversed)	+200,055

Below we provide a brief description of each line item that appears on this abbreviated balance of payments record.

Current Account

- Line 1, $2.59 trillion, shows the value of all U.S. exports of goods, services, and income. This value is equal to the sum of lines 3, 4, and 13.
- Line 3, $1.27 trillion, shows exports of merchandise goods. This includes any physical items that leave the country.
- Line 4, $549 billion, shows exports of services to foreigners. This category includes travel services, passenger fares, royalties, license fees, insurance legal services, and other private services.
- Line 13, $761 billion, shows income receipts on U.S. assets abroad. This represents profits and interest earned by U.S. residents on investments in other countries. In a sense, these are payments for services rendered where the services include entrepreneurial services in the case of foreign-operated factories, or monetary services in the case of interest and dividend payments on foreign securities. This line is included in a measure of gross national product (GNP) since this income is accruing to U.S. factors of production. However, the line is excluded from a measure of gross domestic product (GDP) since production did not take place within the borders of the country. Income receipts are divided into four subcategories: direct investment receipts, other private receipts, U.S. government receipts, and compensation of employees.

- Line 14, $370 billion, shows direct investment receipts. This represents profit earned by U.S. companies on foreign direct investment (FDI), where FDI is defined as a greater than 10 percent ownership share in a foreign company. Note that this is not new investments but rather the profit and dividends earned on previous investments.
- Line 15, $385 billion, shows other private receipts. This category includes interest and profit earned by individuals, businesses, investment companies, mutual funds, pension plans, and so on. In effect, all private investment income that accrues on investments worth less than 10 percent of a company would be included here.
- Line 16, $4.9 billion, shows U.S. government income receipts. This refers to interest and other income earned by government investments abroad. Notice that this item is very small compared to the other two income categories.
- Line 18, $3.1 trillion, records imports of goods, services, and income. This value is equal to the sum of lines 20, 21, and 30.
- Line 20, $2.1 trillion, shows imports of merchandise goods. Notice that goods imports make up about two-thirds of total imports.
- Line 21, $405 billion, shows imports of services such as travel services, passenger fares, insurance, and so on.
- Line 30, $636 billion, shows income payments on foreign assets in the United States. This corresponds to income earned by foreigners who operate companies in the United States or income earned on other U.S.-based assets held by foreigners. This entry is further divided into four components: direct investment payments, other private payments, U.S. government payments, and compensation of employees.
- Line 31, $120 billion, records direct investment payments to foreigners in the United States. This represents profit earned on foreign direct investment by foreign residents' companies, where FDI is defined as a greater than 10 percent ownership share in a U.S. company. Note that this is not new investments but rather the profit and dividends earned on previous investments.
- Line 32, $349 billion, reports other private payments. This category includes interest and profit earned by individuals, businesses, investment companies, mutual funds, pension plans, and so on. In effect, all private investment income that accrues on investments worth less than 10 percent of a company would be included here.
- Line 33, $165 billion, records payments made by the U.S. government to foreigners. This item represents mostly interest payments on U.S. Treasury bills owned by foreigners.

- Line 35, $128 billion, records net unilateral transfers. These transfers refer to government grants to foreign nations, government pension payments, and private remittances to family and friends abroad. A debit entry here means that the net transfers are outbound, that is, more transfers are made from the U.S. to individuals abroad than are made in the reverse direction.

Capital Account

Line 39, $953 million, represents net capital account transactions.

Financial Account

- Line 40, $106 million, shows the value of purchases of foreign assets by U.S. residents, hence it is referred to as a capital outflow. The line is the sum of U.S. official reserve assets (line 41), U.S. government assets (line 46), and U.S. private assets (line 50).
- Line 41, $4.8 billion, represents net U.S. official reserve transactions. Any purchases or sales of foreign currency in a foreign exchange intervention by the central bank would be recorded here. Since the item is a debit entry, it means that the U.S. central bank made net purchases of foreign assets (currencies) in 2008.
- It is worth noting that this line is more important for a country maintaining a fixed exchange rate. To maintain a credible fixed exchange rate, central banks must periodically participate in the foreign exchange market. This line measures the extent of that participation and is sometimes referred to as the "balance of payments" in a fixed exchange rate system.
- Line 46, $529 billion, represents net purchases of assets by the U.S. government, though not by the Federal Reserve.
- Line 50, $534 billion, shows private purchases of foreign assets by U.S. residents. It is the primary component of total U.S. assets abroad. The item is composed of direct investment (line 51), foreign securities (line 52), U.S. claims reported by U.S. nonbanks (line 53), and U.S. claims reported by U.S. banks (line 54).
- Line 51, $332 billion, shows direct investment by U.S. residents abroad. It would include purchases of factories, stocks, and so on by U.S. businesses and affiliates in foreign countries as long as there is a controlling interest in excess of 10 percent voting share.
- Line 52, $60 billion, shows net purchases of foreign stocks and bonds by U.S. individuals and businesses when there is no controlling interest in the foreign company. Most purchases by U.S. mutual funds, pension funds, and insurance companies would be classified here.

- Line 53, $372 billion, shows U.S. resident purchases of foreign assets reported by nonbanks.
- Line 54, $433 billion, reports U.S. resident purchases of foreign assets reported by U.S. banks. This may include items like foreign currency denominated demand deposits held by U.S. businesses and individuals in U.S. banks.
- Line 55, $534 billion, shows the sum total of foreign assets in the United States. This item refers to all purchases of U.S. assets by foreign residents, thus, it is listed as a capital inflow. This line is composed of the sum of foreign official assets in the United States (line 56), and other foreign assets in the United States (line 63).
- Line 56, $487 billion, refers to purchases of U.S. assets by foreign governments or foreign central banks.
- Line 63, $47 billion, refers to all other foreign assets purchases of U.S. assets and is the main component of capital inflows. It is composed of direct investment (line 64), U.S. Treasury securities (line 65), U.S. securities other than T-bills (line 66), U.S. currency (line 67), U.S. liabilities reported by U.S. nonbanks (line 68), and U.S. liabilities reported by U.S. banks (line 69).
- Line 64, $319 billion, refers to purchases of U.S. factories and stocks when there is a greater than 10 percent ownership share.
- Line 65, $196 billion, shows total purchases of U.S. Treasury bills by foreigners. This corresponds to foreign loans to the U.S. government.
- Line 66, $126 billion, shows non-U.S. Treasury bill and nondirect investment purchases of stocks and bonds by foreigners.
- Line 67, $29 billion, a credit entry, represents U.S. currency that has been repatriated (net). Typically, this flow is a credit indicating an outflow of U.S. currency. Because of the expectation that the U.S. dollar will remain stable in value, it is often held by residents in inflationary countries to prevent the deterioration of purchasing power. It is estimated that over $270 billion of U.S. currency circulates abroad and is used in exchange for foreign goods and services or simply held to store value. The value on line 67 represents only the amount that flowed back in 2007.
- Line 68, $45 billion, shows deposits and purchases of U.S. assets by foreigners reported by U.S. nonbanks.
- Line 69, $326 billion, reports deposits and purchases of U.S. assets by foreigners reported by U.S. banks. Thus if a foreign resident opens a checking account in a U.S. bank denominated in U.S. dollars, that value would be recorded here.

- Line 71, $200 billion, represents the statistical discrepancy. It is the sum of all the above items with the sign reversed. It is included to satisfy the accounting requirement that all debit entries be balanced by credit entries of equal value. Thus when the statistical discrepancy is included, the balance on the complete balance of payments is zero.

Summary Balances on the U.S. Balance of Payments (2008)

Table 2.6 "Balances on the U.S. Balance of Payments, 2008 (Millions of Dollars Seasonally Adjusted) (Credits [+], Debits [-])" reports a number of noteworthy balance of payments "balances" for 2008. In effect these subaccount balances allow us to identify net inflows or outflows of specific categories of goods, services, income, and assets.

Table 2.6 Balances on the U.S. Balance of Payments, 2008 (Millions of Dollars Seasonally Adjusted) (Credits [+], Debits [-])

Lines 1 + 18 + 35	Current account balance	-706, 068
Lines 3 + 20	Trade (goods) balance	-840, 251
Lines 4 + 21	Services balance	+144, 315
Lines 3 + 4 + 20 + 21	Goods and services balance	-695, 936
Lines 12 + 29 (not listed)	Investment income balance	+118, 231
Lines 40 + 55	Financial account balance	+533, 965
Line 71	Statistical discrepancy	+200,055

The sum of lines 1, 18, and 35 (i.e., exports of goods, services, and income; imports of goods, services, and income; and unilateral transfers [maintaining signs]) represents the current account (CA) balance. In 2008 in the United States, the CA balance was -706 billion dollars where the minus sign indicates a deficit. Thus the United States recorded a current account deficit of $706 billion. Note that the current account balance is often reported as the "trade balance using a broad measure of international trade."

Because unilateral transfers are relatively small and because investment income can be interpreted as payments for a service, it is common to say that a current account deficit means that imports of goods and services exceed exports of goods and services.

The sum of lines 3 and 20 (i.e., exports of goods and imports of goods) is known as the merchandise trade balance, or just trade balance for short. In 2008, the United States recorded a trade deficit of over $840 billion. This means that the United States imported more physical goods than it exported.

The sum of lines 4 and 21, service exports and service imports, represents the service trade balance or just service balance. The table shows that the United States recorded a service surplus of over $144 billion in 2008. In other words, the U.S. exports more services than it imports from the rest of the world.

The sum of lines 2 and 19 (not listed), exports of goods and services and imports of goods and services, is a noteworthy trade balance because this difference is used in the national income identity for GDP. In contrast, the national income identity for GNP includes the current account balance instead. In 2008, the United States recorded a goods and services trade deficit of over $695 billion.

The sum of lines 12 and 29 (not listed), income receipts on U.S. assets abroad and income payments on foreign assets in the United States, represents the balance on investment income. In 2008, there was a recorded investment income surplus of over $118 billion in the United States. This means that U.S. residents earned more on their investments abroad than foreigners earned on their investments in the United States.

The sum of lines 40 and 55, U.S. assets abroad and foreign assets in the United States, represents the financial account balance. In 2008, the United States recorded a financial account surplus of over $533 billion. A surplus on capital account means that foreigners are buying more U.S. assets than U.S. residents are buying of foreign assets. These asset purchases, in part, represent international borrowing and lending. In this regard, a capital account surplus implies that the United States is borrowing money from the rest of the world.

Finally, line 71 records the 2008 U.S. statistical discrepancy as a $200 billion credit entry. This implies that recorded debit entries on the balance of payments exceeded recorded credit entries. Thus an additional $200 billion credit entry is needed to make the accounts balance. This is the largest statistical discrepancy recorded since the BEA records began in 1960.

The presence of a statistical discrepancy means that there are international transactions that have taken place but have not been recorded or accounted for properly. One might conclude that the size of the errors is $200 billion, but this does not follow. The discrepancy only records the net effect. It is conceivable that $400 billion of credit entries and $200 billion of debit entries were missed. Or possibly, $800 billion of debit entries and $600 billion of credit entries were missed. In each case, the difference is $200 billion dollars, but clearly the amount of error is substantially more in the latter case.

Based on the way the balance of payments data are collected, it seems likely that the primary source of the statistical discrepancy is on the capital account side rather than the current account side. This is because trade in goods, the primary component of the current account, is measured directly and completely by customs officials, while capital account data are acquired through surveys completed by major banks and financial institutions. This does not mean that errors cannot occur, however. Goods trade is tangible and thus is easier to monitor. Capital transactions, in contrast, can be accomplished electronically and invisibly and thus are more prone to measurement errors. Service and income transactions on the current account are also likely to exhibit the same difficulty in monitoring, implying that errors in the current account are more likely to arise in these subcategories.

KEY TAKEAWAYS

- The U.S. balance of payments records transactions on both the current and financial accounts concluding with several important balances.
- The United States had a current account deficit of $706 billion in 2008.
- The U.S. had a merchandise trade deficit that was larger than its current account deficit at over $840 billion in 2008.
- The U.S. had a financial account surplus of over $533 billion.
- The statistical discrepancy at $200 billion in 2008 demonstrates that all international transactions are not being recorded since the sum of the balance on the current account and the financial accounts does not equal zero.

EXERCISE

Jeopardy Questions:As in the popular television game show, you are given an answer to a question and you must respond with the question. For example, if the answer is "a tax on imports," then the correct question is "What is a tariff?"

- The value of the statistical discrepancy if a country has a current account deficit of $250 billion and a financial account surplus of $230 billion.
- The approximate value of the U.S. current account deficit in 2008.
- The approximate value of the U.S. merchandise trade deficit in 2008.
- Of U.S. domestic residents or foreign residents, this group profited more on its foreign investments because the United States ran a surplus on its investment income balance.
- The approximate value of the U.S. financial account surplus in 2008.
- The approximate value of the statistical discrepancy in the U.S. balance of payments in 2008.

2.7 THE TWIN-DEFICIT IDENTITY

One of the important relationships among aggregate economic variables is the so-called twin-deficit identity, a term in reference to a country's government budget deficit and a simultaneous current account deficit. The name for this identity became commonplace during the 1980s and 1990s because at that time the United

States experienced deficits in both of these accounts. Now, as we will see later, the identity will be a misnomer in many circumstances since there is no reason that "twin" deficits need to always appear together on these two national accounts. In fact, some countries will, at times, experience a deficit on one account and a surplus on the other. Also, at times, a country will experience a surplus on both accounts.

Thus a better title to this section would be "The Relationship between a Country's Government Budget Deficit and Its Current Account Deficit." However, since 2004, the United States finds itself back in the twin-deficit scenario, and since "twin-deficit identity" rolls off the tongue much more easily, we will stick to this title.

To understand this identity it will be helpful to take a much more careful look at the national income identity. This time I will build up the identity in a stepwise fashion using a circular flow diagram to better visualize the flows of money within an economy. A circular flow diagram is typically one of the first principles shown to students in an introductory macroeconomics class. Its purpose is to show the flow of money between the major players (or agents) within an economy. Circular flow diagrams can be either simple or complex depending on how many agents one introduces into the system and how finely one wishes to break down the monetary flows.

Circular Flow: Version 1

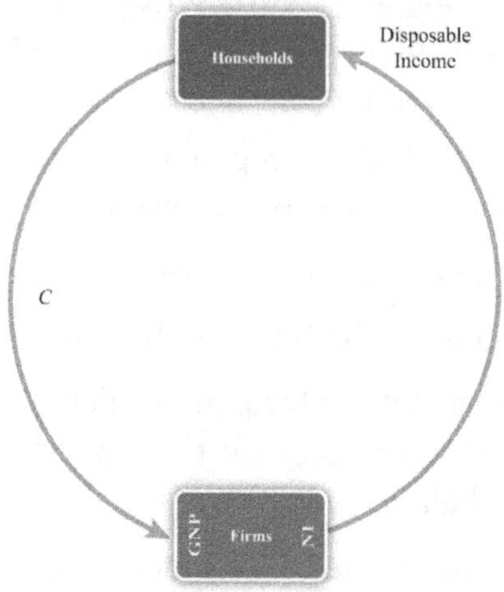

Figure 2.2 The Simplest Circular Flow

The simplest version of a circular flow diagram considers an economy consisting of two agents: households and firms. We imagine that firms produce goods and services using labor as an input.

The flow of money is shown in Figure 2.2 "The Simplest Circular Flow". The C arrow represents the dollar value of consumption expenditures made by households to purchase the goods and services produced and sold by firms. (The goods and services flow could be represented by an arrow in the opposite direction to C, but we leave that out for simplicity.) Since we assume in this case that there are only households buying goods, all GNP consists of C. The money that flows to firms from sales of consumption goods is given to the workers in exchange for their labor services. This monetary flow is represented by the arrow labeled "disposable income." Disposable income is all the money households have to spend, which in this case is equal to the national income (NI).

Note especially that we use GNP rather than GDP as our measure of national income so that flows with the rest of the world later are properly defined.

Circular Flow: Version 2

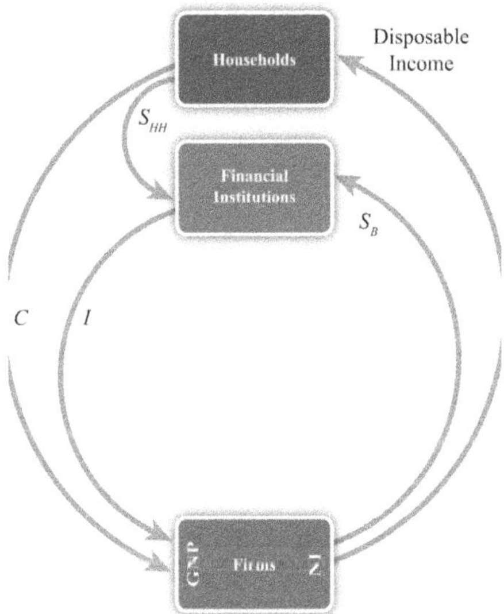

Figure 2.3 The Circular Flow Adding Financial Institutions

The circular flow can be extended one step by adding financial institutions in Figure 2.3 "The Circular Flow Adding Financial Institutions". Financial institutions represent any company that facilitates borrowing and lending; the prime example is a bank. However, they may also include investment companies, pension funds, and mutual funds. The presence of financial institutions allows some money to be diverted from the consumption flow. In Figure 2.3 "The Circular Flow Adding Financial Institutions", these diversions are represented by SHH, representing household savings and SB, representing business saving. Some of the revenue earned by firms is not actually given out to workers in the form of wages. Instead some money is "retained" in the form of profit and excess earnings. These retained earnings are generally used to purchase investment goods to help an industry replace worn-out capital equipment and to add new capital. Much of these retained earnings may be used directly to purchase new capital equipment, although some of it will be saved by depositing it in a financial institution. For simplicity we will imagine that all such business saving flows through the financial system, hence the SB arrow. In addition, households generally hold back some of their income from spending and deposit it into pension plans, savings accounts, and so on. Thus we include the arrow from households. The easiest way to think of the diagram is to imagine that financial institutions take deposits from firms and households and then lend out the money to finance investment spending, I. With some exceptions, this is the way it will often work. One notable exception is that some of the money lent by banks is often used to finance consumption rather than investment. This occurs whenever households finance consumption spending using a credit card. However, we can avoid this complication by defining SHH as being "net" savings, where the net means "after subtracting household borrowing." With this definition in mind, it should be clear that SHH can be negative—that is, its flow reversed—if household borrowing exceeds household saving.

We can now identify several important relationships. The first one relates to an important decision made by households. They choose how much of their disposable income should be spent on consumption and how much should be saved. You may recall from previous courses that the fraction of income spent on consumption goods (from an extra dollar of income) is called the marginal propensity to consume, while the fraction of income saved is called the marginal propensity to save.

A second relationship is shown on the left side of the Firms box. This indicates that GNP is equal to the sum of C and I. This version of the national income identity would only be valid if there were no government sector and no trade with the rest of the world.

A third important relationship is shown by noting the flow of money in and out of the financial sector. There we see two arrows flowing in (i.e., S_{HH} and S_B) and one flow outward (i.e., I). This leads to the identity

$$S_{HH + SB = I,}$$

indicating that the sum of household and business saving equals investment. A more common simplification of this relationship is shown by noting the following:

$$S_{P = SHH + SB,}$$

where S_P is called private saving. Thus private saving equals the sum of household saving and business saving. This will simplify the above identity to

$$S_{P = I,}$$

or simply, private saving equals investment. Note that the term "private" is used here to distinguish it from government (or public sector) saving, which we'll include next.

Circular Flow: Version 3

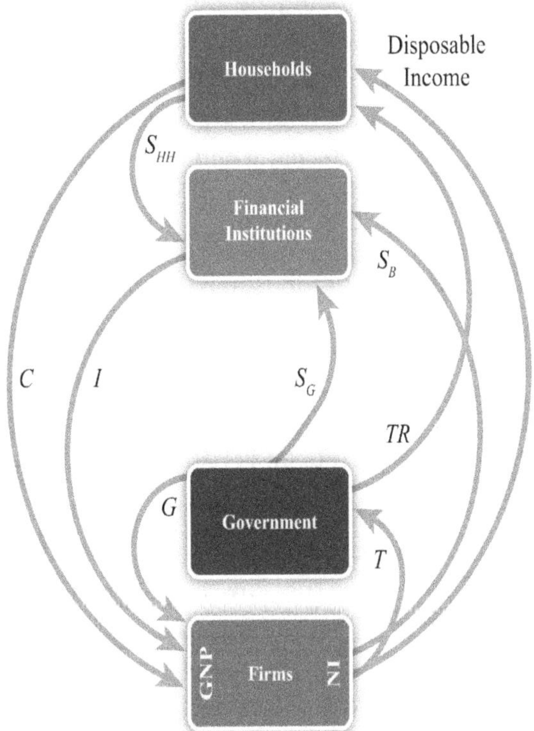

Figure 2.4 The Circular Flow Adding Government

Next, let's add in the government sector in Figure 2.4 "The Circular Flow Adding Government". The government is shown both to take money out of the circular flow and to inject money back in. Money is withdrawn first in the form of taxes (T). In the adjoining diagram, taxes are represented as a flow of money directly from firms, as if it is entirely a tax on income. This is a simplification since in reality taxes are collected in many forms from many different agents. For example, governments collect profit taxes from firms and financial institutions, sales and property taxes from households, and tariffs on traded goods (not included yet). All of these taxes are assumed to be lumped together in the T flow and withdrawn directly from national income.

Tax revenues (TR) can be spent in two separate ways. The TR flow represents transfer payments injected into the household income stream. Transfer payments include social security paid to retired workers, Medicaid and welfare payments, unemployment, and so on. These are government expenditures that do not exchange for a particular good or service. The second type of expenditure is G. G represents spending by government for the purchase of goods and services produced by firms. It includes defense spending, education, police and fire protection, and so on.

The final monetary flow, shown flowing out of the government, is labeled SG and refers to government saving. It should be obvious that the money collected by government in the form of taxes need not always equal government expenditures. In the event that tax revenues exceed expenditures, the government would have extra money left over. We imagine that this money would be saved in the financial sector since it is always better to collect interest when possible. Hence we draw the flow of excess funds, government saving (SG), flowing from government into the financial sector.

We can now represent the flow of funds in and out of the government sector with the following identity:

$$S_{G = T - TR - G.}$$

When T exceeds the sum of TR and G, the government has extra saving that flows into the financial sector. These funds would then be available to lend out and finance additional investment.

Of course, what is more typical of many governments is for the sum of TR and G to exceed tax revenue, T. In this case, the flow of government saving (S_G) would be negative and would be represented in the diagram as a flow in the opposite direction. In this case, the government would be borrowing money from the financial sector to finance its excess expenditures. We would also say that the government is running a budget deficit.

In short, negative government saving, that is, SG < 0, implies a government budget deficit, which the government finances by borrowing from the financial sector.

Otherwise, positive government saving, that is, $S_G > 0$, implies a government budget surplus, which results either in additions to saving or a repayment of previous debt.

Next, in this version of the circular flow, we can represent the national income identity as the flow of money into firms. In this case, GNP equals the sum of C, I, and G. This version would only be Accurate when there is no trade with the rest of the world.

Lastly, with government included, we must rewrite the relationship representing the flows in and out of the financial sector. This now becomes

$$S_{HH + SB + SG = I.}$$

This identity says that the sum of household, business, and government saving must equal private investment expenditures.

Circular Flow: Version 4

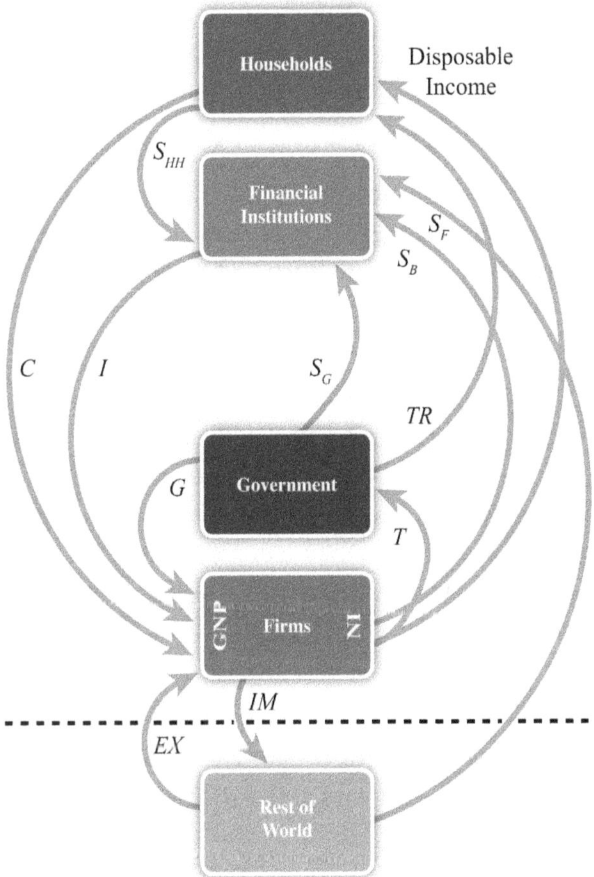

Figure 2.5 The Circular Flow Adding the RoW

The final circular flow diagram shown in Figure 2.5 "The Circular Flow Adding the RoW" extends the previous version to include trade flows with the rest of the world. The rest of the world (RoW) is shown at the very bottom of the adjoining diagram, below the dotted line, which represents the border. Trade with the RoW consists first of exports of goods, services, income and transfers, and expenditures on exports (EX), represented by a flow into firms since money is being used by foreigners to purchase the exported products. Second, imports of goods, services, income and transfers, and imports (IM) are subtracted from firms, resulting in an arrow from firms to the RoW. This adjustment accounts for the fact that measured expenditures made by households, the government, and firms in a open economy will consist of purchases of both domestic and imported goods. Thus the C, I, and G flows will include their purchases of imports, and these should not be included as part of GNP. In essence, the money used to buy imported products is redirected to the foreign firms, hence we have the outflow of money. (For a more complete explanation see

Chapter 2 «National Income and the Balance of Payments Accounts», Section 2.1 "National Income and Product Accounts".)

This completes the national income identity with all major sectors included and now becomes

$$GNP = C + I + G + EX - IM,$$

which is represented by the flow of money into (and away from) firms on the left side of the diagram. However, as noted elsewhere, EX - IM, the balance on the current account, need not be equal to zero. If EX - IM > 0, then the country would have a current account (CA) surplus, whereas if EX - IM < 0 the country would have a CA deficit.

Consider when EX - IM < 0. In this case, more money flows out to purchase imports than flows back in to purchase exports. Essentially, there is a loss of money to the RoW despite some exceptions; however, this money does not remain outside the country. Instead, it is brought right back in and deposited into financial institutions (shown as the SF flow on the diagram). In other words, it is saved. This saving represents the country's financial account surplus, which is equal and opposite to the CA deficit (see Chapter 2 «National Income and the Balance of Payments Accounts», Section 2.5 "Recording Transactions on the Balance of Payments" for a more complete explanation).

The key point is that foreign saving offsets the CA deficit. This can be represented by the relationship showing the inflows and outflows from the RoW, namely,

$$S_{F = IM - EX.}$$

This says that foreign saving equals the CA deficit. From the perspective of the foreigners, we would refer to SF as money saved or lent to the domestic country. From the perspective of the domestic country, SF would be considered money borrowed from the RoW.

Clearly, since a country may run a surplus on trade (i.e., EX - IM > 0), S_F could also be negative. In this case, the RoW would either be dissaving, meaning it is withdrawing previously accumulated saving from the domestic country, or the RoW would be borrowing money from the domestic country. This would occur if a domestic bank makes a loan to someone abroad. Alternatively, from the perspective of the domestic country, we can say it is lending money to the RoW when $S_F < 0$.

Finally, the Twin-Deficit Identity

The twin-deficit identity is derived by accounting for the monetary flows in and out of the financial sector in version four of the circular flow. This results in the following identity:

$$S_{HH + SB + SG + SF = I.}$$

This says that the sum of household saving, business saving, government saving, and foreign saving must equal private investment spending. An equivalent version can be written by recalling that household plus business saving equals private saving to get

$$S_{P + SG + SF = I.}$$

The identity is best interpreted by noting that there are four key sources for funds in the financial sector that are not part of the consumption stream. The pool of funds to finance investment can be drawn from households, businesses, the government, or from the RoW. Also, the sum of all funds not used for consumption must be equal to the amount spent on investment goods.

It is important to note that this relationship is an accounting identity. This means that the relationship must be true as long as all variables are measured properly. This is not an economic theory, which is a proposition that may or may not be true. In practice, this identity rarely adds up, however, because the variables are not typically measured accurately.

To turn this identity into the "twin-deficit" identity, we must merely take note of several previous definitions. Recall that

$$S_{G = T - TR - G, SF = IM - EX,}$$

and

$$S_{P = SHH + SB.}$$

Plugging these into identity 1 above yields

$$S_{P + T - TR - G + IM - EX = I.}$$

Reorder these to get the following twin-deficit identity:

$$(S_{P - I) + (IM - EX) = (G + TR - T).}$$

This is a popular way of writing the twin-deficit identity since it explicitly indicates two deficits. If the second expression (IM - EX) > 0, then the country has a current account deficit (i.e., a trade deficit). If the right-hand-side expression (G + TR - T) > 0, then the country has a government budget deficit. The expression in total, then, demonstrates that these two deficits are related to each other according to this accounting identity. Indeed, the difference between the government budget deficit and the trade deficit must equal the difference between private saving and investment as shown here:

$$(S_{P - I) = (G + TR - T) - (IM - EX).}$$

The Twin-Deficit Relationship in the United States and China

Perhaps the best way to get a feel for the twin-deficit relationship in a country is to look at the numbers. Table 2.7 "U.S. Twin-Deficit Figures (GDP), 1997–2008" and

Table 2.8 «China Twin-Deficit Figures (GDP), 1997–2007» show values for the twin-deficit identity in the United States and in China over the past ten years or so. All values are presented as a percentage of GDP. Also, because the data on the balance of payments never add up, which results in a statistical discrepancy term, the twin-deficit identity numbers do not add up. To avoid that problem, the private saving numbers presented are not the actual reported values but the values saving would have to be to assure the twin-deficit identity adds up—that is, it is derived as a residual value.

Table 2.7 U.S. Twin-Deficit Figures (GDP), 1997–2008

$(S_p - I)$ + Current Account Deficit = Govt. Budget Deficit				
Year	**Private Saving* (%)**	**Investment (%)**	**Current Account Deficit (%)**	**Govt. Budget Deficit (%)**
2008	13.5	14.0	4.7	4.2
2007	11.7	15.4	5.3	1.6
2006	12.1	16.7	6.1	1.5
2005	12.9	16.5	6.1	2.5
2004	14.0	16.1	5.5	3.4
2003	14.0	15.2	4.8	3.6
2002	13.4	15.1	4.4	2.7
2001	11.6	15.9	3.8	-0.5
2000	11.0	17.7	4.2	-2.4
1999	12.6	17.5	3.2	-1.7
1998	13.8	17.3	2.4	-1.0
1997	15.2	16.7	1.7	0.2
*** Private saving is calculated as a residual.**				

Source: U.S. Bureau of Economic Analysis, National Economic Accounts, Frequently Requested NIPA Tables. See U.S. BEA interactive tables for the years indicated at http://www.bea.gov/national/nipaweb/SelectTable.asp?Popular=Y.

Table 2.8 China Twin-Deficit Figures (GDP), 1997–2007

$(S_p - I)$ + Current Account Deficit = Govt. Budget Deficit				
Year	**Private Saving* (%)**	**Investment (%)**	**Current Account Deficit (%)**	**Govt. Budget Deficit (%)**
2007	53.0	42.3	-11.3	-0.6
2006	52.8	42.6	-9.4	0.8
2005	51.1	42.7	-7.2	1.2
2004	48.1	43.2	-3.6	1.3

$(S_p\text{-}I)$ + Current Account Deficit = Govt. Budget Deficit				
Year	Private Saving* (%)	Investment (%)	Current Account Deficit (%)	Govt. Budget Deficit (%)
2003	46.0	41.0	-2.8	2.2
2002	43.0	37.9	-2.4	2.6
2001	40.1	36.5	-1.3	2.3
2000	39.5	35.3	-1.7	2.5
1999	39.6	36.2	-1.4	1.9
1998	40.2	36.2	-2.9	1.1
1997	40.6	36.7	-3.1	0.7
* Private saving is calculated as a residual.				

Source: China Data Online, China Statistical Yearbook. See China Statistical Yearbooks located at http://chinadataonline.org/member/yearbooksp/default.asp?Start Year=1981 & End Year=2009 & IFFirst=yes & page=2.

The twin-deficit numbers reveal some interesting patterns. As of the most recent data (2008), the United States has twin deficits, with a CA deficit of 4.7 percent of GDP and a government budget deficit of 4.2 percent. Since these numbers are almost equal, it is as if the U.S. government deficit, which must be financed with borrowing, is being financed by borrowed funds from abroad. In the previous year, 2007, government borrowing requirements were much lower, at 1.6 percent, but borrowing from foreigners was higher at 5.3 percent. The extra borrowing allowed the U.S. savings rate to remain much lower than the private investment requirement. We can interpret this year as one in which private investment was mostly financed with borrowings from abroad.

The United States has had twin deficits since 2001, when it finished a four-year run with a trade deficit and a government budget surplus. This demonstrates that twin "deficits" do not always arise despite the label used to describe the identity. During the budget surplus years the government was able to retire some of its outstanding debt, but the country also ran CA deficits implying, essentially, borrowings from foreigners. As in 2007, these years also describe periods in which foreign borrowings are used to maintain a higher investment level than can be sustained with the lower national savings rate.

In contrast, consider the twin-deficit numbers calculated in the same way for China during the same period. The differences with the U.S. numbers are striking. The two things that stand out immediately are the significantly higher values for private saving and investment. Instead of numbers in the midteens in the United States, China's percentages are in the midforties to low fifties. Again, the savings terms are calculated as residuals, so there may be some error there, but nonetheless it is clear that China both saves and invests about three times more than the United States as a percentage of GDP. Because it invests so much more, the implication from the national income identity is that China consumes much less than the United States as a percentage. Indeed, China's consumption figures (not shown) are usually less than 50 percent of GDP.

Indeed, this is why China and many other Asian economies are described as high-saving and low-consuming countries. The United States in comparison is described as a high-consumption country and low-saving country.

The negative number on China's CA deficit in all the years means that China has run a trade surplus. A surplus means it is lending money abroad and forgoing consumption, by another 11 percent in 2007. (This will be explained in more detail in Chapter 3 "The Whole Truth about Trade Imbalances".) Also, the negative number for China's budget balance means that it was running a government budget surplus in 2007. So in 2007, China had twin surpluses—a much rarer occurrence—rather than twin deficits. In previous years China didn't have twin anything: running trade surpluses that were increasing through the past decade, and government budget deficits.

It is worth reflecting briefly on the large investment and trade surpluses in China in comparison with the United States. The U.S. per capita GDP is about $47,000. Comprising that per person production is about 15 percent that goes into investment. That still leaves a considerable percentage left for the consumption and government spending that enhance Americans' standard of living. In contrast, China's per capita GDP, in purchasing power parity (PPP) terms, is about $6,000. Per person, it produces much less than in the United States. But curiously, despite being a much poorer country, the high investment rate means that it consumes and spends on government programs a much smaller percentage of its income than the United States; perhaps as little as $3,000 per person.

This seems to fly in the face of simple logic. One might expect that a richer country like the United States would save more and consume less since it can do so while still maintaining a high standard of living. For a poorer country like China, we might expect it would save less and try to consume a larger proportion of its income in order to catch up (i.e., in terms of its standard of living) with the rest of the world. Instead, it is the exact opposite.

KEY TAKEAWAYS

- Twin deficits occur when a country has both a current account deficit and a government budget deficit at the same time.
- When twin deficits occur, the sum of net private saving (S_p-I) and the current account deficit must equal the government budget deficit.

- A government budget deficit represents a use of funds drawn from the financial sector.
- A trade deficit represents a source of funds for the financial sector.
- Private saving represents a source of funds for the financial sector.
- Private investment represents a use of funds drawn from the financial sector.
- The United States has run twin deficits for the past seven years. It can be reasonably described as a low-investment, low-saving, and high-consumption country.
- China has mostly run trade surpluses and budget deficits in the past decade. It can be reasonably described as a high-investment, high-saving, and low-consumption country.

EXERCISES

Jeopardy Questions: As in the popular television game show, you are given an answer to a question and you must respond with the question. For example, if the answer is "a tax on imports," then the correct question is "What is a tariff?"

- An excess of government receipts over expenditures.
- National income minus taxes plus transfer payments.
- The level of government spending when the government deficit is $100 billion, transfer payments are $800 billion, and tax revenues are $1,300 billion.
- The four different sources of saving described in this chapter.
- Of deficit, surplus, or balance, the balance on the current account if the expression IM - EX in the twin-deficit identity is positive.
- Of deficit, surplus, or balance, the balance on the government budget if the expression (G+TR−T) in the twin-deficit identity is positive.
- What is the government's budget balance if government spending is $40 billion, private saving is $60 billion, government transfer payments are $10 billion, private investment is $80 billion, and tax revenues are $50 billion? Show your work.
- Below are the economic data for the fictional country of Sandia. Write out the twin-deficit identity. Verify whether Sandia's data satisfy the identity.

TABLE 2.9 SANDIA'S ECONOMIC DATA (BILLIONS OF DOLLARS)

Gross Domestic Product	400
Imports of Goods and Services	140
Investment Spending	20

Private Saving	30
Exports of Goods and Services	100
Government Transfers	40
Government Tax Revenues	140
Government Spending	140
Consumption Spending	280

Japan once argued that the main reason the United States had large trade deficits during the 1980s and 1990s was because of its large federal government budget deficit. If the United States wanted to reduce its trade deficit, Japan said, then the United States should reduce its budget deficit. Use the twin-deficit identity to answer the following questions:

Explain what also would have to hold for there to be a direct relationship between budget deficit changes and trade deficit changes.

- Is it possible to account for a reduction in the federal government budget deficit and a simultaneous increase in the current account deficit? Explain.
- Is it possible to reduce the federal government budget deficit, maintain the same level of net private saving (i.e., S_p - I), and still experience an increase in the current account deficit? Explain.
- Explain whether the following economic changes are consistent with the twin-deficit identity. Assume ceteris paribus, meaning all other variables in the identity remain fixed.
- A $10 billion increase in the government budget deficit and a $10 billion increase in the current account deficit.
- A $50 billion decrease in the government budget deficit and a $50 billion increase in private investment.
- A $10 billion increase each in the government budget surplus, the current account deficit, private saving, and private investment.
- A $30 billion increase in the current account surplus and a $30 billion increase in the government budget deficit.

Refer to the table below to answer the following questions:

Use the twin-deficit identity to fill in the blank values in the table below for the three fictitious countries.

	Private Saving (S_p)	Investment	Current Account Deficit	Government Budget Deficit
Metis	500	500		200
Thebe		150	0	300
Leda	75	100	0	

- Which country is best described as financing its government budget deficit with domestic saving?
- Which country is best described as financing its government budget deficit with foreign saving?
- Which country is best described as financing extra domestic investment with government saving?

2.8 INTERNATIONAL INVESTMENT POSITION

LEARNING OBJECTIVES

- Learn how to define and interpret a country's international investment position.
- Understand how the international investment position is updated from year to year.

A country's international investment position (IIP) is like a balance sheet in that it shows the total holdings of foreign assets by domestic residents and the total holdings of domestic assets by foreign residents at a point in time. In the International Monetary Fund's (IMF) financial statistics, these are listed as domestic assets (foreign assets held by domestic residents) and domestic liabilities (domestic assets owned by foreign residents). The financial account balance, whose counterpart is the current account balance, is more like an income statement that shows the changes in asset holdings during the past year. In other words, the financial account balance consists of flow variables since it records changes in the country's asset holdings during the year, while the international asset position of a country consists of stock variables since it records the total value of assets at a point in time.

A country's net international asset position may be in surplus, deficit, or balance. If in surplus, then the value of foreign assets (debt and equity) held by domestic residents exceeds the value of domestic assets held by foreigners. Alternatively, we could say that domestic assets exceed domestic liabilities. This country would then be referred to as a creditor country. If the reverse is true, so that domestic liabilities to foreigners exceed domestic assets, then the country would be called a debtor country.

Asset holdings may consist of either debt obligations or equity claims. Debt consists of IOUs (i.e., I owe you) in which two parties sign a contract agreeing to an initial transfer of money from the lender to the borrower followed by a repayment according to an agreed schedule. The debt contract establishes an obligation for the borrower to repay principal and interest in the future. Equity claims represent ownership shares in potentially productive assets. Equity holdings do not establish obligations between parties, at least not in the form of guaranteed repayments. Once ownership in an asset is transferred from seller to buyer, all advantages and disadvantages of the asset are transferred as well.

Debt and equity obligations always pose several risks. The first risk with debt obligations is the risk of possible default (either total or partial). To the lender, default risk means that the IOU will not be repaid at all, that it will be repaid only in part, or that it is repaid over a much longer period of time than originally contracted. The risk of default to the borrower is that future borrowing will likely become unavailable. The advantage of default to the borrower, of course, is that not all the borrowed money is repaid. The second risk posed by debt is that the real value of the repayments may be different than expected. This can arise because of unexpected inflation or unexpected currency changes. Consider inflation first. If inflation is higher than expected, then the real value of debt repayment (if the nominal interest rate is fixed) will be lower than originally expected. This will be an advantage to the borrower, who repays less in real terms, and a disadvantage to the lender, who receives less in real terms. If inflation turns out to be less than expected, then the advantages are reversed. Next, consider currency fluctuations. Suppose a domestic resident, who receives income in the domestic currency, borrows foreign currency in the international market. If the domestic currency depreciates, then the value of the repayments in domestic currency terms will rise even though the foreign currency repayment value remains the same. Thus currency depreciations can be harmful to borrowers of foreign currency. A similar problem can arise for a lender. Suppose a domestic resident purchases foreign currency and then lends it to a foreign resident (note that this is the equivalent of saving money abroad). If the domestic currency appreciates, then foreign savings, once cashed in, will purchase fewer domestic goods and the lender will lose.

The risk of equity purchases arises whenever the asset's rate of return is less than expected. This can happen for a number of different reasons. First, if the equity purchases are direct investment in a business, then the return on that investment will depend on how well the business performs. If the market is vibrant and management is good, then the investment will be profitable. Otherwise, the rate of return on the investment could be negative. All the risk, however, is borne by the investor. The same holds true for stock purchases. Returns on stocks may be positive or negative, but it is the purchaser who bears full responsibility for the return on the investment.

Equity purchases can suffer from exchange rate risk as well. When foreign equities are purchased, their rate of return in terms of domestic currency will depend on the currency value. If the foreign currency in which assets are denominated falls substantially in value, then the value of those assets falls along with it.

The U.S. International Investment Position

The United States is the largest debtor nation in the world. This means that its international investment position is in deficit and the monetary value of that deficit is larger than that of any other country in the world. The data for the U.S. international investment position in 2008 are available in this U.S. BEA international investment position spreadsheet.The data for the U.S. international investment position are available from the Bureau of Economic Analysis, International Economic Accounts, International Investment Position, at http://www.bea.gov/international/xls/intinv08_t1.xls. At market values the preliminary estimate for 2008 is that the U.S. was in debt to the rest of the world in the amount of $3.469 trillion. (Refer to cell I22 in spreadsheet.) Excluding financial derivatives that refer to interest rate and foreign exchange contracts, the United States was in debt in the amount -$3.628 trillion (cell I24).

Note that this valuation is the U.S. "net" investment position, meaning that it is the difference between the sum total value of foreign assets owned by U.S. residents (U.S. assets abroad) minus U.S. assets owned by foreigners (foreign-owned assets in the United States). The first of these, U.S. assets abroad, represents our purchases of foreign equities and money we have lent to foreigners. The total value stood at $19.888 trillion in 2008 using market value methods (cell I26). The second, foreign-owned assets in the United States, represents foreign purchases of U.S. equities and money foreigners have lent to us or, equivalently, that we have borrowed. The total in 2008 stood at $23.357 trillion (cell I50).

The size of the U.S. debt position causes worry for some. Thirty years ago the United States had a sizable creditor position. However, as a result of trade deficits run throughout the 1980s and 1990s, the United States quickly turned from a net creditor to a net debtor. The changeover occurred in 1989. In the early 1990s, the size of this debt position was not too large compared to the size of the economy; however, by the late 1990s and early 2000s, the debt ballooned. In 2008, the U.S. debt position stood at 24.6 percent of GDP, which interestingly is down slightly from 24.9 percent of GDP in 2002 despite annual current account deficits since then. The reason for these changes is changes in the valuations of assets, as reflected in stock market prices, real estate price changes, and changes in the exchange rate. Notice in the 2008 BEA IIP spreadsheet that the investment position is derived from the 2007 position in the following way. First, the current account deficit caused an addition to U.S. external debt of $505 billion (cell D22). Changes in asset prices both here and abroad further increased U.S. external debt by $720 billion (cell E22). This could be because either real estate prices abroad fell by more than in the United States or security prices abroad fell by more than in the United States. Next, there was another increase of $583 billion in external U.S. debt because of changes in exchange rates. In this case, an appreciation of the U.S. dollar increased the values of foreign-held U.S. assets and reduced the value of U.S.-held foreign assets. Finally, U.S. external debt decreased by $479 billion due to other factors that don't neatly fit into the first two categories. (See footnote 2 in the BEA IIP spreadsheet.)

For several reasons, the debt is not a cause for great worry, although it is growing quickly. First, despite its large numerical size, the U.S. international debt position is still less than 25 percent of its annual GDP. Although this is large enough to be worrisome, especially with a trend toward a future increase, it is not nearly as large as some other countries have experienced in the past. In Argentina and Brazil, international debt positions exceeded 60 percent of their GDPs. For some less-developed countries, international debt at times has exceeded 100 percent of their annual GDP.

A second important point is that much of our international obligations are denominated in our own home currency. This means that when international debts (principal + interest) are paid to foreigners, they will be paid in U.S. currency rather than foreign currency. This relieves the U.S. from the requirement to sell products abroad to acquire sufficient foreign currency to repay its debts. Many other countries that have experienced international debt crises have had great problems financing interest and principal repayments especially when bad economic times make it difficult to maintain foreign sales. Finally, it is worth noting that, despite the name applied to it, our international "debt" position does not correspond entirely to "debt" in the term's common usage. Recall that debt commonly refers to obligations that must be repaid with interest in the future. Although a sizable share of our outstanding obligations is in the form of debt, another component is in equities. That means some of the money "owed" to foreigners is simply the value of their shares of stock in U.S. companies. These equities either will make money or will not be based on the success of the business, but they do not require a formal obligation for repayment in the future.

KEY TAKEAWAYS

- The IIP measures the difference between the total value of domestic holdings of foreign assets and the value of foreign assets held in the domestic country. If the IIP is negative, we say the country is a debtor country. If the IIP is positive, we say the country is a creditor country.
- Asset holdings include both debt and equities. Debt involves an obligation to repay principal and interest, whereas equities involve either profit or loss to the foreign asset holder.

- The U.S. IIP stands at $3.5 trillion in 2008, making the United States the largest debtor nation in the world.

EXERCISE

Jeopardy Questions: As in the popular television game show, you are given an answer to a question and you must respond with the question. For example, if the answer is "a tax on imports," then the correct question is "What is a tariff?"

- A complete record of a country's holdings of foreign assets and foreigners' holdings of domestic assets at a point in time.
- The term describing a country whose total domestic assets held abroad exceed total domestic liabilities held by foreigners.
- The term describing a country whose total domestic liabilities held by foreigners exceed total domestic assets held abroad.
- The name for the type of asset that establishes an obligation for the borrower to repay principal and interest in the future.
- The name for the type of asset that represents ownership shares in potentially productive assets.

CHAPTER

THE COMPLETE TRUTH REGARDING TRADE IMBALANCES 3

INTRODUCTION

One of the most misinterpreted and misunderstood concepts in international finance is the implication of a country's trade deficit or surplus. Often it is incorrectly presumed that a trade deficit is problematic while a trade surplus is a sign of economic strength. This chapter walks the reader through a thorough investigation of trade imbalances—what they mean and how to interpret them. The chapter concludes that trade deficits can indeed be a big problem for a country, but not always. Trade surpluses can also be a sign of strength, but again, not always. Whether a trade imbalance for a particular country should be viewed as good, bad, or benign depends on many other economic circumstances. This chapter spells out what those circumstances are.

3.1 TRADE IMBALANCES: AN OVERVIEW

Unfortunately, these perceptions and beliefs are somewhat misguided. In general, it is simply not true that a trade deficit is a sign of a weak economy and a trade surplus is a sign of a strong economy. Merely knowing that a country has a trade deficit, or that a trade deficit is rising, is not enough information to say anything about the current or future prospects for a country—and yet that is precisely how the statistics are often reported.

The truth about trade deficits is that sometimes they are good, sometimes they are bad, but most times, they are benign (i.e., they just don't matter). There are situations in which trade deficits could be interpreted as a sign of a strong thriving economy. There are other situations in which trade deficits could be indicative of economic problems. In most situations, however, trade deficits are not large enough to warrant a positive or negative interpretation. In this case, they should be viewed without interest. These same points apply to trade surpluses as well.

The purpose of this chapter is to explain, clearly and intuitively, the circumstances in which trade imbalances should be interpreted as good and the circumstances in which they are bad. The section will show situations in which trade deficits can indeed lead to long-term harm for an economy. However, it will also show cases in which trade deficits significantly improve a country's long-term economic prospects. We will highlight cases in which trade surpluses are appropriate and a sign of strength for a country, and we will show other cases in which trade surpluses may correspond to current demise or even an eventual collapse of an economy.

Most important, one should realize after reading this chapter that merely knowing that a country has a trade deficit or surplus is not enough information to say anything substantive about the strength of a country or its economic prospects.

KEY TAKEAWAY

- Trade deficits or trade surpluses can be good, bad, or benign depending on the underlying economic circumstances.

EXERCISE

JEOPARDY QUESTIONS: As in the popular television game show, you are given an answer to a question and you must respond with the question. For example, if the answer is "a tax on imports," then the correct question is "What is a tariff?"

- Of good, bad, or benign, this is what the common myth is about the nature of trade deficits.
- Of good, bad, or benign, this is what the common myth is about the nature of trade surpluses.
- Of good, bad, benign, or all of the above, in general, this is what trade deficits can be.
- Of good, bad, benign, or all of the above, in general, this is what trade surpluses can be.
- Of good, bad, benign, or all of the above, perhaps most of the time, this is what trade deficits are.
- Of good, bad, benign, or all of the above, perhaps most of the time, this is what trade surpluses are.

3.2 JOBS AND TRADE IMBALANCES

One of the main reasons trade deficits are considered deleterious is because of a common argument that trade deficits result in job losses. The rationale behind this argument is simple and convincing. There are two parts to the story that begin with the definition of a trade deficit.

First, a trade deficit arises whenever imports exceed exports. One simple reason for an imbalance of this kind is that imports are too large or at least larger than they would be under balanced trade. The most common reason offered in developed countries for why imports are too large is that low import prices arise because less-developed countries have exceedingly low wages paid to workers, lax health and safety standards, or more lenient environmental policies, all of which contribute to a veritable flood of imports.

The effect of excessive imports is said to be the purchase of cheaper foreign goods by domestic consumers rather than purchasing the slightly more expensive domestic varieties. As demand for domestic firms' products falls, these firms are forced to downsize, resulting in the layoff of domestic workers. Thus it is said that trade deficits cause the loss of domestic jobs.

The second story argues that the reason imports exceed exports is because exports are too low; they are smaller than they should be. The most common reason given for low exports, especially in the developed countries, is the relatively high barriers to trade in developing countries. Although many countries participate in the World Trade Organization (WTO), the average applied tariffs still remain considerably higher in developing countries.

The effect of insufficient exports is that products that could be produced and sold abroad are not produced and sold abroad because of the barriers to trade. If the barriers were only removed, then exports would expand and jobs would be created in the country.

Thus since both of these stories can operate simultaneously, most observers are convinced that trade deficits indeed will cause job losses. Turn the deficit around, perhaps so much so as to induce a trade surplus, and this logic suggests that more jobs will be created.

This argument is very convincing because there is an element of truth to it. Changes in import and export patterns will certainly have competitive impacts on some industries and could produce temporary job losses. However, this doesn't mean that a country with a trade deficit generates fewer overall jobs than a country with a trade surplus. Nor does it mean that increases in a country's trade deficit will necessarily lead to economy-wide job losses.

One reason job losses may not occur has to do with the deceptive nature of the previous job loss stories. The stories are convincing as far as they go, but unfortunately, they don't go far enough. In other words, the job loss stories have some validity, but they are incomplete; they don't tell the full story, and as a result they tend to mislead.

The rest of the story (as Paul Harvey would have said) is to recognize that when trade deficits arise on the current account, there is an equal and opposite trade surplus on the financial account of the balance of payments. A financial account surplus means that foreigners are purchasing domestic assets. Some of these purchases consist of equities such as stocks and real estate, while other asset purchases involve the lending of money as when foreigners purchase a government bond. In any case, that money flows back into the deficit country and ultimately is spent by someone. That someone could be the previous holder of the real estate or it could be the domestic government. When it is spent, it creates demands for goods and services that in turn create jobs in those industries.

Now consider for a moment the following thought experiment. Suppose we could instantly change the behavior of the foreign lenders generating the financial account surplus (and the related trade deficit). Suppose they decide at once not to lend the money to the government or not to purchase real estate but instead decide to purchase domestic goods. The increase in goods purchases by foreigners would imply that export demand and hence exports will rise. Indeed, they will rise sufficiently to eliminate the trade deficit. And because of the increase in exports, jobs will be created in the export industries. However, at the same time export jobs are created, other jobs in the economy are being lost. That's because now less money is there to purchase the real estate or to lend to the government. Thus the elimination of the trade deficit doesn't create jobs in the aggregate, but it will change which sectors have more and less demand for its products. In other words, changes in the trade deficit will ultimately affect only where the jobs are in the economy (i.e., in which industries), not how many jobs there are.

The one exception to this, and one of the main reasons the job loss stories remain so convincing, is when there are rapid changes in the trade deficit or surplus. Rapid changes, like the thought experiment above, would require adjustments of workers between industries. During that adjustment process, some workers will be temporarily unemployed. If that adjustment involves an increase in the trade deficit or a decrease in the trade surplus, the temporary jobs effect will be very noticeable in the tradable products industries. However, if the adjustment involves a decrease in the deficit or an increase in the surplus, then the job losses will more likely occur in the nontradable products sectors and it will be difficult to connect those job losses to the changes in the trade balance.

To provide some validation of this point—that is, that changes in the trade balances do not have effects on the aggregate number of jobs in an economy—consider Figure 3.1 "U.S. Trade Deficits and Unemployment, 1980–2009", showing two U.S. macroeconomic variables plotted over the past twenty years: the current account balance and the national unemployment rate. Now if the jobs stories suggesting that trade deficits cause job losses were true, we might expect to see an inverse relationship between the trade balance and the unemployment rate. Alternatively, if an increase in a country's trade deficit causes job losses in the economy, we might expect an increase in the unemployment rate to occur as well. Similarly, a decrease in the trade deficit should create jobs and lead to a decrease in the unemployment rate.

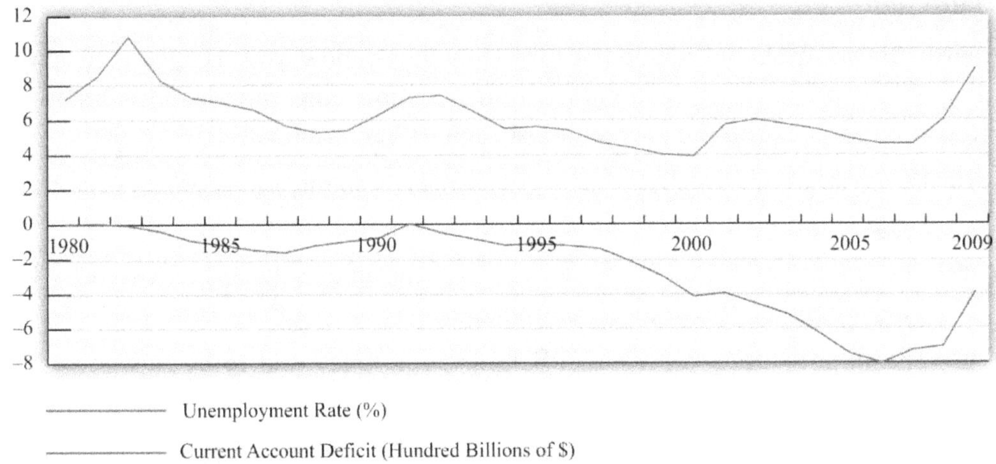

Figure 3.1 U.S. Trade Deficits and Unemployment, 2009–1980

Interestingly, what Figure 3.1 "U.S. Trade Deficits and Unemployment, 1980–2009" shows is that during the periods when the U.S. trade deficit is rising (i.e., the trade balance is falling), the unemployment rate is falling; whereas when the trade deficit is falling, the unemployment rate is rising. This is precisely the opposite effect one would expect if the job-loss stories of trade deficits were true.

Of course this evidence does not prove that trade deficits will reduce unemployment in every country in all circumstances. However, the evidence does suggest that it is inappropriate to jump to the popular conclusion that trade deficits are bad for jobs and thus bad for the economy.

KEY TAKEAWAYS

- Trade deficits are often incorrectly presumed to cause job losses in an economy.
- The job-loss stories suggest that trade deficits arise due to excessive imports or insufficient exports and that by eliminating a deficit a country can create jobs in the economy.
- The job-loss story is incomplete though because it ignores the demand and jobs caused by the financial account surplus.
- When all effects of trade imbalances are accounted for, trade deficits may cause no more than temporary job losses in transition but not affect the aggregate level of jobs in an economy.

Evidence from the United States over the past twenty years is used to show that the relationship between trade deficits and the unemployment rate is the opposite from what the popular "trade deficits cause job losses" stories would suggest.

EXERCISE

Jeopardy Questions:As in the popular television game show, you are given an answer to a question and you must respond with the question. For example, if the answer is "a tax on imports," then the correct question is "What is a tariff?"

- Of too large, too small, or just right, concerns about trade deficits sometimes suggest this about imports.
- The import effect on trade deficits is sometimes said to be caused by this wage phenomenon in foreign countries.
- The import effect on trade deficits is sometimes said to be caused by this environmental legal phenomenon in foreign countries.
- Of too large, too small, or just right, concerns about trade deficits sometimes suggest this about exports.
- The export effect on trade deficits is sometimes said to be caused by this trade barrier phenomenon in foreign countries.
- The "trade deficits cause job losses" story ignores the effects of international transactions recorded on this balance of payments account.
- Of increase, decrease, or stay the same, this has been the typical corresponding change in the U.S. unemployment rate whenever the U.S. trade deficit was rising since 1980.

3.3 THE NATIONAL WELFARE IMPACTS OF TRADE IMBALANCES

In this section, a series of simple scenarios (or stories) are presented to demonstrate how the well-being of a country may be affected when it runs a trade imbalance. The scenarios compare national output with domestic spending over two periods of time under alternative assumptions about the country's trade imbalance and its economic growth rate between the two periods. After each aggregate scenario is presented, we also provide an analogous situation from the point of view of an individual. Finally we present an evaluation of each scenario and indicate countries that may be displaying similar trade patterns.

Two periods are used as a simple way to introduce the dynamic characteristics of trade imbalances. The amount of time between the two periods can be varied to provide alternative interpretations. Thus the two periods could be labeled as today and tomorrow, this year and next year, or this generation and next generation.

We assume that all trade imbalances correspond to debt obligations or IOUs (i.e., I owe you). In other words, the financial account imbalances that offset the trade imbalances will be interpreted as international borrowing and lending rather than, say, foreign direct investment flows or real estate purchases.

Afterward, we will comment on how the interpretations of these scenarios may change with the alternative type of asset flow.

National welfare is best measured by the amount of goods and services that are "consumed" by households. What we care about, ultimately, is the standard of living obtainable by the average citizen, which is affected not by how much the nation produces but by how much it consumes. Although gross domestic product (GDP) is often used as a proxy for national welfare, it is an inadequate indicator for many reasons, especially when a country runs trade imbalances. To quickly see why, consider the extreme situation in which a country runs the largest trade surplus possible. This would arise if a country exports all of its GDP and imports nothing. The country's trade surplus would then equal its GDP, but the citizens in the country would have no food, clothing, or anything else to consume. The standard of living would be nonexistent.

To avoid this problem we use domestic spending (DS), or the sum of domestic consumption, investment, and government spending, as a proxy for national welfare. More formally, let

$$DS = C + I + G,$$

where C, I, and G are defined as in the national income accounts. Recall from Chapter 2 «National Income and the Balance of Payments Accounts» that C, I, and G each can be segmented into spending on domestically produced goods and services and spending on imported goods and services. Thus domestic spending includes imported goods in the measure of national welfare. This is appropriate since imported goods are consumed by domestic citizens and add to their well-being and standard of living.

One problem with using domestic spending as a proxy for average living standards is the inclusion of investment (note that this problem would also arise using GDP as a proxy). Investment spending measures the value of goods and services used as inputs into the productive process. As such, these items do not directly raise the well-being of citizens, at least not in the present period. To clarify this point, consider an isolated, self-sufficient corn farmer. Each year the farmer harvests corn, using part of it to sustain the family during the year, while allocating some of the kernels to use as seed corn for the following year. Clearly, the more kernels the farmer saves for next year's crop, the less corn the family will have to consume this year. As with the farmer, the same goes for the nation: the more that is invested today, the lower will be today's standard of living, ceteris paribus. Thus we must use domestic spending cautiously as a measure of national welfare and take note of changes in investment spending if it occurs.

The analysis below will focus on the interpretation of differences between national income (GDP) and domestic spending under different scenarios concerning the trade imbalance. The relationship between them can be shown by rewriting the national income identity.

The national income identity is written as

$$GDP = C + I + G + EX - IM.$$

Substituting the term for domestic spending yields

$$GDP = DS + EX - IM,$$

and rearranging it gives

$$EX - IM = GDP - DS.$$

The last expression implies that when a country has a current account (or trade) surplus, GDP must exceed domestic spending by the equivalent amount. Similarly, when a country has a trade deficit, domestic spending exceeds GDP.

Note that to be completely accurate, we should use growth national product (GNP) rather than GDP in the analysis. This is because we are interpreting EX - IM as the current account balance that includes income payments and receipts. With income flows included on the trade side, the measure of national output we get is GNP not GDP. Because conceptually both are measures of national output, we will use GNP in everthing that follows in this section.

Case 1: No Trade Imbalances; No GNP Growth between Periods

Case one, what we will call the base case, is used to demonstrate how GNP compares with domestic spending in the simplest scenario. Here we assume that the country does not run a trade deficit or surplus in either of the two periods and that no GNP growth occurs between periods. No trade imbalance implies that no net international borrowing or lending occurs on the financial account. The case mimics how things would look if the country were in autarky and did not trade with the rest of the world.

Note from Figure 3.2 "Case 1" that domestic spending is exactly equal to GNP in both periods. Since domestic spending is used to measure national welfare, we see that the average standard of living remains unchanged between the two periods. Overall, nothing very interesting happens in this case, but it will be useful for comparison purposes.

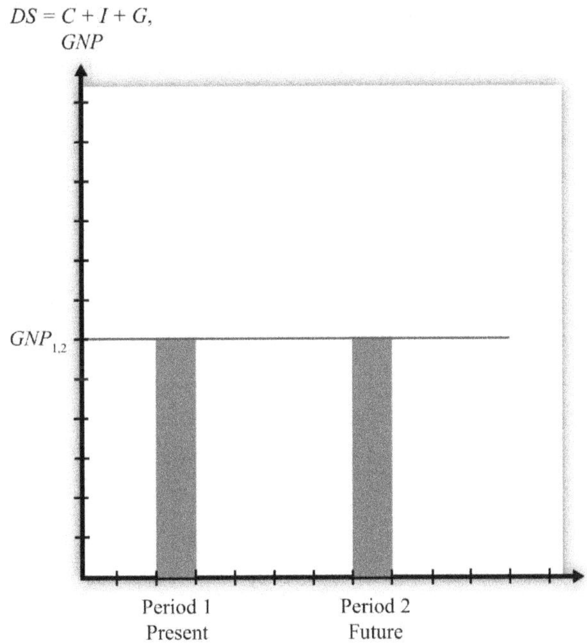

Figure 3.2 Case 1

The Individual Analogy

Consider an individual named Rajiv. For an individual, GNP is analogous to Rajiv's annual income since his income represents the value of goods and services produced with his labor services. Domestic spending is analogous to the value of the goods and services purchased by Rajiv during the year. It corresponds to Rajiv's consumption of goods and services that serves as a proxy for his welfare level. Trade for an individual occurs whenever a transaction occurs with someone outside his household.

Let's assume for simplicity that Rajiv earns $30,000 per year. The assumption of no GNP growth in the base case implies that he continues to earn $30,000 in the second period and thus experiences no income growth. The assumption of no trade imbalances implies that Rajiv engages in no borrowing or lending outside of his household. That implies that he spends all of his income on consumption goods and thus purchases $30,000 worth of goods and services. This level of consumption remains the same in both periods, implying that his standard of living is unchanged.

Another way of interpreting balanced trade for an individual is to imagine that he exports $30,000 worth of labor services and afterward imports $30,000 worth of consumption goods and services. Since exports equal imports, trade is balanced.

Case 2: Current Account Deficit Period 1; No GDP Growth between Periods

In this case, we assume that the country runs a current account (or trade) deficit in the first period. We'll also assume that the resultant financial account surplus corresponds to borrowing from the rest of the world, rather than asset purchases. These borrowed funds are assumed to be repaid in their entirety in the second period. In other words, we'll assume that loans are taken out in the first period and that the principal and interest are repaid completely in the second period. We also assume that there is no GNP growth between periods.

As shown in Figure 3.3 "Case 2", the trade deficit in the first period implies that domestic spending, DS_1, exceeds GNP_1. The difference between DS_1 and GNP_1 represents the current account deficit as well as the value of the outstanding principal on the foreign loans. The extra consumption the country can enjoy is possible because it borrows funds from abroad and uses them to purchase extra imports. The result is the potential for a higher standard of living in the country in the period in which it runs a current account deficit if the extra funds are not directed into domestic investment.

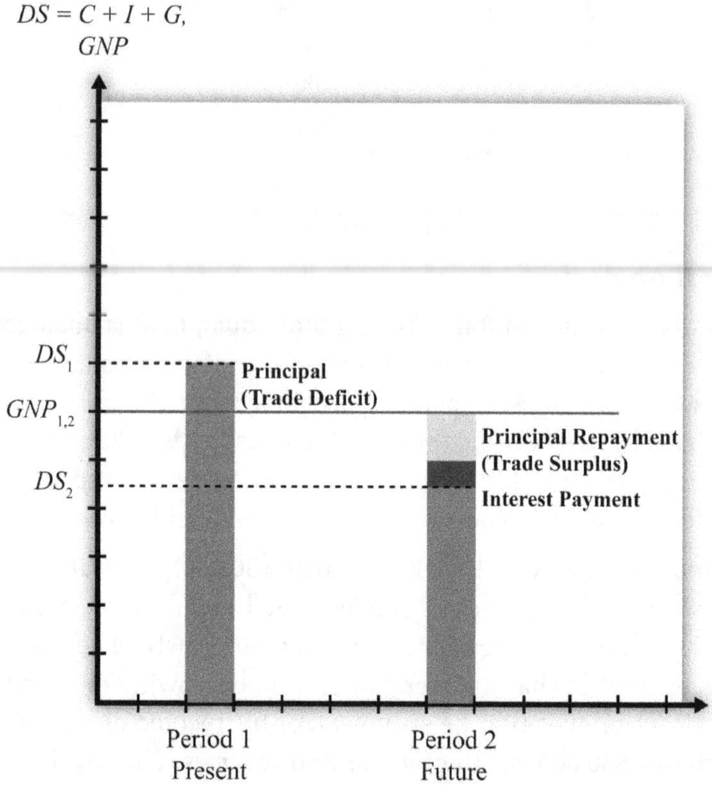

Figure 3.3 Case 2

In the second period, the borrowed funds must be repaid with interest. The repayment reduces domestic spending below the level of GNP by the amount of the principal and interest repayment as shown by the light-colored areas in the diagram.In actuality, the interest repayment component may be included as part of domestic spending since interest represents a payment for services received—those services being the privilege of consuming earlier. However, since this service is unlikely to raise one's standard of living in period two, we have excluded it from domestic spending. Since GNP does not change between the two periods, DS_2 will lie below GNP_1. What this means is that the average standard of living can fall during the period in which the loan repayment is being made.

This outcome highlights perhaps the most important concern about trade deficits. The fear is that large and persistent trade deficits may require a significant fall in living standards when the loans finally come due. If the periods are stretched between two generations, then there is an intergenerational concern. A country running large trade deficits may raise living standards for the current generation, only to reduce them for the next generation. It is then as if the parents' consumption binge is being subsidized by their children.

The Individual Analogy

In case two, our individual, Rajiv, would again have a $30,000 income in two successive periods. In the first period, suppose Rajiv borrows money, perhaps by running up charges on his credit card. Suppose these charges amount to $5,000 and that the interest rate is a generous 10 percent. Assuming Rajiv does not save money in the first period, his consumption level in the first period would be the sum of his income and his borrowed funds. Thus he would enjoy $35,000 worth of goods and services reflecting a standard of living higher than his actual income.

In the second period, Rajiv must pay back the $5,000 in loans plus the interest charges, which, at a 10 percent interest rate, would amount to $500. Thus $5,500 of Rajiv's $30,000 income would go toward debt repayment, leaving him with only $24,500 to spend on consumption.

In this case, extra consumption, or a higher living standard in period one, is achieved by sacrificing a lower living standard in the future.

Note that in the first period Rajiv imports more goods and services in consumption than he exports in terms of labor services. Hence, this corresponds to a trade deficit. In the second period, Rajiv imports fewer goods and services in consumption than the labor services he exports; hence, this corresponds to a trade surplus.

Evaluation

Case two reflects legitimate concerns about countries that run large or persistent trade deficits. The case highlights the fact that trade deficits, which arise from international borrowing, may require a reduced average standard of living for the country in the future when the loans must be repaid.

An example of this situation would be Mexico during the 1970s and 1980s. Mexico ran sizeable current account deficits in the 1970s as it borrowed liberally in international markets.

In the early 1980s, higher interest rates reduced its ability to fulfill its obligations to repay principal and interest on its outstanding loans. Their effective default precipitated the third world debt crisis of the 1980s. During the 1980s, as arrangements were made for an orderly, though incomplete, repayment of Mexico's loans, the country ran sizeable current account surpluses. As in case two here, Mexico's current account deficits in the 1970s allowed it to raise its average living standards, above what would have been possible otherwise, while its current account surpluses in the 1980s forced a substantial reduction in living standards.

It is worth emphasizing that current account deficits are not detrimental in the periods in which the deficits are occurring. In fact, current account deficits correspond to higher consumption, investment, and government spending levels than would be possible under balanced trade. Instead, current account deficits pose a problem only when the debt repayment occurs, which is when the country is running current account surpluses. Trade deficits raise national welfare in the periods in which they occur, while trade surpluses reduce welfare in the periods in which they occur.

In other words, in terms of the national welfare effects, the problem here isn't large or persistent trade deficits but rather the large and persistent trade surpluses that might arise in the future as a result.

It is also worth noting that trade deficits in this case need not be a problem in the long run if they are not too large. Just as an individual may make a choice to substitute future consumption for present consumption, so might a nation. For example, an individual may reasonably decide while young to take exotic vacations, engage in daredevilish activities, or maybe purchase a fast car, even if it means taking out sizeable loans. Better to enjoy life while healthy, he may reason, even if it means that he will have to forgo similar vacations or activities when he is older. Similarly, a nation, through an aggregation of similar individual decisions, may "choose" to consume above its income today even though it requires reduced consumption tomorrow. As long as the future reduced consumption "costs" are borne by the individuals who choose to overconsume today, deficits for a nation need not be a problem. However, if the decision to overconsume is made through excessive government spending, then the burden of reduced consumption could fall on the future generation of taxpayers, in which case there would be an intergenerational welfare transfer.

Case 3: Current Account Deficit Period 1; Positive GDP Growth between Periods

In the third case, we assume, as in case two, that the country runs a trade deficit in the first period, that the trade deficit corresponds to borrowing from the rest of the world, and that in period two all the loans are repaid with interest. What differs here is that we will assume GNP growth occurs between the first and second periods. As we'll see, growth can significantly affect the long-term effects of trade deficits.

In Figure 3.4 "Case 3", note that the first period domestic spending (DS_1) lies above GNP in the first period (GNP_1). This arises because a trade deficit implies that the country is borrowing from the rest of the world, allowing it to spend (and consume) more than it produces.

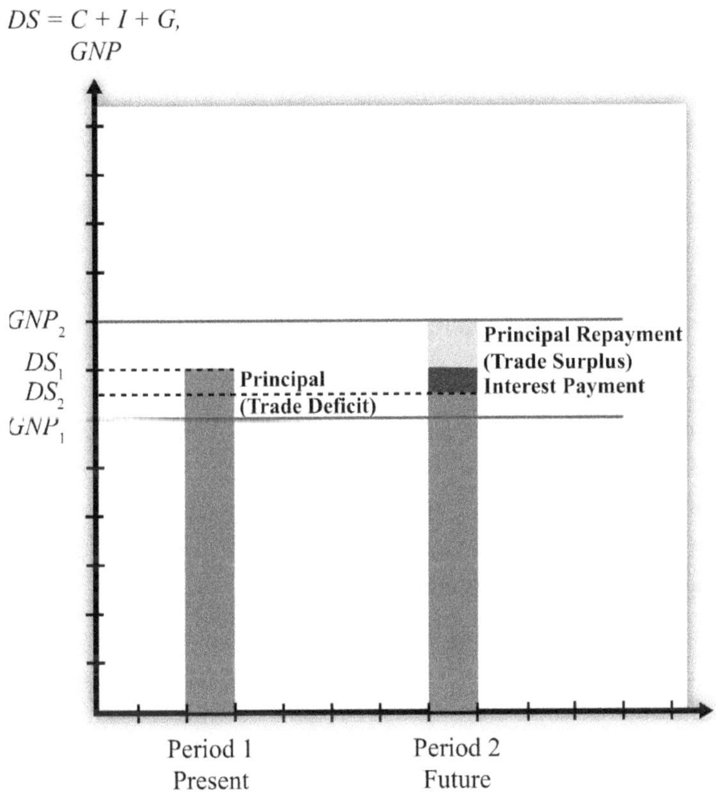

Figure 3.4 Case 3

In the second period, we assume that GNP has grown to GNP_2 as shown in the graph. The principal and interest from first period loans are repaid, which lowers domestic spending to DS_2. Note that since domestic spending is less than GNP_2, the country must be running a trade surplus. Also note that the trade surplus implies that consumption and the average standard of living are reduced below the level that is obtainable with balanced trade in that period. In a sense, the trade deficit has a similar long-term detrimental effect as in case two.

However, it is possible that the first period trade deficit, in this case, may actually be generating a long-term benefit. Suppose for a moment that this country's balanced trade outcome over two periods would look like the base case. In that case, balanced trade prevails but no GDP growth occurs, leaving the country with the same standard of living in both periods. Such a country may be able to achieve an outcome like case three if it borrows money from the rest of the world in period one—thus running a current account deficit—and uses those funds to purchase investment goods, which may in turn stimulate GNP growth. If GNP rises sufficiently, the country will achieve a level of domestic spending that exceeds the level that would have been obtained in the base case.

Indeed, it is even possible for a country's standard of living to be increased in the long term entirely because it runs a trade deficit. In case three, imagine that all the borrowed funds in period one are used for investment. This means that even though domestic spending rises, the average standard of living would remain unchanged relative to the base case because investment goods generate no immediate consumption pleasures. In period two, the higher level of domestic spending may be used for increased consumption that would cause an increase in the country's average living standards. Thus the country is better off in both the short term and long term with the unbalanced trade scenario compared to the balanced trade case.

The Individual Analogy

The third case is analogous to our individual Rajiv with, say, a $30,000 income in period one. The trade deficit in the first period means that he borrows money using his credit card to purchase an additional, say, $5,000 worth of "imported" consumption goods. Thus in period one the person's consumption and standard of living are higher than reflected by his income.

In the second period, the GNP rises, corresponding to an increase in Rajiv's income. Let say that his income rises to $40,000 in the second period. We'll also assume that all credit card loans must be repaid along with 10 percent interest charges in the second period. Consumption spending for Rajiv is now below his income. Subtracting the $5,000 principal repayment and the $500 interest payment from his $40,000 income yields consumption of $34,500.

The investment story above is similar to the case in which an individual takes out $5,000 in student loans in period one and earns an advanced degree that allows him to acquire a better-paying job. Assuming the educational investment does not add to his consumption pleasures (a seemingly reasonable assumption for many students), his welfare is unaffected by the additional spending that occurs in period one. However, his welfare is increased in period two since he is able to consume an additional $4,500 worth of goods and services even after paying back the student loans with interest.

Evaluation

The lesson of case three is that trade deficits, even if large or persistent, will not cause long-term harm to a nation's average standard of living if the country grows rapidly enough. Rapid economic growth is often a cure-all for problems associated with trade deficits.

In some cases, it is possible for growth to be induced by investment spending made possible by borrowing money in international markets. A trade deficit that arises in this circumstance could represent economic salvation for a country rather than a sign of economic weakness.

Consider a less-developed country. Countries are classified as less developed because their average incomes are very low. Indeed, although many less-developed countries, or LDCs, have a small, wealthy upper class, most of the population lives in relative poverty. Individuals who are poor rarely save very much of their incomes, therefore, LDCs generally have relatively small pools of funds at home that can be used to finance domestic investment. If investment is necessary to fuel industrialization and economic growth, as is often the case especially in early stages of development, an LDC might be forced to a slow or nonexistent growth path if it restricts itself to balanced trade and limits its international borrowing.

On the other hand, if an LDC borrows money in international financial markets, it will run a trade deficit by default. If these borrowed funds are used for productive investment, which in turn stimulates sufficient GDP growth, then the country may be able to raise average living standards even after repaying the principal and interest on international loans. Thus trade deficits can be a good thing for less-developed countries.

The same lesson can be applied to the economies in transition in the former Soviet bloc. These countries suffered from a lack of infrastructure and a dilapidated industrial base after the collapse of the Soviet Union. One obvious way to spur economic growth in the transition is to replace the capital stock with new investment: build new factories, install modern equipment, improve the roads, improve telecommunications, and so on. However, with income falling rapidly after the collapse, there were few internal sources to fund this replacement investment. It was also not obvious which sectors were the best to invest in. Nevertheless, one potential option was for these countries to borrow funds on international financial markets. Trade deficits that would occur under this scenario could be justified as an appropriate way to stimulate rapid economic growth.

Of course, just because trade deficits can induce economic growth and generate long-term benefits for a country doesn't mean that a trade deficit will spur long-term economic growth. Sometimes investments are made in inappropriate industries. Sometimes external shocks cause once profitable industries to collapse. Sometimes borrowed international funds are squandered by government officials and used to purchase large estates and big cars. For many reasons good intentions, and good theory, do not always produce good results. Thus a country that runs large and persistent trade deficits, hoping to produce the favorable outcome shown in case three, might find itself with the unfavorable outcome shown in case two.

Finally, a country running trade deficits could find itself with the favorable outcome even if it doesn't use borrowed international funds to raise domestic investment. The United States, for example, has had rather large trade deficits since 1982. By the late 1980s, the United States achieved the status of the largest debtor nation in the world. During the same period, domestic investment remained relatively low especially in comparison to other developed nations in the world. One may quickly conclude that since investment was not noticeably increased during the period, the United States may be heading for the detrimental outcome. However, the United States maintained steady GNP growth during the 1980s and 1990s, except during the recession year in 1992. As long as growth proceeds rapidly enough, for whatever reason, even a country with persistent deficits can wind up with the beneficial outcome.

Case 4: Current Account Surplus Period 1; No GDP Growth between Periods

In this case, we assume that the country runs a trade surplus in the first period and that no GDP growth occurs between periods. A surplus implies that exports exceed imports of goods and services and that the country has a financial account deficit. We will assume that the financial account deficit corresponds entirely to loans made to the rest of the world. We can also refer to these loans as savings, since the loans imply that someone in the country is forgoing current consumption. In the future, these savings will be redeemed along with the interest collected in the interim. We shall assume that all of these loans are repaid to the country with interest in the second period.

In Figure 3.5 "Case 4", we see that in the first period, when the trade surplus is run, domestic spending (DS_1) is less than national income or GDP. This occurs because the country is lending rather than consuming some of the money available from production. The excess of exports over imports represents goods that could have been used for domestic consumption, investment, and government spending but are instead being consumed by foreigners. This means that a current account surplus reduces a country's potential for consumption and investment below what is achievable in balanced trade. If the trade surplus substitutes for domestic consumption and government spending, then the trade surplus will reduce the country's average standard of living. If the trade surplus substitutes for domestic investment, average living standards would not be affected, but the potential for future growth can be reduced. In this sense, trade surpluses can be viewed as a sign of weakness for an economy, especially in the short run during the periods when surpluses are run. Surpluses can reduce living standards and the potential for future growth.

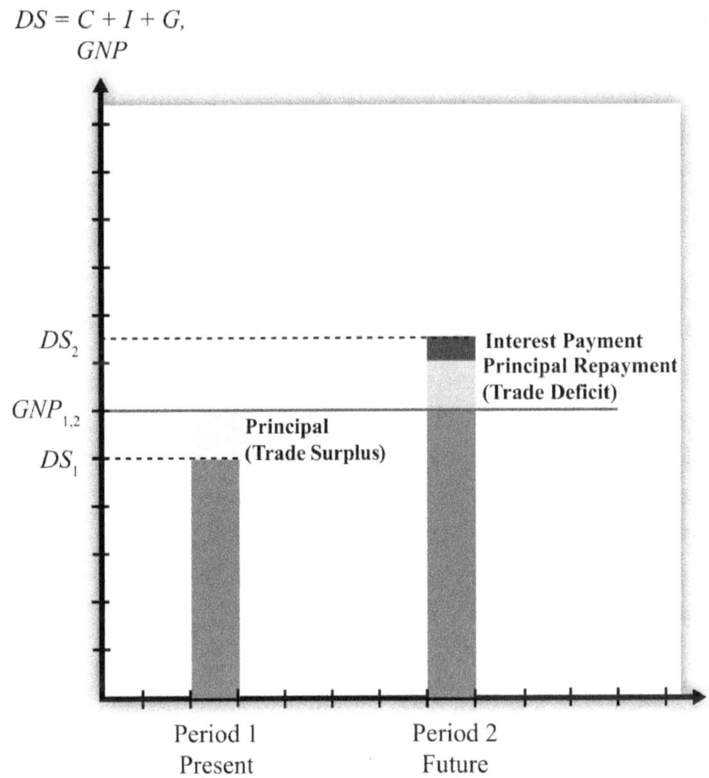

Figure 3.5 Case 4

Nevertheless, this does not mean that countries should not run trade surpluses or that trade surpluses are necessarily detrimental over a longer period. As shown in the diagram, when period two arrives the country redeems its past loans with interest. This will force the country to run a trade deficit, and domestic spending (DS_2) will exceed GDP. The trade deficit implies imports exceed exports, and these additional imports can be used to raise domestic consumption, investment, and government spending. If the deficit leads to greater consumption and government spending, then the country's average standard of living will rise above what is achievable in balanced trade. If the deficit leads to greater investment, then the country's potential for GDP growth in the third period (not shown) is enhanced.

Briefly, this case describes the situation in which a country forgoes first period consumption and investment so that in period two it can enjoy even greater consumption and investment.

The Individual Analogy

Consider our individual, Rajiv, who has an annual income of $30,000 over two periods. This corresponds to the constant GDP in the above example. Rajiv would run a trade surplus in period one if he lends money to others. One way to achieve this is simply to put money into a savings account in the local bank. Suppose Rajiv deposits $5,000 into a savings account. That money is then used by the bank to make loans to other individuals and businesses. Thus in essence Rajiv is making loans to them with the bank acting as an intermediary. The $5,000 also represents money that Rajiv does not use to buy goods and services. Thus in period one Rajiv exports $30,000 of labor services, but imports only $25,000 of consumption goods. The excess is loaned to others so that they may be consumed instead in the first period. It is clear that Rajiv's standard of living at $25,000 is lower in the first period than the $30,000 he could have achieved had he not deposited money into savings.

In the second period, we imagine that Rajiv again earns $30,000 and withdraws all the money plus interest from the savings account. Suppose he had earned 10 percent interest between the periods. In this case, his withdrawal would amount to $5,500. This means that in period two Rajiv can consume $35,500 worth of goods and services. This outcome also implies that Rajiv's domestic spending capability exceeds his income and so he must be running a trade deficit. In this case, Rajiv's imports of goods and services at $35,500 exceed his exports of $30,000 worth of labor services; thus he has a trade deficit.

Is this outcome good or bad for Rajiv? Most would consider this a good outcome. One might argue that Rajiv has prudently saved some of his income for a later time when he may have a greater need. The story may seem even more prudent if Rajiv suffered a significant drop in income in the second period to, say, $20,000. In this case, the savings would allow Rajiv to maintain his consumption at nearly the same level in both periods despite the shock to his income stream. This corresponds to the words of wisdom that one should save for a rainy day. Savings can certainly allow an individual to smooth his consumption stream over time.

Alternatively, one might consider the two periods of the story to be middle age and retirement. In this case, it would make sense to save money out of one's income in middle age so that one can draw on those savings and their accumulated earnings during retirement when one's income has fallen to zero.

On the other hand, excessive saving in the first period might make Rajiv seem miserly. Few people would advise that one save so much as to put oneself into poverty or to reduce one's living standard below some reasonable norm. Excessive prudence can seem inappropriate as well.

Evaluation

The prime example of a country that mimics the first period of case four is Japan during the 1980s and 1990s. Japan ran sizeable trade surpluses during those two decades. As this story suggests, the flip side of the trade surplus is a financial account deficit that implied a considerable increase in the amount of loans that Japan made to the rest of the world. Although Japan's trade surplus has often been touted as a sign of strength, an important thing to keep in mind is that Japan's trade surpluses implied lower consumption and government purchases, and thus a lower standard of living than would have been possible with balanced trade. Although trade surpluses can also result in lower investment, this effect was not apparent for Japan. During those two decades of investment, spending as a percentage of GDP always exceeded 25 percent, higher than most other developed countries.

These surpluses may turn out to be especially advantageous for Japan as it progresses in the twenty-first century. First of all, it is clear that Japan's surpluses did not usher in an era of continual and rapid GDP growth. By the early 1990s, Japan's economy had become stagnant and finally began to contract by 1998. However, rather than allowing a decline in GDP to cause a reduction in living standards, Japan could use its sizeable external savings surplus to maintain consumption at the level achieved previously. Of course, this would require that Japan increase its domestic consumption and begin to run a trade deficit, two things that did not occur even by 2009.

In another respect, Japan's trade surpluses may be advantageous over the longer run. Japan, along with most other developed nations, will experience a dramatic demographic shift over the next three decades. Its retired population will continue to grow as a percentage of the total population of the baby boomers reach retirement and people continue to live longer. The size of the Japan's working population will consequently decline as a percentage of the population. This implies an increasing burden on Japan's pay-as-you-go social retirement system as a smaller number of workers will be available per retiree to fund retiree benefits. If at that time Japan draws down its accumulated foreign savings and runs trade deficits, it will be able to boost the average consumption level of its population while reducing the need to raise tax burdens to fund its social programs. Of course, this outcome may never be realized if Japan's economy does not rebound strongly from its recent stagnant condition.

Overall, regardless of the outcome, Japan's economy today, faced with a potentially severe recession, is certainly in a stronger position by virtue of its accumulated foreign savings than it would be if it had run trade deficits during the past two decades.

Concise Summary

These stories suggest that trade imbalances, when evaluated in terms of their momentary effects and their long-term economic consequences, can be either good, bad, or benign, depending on the circumstances.

Trade deficits may signal excessive borrowing that could in the future lead to possible default, or worse, an excessive reduction in living standards needed to repay the accumulated debt. In this case, the trade deficit is clearly bad for the nation. Alternatively, trade deficits may represent a country that is merely drawing down previously accumulated foreign savings or selling other productive assets, in which case there is no potential for default or reduced living standards in the future. Here, the trade deficit is either immaterial or even beneficial in that the nation is able to achieve a higher current living standard because of the deficit. Trade deficits might also make an expansion of domestic investment possible, which could spur future economic growth sufficiently to make repayment consistent with growing living standards. In this case, trade deficits are clearly good as they stimulate future economic prosperity. Finally, in a free market economy, trade deficits may simply reflect the aggregated choices of many individuals to forgo future consumption to achieve more current consumption. In this case, the trade deficit should be viewed as immaterial since it merely reflects the free choices of the nation's people.

On the other hand, a trade surplus may correspond to prudent foreign saving and purchases of foreign productive assets, which may be used to support a growing retired population in the future. In this case, the trade surplus is a good thing for the nation. The trade surplus might also represent a period of repayment of past debt. This outcome may be acceptable if achieved together with growing living standards. However, if the surplus arises in a period of slow growth or falling GDP, then the surplus would correspond to painful reductions in living standards, which is clearly a bad outcome for the country. Finally, the trade surplus may occur as a result of the aggregated choices of many individuals who have acquired greater past consumption by forgoing current consumption. In this case, the surplus should be viewed as immaterial to the nation as a whole.

KEY TAKEAWAYS

- Domestic spending measures the total value of purchases of goods and services in a country regardless of where the goods and services were produced. As such, it is a better way to measure the "consumption" in an economy affecting the nation's standard of living as compared to "production" or GDP.
- When a country has a current account deficit, its national consumption exceeds its national production. When a country has a current account surplus, its national production exceeds its national consumption.
- Trade deficits become a problem over time if accumulated borrowings result in a substantial reduction in consumption and standard of living for its citizens during the repayment periods.
- The problems associated with a deficit occur not when the trade deficit is being run but in later periods when a trade surplus becomes necessary.
- Trade deficit problems are mitigated with GNP growth. The faster GNP grows, the lesser the decline in future consumption during the repayment period.

EXERCISES

Consider the Japanese economy over two periods of time: first period (today) and second period (the future). Suppose Japanese GDP today is $2,000 billion (we'll use the U.S. dollar rather than the yen). Suppose Japan runs a current account surplus of 5 percent of GDP in the first period and lends money at the market interest rate of 5 percent.

- What is the value of domestic spending on C, I, and G in the first period?
- What would be the value of domestic spending in Japan in the second period if all the first period loans are repaid with interest and no economic growth occurs between periods?
- Consider the following situations describing the actions of an individual household. Explain whether each situation is analogous to a country running a trade deficit, a trade surplus, or neither. Briefly explain why.
- A student takes out a bank loan to finance a spring break vacation.
- A family sells an antique watch to finance a purchase of 100 shares of a "hot" stock.
- A retired couple cashes in a portion of their savings to finance their daily living expenses.
- A carpenter builds a deck for a dentist in exchange for dental checkups for his kids.
- A family pays off the last $3,000 of its student loans.
- Suppose that each situation listed is the dominant effect on a country's balance of payments. Indicate by filling in the blank spaces whether the current account and capital account will be in surplus or deficit.

	Current Account Balance	Financial Account Balance
a. A country is a net borrower from the rest of the world		
b. A country is repaying past debts		
c. A country exports more goods and services than it imports		
d. A country sells foreign assets and repatriates the proceeds		
e. A country is a net lender to the rest of the world		
f. A country earns more income on foreign assets than foreigners earn in its country		

3.4 A FEW NEW COMPLICATIONS

The analysis of trade imbalances is further complicated by the fact that not all financial flows are debt obligations or IOUs (i.e., I owe you). In the previous stories, we assumed that all financial account transactions corresponded to international lending or borrowing. In actuality, many international asset transactions involve sales or purchases of productive assets. For example, if a foreigner purchases shares of Microsoft stock in the U.S. market, the transaction would be recorded as a credit entry on the financial account and would add to a financial account surplus. However, in this case we could not claim that someone in the United States borrowed money from the rest of the world because there is no obligation to repay principal and interest in the future. Instead the foreign purchaser of the U.S. asset has purchased an ownership claim in a U.S. corporation that entitles him to the future stream of dividends plus capital gains if he sells the stock later at a higher price. If the company is profitable in the future, then the investors will earn a positive return. However, if the company suffers economic losses in the future, then the dividends may be discontinued and the stock's price may fall. Alternatively, the U.S. dollar could experience a significant depreciation. The end result could be losses for the foreign investor and a negative rate of return. In either case the foreign investor is not "entitled" to a return of his original investment or any additional return beyond. This same type of relationship arises for international real estate transactions and for foreign direct investment, which occurs when a foreign firm substantially owns and operates a company in another country.

To the extent that financial account flows correspond to asset purchases without repayment obligations, the stories above change somewhat. For example, suppose a country runs a trade deficit in period one and suppose further that the resulting financial account surplus corresponds to foreign purchases of U.S. real estate and businesses. In the first period, a country's standard of living could be raised above what is possible with balanced trade—not by borrowing money but by selling ownership claims on productive assets. In the second period, the country's standard of living need not be reduced since there is no repayment obligation.

This case is analogous to an individual who sells his watch at a pawnshop. In that period he is able to buy more than his income because he has divested some of his previously accumulated wealth. In the following period, he can once again make purchases equal to his income and thus need not suffer a reduction in his living standards.

The implication here is that nondebt asset flows may be less problematic than international loans because they do not require a reduction in living standards in the future. Of course, in this case, there is an additional concern that the country that sells off its assets may also be losing control of its productive assets and thus its citizens will not be the ones to earn positive returns on these domestic activities. This concern should be tempered for a few reasons. First, foreign-owned firms remain subject to the laws of the domestic country. Countries can prevent exorbitant profit taking by applying profit taxes. What's more, the foreign owners do not enjoy voting privileges and thus have less say over laws that might affect them. Second, foreign-owned firms generate employment opportunities for domestic citizens, and that serves to benefit the country. Finally, owners of firms, whether foreign or domestic, are generally motivated by similar desires—namely, to make the business successful— and successful businesses generally benefit the owners, the employees, and the consumers of the product.

As an example, consider the purchase in the 1980s of Rockefeller Center in New York City by a group of Japanese investors. Rockefeller Center is a centrally located building in New York City whose owners lease office space to businesses that wish to locate their offices there. Any owner of the building must compete with other businesses leasing office space throughout the city and thus must provide as high a quality and as low a price as possible. If the owners manage the property well and provide quality services, then they will have a lot of tenants and they will make a profit. If they provide poor services, then businesses will move out and the owners will lose money. Thus it really shouldn't matter to the tenants whether the owners are American or Japanese, only whether they are good managers of the office space. Similarly, the owners, regardless of nationality, will hire workers to maintain the facilities. These workers will benefit if the management is good and will suffer if it is poor, regardless of the owners' nationality. Finally, if the owners of the building are successful, then they deserve to earn a profit or return on their investment. If they provide poor services at high prices, then they will deserve to make a loss. Indeed, it shouldn't matter to anyone whether the owners are American or Japanese nationals.

KEY TAKEAWAY

- A trade deficit financed by sales of equity rather than debt does not require a repayment in the future or a subsequent decline in consumption. However, it does imply that a flow of the profits from domestic activities will accrue to foreigners rather than domestic residents.

EXERCISE

Jeopardy Questions: As in the popular television game show, you are given an answer to a question and you must respond with the question. For example, if the answer is "a tax on imports," then the correct question is "What is a tariff?"

- The full form of the abbreviation "IOU."
- The terms representing the two broad types of assets; one is related to borrowing and lending and the other is related to ownership.

- The type of asset represented by a bank certificate of deposit.
- The type of asset represented by a common or preferred share of stock.
- The type of asset represented by a checking account deposit.
- The type of asset represented by the deed to a private golf course.
- International purchases of this type of asset require repayment of principal and interest in the future.
- International purchases of this type of asset do not require repayment of principal and interest.

3.5 EVALUATION METHODS FOR TRADE IMBALANCES

A quick reading of business and financial newspapers and magazines often reveals a number of misunderstandings about economic relationships. One of the most notable is the widespread conviction that trade deficits are a troubling economic condition that indicates weakness in an economy, while trade surpluses are a sign of strength for an economy. Although these beliefs are well founded in some circumstances, they are not valid as a general principle. A careful look at the implications of trade imbalances reveals that trade deficits can, at times, be an indicator of rising economic stature, while trade surpluses can be associated with economic disaster. In many other cases, perhaps most, trade imbalances are simply benign—that is, they do not represent a serious threat or imply a notable benefit.

There are several reasons why misunderstandings about trade imbalances persist. The first problem relates to the terminology. A deficit, regardless of the context, sounds bad. To say that a business's books are in deficit, that a government's budget is in deficit, or that a country's trade balance is in deficit, simply sounds bad. A surplus, in contrast, sounds pretty good. For a business, clearly we'd prefer a surplus, to be in the black, to make a profit. Likewise, a budget surplus or a trade surplus must be good as well. Lastly, balance seems either neutral or possibly the ideal condition worth striving for. From an accountant's perspective, balance is often the goal. Debits must equal credits, and the books must balance. Surely, this terminology must contribute to the confusion, at least in a small way, but it is not accurate in describing trade imbalances in general.

A second reason for misunderstandings, especially with regard to deficits, may be a sense of injustice or inequity because foreigners are unwilling to buy as many of our goods as we buy of theirs. Fairness would seem to require reciprocity in international exchanges and therefore balanced trade. This misunderstanding could be easily corrected if only observers were aware that a country's balance of payments, which includes trade in goods, services, and assets, is always in balance. There are no unequal exchanges even when a country runs a trade deficit.

A third reason for the misunderstanding is that trade deficits are indeed bad for some countries in some situations while surpluses are sometimes associated with good economic outcomes. One needs only to note the many international debt crises experienced by countries after they had run persistent and very large trade deficits. One could also look at the very high growth rates of Japan in the 1980s and China in the last few decades for examples of countries with large trade surpluses that have seemingly fared very well.

However, despite these examples, one should not conclude that any country that has a trade deficit or whose trade deficit is rising is necessarily in a potentially dangerous situation; nor should we think that just because a country has a trade surplus that it is necessarily economically healthy. To see why, we must recognize that trade imbalances represent more than just an imbalance in goods and services trade.

Any imbalance in goods and services trade implies an equal and opposite imbalance in asset trade. When a country runs a trade deficit (more exhaustively labeled a current account deficit), it is also running a financial account surplus; similarly, a trade surplus corresponds to a financial account deficit. Imbalances on the financial account mean that a country is a net seller of international assets (if a financial account surplus) or a net buyer of international assets (if a financial account deficit).

One way to distinguish among good, bad, or benign trade imbalances is to recognize the circumstances in which it is good, bad, or benign to be a net international borrower or lender, a net purchaser, or seller of ownership shares in businesses and properties.

The International Investment Position

An evaluation of a country's trade imbalance should begin by identifying the country's net international asset or investment position. The investment position is like a balance sheet in that it shows the total holdings of foreign assets by domestic residents and the total holdings of domestic assets by foreign residents at a point in time. In the International Monetary Fund's (IMF) financial statistics, these are listed as domestic assets (foreign assets held by domestic residents) and domestic liabilities (domestic assets owned by foreign residents). In contrast, the financial account balance is more like an income statement that shows the changes in asset holdings during the past year. In other words, the international asset position of a country consists of stock variables while the financial account balance consists of flow variables.

A country's net international investment balance may either be in a debtor position, a creditor position, or in balance. If in a creditor position, then the value of foreign assets (debt and equity) held by domestic residents exceeds the value of domestic assets held by foreigners. Alternatively, we could say that domestic assets exceed domestic liabilities. If the reverse is true, so that domestic liabilities to foreigners exceed domestic assets, then the country would be called a debtor nation.

Asset holdings may consist of either debt obligations or equity claims. Debt consists of IOUs in which two parties sign a contract agreeing to an initial transfer of money from the lender to the borrower followed by a repayment according to an agreed schedule. The debt contract establishes an obligation for the borrower to repay principal and interest in the future. Equity claims represent ownership shares in potentially productive assets. Equity holdings do not establish obligations between parties, at least not in the form of guaranteed repayments. Once ownership in an asset is transferred from seller to buyer, all advantages and disadvantages of the asset are transferred as well.

Debt and equity obligations always pose several risks. The first risk with debt obligations is the risk of possible default (either total or partial). To the lender, default risk means that the IOU will not be repaid at all, that it will be repaid only in part, or that it is repaid over a much longer period than originally contracted. To the borrower, the risk of default is that future borrowing will likely become unavailable. In contrast, the advantage of default to the borrower is that not all the borrowed money is repaid.

The second risk posed by debt is that the real value of the repayments may be different than expected. This can arise because of unexpected inflation or unexpected currency value changes. Consider inflation first. If inflation is higher than expected, then the real value of debt repayment (if the nominal interest rate is fixed) will be lower than originally expected. This will be an advantage to the borrower (debtor), who repays less in real terms, and a disadvantage to the lender (creditor), who receives less in real terms. If inflation turns out to be less than expected, then the advantages are reversed.

Next, consider currency fluctuations. Suppose a domestic resident, who receives income in the domestic currency, borrows foreign currency in the international market. If the domestic currency depreciates, then the value of the repayments in domestic currency terms will rise even though the foreign currency repayment value remains the same. Thus currency depreciations can be harmful to borrowers of foreign currency. A similar problem can arise for a lender. Suppose a domestic resident purchases foreign currency and then lends it to a foreign resident (note in this case the domestic resident is saving money abroad). Afterward, if the domestic currency appreciates, then foreign savings, once cashed in, will purchase fewer domestic goods and the lender will lose.

Similarly, various risks arise with equity purchases internationally because the asset's rate of return may turn out to be less than expected. This can happen for a number of different reasons. First, if the equity purchases are direct investment in a business, then the return on that investment will depend on how well the business performs. If the market is vibrant and management is good, then the investment will be profitable. Otherwise, the rate of return on the investment could be negative; the foreign investor could lose money. In this case, all the risk is borne by the investor, however. The same holds for stock purchases. Returns on stocks may be positive or negative, but it is the purchaser who bears full responsibility for the return on the investment. As with debt, equity purchases can suffer from exchange rate risk as well. When foreign equities are purchased, their rate of return in terms of domestic currency will depend on the currency value. If the foreign currency in which assets are denominated falls substantially in value, then the value of those assets falls along with it.

Four Trade Imbalance Scenarios

There are four possible situations that a country might face. It may be

- a debtor nation with a trade deficit,
- a debtor nation with a trade surplus,
- a creditor nation with a trade deficit,
- a creditor nation with a trade surplus.

Figure 3.6 "International Asset Positions" depicts a range of possible international investment positions. On the far left of the image, a country would be a net debtor nation, while on the far right, it would be a net creditor nation. A trade deficit or surplus run in a particular year will cause a change in the nation's asset position assuming there are no capital gains or losses on net foreign investments. A trade deficit would generally cause a leftward movement in the nation's investment position implying either a reduction in its net creditor position or an increase in its net debtor position. A trade surplus would cause a rightward shift in a country's investment position implying either an increase in its net creditor position or a decrease in its net debtor position.

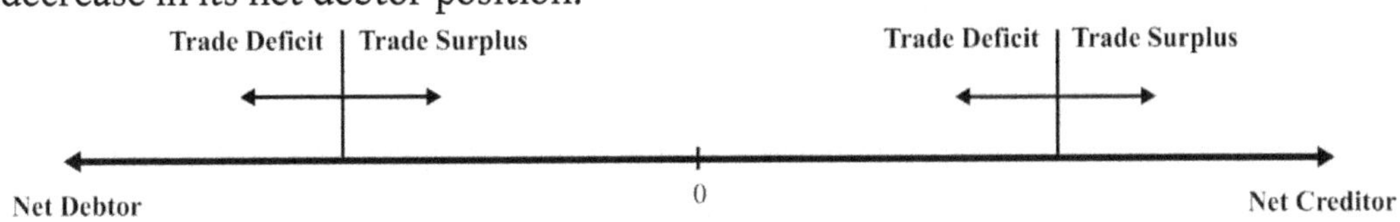

Figure 3.6 International Asset Positions

An exception to this rule occurs whenever there are changes in the market value of foreign assets and when the investment position is calculated using current market values rather than original cost. For example, suppose a country has balanced trade in a particular year and is a net creditor nation. If the investment position is evaluated using original cost, then since the current account is balanced, there would be no change in the investment position. However, if the investment position is evaluated at current market values, then the position can change even with balanced trade. In this case, changes in the investment position arise due to capital gains or losses. Real estate or property valuations may change, portfolio investments in stock markets may rise or fall, and currency value changes may also affect the values of national assets and liabilities.

The pros and cons of a national trade imbalance will depend on which of the four situations describes the current condition of the country. We'll consider each case in turn next.

Case 1: Net Debtor Nation Running a Current Account Deficit

This is perhaps the most common situation in the world, or at least this type of case gets the most attention. The main reason is that large trade deficits run persistently by countries, which are also large debtor nations, can eventually be unsustainable. Examples of international debt crises are widespread. They include the third world debt crisis of the early 1980s, the Mexican crisis in 1994, and the Asian crisis in 1997.

However, not all trade deficits nor all debtor countries face eventual default or severe economic adjustment. Indeed, for some countries, a net debtor position with current account deficits may be an ideal economic situation. To distinguish the good cases from the bad requires us to think about situations in which debt is good or bad.

As mentioned earlier, a current account deficit means that a country is able to spend more on goods and services than it produces during the year. The additional spending can result in increases in consumption, investment, and/or government spending. The country accomplishes this as a net debtor country by borrowing from the rest of the world (incurring debt), or by selling some of its productive assets (equities).

Let's consider a few scenarios.

First, suppose the current account deficit is financed by borrowing money from the rest of the world (i.e., incurring debt). Suppose the additional spending over income is on consumption and government goods and services. In this case, the advantage of the deficit is that the country is able to consume more private and public goods while it is running the deficit. This would enhance the nation's average standard of living during the period the deficit is being run. The disadvantage is that the loans that finance the increase in the standard of living must be repaid in the future. During the repayment period, the country would run a current account surplus, resulting in national spending below national income. This might require a reduction in the country's average standard of living in the future.

This scenario is less worrisome if the choices are being made by private citizens. In this case, individuals are freely choosing to trade off future consumption for current consumption. However, if the additional spending is primarily on government goods and services, then it will be the nation's taxpayers who will be forced to repay government debt in the future by reducing their average living standards. In other words, the future taxpayers' well-being will be reduced to pay for the extra benefits accruing to today's taxpayers.

Possible reductions in future living standards can be mitigated or eliminated if the economy grows sufficiently fast. If national income is high enough in the future, then average living standards could still rise even after subtracting repayment of principal and interest. Thus trade deficits are less worrisome when both current and future economic growth are more rapid.

One way to stimulate economic growth is by increasing spending on domestic investment. If the borrowed funds that result when a country runs a current account deficit are used for investment rather than consumption or if the government spending is on infrastructure, education, or other types of human and physical capital, then the prospects for economic growth are enhanced.

Indeed, for many less-developed countries and countries in transition from a socialist to capitalist market, current account deficits represent potential salvation rather than a curse. Most poor countries suffer from low national savings rates (due to low income) and inadequate tax collection systems. One obvious way to finance investment in these countries is by borrowing from developed countries that have much higher national savings rates. As long as the investments prove to be effective, much more rapid economic growth may be possible.

Thus trade deficits for transitional and less-developed economies are not necessarily worrisome and may even be a sign of strength if they are accompanied by rising domestic investment and/or rising government expenditures on infrastructure.

The main problem with trade deficits arises when they result in a very large international debt position. (Arguably, one could claim that international debt greater than 50 percent of GDP is very large.) In this circumstance, it can lead to a crisis in the form of a default on international obligations. However, the international debt position figures include both debt and equities, and only the debt can be defaulted on. Equities, or ownership shares, may yield positive or negative returns but do not represent the same type of contractual obligations. A country would never be forced to repay foreign security holders for its losses simply because its value on the market dropped. Thus a proper evaluation of the potential for default should only look at the net international "debt" position after excluding the net position on equities.

Default becomes more likely the larger the external debt relative to the countries' ability to repay. Ability to repay can be measured in several ways. First, one can look at net debt relative to GDP. Since it measures annual national income, GDP represents the size of the pool from which repayment of principal and interest is drawn—the larger the pool, the greater the ability of the country to repay. Alternatively, the lower the country's net debt to GDP ratio, the greater the country's ability to repay.

A second method to evaluate ability to repay is to consider net debt as a percentage of exports of goods and services. This is especially relevant when international debt is denominated in foreign currencies. In this case, the primary method to acquire foreign currencies to make repayment of debt is through the export of goods and services. (The alternative method is to sell domestic assets.) Thus the potential for default may rise if the country's ratio of net external debt to exports is larger.

Notice, though, that the variable to look at to evaluate the risk of default is the net debt position, not the trade deficit. The trade deficit merely reveals the change in the net debt position during the past year and does not record total outstanding obligations. In addition, a trade deficit can be run even while the net "debt" position falls. This could occur if the trade deficit is financed primarily with net equity sales rather than net debt obligations. Thus the trade deficit, by itself, does not reveal a complete picture regarding the potential for default.

Next, we should consider what problems are associated with default. Interestingly, it is not really default itself that is immediately problematic but the actions taken to avoid default. If default on international debt does occur, international relationships with creditor countries would generally suffer. Foreign banks that are not repaid on past loans will be reluctant to provide loans in the future. For a less-developed country that needs foreign loans to finance productive investment, these funds may be cut off for a long period and thus negatively affect the country's prospects for economic growth. On the positive side, default is a benefit for the defaulting country in the short-run since it means that borrowed funds are not repaid. Thus the country enjoys the benefits of greater spending during the previous periods when trade deficits are run but does not have to suffer the consequences of debt repayment. With regard to the country's international debt position, default would cause an immediate discrete reduction in the country's debt position.

The real problem arises when economic shocks suddenly raise external obligations on principal and interest, making a debt that was once sustainable suddenly unsustainable. In these cases, it is the effort made to avoid default that is the true source of the problem.

Inability to repay foreign debt arises either if the value of payments suddenly increases or if the income used to finance those payments suddenly falls. Currency depreciations are a common way in which the value of repayments can suddenly rise. If foreign debt is denominated in foreign currency, then domestic currency depreciation implies an appreciation in the value of external debt. If the currency depreciation is large enough, a country may become suddenly unable to make interest and principal repayments. Note, however, that if external debt were denominated in domestic currency, then the depreciation would have no effect on the value of interest and principal repayments. This implies that countries with large external debts are in greater danger of default if (1) their currency value is highly volatile and (2) the external debt is largely denominated in foreign currency.

A second way in which foreign interest obligations can suddenly rise is if the obligations have variable interest rates and if the interest rates suddenly rise. This was one of the problems faced by third world countries during the debt crisis in the early 1980s. Loans received from the U.S. and European banks carried variable interest rates to reduce the risk to the banks from unexpected inflation. When restrictive monetary policy in the United States pushed up U.S. interest rates, interest obligations by foreign countries also suddenly rose. Thus international debt with variable interest rates potentially raises the likelihood of default.

Default can also occur if a country's ability to repay suddenly falls. This can occur if the country enters into a recession. Recessions imply falling GDP, which reduces the pool of funds available for repayment. If the recession is induced by a reduction in exports, perhaps because of recessions in major trading partner countries, then the ability to finance foreign interest and principal repayments is reduced. Thus a recession in the midst of a large international debt position can risk potential default on international obligations.

But what are the problems associated with a sudden increase in debt repayment if default on the debt does not occur? The problem, really, is that the country might suddenly have to begin running current account surpluses to maintain repayments of its international obligations. Remember that trade deficits mean that the country can spend more than its income. By itself, that's a good thing. Current account surpluses, though, mean that the country must spend less than its income. That's the bad thing, especially if it occurs in the face of an economic recession.

Indeed, this is one of the problems the U.S. economy is facing in the midst of the current recession. As the U.S. GDP began to fall in the fall of 2008, the U.S. trade deficit also fell. For the "trade deficits are bad" folks, this would seem to be a good thing. However, it really indicated that not only was U.S. production falling but, because its trade deficit was also falling, its consumption was falling even faster. In terms of standard of living, the drop in the U.S. trade deficit implied a worsening of the economic conditions of its citizens.

However, since this problem arises only when a net debtor country runs a current account surplus, we'll take up this case in the next section. Note well though that the problems associated with a trade deficit run by a net debtor country are generally not visible during the period in which the trade deficit is run. It is more likely that a large international debt will pose problems in the future if or when substantial repayment begins.

- In summary, the problem of trade deficits run by a net debtor country is more worrisome the larger the net debtor position,
- the larger the net debt (rather than equity) position,
- the larger the CA deficit (greater than 5 percent of GDP is large according to some, although large deficit with small net debtor position is less worrisome),
- the more net debt is government obligations or government backed,
- the larger the government deficit,
- if a high percentage of debt is denominated in foreign currency and if the exchange rate has or will depreciate substantially,
- if rising net debt precedes slower GDP growth,
- if rising net debt correlates with falling investment,
- if deficits correspond to "excessive" increase in (C + G) per capita (especially if G is not capital investment),
- if interest rate on external debt is variable,
- if a large recession is imminent.

The situation is benign or beneficial if the reverse occurs.

Case 2: Net Debtor Nation Running a Current Account Surplus

This case generally corresponds to a country in the process of repaying past debt. Alternatively, foreigners may be divesting themselves of domestic equity assets (i.e., selling previously purchased equities, like stocks and real estate, back to domestic residents). In either case, the trade surplus will reduce the country's net debtor position and will require that domestic spending is less than national income. This case is especially problematic if it arises because currency depreciation has forced a sudden change in the country's required repayments on international debt. This is the outcome when a series of trade deficits proves to be unsustainable. What unsustainability means is that the deficits can no longer be continued. Once external financing is no longer available, the country would not have the option to roll over past obligations. In this case, in the absence of default, the country's net repayment on current debt would rise and push the financial account into deficit and hence the trade account into surplus.

When this turnaround occurs rapidly, the country suddenly changes from a state in which it spends more on consumption, investment, and government than its income to a state in which it spends less on these items than its income. Even if GDP stayed the same, the country would suffer severe reductions in its standard of living and reductions in its investment spending. The rapid reduction in domestic demands is generally sufficient to plunge the economy into a recession as well. This reduction in GDP further exacerbates the problem.

This problematic outcome is made worse nationally when most of the debt repayment obligations are by the domestic government or if the external obligations are government-backed. A government that must suddenly make larger than expected repayments of debt must finance it either by raising taxes or by reducing government benefits. The burden of the repayment is then borne by the general population because it must all come from taxpayers. Exactly who suffers more or less will depend on the nature of the budget adjustments, although it often seems that poorer segments of the population bear the brunt of the adjustment costs.

If the sudden increase in debt repayment were primarily by private firms, then the burdens would fall on the associates of those firms rather than the general population. If this occurs on a small scale, we can view this as normal adjustments in a free market system: some firms always go bust, forcing dislocations of labor and capital. The general population in this case would not bear the burden of adjustment unless they are affiliated with the affected firms.

However, even if the debt repayment burden is private and even if the government had not previously guaranteed that debt, the government may feel compelled to intervene with assistance if many private firms are negatively affected. This will perhaps be even more likely if the affected private debt is held by major national banks. Default by enough banks can threaten the integrity of the banking system. Government intervention to save the banks would mean that the general population would essentially bear the burdens of private mistakes.

This kind of rapid reversal is precisely what happened to Indonesia, Thailand, Malaysia, and South Korea in the aftermath of the Asian currency crisis in 1997. Afterward, these countries recorded substantial current account surpluses. These surpluses should not be viewed as a sign of strong vibrant economies; rather, they reflect countries that are in the midst of recessions, struggling to repay their past obligations, and that are now suffering a reduction in average living standards as a consequence.

The most severe consequences of a current account surplus as described above arise when the change from trade deficit to surplus is abrupt. If, on the other hand, the transition is smooth and gradual, then the economy may not suffer noticeably at all. For example, consider a country that has financed a period of extra spending on infrastructure and private investment by running trade deficits and has become a net international debtor nation. However, once the investments begin to take off, fueling rapid economic growth, the country begins to repay more past debt than the new debt that it incurs each period. In this case, the country could make a smooth transition from a trade deficit to a trade surplus. As long as GDP growth continued sufficiently fast, the nation might not even need to suffer reductions in its average living standards even though it is spending less than its income during the repayment period.

In summary, the situation of a net debtor nation running current account surpluses is more worrisome if:

- surpluses follow default,
- GDP growth rate is low or negative,
- the investment rate is low or falling,
- real C + G per capita is falling,
- surplus corresponds to rising net debt and larger equity sales.

The situation is benign or beneficial if the reverse occurs.

Case 3: Net Creditor Nation Running a Current Account Surplus

A net creditor country with trade surpluses is channeling savings to the rest of the world either through lending or through the purchase of foreign productive assets. The situation is generally viewed as prudent but may have some unpleasant consequences. Recall that a country with a trade surplus is spending less on consumption, investment, and government combined than its national income. The excess is being saved abroad. Net creditor status means that the country has more total savings abroad than foreigners have in their country.

The first problem may arise if the surplus corresponds to the substitution of foreign investment for domestic investment. In an era of relatively free capital mobility, countries may decide that the rate of return is higher and the risk is lower on foreign investments compared to domestic investments. If domestic investment falls as a result, future growth prospects for the country are reduced as well. This situation has been a problem in Russia and other transition economies. As these economies increased their private ownership of assets, a small number of people became extremely wealthy. In a well-functioning economy with good future business prospects, wealth is often invested internally helping to fuel domestic growth. However, in many transition economies, wealth holders decided that it was too risky to invest domestically because uncertainty about future growth potential was very low. So instead, they saved their money abroad, essentially financing investment in much healthier and less risky economies.

China is another creditor country running a trade surplus today. It is, however, in a different situation than Russia or the transition economies in the 1990s. China's internal investment rate is very high and its growth rate has been phenomenal over the past twenty years or more. The fact that it has a trade surplus means that as a nation it is saving even more than necessary to finance its already high investment levels. The excess it is lending abroad, thereby raising its international creditor position. (See Chapter 1 for more details.) If it was to redirect that saving domestically, it may not be able to fuel additional growth since their investment spending is already so high. Their trade surplus also means that its average standard of living is well below what is possible because it is saving the surplus abroad rather than spending it on consumption or government goods at home.

A second problem arises even if domestic investment remains high. With domestic investment kept high, the cost of the large surpluses must be felt as a reduction in consumption and government spending. In this case, a large trade surplus leads to a reduction in average living standards for the country. This is a point worth emphasizing. Countries that run trade surpluses suffer a reduction in living standards, not an increase, relative to the case of balanced trade.

Another potential problem with being a net creditor country is the risk associated with international lending and asset purchases. First of all, foreign direct investments may not pay off as hoped or expected. Portfolio investments in foreign stock markets can suddenly be reduced in value if the foreign stock market crashes. On international loans, foreign nations may default on all or part of the outstanding loans, may defer payments, or may be forced to reschedule payments. This is a more likely event if the outstanding loans are to foreign countries with national external debts that may prove unsustainable. If the foreign country suffers rapid currency depreciation and if the foreign loans are denominated in domestic currency, then the foreign country may be forced to default. Defaults may also occur if the foreign debtor countries suffer severe recessions. The creditor nation in these cases is the one that must suffer the losses.

It was this situation that was especially serious for the United States at the onset of the third world debt crisis in the early 1980s. At that time, a number of large U.S. banks had a considerable proportion of their asset portfolios as loans to third world countries. Had these countries defaulted en masse, it would have threatened the solvency of these banks and could have led to a serious banking crisis in the U.S. economy.

Alternatively, suppose the surplus country has made external loans in the foreign countries' currency. If the foreign currency depreciates, even if only gradually, then the value of the foreign assets falls in terms of the domestic currency. The realized rates of return on these assets could then become negative, falling far short of returns on comparable domestic assets.

This is the dilemma that China faces today. The Chinese government has accumulated almost $1 trillion of U.S. Treasury bonds as a result of its persistent current account surpluses over the past decade. All of this debt is denominated in U.S. dollars, making it subject to exchange rate risk. If the Chinese relent to U.S. pressure to allow their fixed currency value appreciate to the U.S. dollar, then the value of these U.S. assets falls in value and reduces their future returns. The Chinese are also worried about the potential for future U.S. inflation due to the expansionary monetary policy used during the current economic crisis. If inflation does arise in the future, the value of the trillion dollars of foreign debt would also be reduced. This situation is epitomized with a popular parable that says, “If you owe me a thousand dollars, then you have a problem, but if you owe me a million dollars, then I have a problem.” Even though the United States is the debtor and the Chinese the creditor, the Chinese now have a problem because they may have lent too much to the United States.

In summary, the situation of a net creditor nation running current account surpluses is worrisome if the:

- net credit position is very large,
- current account surplus is very large,
- GDP growth rate is low,
- investment rate is low or falling,
- C + G per capita is low or falling,
- surplus involves lending denominated in a foreign currency that may afterward depreciate,
- domestic currency has appreciated substantially,
- foreign asset values have fallen substantially.

The situation is benign or beneficial if the reverse occurs.

Case 4: Net Creditor Nation Running a Current Account Deficit

In general, a deficit run by a country that is a net creditor is least likely to be problematic. Essentially, this describes a country that is drawing down previously accumulated savings. The deficit also implies that the country is spending more than its income. This situation is especially good if it allows the country to maintain living standards during a recession. This case would also be good if a country with a rapidly aging population is drawing down previous savings to maintain average living standards.

The current account deficit can cause problems if as in case one, the deficit corresponds to falling investment and increases in consumption and government expenditures. If these changes occur while the economy continues to grow, then it may indicate potential problems for future economic growth. However, if the same changes occur while the economy is in a recession, then the effect would be to maintain average living standards by drawing down external savings. If this occurs only during the recession, then the long-term effect on growth would be mitigated.

This case can be a problem if the net creditor position is extremely large. A large amount of foreign savings can always potentially drop in value given currency fluctuations as described above in case three. However, the current account deficit only serves to reduce this potential problem since it reduces the country's net creditor position.

In summary, the situation of a net creditor nation running current account deficits is worrisome if the net creditor status is smaller and the deficit is larger (although this is generally less worrisome than if the country were a net debtor), investment is falling (although a temporary drop in investment is likely in a recession), C + G per capita is rising rapidly.

The situation is benign or beneficial if the reverse occurs.

KEY TAKEAWAYS

- Since trade deficits are not always bad and trade surpluses not always good, it is important to know how to judge a country's trade imbalance.
- Trade deficits are more worrisome when a country is a large international debtor and when growth or prospective growth is low.
- Trade deficits are less worrisome if international debt is low or if the country is a creditor nation.
- Trade deficits are less worrisome if they accompany increased investment and other stimuli to economic growth.
- Trade surpluses are more worrisome when the foreign credits reduce domestic investment sufficiently to reduce growth.
- Trade surpluses are more worrisome when future repayments will likely be lower than anticipated. This can occur if the credits are exceedingly large or denominated in foreign currency.
- Trade surpluses are more worrisome when they arise suddenly in association with a large international debtor position.

EXERCISES

Suppose the hypothetical country of Avalon has a current account deficit of $20 billion this year. From the two scenarios listed in each part below, identify which scenario would make this deficit more worrisome to an economic analyst and which scenario would be less worrisome. Briefly explain why.

- Scenario 1: Avalon's GDP is $80 billion dollars per year.
- Scenario 2: Avalon's GDP is $800 billion per year.
- Scenario 1: Avalon is a net debtor country.
- Scenario 2: Avalon is a net creditor country.
- Scenario 1: Avalon's annual consumption spending is 50 percent of GDP.
- Scenario 2: Avalon's annual consumption spending is 90 percent of GDP.

- Scenario 1: Avalon's GDP grew 1 percent last year.
- Scenario 2: Avalon's GDP grew 10 percent last year.

Below are the economic data for five fictitious countries running trade deficits. Dollar amounts are in billions, and percentages are relative to GDP.

	Alpha (%)	Beta (%)	Gamma (%)	Delta (%)	Epsilon (%)
GDP	$260	$340	$135	$400	$840
Trade Deficit (TD)	9.1	9.7	2.5	5.7	6.0
Projected GDP Growth	+2.0	+10.2	+3.0	+1.0	+5.5
Net International Investment Position (IIP)	75 debtor	30 creditor	20 debtor	60 debtor	5 debtor
Domestic Investment (I)	18	35	16	13	27

Suppose you work for the International Monetary Fund, and it has asked you to assess which two of these five countries' trade deficits are most likely to pose future repayment problems. Provide a brief explanation justifying your assessment.

Consider the fictitious country of Malamar. Economic data for Malamar are presented in the table below. Note that Malamar is currently running a trade deficit of $60 billion.

Trade Deficit (TD)	$60 billion
GDP	$1,000 billion
GDP Growth—Past 3 Years (Growth -)	-1.2%
Projected GDP Growth—Next 3 Years (Growth +)	8.5%
Net International Investment Position (IIP)	-$800 billion (debtor)
Domestic Investment (I)	$350 billion

In the table below, reference the above data (either directly or in combination) in the first column and indicate in the second column whether this information tends to make Malamar's deficit more worrisome or less worrisome. One example is provided to illustrate.

Data	More or Less Worrisome
TD/GDP = 6 percent	More

Consider the following statements concerning current account balances. Explain in what sense, if any, the statements are valid. In what sense, if any, are the statements misguided?

- A current account deficit implies that our nation is giving away money to the rest of the world.
- A current account deficit indicates that a country has exported jobs to the rest of the world.
- A current account deficit implies that the nation must have a reduced standard of living in the future.

CHAPTER

RATES OF RETURN AND FOREIGN EXCHANGE MARKETS 4

INTRODUCTION

People trade one national currency for another for one reason: they want to do something with the other currency. What they might do consists of one of two things: either they wish to spend the money, acquiring goods and services, or they wish to invest the money.

This chapter introduces the foreign exchange market for currency trades. It highlights some of the more obvious, although sometimes confusing, features and then turns attention to the motivations of foreign investors. One of the prime motivations for investing in another country is because one hopes to make more money on an investment abroad. How an investor calculates and compares those rates of returns are explored in this chapter.

4.1 PARTICIPANTS AND OBJECTIVES IN THE FOREX

The foreign exchange market (Forex) is not a market like the New York Stock Exchange, where daily trades of stock are conducted in a central location. Instead, the Forex refers to the activities of major international banks that engage in currency trading. These banks act as intermediaries between the true buyers and sellers of currencies (i.e., governments, businesses, and individuals). These banks will hold foreign currency deposits and stand ready to exchange these for domestic currency upon demand. The exchange rate (ER) will be determined independently by each bank but will essentially be determined by supply and demand in the market. In other words, the bank sets the exchange rate at each moment to equalize its supply of foreign currency with the market demand. Each bank makes money by collecting a transactions fee for its "exchange services."

It is useful to categorize two distinct groups of participants in the Forex, those whose transactions are recorded on the current account (importers and exporters) and those whose transactions are recorded on the financial account (investors).

Importers and Exporters

Anyone who imports or exports goods and services will need to exchange currencies to make the transactions. This includes tourists who travel abroad; their transactions would appear as services in the current account. These businesses and individuals will engage in currency trades daily; however, these transactions are small in comparison to those made by investors.

International Investors, Banks, Arbitrageurs, and Others

Most of the daily currencies transactions are made by investors. These investors, be they investment companies, insurance companies, banks, or others, are making currency transactions to realize a greater return on their investments or holdings. Many of these companies are responsible for managing the savings of others. Pension plans and mutual funds buy and sell billions of dollars worth of assets daily. Banks, in the temporary possession of the deposits of others, do the same. Insurance companies manage large portfolios that act as their capital to be used to pay off claims on accidents, casualties, and deaths. More and more of these companies look internationally to make the most of their investments.

It is estimated by the Bank of International Settlements that over $3 trillion (or $3,000 billion) worth of currency is traded every day. Only about $60 to $100 billion of trade in goods and services takes place daily worldwide. This suggests that many of the currency exchanges are done by international investors rather than importers and exporters.

Investment Objectives

Investors generally have three broad concerns when an investment is made. They care about how much money the investment will earn over time, they care about how risky the investment is, and they care about how liquid, or convertible, the asset is.

Rate of return (RoR). The percentage change in the value of an asset over some period.

Investors purchase assets as a way of saving for the future. Anytime an asset is purchased, the purchaser is forgoing current consumption for future consumption. To make such a transaction worthwhile the investors hope (sometimes expect) to have more money for future consumption than the amount they give up in the present. Thus investors would like to have as high a rate of return on their investments as possible.

Example 1: Suppose a Picasso painting is purchased in 1996 for $500,000. One year later, the painting is resold for $600,000. The rate of return is calculated as

Example 2: $1,000 is placed in a savings account for one year at an annual interest rate of 10 percent. The interest earned after one year is $1,000 × 0.10 = $100. Thus the value of the account after one year is $1,100. The rate of return is

This means that the rate of return on a domestic interest-bearing account is merely the interest rate.

Risk. The second primary concern of investors is the riskiness of the assets. Generally, the greater the expected rate of return, the greater the risk. Invest in an oil wildcat endeavor and you might get a 1,000 percent return on your investment—that is, if you strike oil. The chances of doing so are likely to be very low, however. Thus a key concern of investors is how to manage the trade-off between risk and return.

Liquidity. Liquidity essentially means the speed with which assets can be converted to cash. Insurance companies need to have assets that are fairly liquid in the event that they need to pay out a large number of claims. Banks also need to be able to make payouts to their depositors, who may request their money back at any time.

KEY TAKEAWAYS

- Participants in the foreign exchange markets can be classified into traders and investors.
- Traders export or import goods and services whose transactions appear on the current account of the balance of payments.
- Investors purchase or sell assets whose transactions appear on the financial account of the balance of payments.
- The three main concerns for any investor are first to obtain a high rate of return, second to minimize the risk of default, and third to maintain an acceptable degree of liquidity.
- The rate of return on an asset is the percentage change in its value over a period.

Jeopardy Questions:As in the popular television game show, you are given an answer to a question and you must respond with the question. For example, if the answer is "a tax on imports," then the correct question is "What is a tariff?"

- This group enters the foreign exchange market to make transactions that will be recorded on the current account.
- This group enters the foreign exchange market to make transactions that will be recorded on the financial account.
- The percentage change in the value of an asset over some period.
- The term used to describe the ease with which an asset can be converted to cash.
- The term used to describe the possibility that an asset will not return what is originally expected.

- A list of three main objectives for international investors.
- The rate of return on a share of stock whose value rises during the year from \$5.50 per share to \$6.50 per share.
- The rate of return on a commercial office building that was purchased one year ago for \$650,000 and sold today for \$600,000.

4.2 EXCHANGE RATE: DEFINITIONS

Anyone who has ever traveled to another country has probably had to deal with an exchange rate between two currencies. (I say "probably" because a person who travels from, say, Italy to Spain continues to use euros.) In a sense, exchange rates are very simple. However, despite their simplicity they never fail to generate confusion. To overcome that confusion this chapter begins by offering straightforward definitions and several rules of thumb that can help with these problems.

The exchange rate (ER) represents the number of units of one currency that exchanges for a unit of another. There are two ways to express an exchange rate between two currencies (e.g., between the U.S. dollar [\$] and the British pound [£]). One can either write \$/£ or £/\$. These are reciprocals of each other. Thus if E is the \$/£ exchange rate and V is the £/\$ exchange rate, then $E = 1/V$.

For example, on January 6, 2010, the following exchange rates prevailed:

$$E_{\$/£} = 1.59, \text{ which implies } V_{£/\$} = 0.63,$$

and

$$V_{¥/\$} = 92.7, \text{ which implies } E_{\$/¥} = 0.0108.$$

Currency Value

It is important to note that the value of a currency is always given in terms of another currency. Thus the value of a U.S. dollar in terms of British pounds is the £/\$ exchange rate. The value of the Japanese yen in terms of dollar is the \$/¥ exchange rate.

Note that we always express the value of all items in terms of something else. Thus the value of a quart of milk is given in dollars, not in quarts of milk. The value of car is also given in dollar terms, not in terms of cars. Similarly, the value of a dollar is given in terms of something else, usually another currency. Hence, the rupee/dollar exchange rate gives us the value of the dollar in terms of rupees.

This definition is especially useful to remember when one is dealing with unfamiliar currencies. Thus the value of the euro (€) in terms of British pounds is given as the £/€ exchange rate.

Similarly, the peso/euro exchange rate refers to the value of the euro in terms of pesos.

Currency appreciation means that a currency appreciates with respect to another when its value rihme period.

Example 1: U.S. dollar (US$) to the Canadian dollar (C$)

On January 6, 2010, $E_{C\$/US\$}$ = 1.03.On January 6, 2009, $E_{C\$/US\$}$ = 1.19.

Use the percentage change formula, (new value - old value)/old value:

Multiply by 100 to write as a percentage to get

$-0.134 \times 100 = -13.4\%$.

Since we have calculated the change in the value of the U.S. dollar in terms of Canadian dollar, and since the percentage change is negative, this means that the dollar has depreciated by 13.4 percent with respect to the C$ during the previous year.

Example 2: U.S. dollar ($) to the Pakistani rupee (R)

On January 6, 2010, $E_{R/\$}$ = 84.7.On January 6, 2010, $E_{R/\$}$ = 79.1.

Use the percentage change formula, (new value - old value)/old value:

Multiply by 100 to write as a percentage to get

$+0.071 \times 100 = +7.1\%$.

Since we have calculated the change in the value of the U.S. dollar, in terms of rupees, and since the percentage change is positive, this means that the dollar has appreciated by 7.1 percent with respect to the Pakistani rupee during the past year.

Other Exchange Rate Terms

Arbitrage generally means buying a product when its price is low and then reselling it after its price rises in order to make a profit. Currency arbitrage means buying a currency in one market (e.g., New York) at a low price and reselling, moments later, in another market (e.g., London) at a higher price.

The spot exchange rate refers to the exchange rate that prevails on the spot, that is, for trades to take place immediately. (Technically, it is for trades that occur within two days.)

The forward exchange rate refers to the rate that appears on a contract to exchange currencies either 90 ,60 ,30, or 180 days in the future.

For example, a corporation might sign a contract with a bank to buy euros for U.S. dollars sixty days from now at a predetermined ER. The predetermined rate is called the sixty-day forward rate. Forward contracts can be used to reduce exchange rate risk.

For example, suppose an importer of BMWs is expecting a shipment in sixty days. Suppose that upon arrival the importer must pay €1,000,000 and the current spot ER is 1.20 $/€.

Thus if the payment were made today it would cost $1,200,000. Suppose further that the importer is fearful of a U.S. dollar depreciation. He doesn't currently have the $1,200,000 but expects to earn more than enough in sales over the next two months. If the U.S. dollar falls in value to, say, 1.30 $/€ within sixty days, how much would it cost the importer in dollars to purchase the BMW shipment?

The shipment would still cost €1,000,000. To find out how much this is in dollars, multiply €1,000,000 by 1.30 $/€ to get $1,300,000.

Note that this is $100,000 more for the cars simply because the U.S. dollar value changed.

One way the importer could protect himself against this potential loss is to purchase a forward contract to buy euros for U.S. dollars in sixty days. The ER on the forward contract will likely be different from the current spot ER. In part, its value will reflect market expectations about the degree to which currency values will change in the next two months. Suppose the current sixty-day forward ER is 1.25 $/€, reflecting the expectation that the U.S. dollar value will fall. If the importer purchases a sixty-day contract to buy €1,000,000, it will cost him $1,250,000 (i.e., $1,000,000 × 1.25 $/€). Although this is higher than what it would cost if the exchange were made today, the importer does not have the cash available to make the trade today, and the forward contract would protect the importer from an even greater U.S. dollar depreciation.

When the forward ER is such that a forward trade costs more than a spot trade today costs, there is said to be a forward premium. If the reverse were true, such that the forward trade were cheaper than a spot trade, then there is a forward discount.

A currency trader is hedging if he or she enters into a forward contract to protect oneself from a downside loss. However, by hedging the trader also forfeits the potential for an upside gain. Suppose in the story above that the spot ER falls rather than rises. Suppose the ER fell to 1.10 $/€. In this case, had the importer waited, the 1,000,000€ would only have cost 1,100,000$ (i.e., 1.10 × 1,000,000$ $/€). Thus hedging protects against loss but at the same time eliminates potential unexpected gain.

KAn exchange rate denominated x/y gives the value of y in terms of x. When an exchange rate denominated x/y rises, then y has appreciated in value in terms of x, while x has depreciated in terms of y.

Spot exchange rates represent the exchange rate prevailing for currency trades today. Forward, or future, exchange rates represent the exchange values on trades that will take place in the future to fulfill a predetermined contract.

Currency arbitrage occurs when someone buys a currency at a low price and sells shortly afterward at a higher price to make a profit.

Hedging refers to actions taken to reduce the risk associated with currency trades.

EXERCISES

Jeopardy Questions:As in the popular television game show, you are given an answer to a question and you must respond with the question. For example, if the answer is "a tax on imports," then the correct question is "What is a tariff?"

- The term used to describe an increase in the value of the yen.
- This currency value is expressed by the euro/peso exchange rate.
- This has happened to the value of the U.S. dollar if the dollar/euro exchange rate rises from 1.10 $/€ to 1.20 $/€.
- The term used to describe the process of buying low and selling high to make a profit.
- The term used to describe the exchange rate that appears on a contract to exchange currencies either 30, 60, 90, or 180 days in the future.
- The term used to describe the exchange rate that prevails for (almost) immediate trades.
- The term used to describe process of protecting oneself from the riskiness of exchange rate movements.
- Use the exchange rate data in the table to answer the following questions. The first two exchange rates are the spot rates on those dates. The third exchange rate is the one-year forward exchange rate as of February 2004.

	February 4, 2003	February 4, 2004	Forward February 4, 2005
United States–Europe	1.08 $/€	1.25 $/€	1.24 $/€
South Africa–United States	8.55 rand/$	6.95 rand/$	7.42 rand/$

- Calculate the rate of change in the euro value relative to the dollar between 2003 and 2004.
- Calculate the rate of change in the dollar value relative to the euro between 2003 and 2004.
- Calculate the rate of change in the dollar value relative to the South African rand between 2003 and 2004.
- Calculate the expected change in the dollar value relative to the euro between 2004 and 2005.
- Calculate the expected change in the dollar value relative to the rand between 2004 and 2005.

4.3 RETURN ON INTERNATIONAL INVESTMENTS RATES CALCULATION

Suppose that an investor holding U.S. dollars must decide between two investments of equal risk and liquidity. Suppose one potential investment is a one-year certificate of deposit (CD) issued by a U.S. bank while a second potential investment is a one-year CD issued by a British bank. For simplicity we'll assume that interest is calculated on both CDs using a simple interest rather than with a compounding formula. A CD is a type of deposit that provides a higher rate of interest to the depositor in return for a promise to keep the money deposited for a fixed amount of time. The time period could be six months, one year, two years, or any other period decided by the bank. If the depositor wants to withdraw the money earlier, she must pay a penalty.

Since we imagine that an investor wants to obtain the highest rate of return (RoR) possible, given acceptable risk and liquidity characteristics, that investor will choose the investment with the highest rate of return. If the investor acted naively, she might simply compare interest rates between the two investments and choose the one that is higher. However, this would not necessarily be the best choice. To see why, we need to walk through the calculation of rates of return on these two investments.

First, we need to collect some data, which we will do in general terms rather than use specific values. Examples with actual values are presented in a later section.

Let $E_{\$/£}$ = the spot ER.$E_{\$/£}^{e}$ = the expected ER one year from now.$i_{\$}$ = the one-year interest rate on a CD in the United States (in decimal form).$i_{£}$ = the one-year interest rate on a CD in Britain (in decimal form).

U.S. Rate of Return

The rate of return on the U.S. CD is simply the interest rate on that deposit. More formally,

$$RoR_{\$} = i_{\$}.$$

This is because the interest rate describes the percentage increase in the value of the deposit over the course of the year. It is also simple because there is no need to convert currencies.

British Rate of Return

The rate of return on the British CD is more difficult to determine. If a U.S. investor, with dollars, wants to invest in the British CD, she must first exchange dollars for pounds on the spot market and then use the British pound (£) to purchase the British CD. After one year, she must convert pounds back to dollars at the exchange rate that prevails then. The rate of return on that investment is the percentage change in dollar value during the year. To calculate this we can follow the procedure below.

Suppose the investor has P dollars to invest (P for principal).

Step 1: Convert the dollars to pounds.

is the number of pounds the investor will have at the beginning of the year.

Step 2: Purchase the British CD and earn interest in pounds during the year.

is the number of pounds the investor will have at the end of the year. The first term in parentheses returns the principal. The second term is the interest payment.

Step 3: Convert the principal plus interest back into dollars in one year.

is the number of dollars the investor can expect to have at the end of the year.

The rate of return in dollar terms from this British investment can be found by calculating the expected percentage change in the value of the investor's dollar assets over the year, as shown below:

After factoring out the P, this reduces to

Thus the rate of return on the foreign investment is more complicated because the set of transactions is more complicated. For the U.S. investment, the depositor simply deposits the dollars and earns dollar interest at the rate given by the interest rate. However, for the foreign deposit, the investor must first convert currency, then deposit the money abroad earning interest in foreign currency units, and finally reconvert the currency back to dollars. The rate of return depends not only on the foreign interest rate but also on the spot exchange rate and the expected exchange rate one year in the future.

Note that according to the formula, the rate of return on the foreign deposit is positively related to changes in the foreign interest rate and the expected foreign currency value and negatively related to the spot foreign currency value.

For a dollar investor, the rate of return on a U.S. deposit is equal to the interest rate: $RoR_\$ = i_\$$.

For a dollar investor, the rate of return on a foreign deposit depends on the foreign interest rate, the spot exchange rate, and the exchange rate expected to prevail at the time the deposit is redeemed: In particular, .

EXERCISE

Jeopardy Questions: As in the popular television game show, you are given an answer to a question and you must respond with the question. For example, if the answer is "a tax on imports," then the correct question is "What is a tariff?"

- These three variables influence the rate of return on a foreign deposit.
- For a U.S. dollar investor, this is the rate of return on a U.S. dollar deposit yielding 3 percent per year.

- The term used to describe the exchange rate predicted to prevail at some point in the future.
- The term for the type of bank deposit that offers a higher yield on a deposit that is maintained for a predetermined period of time.

4.4 RETURN RATE FORMULAS INTERPRETATION

Although the derivation of the rate of return formula is fairly straightforward, it does not lend itself easily to interpretation or intuition. By applying some algebraic "tricks," it is possible to rewrite the British rate of return formula in a form that is much more intuitive.

Step 1: Begin with the British rate of return formula derived in Chapter 4, Section 4.3 :

Step 2: Factor out the term in parentheses. Add $i_{£}$ and then subtract it as well. Mathematically, a term does not change in value if you add and subtract the same value:

Step 3: Change the (-1) in the expression to its equivalent, . Also change $-i_{£}$ to its equivalent, . Since , these changes do not change the value of the rate of return expression:

Step 4: Rearrange the expression:

Step 5: Simplify by combining terms with common denominators:

Step 6: Factor out the percentage change in the exchange rate term:

This formula shows that the expected rate of return on the British asset depends on two things, the British interest rate and the expected percentage change in the value of the pound. Notice that if is a positive number, then the expected $/£ ER is greater than the current spot ER, which means that one expects a pound appreciation in the future. Furthermore, represents the expected rate of appreciation of the pound during the following year. Similarly, if were negative, then it corresponds to the expected rate of depreciation of the pound during the subsequent year.

The expected rate of change in the pound value is multiplied by $(1 + i_{£})$, which generally corresponds to a principal and interest component in a rate of return calculation.

To make sense of this expression, it is useful to consider a series of simple numerical examples.

Suppose the following values prevail,

	5% per year
	1.1 $/£
	1.0 $/£

Plugging these into the rate of return formula yields

which simplifies to

$$RoR_{£} = 0.05 + (1 + 0.05) \times 0.10 = .155 \text{ or } 15.5\%.$$

Note that because of the exchange rate change, the rate of return on the British asset is considerably higher than the 5 percent interest rate.

To decompose these effects suppose that the British asset yielded no interest whatsoever.

This would occur if the individual held pound currency for the year rather than purchasing a CD. In this case, the rate of return formula reduces to

$$RoR_{£} = 0.0 + (1 + 0.0) \times 0.10 = .10 \text{ or } 10\%.$$

This means that 10 percent of the rate of return arises solely because of the pound appreciation. Essentially an investor in this case gains because of currency arbitrage over time. Remember that arbitrage means buying something when its price is low, selling it when its price is high, and thus making a profit on the series of transactions. In this case, the investor buys pounds at the start of the year, when their price (in terms of dollars) is low, and then resells them at the end of the year when their price is higher.

Next, suppose that there was no exchange rate change during the year, but there was a 5 percent interest rate on the British asset. In this case, the rate of return becomes

$$RoR_{£} = 0.05 + (1 + 0.05) \times 0.0 = .05 \text{ or } 5\%.$$

Thus with no change in the exchange rate, the rate of return reduces to the interest rate on the asset.

Finally, let's look back at the rate of return formula:

The first term simply gives the contribution to the total rate of return that derives solely from the interest rate on the foreign asset. The second set of terms has the percentage change in the exchange rate times one plus the interest rate. It corresponds to the contribution to the rate of return that arises solely due to the exchange rate change. The one plus interest rate term means that the exchange rate return can be separated into two components, a principal component and an interest component.

Suppose the exchange rate change is positive. In this case, the principal that is originally deposited will grow in value by the percentage exchange rate change. But the principal also accrues interest and as the £ value rises, the interest value, in dollar terms, also rises.

Thus the second set of terms represents the percentage increase in the value of one's principal and interest that arises solely from the change in the exchange rate.

KEY TAKEAWAYS

- The rate of return on a foreign deposit consists of three components: the interest rate itself, the change in the value of the principal due to the exchange rate change, and the change in the value of the interest due to the exchange rate change.
- Another formula, but one that is equivalent to the one in the previous section, for the rate of return on a foreign deposit is.

Consider the following data. Suppose the expected exchange rates are the average expectations by investors for exchange rates in one year. Imagine that the interest rates are for equally risky assets and are annual rates.

	United States	Australia	Singapore
Current Exchange Rate	–	1.80 A$/US$	1.75 S$/US$
Expected Exchange Rate	–	1.90 A$/US$	1.65 S$/US$
Current Interest Rate (%)	2.0	4.0	1.0

- Calculate the rate of return for a U.S. dollar investor investing in the Australian deposit for one year.
- Calculate the rate of return for a U.S. dollar investor investing in the Singapore deposit for one year.
- Among these three options (United States, Australia, and Singapore), which is the best place for the investor to invest? Which is the worst place?

The covered interest parity condition substitutes the forward exchange rate for the expected exchange rate. The condition is labeled "covered" because the forward contract assures a certain rate of return (i.e., without risk) on foreign deposits. The table below lists a spot exchange rate, a ninety-day forward rate, and a ninety-day money market interest rate in Germany and Canada. Use this information to answer the following questions.

	Germany	Canada
Spot Exchange Rate	0.5841 $/DM	0.7451 US$/C$
90-Day Forward Exchange Rate	0.5807 $/DM	0.7446 US$/C$
90-Day Interest Rate (%)	1.442	0.875

What would the U.S. ninety-day interest rate have to be for the United States to have the highest rate of return for a U.S. investor? (Use the exact formulas to calculate the rates of return.)

4.5 RATE OF RETURN FORMULAS APPLICATION

Use the data in the tables below to calculate in which country it would have been best to purchase a one-year interest-bearing asset.These numbers were taken from the Economist, Weekly Indicators, December 17, 2005, p. 90, http://www.economist.com.

Example 1

Consider the following data for interest rates and exchange rates in the United States and Britain:

	2.37% per year
	4.83% per year
	1.96 $/£
	1.75 $/£

We imagine that the decision is to be made in 2004, looking forward into 2005. However, we calculate this in hindsight after we know what the 2005 exchange rate is. Thus we plug in the 2005 rate for the expected exchange rate and use the 2004 rate as the current spot rate. Thus the ex-post (i.e., after the fact) rate of return on British deposits is given by

which simplifies to

$$RoR_{£} = 0.0483 + (1 + 0.0483)(-0.1071) = -0.064 \text{ or } -6.4\%.$$

A negative rate of return means that the investor would have lost money (in dollar terms) by purchasing the British asset.

Since $RoR_{\$}$ = %2.37 > $RoR_{£}$ = %6.4-, the investor seeking the highest rate of return should have deposited her money in the U.S. account.

Example 2

Consider the following data for interest rates and exchange rates in the United States and Japan.

	2.37% per year
	0.02% per year
	104 ¥/$
	120 ¥/$

Again, imagine that the decision is to be made in 2004, looking forward into 2005. However, we calculate this in hindsight after we know what the 2005 exchange is. Thus we plug in the 2005 rate for the expected exchange rate and use the 2004 rate as the current spot rate. Note also that the interest rate in Japan really was 0.02 percent. It was virtually zero.

Before calculating the rate of return, it is necessary to convert the exchange rate to the yen equivalent rather than the dollar equivalent. Thus:

Now, the ex-post (i.e., after the fact) rate of return on Japanese deposits is given by

which simplifies to $RoR_{¥}$ - 0.0002 + (1 + 0.0002)(−0.1354) = −0.1352 or −13.52%.

A negative rate of return means that the investor would have lost money (in dollar terms) by purchasing the Japanese asset.

Since $RoR_{\$}$ = %2.37 > $RoR_{¥}$ = %13.52-, the investor seeking the highest rate of return should have deposited his money in the U.S. account.

Example 3

Consider the following data for interest rates and exchange rates in the United States and South Korea. Note that South Korean currency is in won (W).

	2.37% per year
	4.04% per year
	1,059 W/$
	1,026 W/$

As in the preceding examples, the decision is to be made in 2004, looking forward to 2005. However, since the previous year interest rate is not listed, we use the current short-term interest rate. Before calculating the rate of return, it is necessary to convert the exchange rate to the won equivalent rather than the dollar equivalent. Thus

Now, the ex-post (i.e., after the fact) rate of return on Italian deposits is given by

which simplifies to:

$$RoR_W = 0.0404 + (1 + 0.0404)(0.0328) = 0.0746 \text{ or } +7.46\%.$$

In this case, the positive rate of return means an investor would have made money (in dollar terms) by purchasing the South Korean asset.

Also, since $RoR_{\$}$ = 2.37 percent < RoR_W = 7.46 percent, the investor seeking the highest rate of return should have deposited his money in the South Korean account.

KEY TAKEAWAY

- An investor should choose the deposit or asset that promises the highest expected rate of return assuming equivalent risk and liquidity characteristics.

EXERCISES

Consider the following data collected on February 9, 2004. The interest rate given is for a one-year money market deposit. The spot exchange rate is the rate for February 9. The expected exchange rate is the one-year forward rate. Express each answer as a percentage.

	2.5%
	0.7541 US$/C$
	0[0].7468 US$/C$

Use both RoR formulas (one from Chapter 4 "Foreign Exchange Markets and Rates of Return", Section 4.3 "Calculating Rate of Returns on International Investments", the other from Chapter 4 "Foreign Exchange Markets and Rates of Return", Section 4.4 "Interpretation of the Rate of Return Formula", Step 5) to calculate the expected rate of return on the Canadian money market deposit and show that both formulas generate the same answer.

1. What part of the rate of return arises only due to the interest earned on the deposit?
2. What part of the rate of return arises from the percentage change in the value of the principal due to the change in the exchange rate?
3. What component of the rate of return arises from the percentage change in the value of the interest payments due to the change in the exchange rate?

Consider the following data collected on February 9, 2004. The interest rate given is for a one-year money market deposit. The spot exchange rate is the rate for February 9. The expected exchange rate is the one-year forward rate. Express each answer as a percentage.

	4.5%
	1.8574 $/£
	1.7956 $/£

Use both RoR formulas (one from Chapter 4 "Foreign Exchange Markets and Rates of Return", Section 4.3, the other from Chapter 4 "Foreign Exchange Markets and Rates of Return", Section 4.4 , Step 5) to calculate the expected rate of return on the British money market deposit and show that both formulas generate the same answer.

1. What part of the rate of return arises only due to the interest earned on the deposit?
2. What part of the rate of return arises from the percentage change in the value of the principal due to the change in the exchange rate?
3. What component of the rate of return arises from the percentage change in the value of the interest payments due to the change in the exchange rate?

CHAPTER 5

RATE OF INTEREST PARITY

5

INTRODUCRTION

Interest rate parity is one of the most important theories in international finance because it is probably the best way to explain how exchange rate values are determined and why they fluctuate as they do. Most of the international currency exchanges occur for investment purposes, and therefore understanding the prime motivations for international investment is critical.

The chapter applies the rate of return formula developed in Chapter 4 and shows how changes in the determinants of the rate of return on assets affect investor behavior on the foreign exchange market, which in turn affects the value of the exchange rate. The model is described in two different ways: first, using simple supply and demand curves; and second, using a rate of return diagram that will be used later with the development of a more elaborate macro model of the economy.

5.1 INTEREST RATE PARITY: AN OVERVIEW

Interest rate parity (IRP) is a theory used to explain the value and movements of exchange rates. It is also known as the asset approach to exchange rate determination. The interest rate parity theory assumes that the actions of international investors—motivated by cross-country differences in rates of return on comparable assets—induce changes in the spot exchange rate. In another vein, IRP suggests that transactions on a country's financial account affect the value of the exchange rate on the foreign exchange (Forex) market. This contrasts with the purchasing power parity theory, which assumes that the actions of importers and exporters, whose transactions are recorded on the current account, induce changes in the exchange rate.

Interest Rate Parity Condition

Interest rate parity refers to a condition of equality between the rates of return on comparable assets between two countries. The term is somewhat of a misnomer on the basis of how it is being described here, as it should really be called rate of return parity. The term developed in an era when the world was in a system of fixed exchange rates. Under those circumstances, and as will be demonstrated in a later chapter, rate of return parity did mean the equalization of interest rates. However, when exchange rates can fluctuate, interest rate parity becomes rate of return parity, but the name was never changed.

In terms of the rates of return formulas developed in Chapter 4 "Foreign Exchange Markets and Rates of Return", interest rate parity holds when the rate of return on dollar deposits is just equal to the expected rate of return on British deposits, that is, when

$$RoR_{\$} = RoR_{£}.$$

Plugging in the above formula yields

This condition is often simplified in many textbooks by dropping the final term in which the British interest rate is multiplied by the exchange rate change. The logic is that the final term is usually very small especially when interest rates are low. The approximate version of the IRP condition then is

One should be careful, however. The approximate version would not be a good approximation when interest rates in a country are high. For example, back in 1997, short-term interest rates were 60 percent per year in Russia and 75 percent per year in Turkey. With these interest rates, the approximate formula would not give an accurate representation of rates of return.

Interest Rate Parity Theory

Investor behavior in asset markets that results in interest parity can also explain why the exchange rate may rise and fall in response to market changes. In other words, interest parity can be used to develop a model of exchange rate determination. This is known as the asset approach, or the interest rate parity model.

The first step is to reinterpret the rate of return calculations described previously in more general (aggregate) terms. Thus instead of using the interest rate on a one-year certificate of deposit (CD), we will interpret the interest rates in the two countries as the average interest rates that currently prevail. Similarly, we will imagine that the expected exchange rate is the average expectation across many different individual investors. The rates of return then are the average expected rates of return on a wide variety of assets between two countries.

Next, we imagine that investors trade currencies in the foreign exchange (Forex) market. Each day, some investors come to a market ready to supply a currency in exchange for another, while others come to demand currency in exchange for another.

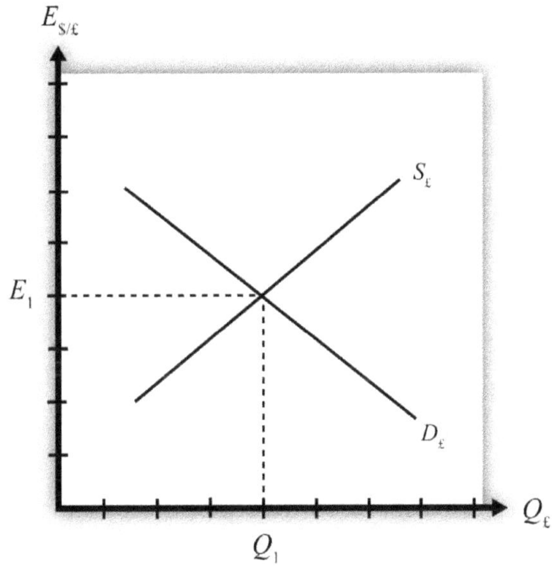

Figure 5.1 The Forex for British Pounds

Consider the market for British pounds (£) in New York depicted in Figure 5.1 "The Forex for British Pounds". We measure the supply and demand of pounds along the horizontal axis and the price of pounds (i.e., the exchange rate $E_{\$/£}$) on the vertical axis. Let $S_£$ represent the supply of pounds in exchange for dollars at all different exchange rates that might prevail. The supply is generally by British investors who demand dollars to purchase dollar denominated assets. However, supply of pounds might also come from U.S. investors who decide to convert previously acquired pound currency. Let $D_£$ the demand for pounds in exchange for dollars at all different exchange rates that might prevail. The demand is generally by U.S. investors who supply dollars to purchase pound-denominated assets. Of course, demand may also come from British investors who decide to convert previously purchased dollars. Recall that

which implies that as $E_{\$/£}$ rises, $RoR_£$ falls. This means that British investors would seek to supply more pounds at higher pound values but U.S. investors would demand fewer pounds at higher pound values. This explains why the supply curve slopes upward and the demand curve slopes downward.

The intersection of supply and demand specifies the equilibrium exchange rate (E_1) and the quantity of pounds (Q_1) traded in the market. When the Forex is at equilibrium, it must be that interest rate parity is satisfied. This is true because the violation of interest rate parity will cause investors to shift funds from one country to another, thereby causing a change in the exchange rate. This process is described in more detail in Chapter 5 "Interest Rate Parity", Section 5.2 "Comparative Statics in the IRP Theory".

KEY TAKEAWAYS

- Interest rate parity in a floating exchange system means the equalization of rates of return on comparable assets between two different countries.
- Interest rate parity is satisfied when the foreign exchange market is in equilibrium, or in other words, IRP holds when the supply of currency is equal to the demand in the Forex.

EXERCISE

- Jeopardy Questions: As in the popular television game show, you are given an answer to a question and you must respond with the question. For example, if the answer is "a tax on imports," then the correct question is "What is a tariff?"
- This theory of exchange rate determination is also known as the asset approach.
- The name of the condition in which rates of return on comparable assets in different countries are equal.
- Of greater, less, or equal, this is how the supply of pounds compares to the demand for pounds in the foreign exchange market when interest rate parity holds.

5.2 IRP THEORY COMPARATIVE STATISTICS

Comparative statics refers to an exercise in a model that assesses how changes in an exogenous variable will affect the values of the endogenous variables. The endogenous variables are those whose values are determined in the equilibrium. In the IRP model, the endogenous variables are the exchange rate value and—of lesser importance—the quantity of currencies exchanged on the Forex market. The exogenous variables are those whose values are given beforehand and are known by the model's decision makers. In the IRP model, the exogenous variables are those that influence the positions of the rate of return curves, including the U.S. interest rate, the British interest rate, and the expected future exchange rate. Another way to describe this is that the endogenous variable values are determined within the model, while the exogenous variable values are determined outside of the model.

Comparative statics exercises enable one to answer a question like "What would happen to the exchange rate if there were an increase in U.S. interest rates?" When assessing a question like this, economists will invariably invoke the ceteris paribus assumption. Ceteris paribus means that we assume all other exogenous variables are maintained at their original values when we change the variable of interest. Thus if we assess what would happen to the exchange rate (an endogenous variable) if there were an increase in the U.S. interest rate (an exogenous variable) while invoking ceteris paribus, then ceteris paribus means keeping the original values for the other exogenous variables (in this case, the British interest rate and the expected future exchange rate) fixed.

It is useful to think of a comparative statics exercise as a controlled economic experiment. In the sciences, one can test propositions by controlling the environment of a physical system in such a way that one can isolate the particular cause-and-effect relationship. Thus, to test whether a ball and a feather will fall at the same rate in a frictionless vacuum, experimenters could create a vacuum environment and measure the rate of descent of the ball versus the feather. In economic systems, such experiments are virtually impossible because one can never eliminate all the "frictions."

However, by creating mathematical economic systems (i.e., an economic model), it becomes possible to conduct similar types of "experiments." A comparative statics exercise allows one to isolate how a change in one exogenous variable affects the value of the equilibrium variable while controlling for changes in other variables that might also affect the outcome.

The Effect of Changes in U.S. Interest Rates on the Spot Exchange Rate

Suppose that the Forex is initially in equilibrium such that $S_£ = D_£$ at the exchange rate E_1. Now let average U.S. interest rates ($i_\$$) rise, ceteris paribus. The increase in interest rates raises the rate of return on U.S. assets ($RoR_\$$), which at the original exchange rate causes the rate of return on U.S. assets to exceed the rate of return on British assets ($RoR_\$ > RoR_£$). This will raise the supply of pounds on the Forex as British investors seek the higher average return on U.S. assets. It will also lower the demand for British pounds (£) by U.S. investors who decide to invest at home rather than abroad.

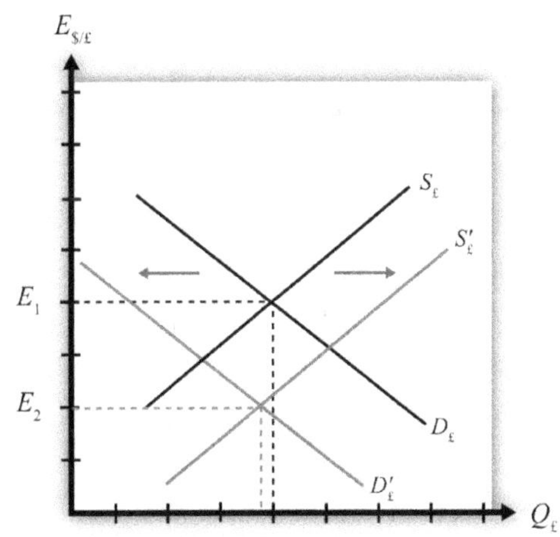

Figure 5. Effects of a U.S. Interest Rate Increase

Thus in terms of the Forex market depicted in Figure 5.2 "Effects of a U.S. Interest Rate Increase", S£ shifts right (black to red) while D£ shifts left (black to red). The equilibrium exchange rate falls to E2. This means that the increase in U.S. interest rates causes a pound depreciation and a dollar appreciation. As the exchange rate falls, RoR£ rises since. RoR£ continues to rise until the interest parity condition, RoR$ = RoR£, again holds.

The Effect of Changes in British Interest Rates on the Spot Exchange Rate

Suppose that the Forex is initially in equilibrium such that $S_£=D_£$ at the exchange rateE_1shown in Figure 5.3 «Effects of a British Interest Rate Increase». Now let average British interest rates ($i_£$) rise, ceteris paribus. The increase in interest rates raises the rate of return on British assets ($RoR_£$), which at the original exchange rate causes the rate of return on British assets to exceed the rate of return on U.S. assets ($RoR_£>RoR_\$$).

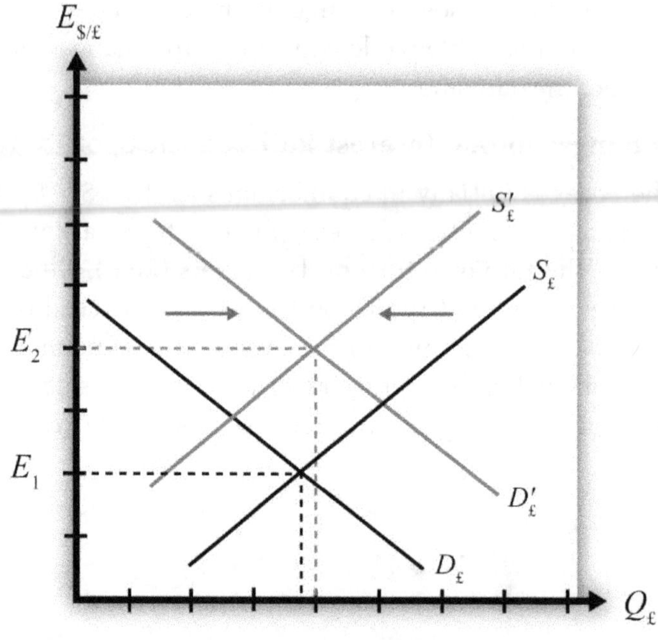

Figure 5.3 Effects of a British Interest Rate Increase

This will raise the demand for pounds on the Forex as U.S. investors seek the higher average return on British assets. It will also lower the supply of British pounds by British investors who decide to invest at home rather than abroad. Thus in terms of the graph, $D_£$ shifts right (black to red) while $S_£$ shifts left (black to red). The equilibrium exchange rate rises to E_2. This means that the increase in British interest rates causes a pound appreciation and a dollar depreciation. As the exchange rate rises, $RoR_£$ falls since. $RoR_£$ continues to fall until the interest parity condition, $RoR_\$$ = $RoR_£$, again holds.

The Effect of Changes in the Expected Exchange Rate on the Spot Exchange Rate

Suppose that the Forex is initially in equilibrium such that $S_£ = D_£$ at the exchange rate E_1. Now suppose investors suddenly raise their expected future exchange rate ($E_{\$/£}^e$), ceteris paribus. This means that if investors had expected the pound to appreciate, they now expect it to appreciate more. Likewise, if investors had expected the dollar to depreciate, they now expect it to depreciate more. Also, if they had expected the pound to depreciate, they now expect it to depreciate less. Likewise, if they had expected the dollar to appreciate, they now expect it to appreciate less.

This change might occur because new information is released. For example, the British Central Bank might release information that suggests an increased chance that the pound will rise in value in the future.

The increase in the expected exchange rate raises the rate of return on British assets ($RoR_£$), which at the original exchange rate causes the rate of return on British assets to exceed the rate of return on U.S. assets ($RoR_£ > RoR_\$$). This will raise the demand for the pound on the Forex as U.S. investors seek the higher average return on British assets. It will also lower the supply of British pounds by British investors who decide to invest at home rather than abroad. Thus, as depicted in Figure 5.4 "Effects of a Change in the Expected Exchange Rate", $D_£$ shifts right (black to red) while $S_£$ shifts left (black to red). The equilibrium exchange rate rises to E_2. This means that the increase in the expected exchange rate ($E_{\$/£}^e$) causes a pound appreciation and a dollar depreciation.

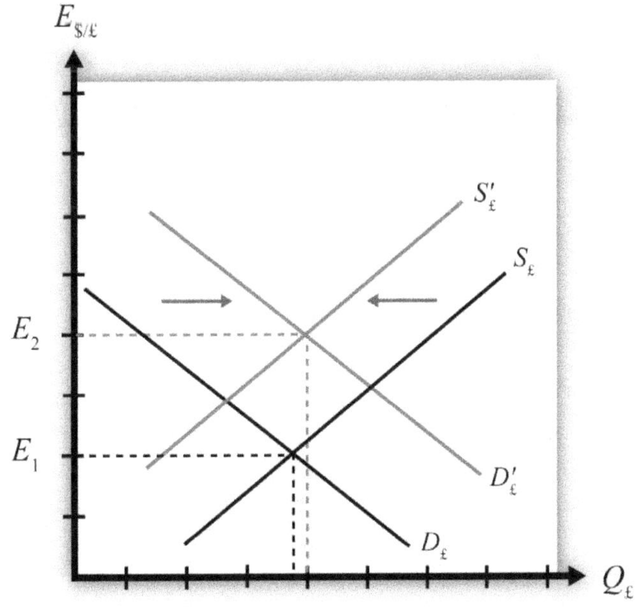

Figure 5.4 Effects of a Change in the Expected Exchange Rate

This is a case of self-fulfilling expectations. If investors suddenly think the pound will appreciate more in the future and if they act on that belief, then the pound will begin to rise in the present, hence fulfilling their expectations.

As the exchange rate rises, $RoR_£$ falls since . $RoR_£$ continues to fall until the interest parity condition, $RoR_\$ = RoR_£$, again holds.

KEY TAKEAWAYS

- An increase in U.S. interest rates causes a pound depreciation and a dollar appreciation.
- An increase in British interest rates causes a pound appreciation and a dollar depreciation.
- An increase in the expected exchange rate ($E_{\$/£}{}^e$) causes a pound appreciation and a dollar depreciation.

EXERCISES

1. Consider the economic changes listed along the left column of the following table. Indicate the effect of each change on the variables listed in the first row. Use insights from the interest rate parity model to determine the answers. Assume floating exchange rates. You do not need to show your work. Use the following notation:

\+ the variable increases

\- the variable decreases

0 the variable does not change

A the variable change is ambiguous (i.e., it may rise, it may fall)

	U.S. Dollar Value	E \$/€
a. A decrease in U.S. interest rates		
b. An increase in expected U.S. economic growth that raises expected asset values		
c. An expected increase in European stock values		

1. On February 5, 2004, the Wall Street Journal reported that Asian central banks were considering selling a significant share of their U.S. government bond holdings. It was estimated at the time that foreign central banks owned over 800\$ billion in U.S. Treasury bonds, or one-fifth of all U.S. federal government debt. Taiwan was considering using some of its foreign reserves to help its businesses purchase U.S. machinery.

What is the likely effect on the U.S. dollar value if Taiwan implements its plan? Explain.

2. What effect would this transaction have on the U.S. trade deficit? Explain.

3. How would the answer to part a change if the Taiwanese government used sales of its foreign reserves to help its businesses purchase Taiwanese-produced machinery? Explain.

5.3 EQUILIBRIUM OF FOREX AND THE RATE OF RETURN DIAGRAM

An alternative graphical approach is sometimes used to depict the equilibrium exchange rate in the foreign exchange (Forex) market. The graph is called the rate of return diagram since it depicts rates of return for assets in two separate countries as functions of the exchange rate. The equilibrium condition depicted in the diagram represents the interest rate parity condition. In effect, the diagram identifies the equilibrium exchange rate that must prevail to satisfy the interest rate parity condition.

Recall the rate of return formulas for deposits in two separate countries. Consider an investor, holding U.S. dollars, comparing the purchase of a one-year certificate of deposit (CD) at a U.S. bank with a one-year CD issued by a British bank. The rate of return on the U.S. deposit works out simply to be the U.S. interest rate shown below:

$$RoR\$ = i\$.$$

The rate of return on the British asset, however, is a more complicated formula that depends on the British interest rate (i£), the spot exchange rate (E$/£), and the expected exchange rate (E$/£e). In its simplest form it is written as follows:

In Figure 5.5 "Rate of Return Diagram", we plot both RoR equations with respect to the exchange rate (E$/£). Since RoR$ is not a function (i.e., not dependent) on the exchange rate, it is drawn as a vertical line at the level of the U.S. interest rate (i$). This simply means that as the exchange rate rises or falls, the RoR$ always remains immutably fixed at the U.S. interest rate.

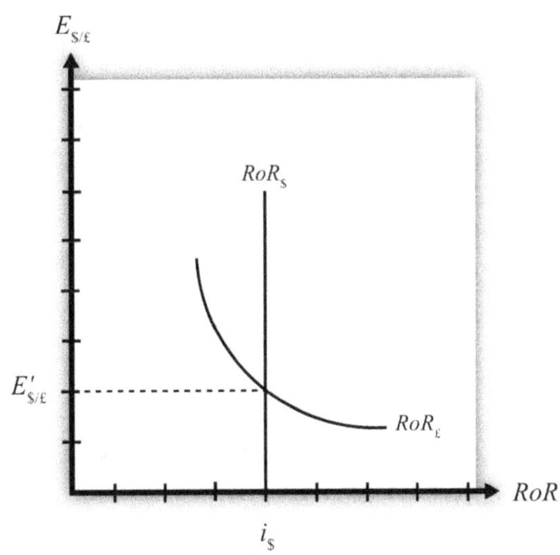

Figure 5.5 Rate of Return Diagram

The $RoR_£$, however, is a function of the exchange rate. Indeed, the relationship is negative since $E_{\$/£}$ is in the denominator of the equation. This means that as $E_{\$/£}$ rises, $RoR_£$ falls, and vice versa.

The intuition behind this negative relationship is obtained by looking at the alternative (equivalent) formula for $RoR_£$:

Recall that the exchange rate ratio represents the expected percentage change in the value of the pound. Suppose, as an example, that this term were positive. That would mean the investor believes the pound will appreciate during the term of the investment. Furthermore, since it is an expected appreciation of the pound, it will add to the total rate of return on the British investment. Next, suppose the spot exchange rate ($E_{\$/£}$) rises today. Assuming ceteris paribus, as we always do in these exercises, the expected exchange rate remains fixed. That will mean the numerator of the exchange rate expression will fall in value, as will the value of the entire expression. The interpretation of this change is that the investor's expected appreciation of the pound falls, which in turn lowers the overall rate of return. Hence, we get the negative relationship between the \$/£ exchange rate and $RoR_£$.

The intersection of the two RoR curves in the diagram identifies the unique exchange rate $E'_{\$/£}$ that equalizes rates of return between the two countries. This exchange rate is in equilibrium because any deviations away from interest rate parity (IRP) will motivate changes in investor behavior and force the exchange back to the level necessary to achieve IRP. The equilibrium adjustment story is next.

KEY TAKEAWAYS

- The rates of return are plotted with respect to the exchange rate. The domestic rate of return does not depend on the exchange rate and hence is drawn as a vertical line. The foreign rate of return is negatively related to the value of the foreign currency.
- The intersection of the rates of return identifies the exchange rate that satisfies the interest rate parity condition.

EXERCISE

- Jeopardy Questions: As in the popular television game show, you are given an answer to a question and you must respond with the question. For example, if the answer is "a tax on imports," then the correct question is "What is a tariff?"
- Of positive, negative, or zero, the relationship between the U.S. interest rate and the rate of return on U.S. assets.
- Of positive, negative, or zero, the relationship between the exchange rate ($E_{\$/£}$) and the rate of return on U.S. assets.

- Of positive, negative, or zero, the relationship between the exchange rate ($E_{\$/£}$) and the rate of return on British assets.
- The name of the endogenous variable whose value is determined at the intersection of two rate of return curves.

5.4 ROR DIAGRAM: EXCHANGE RATE EQUILIBRIUM STORIES

Any equilibrium in economics has an associated behavioral story to explain the forces that will move the endogenous variable to the equilibrium value. In the foreign exchange (Forex) model, the endogenous variable is the exchange rate. This is the variable that is determined as a solution in the model and will change to achieve the equilibrium. Variables that do not change in the adjustment to the equilibrium are the exogenous variables. In this model, the exogenous variables are $E^e_{\$/£}$, $i_\$$, and $i_£$. Changes in the exogenous variables are necessary to cause an adjustment to a new equilibrium. However, in telling an equilibrium story, it is typical to simply assume that the endogenous variable is not at the equilibrium (for some unstated reason) and then explain how and why the variable will adjust to the equilibrium value.

Exchange Rate Too High

Suppose, for some unspecified reason, the exchange rate is currently at $E''_{\$/£}$ as shown in Figure 5.6 «Adjustment When the Exchange Rate Is Too High». The equilibrium exchange rate is at $E'_{\$/£}$ since at this rate, rates of return are equal and interest rate parity (IRP) is satisfied. Thus at $E''_{\$/£}$ the exchange rate is too high. Since the exchange rate, as written, is the value of the pound, we can also say that the pound value is too high relative to the dollar to satisfy IRP.

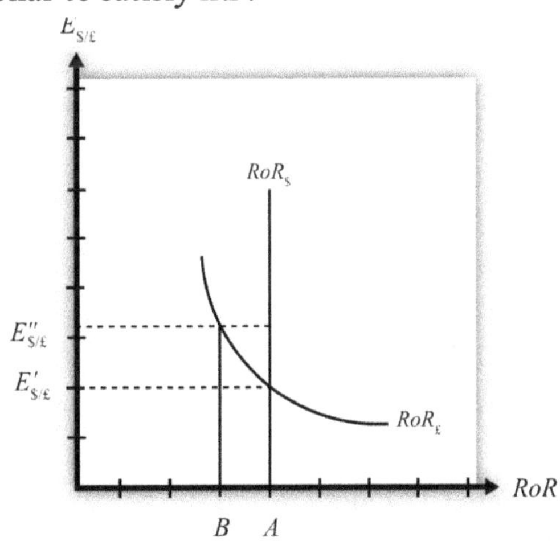

Figure 5.6 Adjustment When the Exchange Rate Is Too High

With the exchange rate at $E''_{\$/£}$, the rate of return on the dollar, $RoR_\$$, is given by the value A along the horizontal axis. This will be the value of the U.S. interest rate. The rate of return on the pound, $RoR_£$ is given by the value B, however. This means that $RoR_£ < RoR_\$$ and IRP does not hold. Under this circumstance, higher returns on deposits in the United States will motivate investors to invest funds in the United States rather than Britain. This will raise the supply of pounds on the Forex as British investors seek the higher average return on U.S. assets. It will also lower the demand for British pounds (£) by U.S. investors who decide to invest at home rather than abroad. Both changes in the Forex market will lower the value of the pound and raise the U.S. dollar value, reflected as a reduction in $E_{\$/£}$.

In more straightforward terms, when the rate of return on dollar deposits is higher than on British deposits, investors will increase demand for the higher RoR currency and reduce demand for the other. The change in demand on the Forex raises the value of the currency whose RoR was initially higher (the U.S. dollar in this case) and lowers the other currency value (the British pound).

As the exchange rate falls from $E''_{\$/£}$ to $E'_{\$/£}$, $RoR_£$ begins to rise up, from B to A. This occurs because $RoR_£$ is negatively related to changes in the exchange rate. Once the exchange rate falls to $E'_{\$/£}$, $RoR_£$ will become equal to $RoR_\$$ at A and IRP will hold. At this point there are no further pressures in the Forex for the exchange rate to change, hence the Forex is in equilibrium at $E'_{\$/£}$.

Exchange Rate Too Low

If the exchange rate is lower than the equilibrium rate, then the adjustment will proceed in the opposite direction. At any exchange rate below $E'_{\$/£}$ in the diagram, $RoR_£ > RoR_\$$. This condition will inspire investors to move their funds to Britain with the higher rate of return. The subsequent increase in the demand for pounds will raise the value of the pound on the Forex and $E_{\$/£}$ will rise (consequently, the dollar value will fall). The exchange rate will continue to rise and the rate of return on pounds will fall until $RoR_£ = RoR_\$$ (IRP holds again) at $E'_{\$/£}$.

KEY TAKEAWAYS

- In the interest rate parity model, when the $/£ exchange rate is less than the equilibrium rate, the rate of return on British deposits exceeds the RoR on U.S. deposits. That inspires investors to demand more pounds on the Forex to take advantage of the higher RoR. Thus the $/£ exchange rate rises (i.e., the pound appreciates) until the equilibrium is reached when interest rate parity holds.
- In the interest rate parity model, when the $/£ exchange rate is greater than the equilibrium rate, the rate of return on U.S. deposits exceeds the RoR on British deposits. That inspires investors to demand more U.S. dollars on the Forex to take advantage of the higher RoR. Thus the $/£ exchange rate falls (i.e., the dollar appreciates) until the equilibrium is reached when interest rate parity holds.

EXERCISE

- Jeopardy Questions: As in the popular television game show, you are given an answer to a question and you must respond with the question. For example, if the answer is "a tax on imports," then the correct question is "What is a tariff?"
- Of increase, decrease, or stay the same, the expected effect on the exchange rate ($E_{\$/£}$) if the rate of return on pound assets is greater than the rate of return on dollar assets.
- Of increase, decrease, or stay the same, the expected effect on the exchange rate ($E_{\$/£}$) if the rate of return on U.S. assets is greater than the rate of return on British assets.
- Of increase, decrease, or stay the same, the expected effect on the value of the dollar if the rate of return on pound assets is greater than the rate of return on dollar assets.
- Of increase, decrease, or stay the same, the expected effect on the value of the dollar if the rate of return on U.S. assets is greater than the rate of return on British assets.
- Of increase, decrease, or stay the same, the expected effect on the value of the dollar if the rate of return on U.S. assets is equal to the rate of return on British assets.

5.5 EXCHANGE RATE EFFECTS OF CHANGES IN U.S. INTEREST RATES USING THE ROR DIAGRAM

Suppose that the foreign exchange market (Forex) is initially in equilibrium such that RoR£ = RoR$ (i.e., interest rate parity holds) at an initial equilibrium exchange rate given by E$/£. The initial equilibrium is depicted in Figure 5.7 "Effects of a U.S. Interest Rate Increase in a RoR Diagram". Next, suppose U.S. interest rates rise, ceteris paribus. Ceteris paribus means we assume all other exogenous variables remain fixed at their original values. In this model, the British interest rate (i£) and the expected exchange rate (E$/£e) both remain fixed as U.S. interest rates rise.

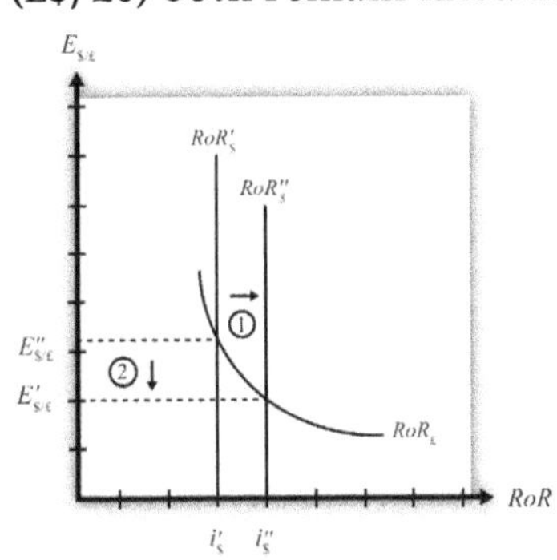

Figure 5.7 Effects of a U.S. Interest Rate Increase in a RoR Diagram

The increase in U.S. interest rates will shift the U.S. RoR line to the right from $RoR'_\$$ to $RoR''_\$$ as indicated by step 1 in Figure 5.7 «Effects of a U.S. Interest Rate Increase in a RoR Diagram». Immediately after the increase and before the exchange rate changes, $RoR_\$ > RoR_£$. The adjustment to the new equilibrium will follow the "exchange rate too high" equilibrium story earlier. Accordingly, higher U.S. interest rates will make U.S. dollar investments more attractive to investors, leading to an increase in demand for dollars on the Forex resulting in an appreciation of the dollar, a depreciation of the pound, and a decrease in $E_{\$/£}$. The exchange rate will fall to the new equilibrium rate $E''_{\$/£}$ as indicated by step 2 in the figure.

In summary, an increase in the U.S. interest rate will raise the rate of return on dollars above the rate of return on pounds, lead investors to shift investments to U.S. assets, and result in a decrease in the $/£ exchange rate (i.e., an appreciation of the U.S. dollar and a depreciation of the British pound).

In contrast, a decrease in U.S. interest rates will lower the rate of return on dollars below the rate of return on pounds, lead investors to shift investments to British assets, and result in an increase in the $/£ exchange rate (i.e., a depreciation of the U.S. dollar and an appreciation of the British pound).

KEY TAKEAWAYS

- An increase in U.S. interest rates will result in a decrease in the $/£ exchange rate (i.e., an appreciation of the U.S. dollar and a depreciation of the British pound).
- A decrease in U.S. interest rates will result in an increase in the $/£ exchange rate (i.e., a depreciation of the U.S. dollar and an appreciation of the British pound).

EXERCISE

- Consider the economic change listed along the top row of the following table. In the empty boxes, indicate the effect of each change, sequentially, on the variables listed in the first column. For example, a decrease in U.S. interest rates will cause a decrease in the rate of return (RoR) on U.S. assets. Therefore a "-" is placed in the first cell under the "A Decrease in U.S. Interest Rates" column of the table. Next in sequence, answer how the RoR on euro assets will be affected. Use the interest rate parity model to determine the answers. You do not need to show your work. Use the following notation:

+ the variable increases

- the variable decreases

0 the variable does not change

A the variable change is ambiguous (i.e., it may rise, it may fall)

	A Decrease in U.S. Interest Rates
RoR on U.S. Assets	–
RoR on Euro Assets	
Demand for U.S. Dollars on the Forex	
Demand for Euros on the Forex	
U.S. Dollar Value	
Euro Value	
$E_{\$/€}$	

5.6 CHANGES IN FOREIGN INTEREST RATES AND THE IMPACT ON EXCHANGE RATES USING THE ROR DIAGRAM

Suppose that the foreign exchange market (Forex) is initially in equilibrium such that $RoR_£ = RoR_\$$ (i.e., interest rate parity holds) at an initial equilibrium exchange rate given by $E'_{\$/£}$. The initial equilibrium is depicted in Figure 5.8 "Effects of a British Interest Rate Increase in a RoR Diagram". Next, suppose British interest rates rise, ceteris paribus. Ceteris paribus means we assume all other exogenous variables remain fixed at their original values. In this model, the U.S. interest rate ($i_\$$) and the expected exchange rate ($E_{\$/£}{}^e$) both remain fixed as British interest rates rise.

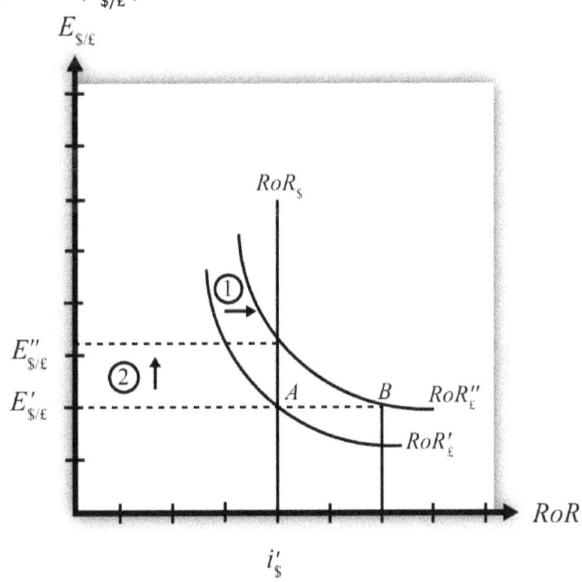

Figure 5.8 Effects of a British Interest Rate Increase in a RoR Diagram

The increase in British interest rates ($i_£$) will shift the British RoR line to the right from $RoR'_£$ to $RoR''_£$ as indicated by step 1 in the figure.

The reason for the shift can be seen by looking at the simple rate of return formula: Suppose one is at the original equilibrium with exchange rate $E'_{\$/£}$. Looking at the formula, an increase in $i_£$ clearly raises the value of $RoR_£$ for any fixed values of $E_{\$/£}^e$. This could be represented as a shift to the right on the diagram, as from A to B. Once at B with a new interest rate, one could perform the exercise used to plot out the downward sloping RoR curve (see Chapter 5 , Section 5.3 . The result would be a curve, like the original, but shifted entirely to the right.

Immediately after the increase and before the exchange rate changes, $RoR_£ > RoR_\$$. The adjustment to the new equilibrium will follow the "exchange rate too low" equilibrium story presented in Chapter 5 , Section 5.4. Accordingly, higher British interest rates will make British pound investments more attractive to investors, leading to an increase in demand for pounds on the Forex, and resulting in an appreciation of the pound, a depreciation of the dollar, and an increase in $E_{\$/£}$. The exchange rate will rise to the new equilibrium rate $E''_{\$/£}$ as indicated by step 2.

In summary, an increase in British interest rates will raise the rate of return on pounds above the rate of return on dollars, lead investors to shift investments to British assets, and result in an increase in the \$/£ exchange rate (i.e., an appreciation of the British pound and a depreciation of the U.S. dollar).

In contrast, a decrease in British interest rates will lower the rate of return on British pounds below the rate of return on dollars, lead investors to shift investments to U.S. assets, and result in a decrease in the \$/£ exchange rate (i.e., a depreciation of the British pound and an appreciation of the U.S. dollar.

KEY TAKEAWAYS

- An increase in British interest rates will result in an increase in the \$/£ exchange rate (i.e., an appreciation of the British pound and a depreciation of the U.S. dollar).
- A decrease in British interest rates will result in a decrease in the \$/£ exchange rate (i.e., a depreciation of the British pound and an appreciation of the U.S. dollar).

EXERCISE

1. Consider the economic change listed along the top row of the following table. In the empty boxes, indicate the effect of each change, sequentially, on the variables listed in the first column. For example, a decrease in U.S. interest rates will cause a decrease in the rate of return (RoR) on U.S. assets. Therefore a "–" is placed in the first box of the table. Next in sequence, answer how the RoR on euro assets will be affected. Use the interest rate parity model to determine the answers. You do not need to show your work. Use the following notation:

+ the variable increases

- the variable decreases

0 the variable does not change

A the variable change is ambiguous (i.e., it may rise, it may fall)

	A Decrease in Euro Interest Rates
RoR on U.S. Assets	-
RoR on Euro Assets	
Demand for U.S. Dollars on the Forex	
Demand for Euros on the Forex	
U.S. Dollar Value	
Euro Value	
$E_{\$/€}$	

5.7 EFFECTS ON EXCHANGE RATE OF CHANGES IN EXPECTED EXCHANGE RATE USING ROR DIAGRAM

Suppose that the foreign exchange market (Forex) is initially in equilibrium such that $RoR_{£} = RoR_{\$}$ (i.e., interest rate parity holds) at an initial equilibrium exchange rate given by $E'_{\$/£}$. The initial equilibrium is depicted in Figure 5.9 "Effects of an Expected Exchange Rate Change in a RoR Diagram". Next, suppose investors' beliefs shift so that $E_{\$/€}^{e}$ rises, ceteris paribus. Ceteris paribus means we assume all other exogenous variables remain fixed at their original values. In this model, the U.S. interest rate ($i_{\$}$) and the British interest rate ($i_{£}$) both remain fixed as the expected exchange rate rises.

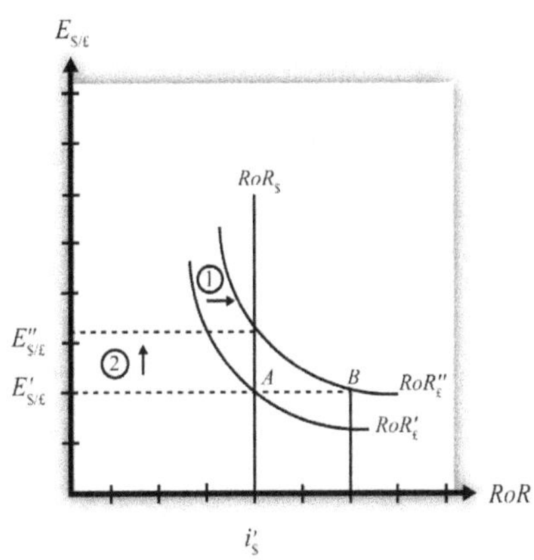

Figure 5.9 Effects of an Expected Exchange Rate Change in a RoR Diagram

An expected exchange rate increase means that if investors had expected the pound to appreciate, they now expect it to appreciate even more. Likewise, if investors had expected the dollar to depreciate, they now expect it to depreciate more. Alternatively, if they had expected the pound to depreciate, they now expect it to depreciate less. Likewise, if they had expected the dollar to appreciate, they now expect it to appreciate less.

This change might occur because new information is released. For example, the British Central Bank might release information that suggests an increased chance that the pound will rise in value in the future.

The increase in the expected exchange rate ($E_{\$/£}^{e}$) will shift the British RoR line to the right from $RoR'_{£}$ to $RoR''_{£}$ as indicated by step 1 in the figure.

The reason for the shift can be seen by looking at the simple rate of return formula:

Suppose one is at the original equilibrium with exchange rate $E'_{\$/£}$. Looking at the formula, an increase in $E_{\$/£}^{e}$ clearly raises the value of $RoR_{£}$ for any fixed values of $i_{£}$. This could be represented as a shift to the right on the diagram from A to B. Once at B with a new expected exchange rate, one could perform the exercise used to plot out the downward sloping RoR curve. The result would be a curve, like the original, but shifted entirely to the right.

Immediately after the increase and before the exchange rate changes, $RoR_{£} > RoR_{\$}$. The adjustment to the new equilibrium will follow the "exchange rate too low" equilibrium story presented in Chapter 5 , Section 5.4 . Accordingly, higher expected British rates of return will make British pound investments more attractive to investors, leading to an increase in demand for pounds on the Forex and resulting in an appreciation of the pound, a depreciation of the dollar, and an increase in $E_{\$/£}$. The exchange rate will rise to the new equilibrium rate $E''_{\$/£}$ as indicated by step 2.

In summary, an increase in the expected future \$/£ exchange rate will raise the rate of return on pounds above the rate of return on dollars, lead investors to shift investments to British assets, and result in an increase in the \$/£ exchange rate (i.e., an appreciation of the British pound and a depreciation of the U.S. dollar).

In contrast, a decrease in the expected future \$/£ exchange rate will lower the rate of return on British pounds below the rate of return on dollars, lead investors to shift investments to U.S. assets, and result in a decrease in the \$/£ exchange rate (i.e., a depreciation of the British pound and an appreciation of the U.S. dollar).

KEY TAKEAWAYS

- An increase in the expected future pound value (with respect to the U.S. dollar) will result in an increase in the spot \$/£ exchange rate (i.e., an appreciation of the British pound and a depreciation of the U.S. dollar).

- A decrease in the expected future pound value (with respect to the U.S. dollar) will result in a decrease in the spot $/£ exchange rate (i.e., a depreciation of the British pound and an appreciation of the U.S. dollar).

EXERCISE

Consider the economic change listed along the top row of the following table. In the empty boxes, indicate the effect of the change, sequentially, on the variables listed in the first column. For example, a decrease in U.S. interest rates will cause a decrease in the rate of return (RoR) on U.S. assets. Therefore a "-" is placed in the first box of the table. Next in sequence, answer how the RoR on euro assets will be affected. Use the interest rate parity model to determine the answers. You do not need to show your work. Use the following notation:

\+ the variable increases

\- the variable decreases

0 the variable does not change

A the variable change is ambiguous (i.e., it may rise, it may fall)

	A Reduction in Next Year's Expected Dollar Value
RoR on U.S. Assets	-
RoR on Euro Assets	
Demand for U.S. Dollars on the Forex	
Demand for Euros on the Forex	
U.S. Dollar Value	
Euro Value	
E$/€	

CHAPTER

PURCHASING POWER PARITY 6

INTRODUCTION

Purchasing power parity is both a theory about exchange rate determination and a tool to make more accurate comparisons of data between countries. It is probably more important in its latter role since as a theory it performs pretty poorly. Its poor performance arises largely because its simple form depends on several assumptions that are not likely to hold in the real world and because the amount of foreign exchange activity due to importer and exporter demands is much less than the amount of activity due to investor demands. Nonetheless, the theory remains important to provide the background for its use as a tool for cross-country comparisons of income and wages, which is used by international organizations like the World Bank in presenting much of their international data.

6.1 PURCHASING POWER PARITY (PPP): AN OVERVIEW

Purchasing power parity (PPP) is a theory of exchange rate determination and a way to compare the average costs of goods and services between countries. The theory assumes that the actions of importers and exporters (motivated by cross-country price differences) induce changes in the spot exchange rate. In another vein, PPP suggests that transactions on a country's current account affect the value of the exchange rate on the foreign exchange (Forex) market. This is in contrast with the interest rate parity theory, which assumes that the actions of investors (whose transactions are recorded on the capital account) induce changes in the exchange rate.

PPP theory is based on an extension and variation of the "law of one price" as applied to the aggregate economy. To explain the theory it is best to first review the idea behind the law of one price.

The Law of One Price (LoOP)

The law of one price says that identical goods should sell for the same price in two separate markets when there are no transportation costs and no differential taxes applied in the two markets. Consider the following information about movie video tapes sold in the U.S. and Mexican markets.

Price of videos in U.S. market ()	$20
Price of videos in Mexican market ()	p150
Spot exchange rate ()	10 p/$

The dollar price of videos sold in Mexico can be calculated by dividing the video price in pesos by the spot exchange rate as shown:

To see why the peso price is divided by the exchange rate rather than multiplied, notice the conversion of units shown in the brackets. If the law of one price held, then the dollar price in Mexico should match the price in the United States. Since the dollar price of the video is less than the dollar price in the United States, the law of one price does not hold in this circumstance.

The next question to ask is what might happen as a result of the discrepancy in prices. Well, as long as there are no costs incurred to transport the goods, there is a profit-making opportunity through trade. For example, U.S. travelers in Mexico who recognize that identical video titles are selling there for 25 percent less might buy videos in Mexico and bring them back to the United States to sell. This is an example of "goods arbitrage." An arbitrage opportunity arises whenever one can buy something at a low price in one location, resell it at a higher price, and thus make a profit.

Using basic supply and demand theory, the increase in demand for videos in Mexico would push up the price of videos. The increase in supply of videos on the U.S. market would force the price down in the United States. In the end, the price of videos in Mexico may rise to, say, p180 while the price of videos in the United States may fall to $18. At these new prices the law of one price holds since

The idea in the law of one price is that identical goods selling in an integrated market in which there are no transportation costs, no differential taxes or subsidies, and no tariffs or other trade barriers should sell at identical prices. If different prices prevailed, then there would be profit-making opportunities by buying the good in the low price market and reselling it in the high price market. If entrepreneurs took advantage of this arbitrage opportunity, then the prices would converge to equality.

Of course, for many reasons the law of one price does not hold even between markets within a country. The price of beer, gasoline, and stereos will likely be different in New York City and in Los Angeles. The price of these items will also be different in other countries when converted at current exchange rates. The simple reason for the discrepancies is that there are costs to transport goods between locations, there are different taxes applied in different states and different countries, nontradable input prices may vary, and people do not have perfect information about the prices of goods in all markets at all times. Thus to refer to this as an economic "law" does seem to exaggerate its validity.

From LoOP to PPP

The purchasing power parity theory is really just the law of one price applied in the aggregate but with a slight twist added. If it makes sense from the law of one price that identical goods should sell for identical prices in different markets, then the law ought to hold for all identical goods sold in both markets.

First, let's define the variable $CB_\$$ to represent the cost of a basket of goods in the United States denominated in dollars. For simplicity we could imagine using the same basket of goods used in the construction of the U.S. consumer price index ($CPI_\$$). The consumer price index (CPI) uses a market basket of goods that are purchased by an average household during a specified period. The basket is determined by surveying the quantity of different items purchased by many different households. One can then determine, on average, how many units of bread, milk, cheese, rent, electricity, and so on are purchased by the typical household. You might imagine it's as if all products are purchased in a grocery store with items being placed in a basket before the purchase is made. $CB_\$$ then represents the dollar cost of purchasing all the items in the market basket. We will similarly define CB_p to be the cost of a market basket of goods in Mexico denominated in pesos.

Now if the law of one price holds for each individual item in the market basket, then it should hold for the market baskets as well. In other words, Rewriting the right-hand side equation allows us to put the relationship in the form commonly used to describe absolute purchasing power parity, which is

If this condition holds between two countries, then we would say PPP is satisfied. The condition says that the PPP exchange rate (pesos per dollar) will equal the ratio of the costs of the two market baskets of goods denominated in local currency units. Note that the reciprocal relationship is also valid.

Because the cost of a market basket of goods is used in the construction of the country's consumer price index, PPP is often written as a relationship between the exchange rate and the country's price indices. However, it is not possible merely to substitute the price index directly for the cost of the market basket used above. To see why, we will review the construction of the CPI in , Section 6.2 .

KEY TAKEAWAYS

- The law of one price says that identical goods should sell for identical prices in two different markets when converted at the current exchange rate and when there are no transportation costs and no differential taxes applied.
- The purchasing power parity theory is an aggregated version of the law of one price.

- The purchasing power parity condition says that identical market baskets should sell for identical prices in two different markets when converted at the current exchange rate and when there are no transportation costs and no differential taxes applied.

EXERCISES

- Jeopardy Questions: As in the popular television game show, you are given an answer to a question and you must respond with the question. For example, if the answer is "a tax on imports," then the correct question is "What is a tariff?"
- The exchange rate value if toothpaste costs $2.50 in the United States and 30 pesos in Mexico and the law of one price holds.
- The exchange rate value if a market basket costs $450 in the United States and 5,400 pesos in Mexico and purchasing power parity holds.
- The term used to describe a collection of goods and services consumed by a typical consumer.
- The term used to distinguish PPP based on price levels rather than inflation rates.
- The term used to describe the economic principle that identical goods should sell at identical prices in different markets.
- Use the information in the table below to answer the following question. Show your work.

	The Economist Price per Issue	Exchange Rate (December 2, 1999)
United States	$3.95	–
Canada	C$ 4.95	1.47 C$/$
Japan	¥920	102 ¥/$

Calculate the implied purchasing power parity exchange rates between Canada and the United States and between Japan and the United States based on the price of the Economist magazine.

6.2 THE PPP AND THE CONSUMER PRICE INDEX (CPI)

The consumer price index (CPI) is an index that measures the average level of prices of goods and services in an economy relative to a base year. To track only what happens to prices, the quantities of goods purchased is assumed to remain fixed from year to year. This is accomplished by determining—with survey methods—the average quantities of all goods and services purchased by a typical household during some period. The quantities of all of these goods together are referred to as the average market basket. For example, the survey might find that the average household in one month purchases 10 gallons of gas, 15 cans of beer, 3.2 gallons of milk, 2.6 pounds of butter, and so on. The basket of goods would also contain items like health and auto insurance, housing services, utility services, and many other items. We can describe the market basket easily as a collection or set of quantities $(Q_1,Q_2,Q_3,\ldots,Q_n)$. Here Q_1 may be the quantity of gasoline, Q_2 the quantity of beer, and so on. The set has n different quantity entries, implying that there are n different items in the market basket.

The cost of the market basket is found by surveying the average prices for each of the n products in the market in question. This survey would yield a collection or set of prices $(P_1, P_2, P_3,\ldots, P_n)$. The cost of the market basket is then found by summing the product of the price and quantity for each item. That is, $CB=P_{1Q1} + P_{2Q2} +P_{3Q3}+\ldots+P_nQ_n$, or

The first year in which the index is constructed is called the base year. Suppose 1982 is the base year for the United States. Let CB_{YY} represent the cost of the market basket evaluated at the prices that prevail in the year (YY) (e.g., CB_{09} is the cost of a market basket evaluated in 2009 prices). The CPI is derived according to the following formula:

where CPI_{YY} is the CPI in the year (YY). The term is multiplied by 100 by convention, probably because it reduces the need to use digits after a decimal point. Notice that the CPI in the base year is equal to 100—that is, CPI_{82} = 100—because CB_{82}/CB_{82} = 1. This is true for all indices—they are by convention set to 100 in the base year.

The CPI in a different year (either earlier or later) represents the ratio of the cost of the market basket in that year relative to the cost of the same basket in the base year. If in 1982 the cost of the market basket rises, then the CPI will rise above 100. If the cost of the market basket falls, then the CPI would fall below 100.

If the CPI rises, it does not mean that the prices of all the goods in the market basket have risen. Some prices may rise more or less. Some prices may even fall. The CPI measures the average price change of goods and services in the basket.

The inflation rate for an economy is the percentage change in the CPI during a year. Thus if CPI_{08} on January 2008 ,1, and CPI_{09} on January 2009 ,1, are the price indices, then the inflation rate during 2008 is given by

PPP Using the CPI

The purchasing power parity relationship can be written using the CPI with some small adjustments. First, consider the following ratio of 2009 consumer price indices between Mexico and the United States:

Given that the base year is 2008, the ratio is written in terms of the market basket costs on the right-hand side and then rewritten into another form. The far right-hand side expression now reflects the purchasing power parity exchange rates in 2009 divided by the PPP exchange rate in 2008, the base year. In other words,

So, in general, if you want to use the consumer price indices for two countries to derive the PPP exchange rate for 2009, you must apply the following formula, derived by rewriting the above as

where represents the PPP exchange rate that prevails in the base year between the two countries. Note that in order for this formula to work correctly, the CPIs in both countries must share the same base year. If they did not, a more complex formula would need to be derived.

KEY TAKEAWAYS

- A country's consumer price index in year (YY) is derived as the ratio of the market basket cost in year (YY) and the market basket cost in the base year.
- The PPP exchange rate between two countries can be written as the ratio of the their consumer price indices in that year multiplied by an adjustment factor given by the PPP exchange rate in the base year of the countries' CPIs.

EXERCISE

- Suppose a consumer purchases the following products each week: ten gallons of gas, fifteen cans of beer, three gallons of milk, and two pounds of butter. Suppose in the initial week the prices of the products are $3 per gallon of gas, $2 per can of beer, $4 per gallon of milk, and $4 per pound of butter. Suppose one year later the prices of the same products are $2 per gallon of gas, $3 per can of beer, $5 per gallon of milk, and $5 per pound of butter.
- Calculate the cost of a weekly market basket in the initial base period.
    - Calculate the cost of a market basket one year later.
    - Construct the price index value for both years.
    - What is the inflation rate between the two years?

6.3 PPP AS A THEORY OF EXCHANGE RATE DETERMINATION

The purchasing power parity (PPP) relationship becomes a theory of exchange rate determination by introducing assumptions about the behavior of importers and exporters in response to changes in the relative costs of national market baskets. Recall the story of the law of one price, when the price of a good differed between two countries' markets and there was an incentive for profit-seeking individuals to buy the good in the low price market and resell it in the high price market. Similarly, if a market basket containing many different goods and services costs more in one market than another, we should likewise expect profit-seeking individuals to buy the relatively cheaper goods in the low-cost market and resell them in the higher-priced market. If the law of one price leads to the equalization of the prices of a good between two markets, then it seems reasonable to conclude that PPP, describing the equality of market baskets across countries, should also hold.

However, adjustment within the PPP theory occurs with a twist compared to adjustment in the law of one price story. In the law of one price story, goods arbitrage in a particular product was expected to affect the prices of the goods in the two markets. The twist that's included in the PPP theory is that arbitrage, occurring across a range of goods and services in the market basket, will affect the exchange rate rather than the market prices.

PPP Equilibrium Story

To see why the PPP relationship represents an equilibrium, we need to tell an equilibrium story. An equilibrium story in an economic model is an explanation of how the behavior of individuals will cause the equilibrium condition to be satisfied. The equilibrium condition is the PPP equation written as

The endogenous variable in the PPP theory is the exchange rate. Thus we need to explain why the exchange rate will change if it is not in equilibrium. In general there are always two versions of an equilibrium story, one in which the endogenous variable ($E_{p/\$}$ here) is too high and one in which it is too low.

PPP equilibrium story 1. Let's consider the case in which the exchange rate is too low to be in equilibrium. This means that where $E_{p/\$}$ is the exchange rate that prevails on the spot market. Since it is less than the ratio of the market basket costs in Mexico and the United States, it is also less than the PPP exchange rate. The right side of the expression is rewritten to show that the cost of a market basket in the United States evaluated in pesos (i.e., $CB_{\$Ep/\$}$) is less than the cost of the market basket in Mexico also evaluated in pesos. Thus it is cheaper to buy the basket in the United States, or in other words, it is more profitable to sell items in the market basket in Mexico.

The PPP theory now suggests that the cheaper basket in the United States will lead to an increase in demand for goods in the U.S. market basket by Mexico. As a consequence, it will increase the demand for U.S. dollars on the foreign exchange (Forex) market. Dollars are needed because purchases of U.S. goods require U.S. dollars. Alternatively, U.S. exporters will realize that goods sold in the United States can be sold at a higher price in Mexico. If these goods are sold in pesos, the U.S. exporters will want to convert the proceeds back to dollars. Thus there is an increase in U.S. dollar demand (by Mexican importers) and an increase in peso supply (by U.S. exporters) on the Forex. This effect is represented by a rightward shift in the U.S. dollar demand curve in Figure 6.1 "Forex Adjustment When ". At the same time, U.S. consumers will reduce their demand for the pricier Mexican goods. This will reduce the supply of dollars (in exchange for pesos) on the Forex, which is represented by a leftward shift in the U.S. dollar supply curve in the Forex market.

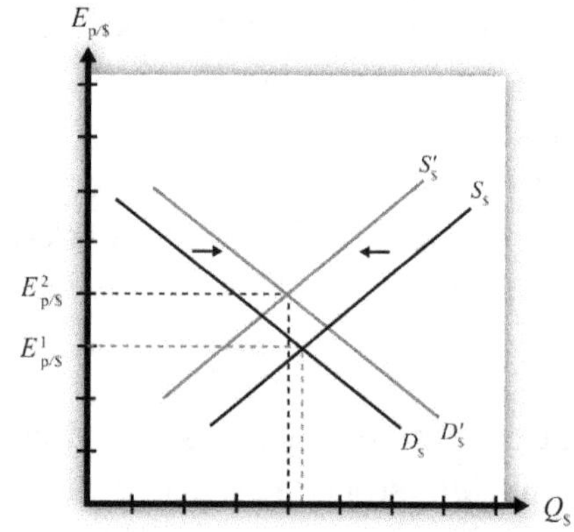

Figure 6.1 Forex Adjustment When Ep/$ Is Low

Both the shift in demand and supply will cause an increase in the value of the dollar and thus the exchange rate ($E_{p/\$}$) will rise. As long as the U.S. market basket remains cheaper, excess demand for the dollar will persist and the exchange rate will continue to rise. The pressure for change ceases once the exchange rate rises enough to equalize the cost of market baskets between the two countries and PPP holds.

PPP equilibrium story 2. Now let's consider the other equilibrium story (i.e., the case in which the exchange rate is too high to be in equilibrium). This implies that

The left-side expression says that the spot exchange rate is greater than the ratio of the costs of market baskets between Mexico and the United States. In other words, the exchange rate is above the PPP exchange rate. The right-side expression says that the cost of a U.S. market basket, converted to pesos at the current exchange rate, is greater than the cost of a Mexican market basket in pesos. Thus, on average, U.S. goods are relatively more expensive while Mexican goods are relatively cheaper.

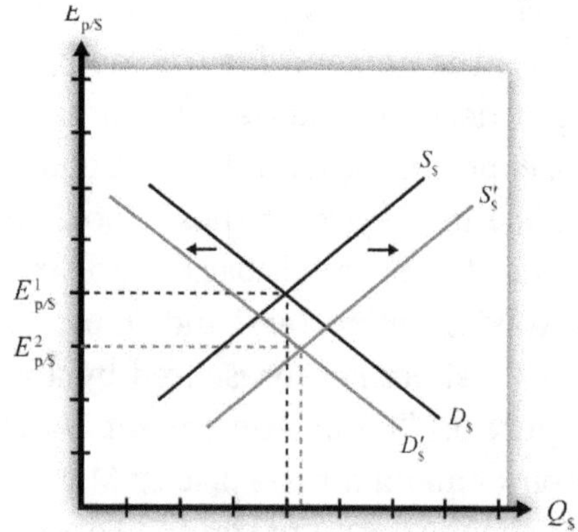

Figure 6.2 Forex Adjustment When Ep/$ Is High

The price discrepancies should lead consumers in the United States or importing firms to purchase less expensive goods in Mexico. To do so, they will raise the supply of dollars in the Forex in exchange for pesos. Thus the supply curve of dollars will shift to the right as shown in Figure 6.2 "Forex Adjustment When ". At the same time, Mexican consumers would refrain from purchasing the more expensive U.S. goods. This would lead to a reduction in demand for dollars in exchange for pesos on the Forex. Hence, the demand curve for dollars shifts to the left. Due to the demand decrease and the supply increase, the exchange rate ($E_{p/\$}$) falls. This means that the dollar depreciates and the peso appreciates.

Extra demand for pesos will continue as long as goods and services remain cheaper in Mexico. However, as the peso appreciates (the dollar depreciates), the cost of Mexican goods rises relative to U.S. goods. The process ceases once the PPP exchange rate is reached and market baskets cost the same in both markets.

Adjustment to Price Level Changes under PPP

In the PPP theory, exchange rate changes are induced by changes in relative price levels between two countries. This is true because the quantities of the goods are always presumed to remain fixed in the market baskets. Therefore, the only way that the cost of the basket can change is if the goods' prices change. Since price level changes represent inflation rates, this means that differential inflation rates will induce exchange rate changes according to the theory.

If we imagine that a country begins with PPP, then the inequality given in equilibrium story 1, can arise if the price level rises in Mexico (peso inflation), if the price level falls in the United States (dollar deflation), or if Mexican inflation is more rapid than U.S. inflation. According to the theory, the behavior of importers and exporters would now induce a dollar appreciation and a peso depreciation. In summary, an increase in Mexican prices relative to the change in U.S. prices (i.e., more rapid inflation in Mexico than in the United States) will cause the dollar to appreciate and the peso to depreciate according to the purchasing power parity theory.

Similarly, if a country begins with PPP, then the inequality given in equilibrium story 2, can arise if the price level rises in the United States (dollar inflation), the price level falls in Mexico (peso deflation), or if U.S. inflation is more rapid than Mexican inflation. In this case, the inequality would affect the behavior of importers and exporters and induce a dollar depreciation and peso appreciation. In summary, more rapid inflation in the United States would cause the dollar to depreciate while the peso would appreciate.

KEY TAKEAWAYS

- An increase in Mexican prices relative to the change in U.S. prices (i.e., more rapid inflation in Mexico than in the United States) will cause the dollar to appreciate and the peso to depreciate according to the purchasing power parity theory.

- More rapid inflation in the United States would cause the dollar to depreciate while the peso would appreciate.

EXERCISE

1. Jeopardy Questions:As in the popular television game show, you are given an answer to a question and you must respond with the question. For example, if the answer is "a tax on imports," then the correct question is "What is a tariff?"
   a. Of increase, decrease, or no change, the effect on the demand for euros in the foreign exchange market if a market basket costs more in the United States than it does in Germany.
   b. Of increase, decrease, or no change, the effect on the supply of dollars in the foreign exchange market if a market basket costs more in the United States than it does in Germany.
   c. Of increase, decrease, or no change, the effect on the U.S. dollar value according to the PPP theory if a market basket costs \$300 in the United States and €200 in Germany and the exchange rate is $E_{\$/€} = 1.30$.
   d. Of increase, decrease, or no change, the effect on the euro value according to the PPP theory if a market basket costs €200 in Germany and ¥22,000 in Japan and the exchange rate is $E_{¥/€} = 115$.
   e. Of increase, decrease, or no change, the effect on the euro value according to the PPP theory if a market basket costs €200 in Germany and ¥22,000 in Japan and the exchange rate is $E_{¥/€} = 100$.

6.4 PPP PROBLEMS AND EXTENSIONS

Problems with the PPP Theory

The main problem with the purchasing power parity (PPP) theory is that the PPP condition is rarely satisfied within a country. There are quite a few reasons that can explain this and so, given the logic of the theory, which makes sense, economists have been reluctant to discard the theory on the basis of lack of supporting evidence. Below we consider some of the reasons PPP may not hold.

Transportation costs and trade restrictions. Since the PPP theory is derived from the law of one price, the same assumptions are needed for both theories. The law of one price assumes that there are no transportation costs and no differential taxes applied between the two markets. These mean that there can be no tariffs on imports or other types of restrictions on trade. Since transport costs and trade restrictions do exist in the real world, this would tend to drive prices for similar goods apart. Transport costs should make a good cheaper in the exporting market and more expensive in the importing market. Similarly, an import tariff would drive a wedge between the prices of an identical good in two trading countries' markets, raising it in the import market relative to the export market price. Thus the greater transportation costs and trade restrictions are between countries, the less likely for the costs of market baskets to be equalized.

Costs of nontradable inputs. Many items that are homogeneous nevertheless sell for different prices because they require a nontradable input in the production process. As an example, consider why the price of a McDonald's Big Mac hamburger sold in downtown New York City is higher than the price of the same product in the New York suburbs. Because the rent for restaurant space is much higher in the city center, the restaurant will pass along its higher costs in the form of higher prices. Substitute products in the city center (other fast food restaurants) will face the same high rental costs and thus will charge higher prices as well. Because it would be impractical (i.e., costly) to produce the burgers at a cheaper suburban location and then transport them for sale in the city, competition would not drive the prices together in the two locations.

Perfect information. The law of one price assumes that individuals have good, even perfect, information about the prices of goods in other markets. Only with this knowledge will profit seekers begin to export goods to the high price market and import goods from the low-priced market. Consider a case in which there is imperfect information. Perhaps some price deviations are known to traders but other deviations are not known, or maybe only a small group of traders know about a price discrepancy and that group is unable to achieve the scale of trade needed to equalize the prices for that product. (Perhaps they face capital constraints and can't borrow enough money to finance the scale of trade needed to equalize prices.) In either case, traders without information about price differences will not respond to the profit opportunities and thus prices will not be equalized. Thus the law of one price may not hold for some products, which would imply that PPP would not hold either.

Other market participants. Notice that in the PPP equilibrium stories, it is the behavior of profit-seeking importers and exporters that forces the exchange rate to adjust to the PPP level. These activities would be recorded on the current account of a country's balance of payments. Thus it is reasonable to say that the PPP theory is based on current account transactions. This contrasts with the interest rate parity theory in which the behavior of investors seeking the highest rates of return on investments motivates adjustments in the exchange rate. Since investors are trading assets, these transactions would appear on a country's capital account of its balance of payments. Thus the interest rate parity theory is based on capital account transactions.

It is estimated that there are approximately \$1–2 trillion dollars worth of currency exchanged every day on international foreign exchange (Forex) markets. That's one-eighth of U.S. GDP, which is the value of production in the United States in an entire year. In addition, the \$1–2 trillion estimate is made by counting only one side of each currency trade. Thus that's an enormous amount of trade. If one considers the total amount of world trade each year and then divides by 365, one can get the average amount of goods and services traded daily. This number is less than \$100 billion dollars. This means that the amount of daily currency transactions is more than ten times the amount of daily trade. This fact would seem to suggest that the primary effect on the daily exchange rate must be caused by the actions of investors rather than importers and exporters. Thus the participation of other traders in the Forex market, who are motivated by other concerns, may lead the exchange rate to a value that is not consistent with PPP.

Relative PPP

There is an alternative version of the PPP theory called the "relative PPP theory." In essence this is a dynamic version of the absolute PPP theory. Since absolute PPP suggests that the exchange rate may respond to inflation, we can imagine that the exchange rate would change in a systematic way given that a continual change in the price level (inflation) is occurring.

In the relative PPP theory, exchange rate changes over time are assumed to be dependent on inflation rate differentials between countries according to the following formula:

Here the percentage change in the dollar value between the first period and the second period is given on the left side. The right side gives the differences in the inflation rates between Mexico and the United States that were evaluated over the same time period. The implication of relative PPP is that if the Mexican inflation rate exceeds the U.S. inflation rate, then the dollar will appreciate by that differential over the same period. The logic of this theory is the same as in absolute PPP. Importers and exporters respond to variations in the relative costs of market baskets so as to maintain the law of one price, at least on average. If prices continue to rise faster in Mexico than in the United States, for example, price differences between the two countries would grow and the only way to keep up with PPP is for the dollar to appreciate continually versus the peso.

KEY TAKEAWAYS

- Purchasing power parity (PPP) will not be satisfied between countries when there are transportation costs, trade barriers (e.g., tariffs), differences in prices of nontradable inputs (e.g., rental space), imperfect information about current market conditions, and when other Forex market participants, such as investors, trade currencies for other reasons.
- Relative PPP is a dynamic version of the theory that relates currency appreciation or depreciation to differences in country inflation rates.

EXERCISE

- Jeopardy Questions: As in the popular television game show, you are given an answer to a question and you must respond with the question. For example, if the answer is "a tax on imports," then the correct question is "What is a tariff?"

- A type of trade cost whose presence is likely to cause deviations in the law of one price and PPP.
- The term used to describe a kind of production input, of which office rental is one type.
- Traders need to have information about this in other markets in order to take advantage of arbitrage opportunities.

6.5 PPP IN THE LONG RUN

In general, the purchasing power parity (PPP) theory works miserably when applied to real-world data. In other words, it is rare for the PPP relationship to hold true between any two countries at any particular point in time. In most scientific disciplines, the failure of a theory to be supported by the data means the theory is refuted and should be thrown out or tossed away. However, economists have been reluctant to do that with the PPP theory. In part this is because the logic of the theory seems particularly sound. In part it's because there are so many "frictions" in the real world, such as tariffs, nontariff barriers, transportation costs, measurement problems, and so on that it would actually be surprising for the theory to work when applied directly to the data. (It is much like expecting an object to follow Newton's laws of motion while sitting on the ground.)

In addition, economists have conceived of an alternative way to interpret or apply the PPP theory to overcome the empirical testing problem. The trick is to think of PPP as a "long-run" theory of exchange rate determination rather than a short-run theory. Under such an interpretation, it is no longer necessary for PPP to hold at any point in time. Instead, the PPP exchange rate is thought to represent a target toward which the spot exchange rate is slowly drawn.

This long-run interpretation requires an assumption that importers and exporters cannot respond quickly to deviations in the cost of market baskets between countries. Instead of immediate responses to price differences between countries by engaging in arbitrage—buying at the low price and selling high—traders respond slowly to these price signals. Some reasons for the delay include imperfect information (traders are not aware of the price differences), long-term contracts (traders must wait till current contractual arrangements expire), and/or marketing costs (entry to new markets requires research and setup costs). In addition, we recognize that the exchange rate is not solely determined by trader behavior. Investors, who respond to different incentives, might cause persistent deviations from the PPP exchange rate even if traders continue to respond to the price differences.

When there is a delayed response, PPP no longer needs to hold at a particular point in time. However, the theory does imagine that traders eventually will adjust to the price differences (buying low and selling high), causing an eventual adjustment of the spot exchange rate toward the PPP rate. However, as adjustment occurs, it is quite possible that the PPP exchange rate also continues to change. In this case, the spot exchange rate is adjusting toward a moving target.

How long will this adjustment take? In other words, how long is the long run? The term itself is generally used by economists to represent some "unspecified" long period of time; it might be several months, years, or even decades. Also, since the target, the PPP exchange rate, is constantly changing, it is quite possible that it is never reached. The adjustment process may never allow the exchange rate to catch up to the target even though it is constantly chasing it.

Perhaps the best way to see what the long-run PPP theory suggests is to consider Figure 6.3 "Hypothetical Long-Term Trend". The figure presents constructed data (i.e., made up) between two countries, A and B. The dotted black line shows the ratio of the costs of market baskets between the two countries over a long period, a century between 1904 and 2004. It displays a steady increase, indicating that prices have risen faster in country A relative to country B. The solid blue line shows a plot of the exchange rate between the two countries during the same period. If PPP were to hold at every point in time, then the exchange rate plot would lie directly on top of the market basket ratio plot. The fact that it does not means PPP did not hold all the time. In fact, PPP held only at times when the exchange rate plot crosses the market basket ratio plot; on the diagram this happened only twice during the century—not a very good record.

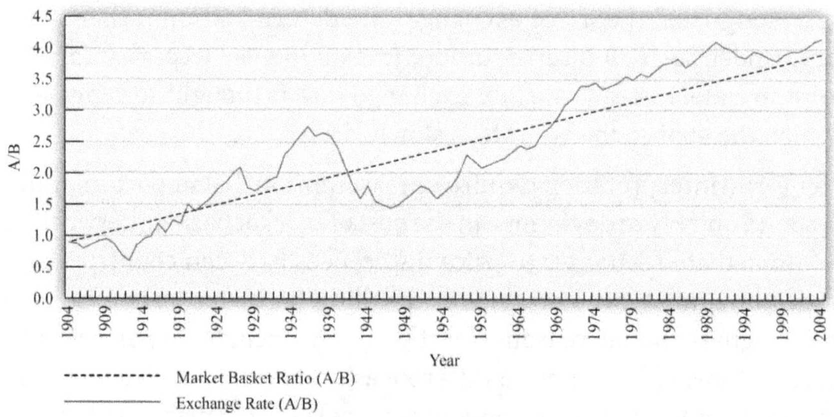

Figure 6.3 Hypothetical Long-Term Trend

Nonetheless, despite performing poorly with respect to moment-by-moment PPP, the figure displays an obvious regularity. The trend of the exchange rate between the countries is almost precisely the trend in the market basket ratio; both move upward at about the same "average" rate. Sometimes the exchange rate is below the market basket ratio, even for a long period of time, but at other times, the exchange rate rises up above the market basket ratio.

The idea here is that lengthy exchange rate deviations from the market basket ratio (i.e., the PPP exchange rate) mean long periods of time in which the cost of goods is cheaper in one country than in another. Eventually, traders will respond to these price discrepancies and begin to import more from the less expensive country. This will lead to the increase in demand for that country's currency and cause the exchange rate to move back toward the market basket ratio. However, in the long-run version of the theory, this will take time, sometimes a considerable amount of time, even years or more.

To see how this relationship works in one real-world example, consider Figure 6.4 "U.S./UK Long-Term Trends". It plots the exchange rate ($E_{\$/£}$) between the U.S. dollar and the British pound between 1913 and 2004 together with an adjusted ratio of the countries' consumer price indices (CPIs) during the same period.A technical point: The ratio of CPIs is adjusted because the ratio of CPIs must be multiplied by the PPP exchange rate that prevailed in the base year for the two countries. However, the CPI series used has 1967 as the base year in the United Kingdom and 1974 as the base year in the United States. This would mean the CPI ratio should be multiplied by the ratio of the cost of a market basket in the United States in 1974 divided by the market basket cost in the United Kingdom in 1967. Unsurprisingly, I don't have that information. Thus I'll assume a number (1.75) that is somewhat greater than the actual exchange rate that prevailed at the time. The higher number may account for the fact that prices rose considerably between 1967 and 1974. In any case, it remains a guess. The adjusted ratio represents an estimate of the ratio of the costs of market baskets between the two countries.

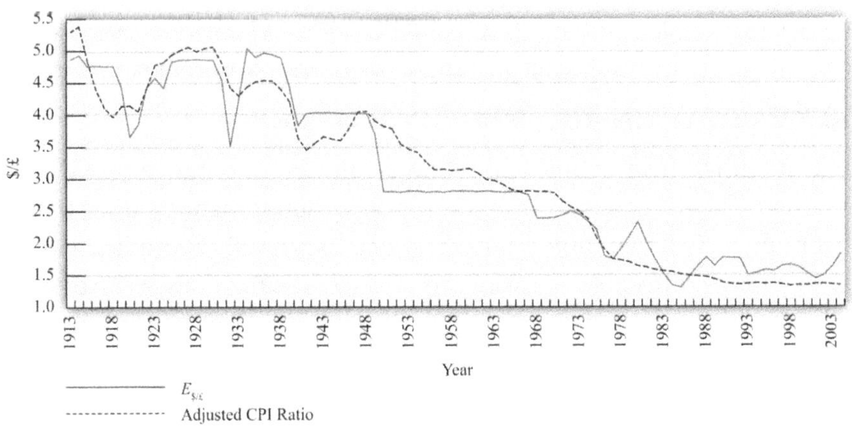

Figure 6.4 U.S./UK Long-Term Trends

In the diagram, the dotted black line represents the estimated ratio of market basket costs and the solid blue line is the exchange rate ($E_{\$/£}$). Note how closely the exchange rate tracks the trend in the market basket ratio. This remains true even though the exchange rate remained fixed during some lengthy periods of time, as in the 1950s and 1960s. While this depiction is just two countries over a long period, it is suggestive that the long-run version of PPP may have some validity.

More sophisticated empirical tests of the long-run version of PPP have shown mixed results, as some studies support the hypothesis while others tend to reject it. Regardless, there is much more support for this version of the theory than for the much more simplistic short-run version.

KEY TAKEAWAYS

- Under the long-run purchasing power parity (PPP) theory, the PPP exchange rate is thought to represent a target toward which the spot exchange rate is slowly drawn over time. The empirical evidence for this theory is mixed.
- Long-run data showing the trend in consumer price index (CPI) ratios between the United States and the United Kingdom relative to the $/£ exchange rate suggest some validity to the theory.

EXERCISE

1. Jeopardy Questions: As in the popular television game show, you are given an answer to a question and you must respond with the question. For example, if the answer is "a tax on imports," then the correct question is "What is a tariff?"
2. The term used by economists to denote an unspecified point in time in the distant future.
3. The term used by economists to denote an unspecified point in time in the near future.
4. The term used to describe the general path along which a variable is changing.
5. Under this version of the PPP theory, the PPP exchange rate represents a target toward which the spot exchange rate is slowly drawn over time.

6.6 OVERVALUATION AND UNDERVALUATION

It is quite common to hear people claim that a country's exchange rate is overvalued or undervalued. The first question one should ask when someone claims the exchange rate is overvalued is "overvalued with respect to what?" There are two common reference exchange rates often considered. The person may mean the exchange rate is overvalued with respect to purchasing power parity (PPP), or he may mean the exchange rate is overvalued relative to the rate presumed Needed to balance the current account (CA).

The mere use of these terms suggests immediately that there is some "proper" value for the exchange rate. However, one should refrain from accepting this implication. As was previously discussed, PPP is unlikely to hold, even over very long periods, for a variety of very good reasons. Also, there is no reason to think that current account balance represents some equilibrium or goal for an economy: countries can run trade deficits or surpluses for an extended period and suffer no ill effects. Thus overvaluation or undervaluation of an exchange rate, for either reason (PPP or current account balance) should be thought of simply as something that happens. Of more interest is what it means when it happens.

OVER- AND UNDERVALUATION WITH RESPECT TO PPP

First let's consider over- and undervaluation with respect to PPP. The PPP exchange rate is defined as the rate that equalizes the cost of a market basket of goods between two countries. The PPP exchange rate between the Mexican peso and the U.S. dollar would be written as which represents the PPP value of the U.S. dollar in terms of pesos.

- If the U.S. dollar is overvalued with respect to the Mexican peso, then the spot exchange rate exceeds the PPP exchange rate:
- This will also mean the exchange rate exceeds the ratio of market basket costs:
- therefore, the following will hold:

The left side (LS) of this expression represents the cost of a U.S. market basket converted to pesos at the current spot exchange rate. The right side (RS) is the cost of the basket in Mexico also evaluated in pesos. Since LS > RS, goods and services cost more on average in the United States than in Mexico at the current exchange rate. Thus for the U.S. dollar to be overvalued with respect to the peso means that goods and services are relatively more expensive in the United States than in Mexico. Of course, it also implies that goods and services are relatively cheaper in Mexico.

A simple guide to judge whether a currency is overvalued is to consider it from the perspective of a tourist. When the U.S. dollar is overvalued, a U.S. tourist traveling to Mexico will find that many products seem cheaper than in the United States, after converting at the spot exchange rate. Thus an overvalued currency will buy more in other countries.

An undervalued currency works in the opposite direction. When the U.S. dollar is undervalued, the cost of a basket of goods in the United States is lower than the cost in Mexico when evaluated at the current exchange rate. To a U.S. tourist, Mexican goods and services would seem more expensive on average. Thus an undervalued currency will buy less in other countries.

Finally, if the U.S. dollar is overvalued with respect to the Mexican peso, it follows that the peso is undervalued with respect to the dollar. In this case, since the U.S. tourists would find Mexican goods comparatively cheap, Mexican tourists would find U.S. goods to be comparatively expensive. If the U.S. dollar were undervalued, then the peso would be overvalued.

Is overvaluation or undervaluation good or bad? That depends on what a person is trying to achieve. For example, if the U.S. dollar is overvalued with respect to the peso, then a U.S. tourist traveling to Mexico will be very happy. In fact, the more overvalued the dollar is, the better. However, for an exporter of U.S. goods to Mexico, its price in peso terms will be higher the more overvalued is the dollar. Thus an overvalued dollar will likely reduce sales and profits for these U.S. firms.

Over- and Undervaluation with Respect to Current Account Balance

The second way over- and undervaluation is sometimes applied is in comparison to an exchange rate presumed necessary to induce trade balance, or balance on the current account. If one imagines that a trade deficit, for example, arises primarily because a country imports too much or exports too little (rather than being driven by financial decisions tending to cause a financial account surplus), then one may also look for ways to either reduce imports or raise exports. A change in the exchange rate offers one viable method to affect trade flows.

Suppose the United States has a trade deficit (which it indeed has had for more than thirty years prior to 2010). If the U.S. dollar value were to fall—a dollar depreciation—then foreign goods would all become relatively more expensive to U.S. residents, tending to reduce U.S. imports. At the same time, a dollar depreciation would also cause U.S. goods to become relatively cheaper to foreign residents tending to raise U.S. exports.

Sometimes economists make numerical estimations as to how much the dollar value would have to fall to bring trade into balance. These estimations are enormously difficult to make for several reasons and should be interpreted and used with great caution, if at all. The primary reason is that many different factors on both the trade side and the financial side influence a country's trade imbalance besides just the exchange rate. The exchange rate that balances trade would depend on the values taken by all the other factors that also influence the trade balance. Different values for all the other variables would mean a different exchange rate needed to balance trade. Thus there isn't one exchange rate value that will balance trade. Instead, there is a different exchange rate value that will balance trade in each and every alternative circumstance. Indeed, even the current exchange rate—whatever that is—can balance trade if other factors change appropriately.

Despite these cautions, many observers will still contend that a country's currency needs to depreciate by some percentage to eliminate a trade deficit, or needs to appreciate to eliminate a trade surplus. When it is believed a depreciation of the currency is needed to balance trade, they will say the currency is overvalued. When it is believed an appreciation of the currency is needed to balance trade, they will say the currency is undervalued. However, in a floating exchange rate system, it is hard to argue that the exchange rate is at the "wrong" value since—with competition in the market—it will always be at the rate that equalizes supply and demand. In other words, the "proper" value for the exchange rate can be said to be not the one that will satisfy PPP or not the one that will generate trade balance but rather whatever rate currently prevails. Under this notion, a currency can never be over- or undervalued in a floating exchange rate system. Instead, the spot exchange rate is always at the "proper" value.

In a fixed exchange rate system, a government can sometimes intervene to maintain an exchange rate that is very different from what would arise if allowed to float. In these cases, large trade surpluses can arise because the government maintains an artificially low value for its currency. Calls for a revaluation (appreciation) of the currency, to promote a reduction in a trade surplus, are somewhat more appropriate in these cases since the market does not determine the exchange rate. Similarly, large deficits could be reduced with a devaluation (depreciation) of the currency.

KEY TAKEAWAYS

- A currency can be overvalued or undervalued with respect to two reference values: (1) the value that would satisfy purchasing power parity (PPP) or (2) the value that would generate current account balance.
- Use of the terms overvaluation and undervaluation suggests that there is a "proper" value for the exchange rate. However, there are often valid reasons why exchange rates will not conform to PPP or why trade imbalances will persist.
- In a floating exchange rate system, the "proper" exchange rate can be said to be the rate that equalizes supply and demand for currencies in exchange. Under this notion, there can never be an over- or undervalued exchange rate.

EXERCISES

1. Use the information in the table below to answer the question, "Is the U.S. dollar overvalued or undervalued with respect to the Canadian dollar and the Japanese yen in terms of purchases of the Economist?" State why it is overvalued or undervalued. Show your work.

	The *Economist* Price per Issue	Exchange Rate (December 2, 1999)
United States	\$3.95	-
Canada	C\$4.95	1.47 C\$/\$
Japan	¥920	102 ¥/\$

Use the information in the table below to answer the following questions:

	Big Mac Price	Exchange Rate (June 4, 1998)
United States (dollar)	\$2.53	-
South Korea (won)	W 2,600	1,475 W/\$
Israel (shekel)	sh 12.50	3.70 sh/\$
Poland (zloty)	zl 5.30	3.46 zl/\$

Calculate whether the won, shekel, and zloty are overvalued or undervalued with respect to the U.S. dollar in terms of Big Mac purchases. Explain what it means to be overvalued or undervalued.

- What would the exchange rates have to be in order to equalize Big Mac prices between South Korea and the United States, Israel and the United States, and Poland and the United States?
- If in the long run the exchange rate moves to satisfy Big Mac purchasing power parity (PPP), will the won, shekel, and zloty appreciate or depreciate in terms of dollars? Explain the logic.
- Use the information about the hourly wage for a high school principal and exchange rates to answer the following questions:

	Wage	Actual Exchange Rate	PPP Exchange Rate
United States	$25/hour	–	–
Mexico	P220/hour	10.9 p/$	7.5 p/$
Japan	¥3,000/hour	110 ¥/$	132 ¥/$

- Calculate the hourly wage rate in dollars in Mexico and Japan using the actual exchange rates.
- Calculate the hourly wage rate in dollars in Mexico and Japan using the PPP exchange rates.
- Based on the information above, in which country is it best to be a high school principal? Which country is second best? Which is third best?
- In terms of PPP, is the U.S. dollar overvalued or undervalued with respect to the peso and with respect to the yen?
- According to the PPP theory, given the conditions above, would the dollar be expected to appreciate or depreciate with respect to the peso and with respect to the yen?

6.7 PPP AND CROSS-COUNTRY COMPARISONS

Probably the most important application of purchasing power parity (PPP) exchange rates is in making cross-country comparisons of income, wages, or gross domestic product (GDP). Suppose that we would like to compare per capita GDP between two countries—say, the United States and China. In 2004, GDP in the United States was approximately $12 trillion; in China GDP was about ¥16 trillion. With a population in the United States of 290 million people, per capita U.S. GDP works out to $41,400 per person. China's population was approximately 1.3 billion people in 2004, so its GDP per capita works out to 11,500 yuan (¥) per person. However, we can't compare these two per capita figures since they are in different units—dollars and yuan. Thus we need to convert units, either turn dollars into yuan or yuan into dollars.

The simplest approach to make this conversion is to use the spot exchange rate that prevailed in 2004, which was 8.28 yuan per dollar. Converting yuan to dollars yields a per capita GDP for China of $1,390. Note that at $41,400 per person, U.S. per capita GDP was almost thirty times higher than China's.

However, there is a problem using this method. One thing that is quickly recognized by Americans when they travel in and around China is that many goods and services seem considerably cheaper than they are in the United States. From a Chinese traveler's perspective, many U.S. goods would seem considerably more expensive. The implication is that although U.S. GDP per person is thirty times higher, that income may not purchase thirty times more goods and services in the U.S. because the prices of U.S. goods and services are so much higher when converted at the current exchange rate. Since presumably we are comparing per capita GDPs to compare how "well-off" people are in one country relative to another, these per capita figures will not accurately reflect these differences.

A solution is found in the purchasing power parity theory (PPP). When prices for similar goods differ as described in the previous paragraph, we would say the U.S. dollar is overvalued with respect to the yuan and with respect to PPP. At the same time, we would say the yuan is undervalued vis-à-vis the dollar. One way to reach comparable (or equalized) values of goods and services between the countries is to apply the PPP exchange rate in the conversion. The PPP exchange rate is that exchange rate that would equalize the value of comparable market baskets of goods and services between two countries.

For example, the estimated PPP exchange rate between the U.S. dollar and yuan in 2004 was 1.85 ¥/$. If this exchange rate had prevailed between the countries, the prices of U.S. goods would seem, on average, to be approximately equal to the prices that prevailed in China. Now, if we use this exchange rate to make the conversion to dollars of GDP per capita in China, then we will get a number that reflects the purchasing power of Chinese income in terms of the prices that prevail in the United States—that is, in terms of prices that are equalized between the countries.

Thus if we take China's GDP per capita of ¥11,500 and convert to dollars with the PPP exchange rate, we get $6,250 per person. The units derived in this expression would typically be called "international dollars." What this means is that ¥11,500 will buy a bundle of goods and services in China that would cost $6,250 if purchased in the United States at U.S. prices. In other words, ¥11,500 is equal to $6,250 when the prices of goods and services are equalized between countries.

The PPP method of conversion is a much more accurate way of making cross-country comparisons of values between countries. In this example, although China's per capita GDP was still considerably lower than in the United States ($6,250 vs. $41,400), it is nonetheless four and a half times higher than using the spot exchange rate ($6,250 vs. $1,390). The higher value takes account of the differences in prices between the countries and thus better reflects the differences in purchasing power of per capita GDP.

The PPP conversion method has become the standard method used by the World Bank and others in making cross-country comparisons of GDP, GDP per capita, and average incomes and wages. For most comparisons concerning the size of economies or standards of living, using PPP is a more accurate method and can fundamentally change our perception of how countries compare. To see how, consider Table 6.1 "GDP Rankings (in Billions of Dollars), 2008", constructed from World Bank data. It shows a ranking of the top ten countries in total GDP converting to dollars using both the current exchange rate method and the PPP method.

Table 6.1 GDP Rankings (in Billions of Dollars), 2008

Rank	Country	Using Current Exchange Rate ($)	Country	Using PPP Exchange Rate ($)
1	United States	14,204	United States	14,204
2	Japan	4,909	China	7,903
3	China	4,326	Japan	4,355
4	Germany	3,653	India	3,338
5	France	2,853	Germany	2,925
6	United Kingdom	2,646	Russia	2,288
7	Italy	2,293	United Kingdom	2,176
8	Brazil	1,613	France	2,112
9	Russia	1,608	Brazil	1,977
10	Spain	1,604	Italy	1,841
11	Canada	1,400	Mexico	1,542
12	India	1,217	Spain	1,456

The United States remains at the top of the list using both methods. However, several countries rise up in the rankings. China rises from the third largest economy using current exchange rates to the second largest using PPP. This means that in terms of the physical goods and services produced by the economies, China really does produce more than Japan. PPP conversion gives a better representation of the relative sizes of these countries.

Similarly, India rises from twelfth rank to fourth. Russia also moves up into sixth place from ninth. At the same time, Japan, Germany, the United Kingdom, France, Italy, Brazil, and Spain all move down in the rankings. Canada moves out of the top twelve, being replaced by Mexico, which rises up to eleventh.

For those countries whose GDP rises in value when converting by PPP (i.e., China, India, and Russia), their currencies are undervalued with respect to the U.S. dollar. So using the current exchange rate method underestimates the true size of their economies. For the other countries, their currencies are overvalued to the dollar, so converting their GDPs at current exchange rates gives an overestimate of the true size of their economies.

KEY TAKEAWAYS

- Using purchasing power parity (PPP) exchange rates to convert income data to a common currency is a better way to make international comparisons because it compensates for the differential costs of living.
- "International dollars" is the term used for the units for data converted to U.S. dollars using the PPP exchange rate.
- International rankings can vary significantly between data converted using actual versus PPP exchange rates.

EXERCISES

1. In February 2004, the Mexican peso–U.S. dollar exchange rate was 11 p/$. The price of a hotel room in Mexico City was 1,000 pesos. The price of a hotel room in New York City was $200.
2. Calculate the price of the Mexican hotel room in terms of U.S. dollars.
3. Calculate the price of the U.S. hotel room in terms of Mexican pesos.
4. Now suppose the exchange rate rises to 12 p/$. What does the exchange rate change indicate has happened to the value of the U.S. dollar relative to the value of the Mexican peso?
5. Does the currency change benefit the U.S. tourist traveling to Mexico City or the Mexican tourist traveling to New York City? Explain why.
6. In 2008, Brazil's per capita income in nominal terms was $8,295 while its per capita income in purchasing power parity (PPP) terms was $10,466. Based on this information, if you were an American traveling in Brazil, would Brazilian products seem expensive or inexpensive relative to U.S. products?
7. In 2008, Germany's per capita income in nominal terms was $44,729 while its per capita income in PPP terms was $35,539. Based on this information, if you were a German traveling in the United States, would U.S. products seem expensive or inexpensive relative to German products?

CHAPTER

INTEREST RATE DETERMINATION 7

INTRODUCTION

Money is a critical component of a modern economy because it facilitates voluntary exchanges. What exactly money is and how it fulfills this role is not widely understood. This chapter defines money and explains how a country's central bank determines the amount of money available in an economy. It also shows how changes in the amount of money in a country influence two very important macroeconomic variables: the interest rate and the inflation rate.

7.1 INTEREST RATE DETERMINATION: AN OVERVIEW

This chapter describes how the supply of money and the demand for money combine to affect the equilibrium interest rate in an economy. The model is called the money market model.

A country's money supply is mostly the amount of coin and currency in circulation and the total value of all checking accounts in banks. These two types of assets are the most liquid (i.e., most easily used to buy goods and services). The amount of money available to spend in an economy is mostly determined by the country's central bank. The bank can control the total amount of money in circulation by using several levers (or tools), the most important of which is the sale or purchase of U.S. government Treasury bonds. Central bank sales or purchases of Treasury bonds are called "open market operations."

Money demand refers to the demand by households, businesses, and the government, for highly liquid assets such as currency and checking account deposits. Money demand is affected by the desire to buy things soon, but it is also affected by the opportunity cost of holding money. The opportunity cost is the interest earnings one gives up on other assets to hold money.

If interest rates rise, households and businesses will likely allocate more of their asset holdings into interest-bearing accounts (these are usually not classified as money) and will hold less in the form of money. Since interest-bearing deposits are the primary source of funds used to lend in the financial sector, changes in total money demand affect the supply of loanable funds and in turn affect the interest rates on loans.

Money supply and money demand will equalize only at one average interest rate. Also, at this interest rate, the supply of loanable funds financial institutions wish to lend equalizes the amount that borrowers wish to borrow. Thus the equilibrium interest rate in the economy is the rate that equalizes money supply and money demand.

Using the money market model, several important relationships between key economic variables are shown:

- When the money supply rises (falls), the equilibrium interest rate falls (rises).
- When the price level increases (decreases), the equilibrium interest rate rises (falls).
- When real GDP rises (falls), the equilibrium interest rate rises (falls).

Connections

The money market model connects with the foreign exchange (Forex) market because the interest rate in the economy, which is determined in the money market, determines the rate of return on domestic assets. In the Forex market, interest rates are given exogenously, which means they are determined through some process not specified in the model. However, that process of interest rate determination is described in the money market. Economists will sometimes say that once the money market model and Forex model are combined, interest rates have been "endogenized." In other words, interest rates are now conceived as being determined by more fundamental factors (gross domestic product [GDP] and money supply) that are not given as exogenous.

The money market model also connects with the goods market model in that GDP, which is determined in the goods market, influences money demand and hence the interest rate in the money market model.

KEY TAKEAWAY

- The key results from the money market model are the following:
- When the money supply rises (falls), the equilibrium interest rate falls (rises).
- When the price level increases (decreases), the equilibrium interest rate rises (falls).
- When real gross domestic product (GDP) rises (falls), the equilibrium interest rate rises (falls).

EXERCISE

a. Jeopardy Questions: As in the popular television game show, you are given an answer to a question and you must respond with the question. For example, if the answer is "a tax on imports," then the correct question is "What is a tariff?"
b. The term describing what is mostly composed of coin and currency in circulation and checking account deposits in a country.
c. The term describing the amount of money that households, businesses, and government want to hold or have available.
d. Of increase, decrease, or stay the same, this happens to the interest rate when the money supply falls.
e. Of increase, decrease, or stay the same, this happens to the interest rate when the domestic price level falls.
f. Of increase, decrease, or stay the same, this happens to the interest rate when real GDP falls.

7.2 SOME PRELIMINARIES

There are several sources of confusion that can affect complete understanding of this basic model.

The first source of confusion concerns the use of the term "money." In casual conversation, money is sometimes used more narrowly and sometimes more broadly than the formal definition. For example, someone might say, "I want to be a doctor so I will make a lot of money." In this case, the person is really referring to income, not money, per se. Since income is typically paid using money, the everyday substitution of the term money for income does make sense, but it can lead to confusion in interpreting the forthcoming model. In general, people use the term money whenever they want to refer to a country's coin and currency and anything these items are used for in payment. However, our formal definition of money also includes items that are not coin and currency. Checking account deposits are an example of a type of money included in the formal definition but not more casually thought of as money. Thus pay attention to the definition and description below and be sure to recognize that one's common conception of money may or may not overlap precisely with the formal definition.

A second source of confusion involves our usage of the term interest rate. The model that will be developed will derive an equilibrium interest rate for the economy. However, everyone knows that there are many interest rates in the economy, and each of these rates is different. There are different rates for your checking and savings account, different rates on a car loan and mortgage, different rates on credit cards and government bonds. Thus it is typical to wonder what interest rate we are talking about when we describe the equilibrium interest rate.

It is important to note that financial institutions make money (here I really should say "make a profit") by lending to one group at a higher rate than it borrows. In other words, financial institutions accept deposits from one group of people (savers) and lend it to another group of people (borrowers.) If they charge a higher interest rate on their loans than they do on deposits, the bank will make a profit.

This implies that, in general, interest rates on deposits to financial institutions are lower than interest rates on their loans. When we talk about the equilibrium interest rate in the forthcoming model, it will mostly apply to the interest rates on deposits rather than loans. However, we also have a small problem in interpretation since different deposits have different interest rates. Thus which interest rate are we really talking about?

The best way to interpret the equilibrium interest rate in the model is as a kind of average interest rate on deposits. At the end of this chapter, we will discuss economic changes that lead to an increase or decrease in the equilibrium interest rate. We should take these changes to mean several things. First, that average interest rates on deposits will rise. Now, some of these rates may rise and a few may fall, but there will be pressure for the average to increase. Second, since banks may be expected to maintain their rate of profit (if possible) when average deposit interest rates do increase, average interest rates on loans will also increase. Again, some loan rates may rise and some fall, but the market pressure will tend to push them upward.

The implication is that when the equilibrium interest rate changes we should expect most interest rates to move in the same direction. Thus the equilibrium interest rate really is referring to an average interest rate across the entire economy, for deposits and for loans.

KEY TAKEAWAYS

- The term money is used causally in a different ways than we define it in the model: here money is defined as total value of coin and currency in circulation and checking account deposits at a point in time.
- The equilibrium interest rate in the money market model should be interpreted as an average interest rate across the entire economy, for deposits and for loans.

EXERCISES

- Jeopardy Questions: As in the popular television game show, you are given an answer to a question and you must respond with the question. For example, if the answer is "a tax on imports," then the correct question is "What is a tariff?"
- Of higher, lower, or the same, this is how average interest rates on bank deposits compare with average interest rates on bank loans.
- The term used to describe the amount of money a person earns as wages.

- When a person is asked how much money he has, he typically doesn't think to include the current balance in this type of bank deposit.
- Since there are many different interest rates on many types of loans and deposits, how do we interpret the equilibrium interest rate in the model?

7.3 MONEY

The money supply in a country refers to a stock of assets that can be readily used to purchase goods and services. An asset is anything that has value. Anything that has value could potentially be used in exchange for other goods, services, or assets. However, some assets are more easily exchangeable than other assets.

Examples of assets include currency, checking account balances, stocks, bonds, whole life insurance policies, real estate, and automobiles. Currency—dollar bills in the United States, pounds sterling in Britain, and pesos in Mexico—is an asset that is readily exchangeable for goods and services within its respective countries. In contrast, real estate is an asset that is very difficult to use to buy goods. For example, no grocery store would accept ownership of a few square feet of your house in exchange for your weekly groceries. The idea of this transaction is unimaginable. Yet these two extreme cases can help us understand the distinction we make between assets classified as money and those not considered money. Most textbook definitions of money begin by defining several of money's key features.

Money as a Unit of Account

One of the most important features of money is its application as a unit of account. In other words, we choose to measure the value of goods, services, and assets in terms of currency or money. In ancient societies, shells, shovels, hoes, knives, cattle, and grain were used as money. In these cases, it would have been common to define the value of an item in terms of how many shells, or knives, or cows, and so on the item exchanges for. The standard unit of account in a country is its currency: dollars in the United States, yen in Japan, and euros in the European Union.

Money as a Medium of Exchange

The key distinguishing feature of money, as compared with other nonmoney assets, is its role as a medium of exchange. Coin, and later currency, came into existence primarily to serve as a vehicle for the exchange of goods and services. Rather than hauling around items that you might hope to barter exchange for other goods you need, it is easier and more efficient to carry coin and currency to purchase goods. However, in order for money to function in this role, it must have widespread acceptability. Anyone selling something you want must be willing to accept the coin or currency you have. Their willingness to accept will in turn depend on the expectation that they'll be able to use that coin later to buy the goods they want.

Other types of assets are often not acceptable as a medium of exchange. For example, if I own a $1,000 U.S. savings bond, I am unlikely to be able to use the bond to purchase items in a store. Bonds can be traded at a bank or a bond market, where exchanges of this sort are common, but not anywhere else. Thus bonds do not function as a medium of exchange.

Liquidity is a term used to describe the distinction made here between bonds and currency. An asset is said to be liquid if it is readily exchangeable for goods and services. An asset is illiquid if it is not easily exchangeable. Thus coin and currency are very liquid assets, while bonds are more illiquid. Real estate is an example of a very illiquid asset since it could take a considerable amount of time to convert the ownership share of a home into a spendable form.

Money as a Store of Value

Perhaps the least important characteristic of money is an ability to serve as a store of value. This is less important because it does not distinguish money from other assets. All assets serve as a store of value. As an example, if I want to save some income from each paycheck so that I can go on a vacation next year, I need to hold that income in a form that will maintain its purchasing power. One simple way to hold it is by cashing my paycheck and putting currency into an envelope. That money accumulating in the envelope will be easily used to purchase plane tickets and a hotel room when I take my vacation next year. In this way, holding currency will allow me to store value over time. On the other hand, I could cash each paycheck and deposit some of the money I want to save into my online stock trading account. With these funds I can purchase stocks, another form of asset. Next year, I can sell the stocks and use the money to take my vacation. Thus stocks represent a store of value as well.

KEY TAKEAWAY

- Money is any asset that serves as a unit of account and can be used as a medium of exchange for economic transactions. It is all assets that have a high degree of liquidity. Money also serves as a store of value, but it is not unique in this role.

EXERCISE

- Jeopardy Questions: As in the popular television game show, you are given an answer to a question and you must respond with the question. For example, if the answer is "a tax on imports," then the correct question is "What is a tariff?"
- The three characteristics that are used to define money.
- This characteristic of money is shared by real estate assets.
- This characteristic of money allows us to compare the values of different products.

- Without this characteristic of money, individuals would be forced to trade by barter.

7.4 MONEY SUPPLY MEASURES

In the United States, the Federal Reserve Bank (or "Federal Reserve," and more informally, "the Fed") reports several distinct measures of the aggregate money supply. The narrowest measure, M1, includes only the most liquid assets. Higher numbers following an "M" reflect broader measures of money that include less liquid assets. Below is a description of M1–M3. However, unless otherwise specified, all later references to the money supply will relate to the M1 definition.

Money Supply Measure "M1"

M1 consists of the most highly liquid assets. That is, M1 includes all forms of assets that are easily exchangeable as payment for goods and services. It consists of coin and currency in circulation, traveler's checks, demand deposits, and other checkable deposits.

The first item in M1 is currency and coin in circulation. In the United States, "currency" refers to $1, $5, $10, $20, $50, and $100 bills. U.S. "coin," meanwhile, refers to pennies, nickels, dimes, and quarters. "In circulation" means that it has to be outside of banks, in people's wallets or purses and businesses' cash registers. Once the currency or coin is deposited in a bank, it is no longer considered to be in circulation, thus it is no longer a part of the M1 money supply.

The second item of M1 is traveler's checks. Traveler's checks are like currency, except that they have a form of insurance tied to them. If a traveler's check is lost or stolen, the issuer will reimburse you for the loss.

The third item in M1 is demand deposits or checking account balances in banks. These consist of money individuals and businesses have deposited into an account in which a check can be written to pay for goods and services. When a check is presented to the bank, it represents a demand for transfer of funds from the check writer to the agent receiving the check. Since the funds must be disbursed on demand, we also refer to these as demand deposits.

The final category in M1 is labeled "other checkable deposits." This consists of two items; NOW accounts and ATS accounts. NOW stands for "negotiable orders of withdrawal." A NOW account is exactly like a checking account except for one thing: it can earn interest. Thus checking accounts without interest are demand deposits and those with interest are NOW accounts. ATS stands for "automatic transfer service." ATS accounts are savings accounts (also called time deposits) with one special feature. They can be drawn automatically to cover overdrafts from one's checking account. Thus if an individual has a checking account with "overdraft protection" tied to their savings account, then the savings account is an ATS account.

Table 7.1 "Components of U.S. M1 Money Supply, November 2009" shows the M1 money supply for the U.S. economy as of November 2009. Notice that the largest component of M1, just over half, is the coin and currency in circulation. Traveler's checks are an insignificant share at 7.5$ billion. Demand deposits and other checkable deposits almost equally split the remaining shares of M1 at close to 25 percent each. The total value of the M1 money supply is 1,688$ billion, which is over 10 percent of annual U.S. GDP.

Table 7.1 Components of U.S. M1 Money Supply, November 2009

	Billions ($)	Total M1 (%)
Currency in Circulation	859.1	51
Traveler's Checks	5.1	< 1
Demand Deposits	439.0	26
Other Checkable Deposits	385.4	23
Total M1 Money Supply	1,688.7	100

Source: Federal Reserve Statistical Release, Money Stock Measures, January 14, 2010. http://www.federalreserve.gov/releases/h6/Current.

Money Supply Measure "M2"

M2 is a broader measure of money than M1. It includes all of M1, the most liquid assets, and a collection of additional assets that are slightly less liquid. These additional assets include savings accounts, money market deposit accounts, small time deposits (less than $100,000) and retail money market mutual funds. Excluded are IRA and Keogh deposits in money market accounts. (These are excluded since they are retirement funds and hence are unlikely to be used as payment for goods and services anytime soon.)

Money Supply Measure "M3"

M3 is an even broader definition of the money supply, including M2 and other assets even less liquid than M2. As the number gets larger (i.e., "1, 2, 3..."), the assets included become less and less liquid. The additional assets include large-denomination time deposits (amounts greater than $100,000), balances in institutional money funds (these include pension funds deposits), responsible party (RP) liabilities issued by depository institutions (refers to repurchase agreements), and eurodollars held by U.S. residents at foreign branches of U.S. banks worldwide and all banking offices in Canada and the United Kingdom (eurodollars are any U.S. dollar deposits made in a depository institution outside the United States). M3 excludes assets held by depository institutions, the U.S. government, money funds, and foreign banks and official institutions.

The United States values of all three major money supply definitions are given in Table 7.2 "U.S. Money Supply Measures (in Billions of Dollars), November 2009". Note that the M1 definition of money is just under one-tenth of the value of the annual GDP in the United States. The M2 money supply is almost six times larger, indicating substantial deposits in savings and time deposits and money market funds. M3 was last reported by the U.S. Fed in February 2006. But at that time, it was almost 90 percent of the U.S. annual GDP.

Table 7.2 U.S. Money Supply Measures (in Billions of Dollars), November 2009

M1	1,688.7
M2	8,391.9
M3 (February 2006)	10,298.7

Source: Federal Reserve Statistical Release, Money Stock Measures, January 14, 2010. For the most recent figures, go to http://www.federalreserve.gov/releases/h6/Current. (M3 was last reported for February 2006.)

KEY TAKEAWAYS

- M1 consists of the most highly liquid assets, including coin and currency in circulation, traveler's checks, demand deposits, and other checkable deposits.
- M2 is a broader measure of money than M1. It includes all of M1, plus savings accounts, money market deposit accounts, small-time deposits, and retail money market mutual funds.
- M3 is an even broader definition of the money supply that includes M2 plus large-denomination time deposits, balances in institutional money funds, repurchase liabilities, and eurodollars held by U.S. residents at foreign branches of U.S. banks.
- In 2009, the U.S. M1 was at just over $1.6 trillion, around 10 percent of the U.S. gross domestic product (GDP).

EXERCISE

- Jeopardy Questions: As in the popular television game show, you are given an answer to a question and you must respond with the question. For example, if the answer is "a tax on imports," then the correct question is "What is a tariff?"
- Of M1, M2, or M3, this measure of money is the most liquid.
- Of M1, M2, and/or M3, this measure(s) of money includes checking account deposits.
- Of M1, M2, and/or M3, this measure(s) of money includes savings account deposits.

- Of M1, M2, and/or M3, this measure(s) of money includes coin and currency in circulation.
- Of M1, M2, and/or M3, this measure(s) of money includes eurodollars held by U.S. residents at foreign branches of U.S. banks.

7.5 MANAGING THE MONETARY SUPPLY

The size of the money stock in a country is primarily controlled by its central bank. In the United States, the central bank is the Federal Reserve Bank while the main group affecting the money supply is the Federal Open Market Committee (FOMC). This committee meets approximately every six weeks and is the body that determines monetary policy. There are twelve voting members, including the seven members of the Fed Board of Governors and five presidents drawn from the twelve Federal Reserve banks on a rotating basis. The current Chairman of the Board of Governors is Ben Bernanke (as of January 2010). Because Bernanke heads the group that controls the money supply of the largest economy in the world, and because the FOMC's actions can have immediate and dramatic effects on interest rates and hence the overall United States and international economic condition, he is perhaps the most economically influential person in the world today. As you'll read later, because of his importance, anything he says in public can have tremendous repercussions throughout the international marketplace.

The Fed has three main levers that can be applied to affect the money supply within the economy: (1) open market operations, (2) reserve requirement changes, and (3) changes in the discount rate.

The Fed's First Lever: Open Market Operations

The most common lever used by the Fed is open market operations. This refers to Fed purchases or sales of U.S. government Treasury bonds or bills. The "open market" refers to the secondary market for these types of bonds. (The market is called secondary because the government originally issued the bonds at some time in the past.)

When the Fed purchases bonds on the open market it will result in an increase in the money supply. If it sells bonds on the open market, it will result in a decrease in the money supply.

Here's why. A purchase of bonds means the Fed buys a U.S. government Treasury bond from one of its primary dealers. This includes one of twenty-three financial institutions authorized to conduct trades with the Fed. These dealers regularly trade government bonds on the secondary market and treat the Fed as one of their regular customers. It is worth highlighting that bonds sold on the secondary open market are bonds issued by the government months or years before and will not mature for several months or years in the future. Thus when the Fed purchases a bond from a primary dealer in the future, when that bond matures, the government would have to pay back the Fed, which is the new owner of that bond.

When the open market operation (OMO) purchase is made, the Fed will credit that dealer's reserve deposits with the sale price of the bond (e.g., 1$ million). The Fed will receive the IOU, or "I owe you" (i.e., bond certificate), in exchange. The money used by the Fed to purchase this bond does not need to come from somewhere. The Fed doesn't need gold, other deposits, or anything else to cover this payment. Instead, the payment is created out of thin air. An accounting notation is made to indicate that the bank selling the bond now has an extra $1 million in its reserve account.

At this point, there is still no change in the money supply. However, because of the increase in its reserves, the dealer now has additional money to lend out somewhere else, perhaps to earn a greater rate of return. When the dealer does lend it, it will create a demand deposit account for the borrower and since a demand deposit is a part of the M1 money supply, money has now been created.

As shown in all introductory macroeconomics textbooks, the initial loan, once spent by the borrower, is ultimately deposited in checking accounts in other banks. These increases in deposits can in turn lead to further loans, subject to maintenance of the bank's deposit reserve requirements. Each new loan made creates additional demand deposits and hence leads to further increases in the M1 money supply. This is called the money multiplier process. Through this process, each $1 million bond purchase by the Fed can lead to an increase in the overall money supply many times that level.

The opposite effect will occur if the Fed sells a bond in an OMO. In this case, the Fed receives payment from a dealer (as in our previous example) in exchange for a previously issued government bond. (It is important to remember that the Fed does not issue government bonds; government bonds are issued by the U.S. Treasury department. If the Fed were holding a mature government bond, the Treasury would be obligated to pay off the face value to the Fed, just as if it were a private business or bank.) The payment made by the dealer comes from its reserve assets. These reserves support the dealer's abilities to make loans and in turn to stimulate the money creation process. Now that its reserves are reduced, the dealer's ability to create demand deposits via loans is reduced and hence the money supply is also reduced accordingly.

A more detailed description of open market operations can be found at New York Federal Reserve Bank's Web site at http://www.ny.frb.org/aboutthefed/fedpoint/fed32.html.

The Fed's Second Lever: Reserve Requirement Changes

When the Fed lowers the reserve requirement on deposits, the money supply increases. When the Fed raises the reserve requirement on deposits, the money supply decreases.

The reserve requirement is a rule set by the Fed that must be satisfied by all depository institutions, including commercial banks, savings banks, thrift institutions, and credit unions. The rule requires that a fraction of the bank's total transactions deposits (e.g., this would include checking accounts but not certificates of deposit) be held as a reserve either in the form of coin and currency in its vault or as a deposit (reserve) held at the Fed. The current reserve requirement in the United States (as of December 2009) is 10 percent for deposits over $55.2 million. (For smaller banks—that is, those with lower total deposits—the reserve requirement is lower.)

As discussed above, the reserve requirement affects the ability of the banking system to create additional demand deposits through the money creation process. For example, with a reserve requirement of 10 percent, Bank A, which receives a deposit of $100, will be allowed to lend out $90 of that deposit, holding back $10 as a reserve. The $90 loan will result in the creation of a $90 demand deposit in the name of the borrower, and since this is a part of the money supply M1, it rises accordingly. When the borrower spends the $90, a check will be drawn on Bank A's deposits and this $90 will be transferred to another checking account, say, in Bank B. Since Bank B's deposits have now risen by $90, it will be allowed to lend out $81 tomorrow, holding back $9 (10 percent) as a reserve. This $81 will make its way to another bank, leading to another increase in deposits, allowing another increase in loans, and so on. The total amount of demand deposits (DD) created through this process is given by the formula

$$DD = \$100 + (.9)\$100 + (.9)(.9)\$100 + (.9)(.9)(.9)\$100 + \ldots.$$

This simplifies to

$$DD = \$100/(1 - 0.9) = \$1{,}000$$

or

$$DD = \$100/RR,$$

where RR refers to the reserve requirement.

This example shows that if the reserve requirement is 10 percent, the Fed could increase the money supply by $1,000 by purchasing a $100 Treasury bill (T-bill) in the open market. However, if the reserve requirement were 5 percent, a $100 T-bill purchase would lead to a $2,000 increase in the money supply.

However, the reserve requirement not only affects the Fed's ability to create new money but also allows the banking system to create more demand deposits (hence more money) out of the total deposits it now has. Thus if the Fed were to lower the reserve requirement to 5 percent, the banking system would be able to increase the volume of its loans considerably and it would lead to a substantial increase in the money supply.

Because small changes in the reserve requirement can have substantial effects on the money supply, the Fed does not use reserve requirement changes as a primary lever to adjust the money supply.

A more detailed description of open market operations can be found at New York Federal Reserve Bank Web site at http://www.ny.frb.org/aboutthefed/fedpoint/fed45.html.

The Fed's Third Lever: Discount Rate/Federal Funds Rate Changes

When the Fed lowers its target federal funds rate and discount rate, it signals an expanded money supply and lower overall interest rates.

When the Fed raises its target federal funds rate and discount rate, it signals a reduced money supply and higher overall interest rates.

In news stories immediately after the FOMC meets, one is likely to read that the Fed raised (or lowered) interest rates yesterday. For many who read this, it sounds as if the Fed "sets" the interest rates charged by banks. In actuality, the Fed only sets one interest rate, and that is the discount rate. The rate that is announced every month is not the discount rate, but the federal funds rate. The federal funds rate is the interest rate banks charge each other for short-term (usually overnight) loans. The Fed does not actually set the federal funds rate, but it does employ open market operations to target this rate at a desired level. Thus what is announced at the end of each FOMC meeting is the target federal funds rate.

The main reason banks make overnight loans to each other each day is to maintain their reserve requirements. Each day some banks may end up with excess reserves. Other banks may find themselves short of reserves. Those banks with excess reserves would prefer to loan out as much as possible at some rate of interest rather than earning nothing. Those banks short of reserves are required by law to raise up their reserves to the required level. Thus banks lend money to each other each night.

If there is excess demand for money overnight relative to supply, the Fed keeps the discount window open. The discount window refers to a policy by the Fed to lend money on a short-term basis (usually overnight) to financial institutions. The interest rate charged on these loans is called the discount rate. Before 2003, banks needed to demonstrate that they had exhausted all other options before coming to the discount window. After 2003, the Fed revised its policies and set a primary credit discount rate and a secondary credit discount rate. Primary credit rates are set 100 basis points (1 percent) above the federal funds rate and are available only to very sound, financially strong banks. Secondary credit rates are set 150 basis points above the federal funds target rate and are available to banks not eligible for primary credit. Although these loans are typically made overnight, they can be extended for longer periods and can be used for any purpose.

Before the changes in discount window policy in 2003, very few banks sought loans through the discount window. Hence, it was not a very effective lever in monetary policy.

However, the announcement of the federal funds target rate after each FOMC meeting does remain an important signal about the future course of Fed monetary policy. If the FOMC announces a lower target federal funds rate, one should expect expanded money supply, perhaps achieved through open market operations. If the FOMC announces a higher target rate, one should prepare for a more contractionary monetary policy to follow.

A more detailed description of the discount window can be found on the New York Federal Reserve Bank Web site at http://www.ny.frb.org/aboutthefed/fedpoint/fed18.html. For more information about federal funds, go to http://www.ny.frb.org/aboutthefed/fedpoint/fed15.html.

KEY TAKEAWAYS

- When the Federal Reserve Bank (a.k.a. "Federal Reserve," or more informally, "the Fed") purchases bonds on the open market it will result in an increase in the U.S. money supply. If it sells bonds in the open market, it will result in a decrease in the money supply.
- When the Fed lowers the reserve requirement on deposits, the U.S. money supply increases. When the Fed raises the reserve requirement on deposits, the money supply decreases.
- When the Fed lowers its target federal funds rate and discount rate, it signals an expanded U.S. money supply and lower overall interest rates.
- When the Fed raises its target federal funds rate and discount rate, it signals a reduced U.S. money supply and higher overall interest rates.

EXERCISE

- Jeopardy Questions: As in the popular television game show, you are given an answer to a question and you must respond with the question. For example, if the answer is "a tax on imports," then the correct question is "What is a tariff?"
- Of increase, decrease, or no change, the effect on the money supply if the central bank sells government bonds.
- Of increase, decrease, or no change, the effect on the money supply if the central bank lowers the reserve requirement.
- Of increase, decrease, or no change, the effect on the money supply if the central bank lowers the discount rate.

- The name given to the interest rate charged by the Federal Reserve Bank on loans it provides to commercial banks
- The name given to the interest rate charged by commercial banks on overnight loans made to other banks.

7.6 MONEY DEMAND

The demand for money represents the desire of households and businesses to hold assets in a form that can be easily exchanged for goods and services. Spendability (or liquidity) is the key aspect of money that distinguishes it from other types of assets. For this reason, the demand for money is sometimes called the demand for liquidity.

The demand for money is often broken into two distinct categories: the transactions demand and the speculative demand.

Transactions Demand for Money

The primary reason people hold money is because they expect to use it to buy something sometime soon. In other words, people expect to make transactions for goods or services. How much money a person holds onto should probably depend on the value of the transactions that are anticipated. Thus a person on vacation might demand more money than on a typical day. Wealthier people might also demand more money because their average daily expenditures are higher than the average person's.

However, in this section we are interested not so much in an individual's demand for money but rather in what determines the aggregate, economy-wide demand for money. Extrapolating from the individual to the group, we could conclude that the total value of all transactions in the economy during a period would influence the aggregate transactions demand for money. Gross domestic product (GDP), the value of all goods and services produced during the year, will influence the aggregate value of all transactions since all GDP produced will be purchased by someone during the year. GDP may underestimate the demand for money, though, since people will also need money to buy used goods, intermediate goods, and assets. Nonetheless, changes in GDP are very likely to affect transactions demand.

Anytime GDP rises, there will be a demand for more money to make the transactions necessary to buy the extra GDP. If GDP falls, then people demand less money for transactions.

The GDP that matters here is nominal GDP, meaning GDP measured in terms of the prices that currently prevail (GDP at current prices). Economists often break up GDP into a nominal component and a real component, where real GDP corresponds to a quantity of goods and services produced after eliminating any price level changes that have occurred since the price level base year. To convert nominal to real GDP, simply divide nominal GDP by the current U.S. price level ($P_\$$); thus

real GDP = nominal GDP/$P_\$$.

If we use the variable $Y_\$$ to represent real U.S. GDP and rearrange the equation, we can get

nominal GDP = $P_\$ Y_\$$.

By rewriting in this way we can now indicate that since the transactions demand for money rises with an increase in nominal GDP, it will also rise with either an increase in the general price level or an increase in real GDP.

Thus if the amount of goods and services produced in the economy rises while the prices of all products remain the same, then total GDP will rise and people will demand more money to make the additional transactions. On the other hand, if the average prices of goods and services produced in the economy rise, then even if the economy produces no additional products, people will still demand more money to purchase the higher valued GDP, hence the demand for money to make transactions will rise.

Speculative Demand for Money

The second type of money demand arises by considering the opportunity cost of holding money. Recall that holding money is just one of many ways to hold value or wealth. Alternative opportunities include holding wealth in the form of savings deposits, certificate of deposits, mutual funds, stock, or even real estate. For many of these alternative assets interest payments, or at least a positive rate of return, may be obtained. Most assets considered money, such as coin and currency and most checking account deposits, do not pay any interest. If one does hold money in the form of a negotiable order of withdrawal (NOW) account, a checking account with interest, the interest earned on that deposit will almost surely be less than on a savings deposit at the same institution.

Thus to hold money implies giving up the opportunity of holding other assets that pay interest. The interest one gives up is the opportunity cost of holding money.

Since holding money is costly—that is, there is an opportunity cost—people's demand for money should be affected by changes in its cost. Since the interest rate on each person's next best opportunity may differ across money holders, we can use the average interest rate ($i_\$$) in the economy as a proxy for the opportunity cost. It is likely that as average interest rates rise, the opportunity cost of holding money for all money holders will also rise, and vice versa. And as the cost of holding money rises, people should demand less money.

The intuition is straightforward, especially if we exaggerate the story. Suppose interest rates on time deposits suddenly increased to 50 percent per year (from a very low base). Such a high interest rate would undoubtedly lead individuals and businesses to reduce the amount of cash they hold, preferring instead to shift it into the high-interest-yielding time deposits. The same relationship is quite likely to hold even for much smaller changes in interest rates. This implies that as interest rates rise (fall), the demand for money will fall (rise). The speculative demand for money, then, simply relates to component of the money demand related to interest rate effects.

KEY TAKEAWAYS

- Anytime the gross domestic product (GDP) rises, there will be a demand for more money to make the transactions necessary to buy the extra GDP. If GDP falls, then people demand less money for transactions.
- The interest one gives up is the opportunity cost of holding money.
- As interest rates rise (fall), the demand for money will fall (rise).

EXERCISE

- Jeopardy Questions: As in the popular television game show, you are given an answer to a question and you must respond with the question. For example, if the answer is "a tax on imports," then the correct question is "What is a tariff?"
- Of increase, decrease, or no change, the effect on the transactions demand for money when interest rates fall.
- Of increase, decrease, or no change, the effect on the transactions demand for money when GDP falls.
- Of increase, decrease, or no change, the effect on the speculative demand for money when GDP falls.
- Of increase, decrease, or no change, the effect on the speculative demand for money when interest rates fall.

7.7 FUNCTIONS OF MONEY AND EQUILIBRIUM

Demand

A money demand function displays the influence that some aggregate economic variables will have on the aggregate demand for money. The above discussion indicates that money demand will depend positively on the level of real gross domestic product (GDP) and the price level due to the demand for transactions. Money demand will depend negatively on average interest rates due to speculative concerns. We can depict these relationships by simply using the following functional representation:

Here M^D is the aggregate, economy-wide money demand, $P_\$$ is the current U.S. price level, $Y_\$$ is the United States' real GDP, and $i_\$$ is the average U.S. interest rate.

The f stands for "function." The f is not a variable or parameter value; it simply means that some function exists that would map values for the right-side variables, contained within the brackets, into the left-side variable. The "+" symbol above the price level and GDP levels means that there is a positive relationship between changes in that variable and changes in money demand. For example, an increase (decrease) in $P_\$$ would cause an increase (decrease) in M^D. A "-" symbol above the interest rate indicates that changes in $i_\$$ in one direction will cause money demand to change in the opposite direction.

For historical reasons, the money demand function is often transformed into a real money demand function as follows. First, rewrite the function on the right side to get

In this version, the price level ($P_\$$) is brought outside the function f( ) and multiplied to a new function labeled L( ), called the "liquidity function." Note that L( ) is different from f( ) since it contains only $Y_\$$ and $i_\$$ as variables. Since $P_\$$ is multiplied to L( ) it will maintain the positive relationship to M^D and thus is perfectly consistent with the previous specification. Finally, by moving the price level variable to the left side, we can write out the general form of the real money demand function as

This states that real money demand ($M^D/P_\$$) is positively related to changes in real GDP ($Y_\$$) and the average interest rate ($i_\$$) according to the liquidity function. We can also say that the liquidity function represents the real demand for money in the economy—that is, the liquidity function is equivalent to real money demand.

Finally, simply for intuition's sake, any real variable represents the purchasing power of the variable in terms of prices that prevailed in the base year of the price index. Thus real money demand can be thought of as the purchasing power of money demanded in terms of base year prices.

Supply

Money supply is much easier to describe because we imagine that the level of money balances available in an economy is simply set by the actions of the central bank. For this reason, it will not depend on other aggregate variables such as the interest rate, and thus we need no function to describe it.

We will use the parameter $M_\$^S$ to represent the nominal U.S. money supply and assume that the Federal Reserve Bank (or simply "the Fed"), using its three levers, can set this variable wherever it chooses. To represent real money supply, however, we will need to convert by dividing by the price level. Hence let represent the real money supply in terms of prices that prevailed in the base year.

Equilibrium

The equilibrium interest rate is determined at the level that will equalize real money supply with real money demand. We can depict the equilibrium by graphing the money supply and demand functions on the following diagram.

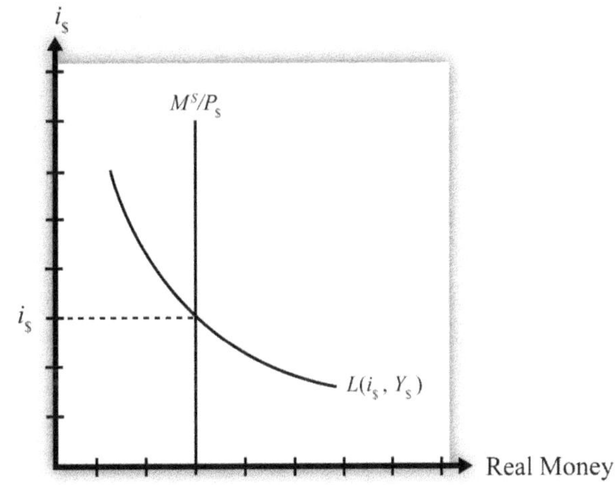

Figure 7.1 The Money Market

The functions are drawn in Figure 7.1 "The Money Market" with real money, both supply and demand, plotted along the horizontal axis and the interest rate plotted along the vertical axis.

Real money supply, , is drawn as a vertical line at the level of money balances, measured best by M1. It is vertical because changes in the interest rate will not affect the money supply in the economy.

Real money demand—that is, the liquidity function $L(i_\$, Y_\$)$—is a downward sloping line in $i_\$$ reflecting the speculative demand for money. In other words, there is a negative relationship presumed to prevail between the interest rate and real money demand.

Where the two lines cross determines the equilibrium interest rate in the economy ($i_\$$) since this is the only interest rate that will equalize real money supply with real money demand.

KEY TAKEAWAYS

- Real money demand is positively related to changes in real gross domestic product (GDP) and the average interest rate.
- Real money supply is independent of the average interest rate and is assumed to be determined by the central bank.
- The intersection of the real money supply function and the real money demand function determines the equilibrium interest rate in the economy.

EXERCISE

a. Jeopardy Questions: As in the popular television game show, you are given an answer to a question and you must respond with the question. For example, if the answer is "a tax on imports," then the correct question is "What is a tariff?"

b. Of positive, negative, or no effect, this is the relationship between the interest rate and real money demand.
c. Of positive, negative, or no effect, this is the relationship between real GDP and real money demand.
d. Of positive, negative, or no effect, this is the relationship between the price level and nominal money demand.
e. Of positive, negative, or no effect, this is the relationship between the interest rate and real money supply.
f. Of positive, negative, or no effect, this is the relationship between real GDP and real money supply.
g. Of positive, negative, or no effect, this is the relationship between the price level and real money supply.
h. The endogenous variable (in the money market model) whose value is determined at the intersection of the real money supply curve and the real money demand curve.

7.8 STORIES ABOUT MONEY MARKET EQUILIBRIUM

Any equilibrium in economics has an associated behavioral story to explain the forces that will move the endogenous variable to the equilibrium value. In the money market model, the endogenous variable is the interest rate. This is the variable that will change to achieve the equilibrium. Variables that do not change in the adjustment to the equilibrium are the exogenous variables. In this model, the exogenous variables are $P_\$$, $Y_\$$, and $M_\$^S$. Changes in the exogenous variables are necessary to cause an adjustment to a new equilibrium. However, in telling an equilibrium story, it is typical to simply assume that the endogenous variable is not at the equilibrium (for some unstated reason) and then to explain how and why the variable will adjust to the equilibrium value.

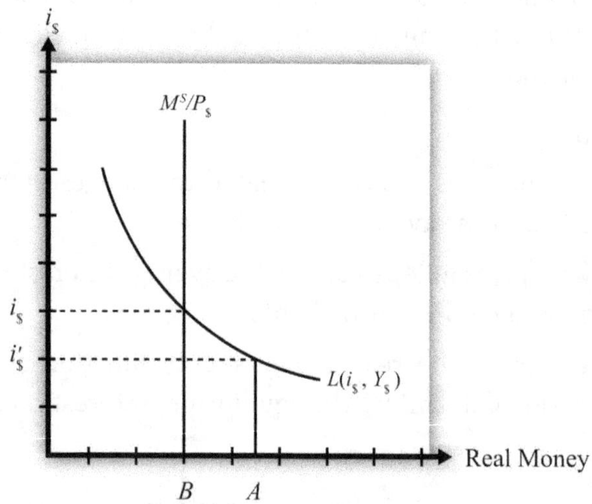

Figure 7.2 Adjustment to Equilibrium: Interest Rate Too Low

Interest Rate Too Low

Suppose that for some reason the actual interest rate, $i'_\$$ lies below the equilibrium interest rate ($i_\$$) as shown in Figure 7.2 "Adjustment to Equilibrium: Interest Rate Too Low". At $i'_\$$, real money demand is given by the value A along the horizontal axis, while real money supply is given by the value B. Since A is to the right of B, real demand for money exceeds the real money supply. This means that people and businesses wish to hold more assets in a liquid, spendable form rather than holding assets in a less liquid form, such as in a savings account. This excess demand for money will cause households and businesses to convert assets from less liquid accounts into checking accounts or cash in their pockets. A typical transaction would involve a person who withdraws money from a savings account to hold cash in his wallet.

The savings account balance is not considered a part of the M1 money supply; however, the currency the person puts into his wallet is a part of the money supply. Millions of conversions such as this will be the behavioral response to an interest rate that is below equilibrium. As a result, the financial sector will experience a decrease in time deposit balances, which in turn will reduce their capacity to make loans. In other words, withdrawals from savings and other type of nonmoney accounts will reduce the total pool of funds available to be loaned by the financial sector. With fewer funds to lend and the same demand for loans, banks will respond by raising interest rates. Higher interest rates will reduce the demand for loans helping to equalize supply and demand for loans. Finally, as interest rates rise, money demand falls until it equalizes with the actual money supply. Through this mechanism average interest rates will rise, whenever money demand exceeds money supply.

Interest Rate Too High

If the actual interest rate is higher than the equilibrium rate, for some unspecified reason, then the opposite adjustment will occur. In this case, real money supply will exceed real money demand, meaning that the amount of assets or wealth people and businesses are holding in a liquid, spendable form is greater than the amount they would like to hold. The behavioral response would be to convert assets from money into interest-bearing nonmoney deposits. A typical transaction would be if a person deposits some of the cash in his wallet into his savings account. This transaction would reduce money holdings since currency in circulation is reduced, but will increase the amount of funds available to loan out by the banks. The increase in loanable funds, in the face of constant demand for loans, will inspire banks to lower interest rates to stimulate the demand for loans. However, as interest rates fall, the demand for money will rise until it equalizes again with money supply. Through this mechanism average interest rates will fall whenever money supply exceeds money demand.

KEY TAKEAWAYS

- If the actual interest rate is lower than the equilibrium rate, the amount of assets people are holding in a liquid form is less than the amount they would like to hold. They respond by converting assets from interest-bearing nonmoney deposits into money. The decrease in loanable funds will cause banks to raise interest rates. Interest rates rise until money supply equals money demand.
- If the actual interest rate is higher than the equilibrium rate, the amount of assets people are holding in a liquid form is greater than the amount they would like to be holding. They respond by converting assets from money into interest-bearing nonmoney deposits. The increase in loanable funds will cause banks to lower interest rates. Interest rates fall until money supply equals money demand.

EXERCISE

- Jeopardy Questions: As in the popular television game show, you are given an answer to a question and you must respond with the question. For example, if the answer is "a tax on imports," then the correct question is "What is a tariff?"
- Of increase, decrease, or stay the same, the effect on the average interest rate when real money supply exceeds real money demand.
- Of increase, decrease, or stay the same, the effect on the average interest rate when real money demand is less than real money supply.
- Of increase, decrease, or stay the same, the effect on the average interest rate when real money demand exceeds real money supply.
- Of increase, decrease, or stay the same, the effect on the average interest rate when households and businesses wish to convert assets from interest-bearing nonmoney deposits into money.
- Of increase, decrease, or stay the same, the effect on the average interest rate when households and businesses wish to convert assets from money into interest-bearing nonmoney deposits.

7.9 EFFECTS OF A RISE IN MONEY SUPPLY

Expansionary monetary policy refers to any policy initiative by a country's central bank to raise (or expand) its money supply. This can be accomplished with open market purchases of government bonds, with a decrease in the reserve requirement, or with an announced decrease in the discount rate. In most growing economies the money supply is expanded regularly to keep up with the expansion of gross domestic product (GDP). In this dynamic context, expansionary monetary policy can mean an increase in the rate of growth of the money supply, rather than a mere increase in money. However, the money market model is a nondynamic (or static) model, so we cannot easily incorporate money supply growth rates. Nonetheless, we can project the results from this static model to the dynamic world without much loss of relevance. (In contrast, any decrease in the money supply or decrease in the growth rate of the money supply is referred to as contractionary monetary policy.)

Suppose the money market is originally in equilibrium in Figure 7.3 at point A with real money supply MS'/P$ and interest rate i$' when the money supply increases, ceteris paribus. The ceteris paribus assumption means we assume that all other exogenous variables in the model remain fixed at their original levels. In this exercise, it means that real GDP (Y$) and the price level (P$) remain fixed. An increase in the money supply (MS) causes an increase in the real money supply (MS/P$) since P$ remains constant. In the diagram, this is shown as a rightward shift from MS'/P$ to MS"/P$. At the original interest rate, real money supply has risen to level 2 along the horizontal axis while real money demand remains at level 1. This means that money supply exceeds money demand, and the actual interest rate is higher than the equilibrium rate. Adjustment to the lower interest rate will follow the "interest rate too high" equilibrium story.

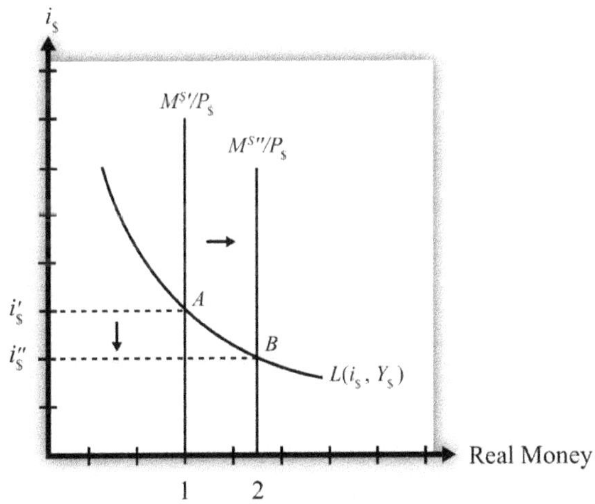

Figure 7.3 Effects of a Money Supply Increase

The final equilibrium will occur at point B on the diagram. The real money supply will have risen from level 1 to 2 while the equilibrium interest rate has fallen from $i_\$'$ to $i_\$''$. Thus expansionary monetary policy (i.e., an increase in the money supply) will cause a decrease in average interest rates in an economy. In contrast, contractionary monetary policy (a decrease in the money supply) will cause an increase in average interest rates in an economy.

Note this result represents the short-run effect of a money supply increase. The short run is the time before the money supply can affect the price level in the economy. In Chapter 7 , Section 7.14 , we consider the long-run effects of a money supply increase. In the long run, money supply changes can affect the price level in the economy. In the previous exercise, since the price level remained fixed (i.e., subject to the ceteris paribus assumption) when the money supply was increased, this exercise provides the short-run result.

KEY TAKEAWAY

- An increase (decrease) in the money supply, ceteris paribus, will cause a decrease (increase) in average interest rates in an economy.

EXERCISE

- Jeopardy Questions: As in the popular television game show, you are given an answer to a question and you must respond with the question. For example, if the answer is "a tax on imports," then the correct question is "What is a tariff?"
- Term often used to describe the type of monetary policy that results in a reduction of the money supply.
- Term often used to describe the type of monetary policy that results in an increase in the money supply.
- Of increase, decrease, or stay the same, the effect on the equilibrium interest rate when the nominal money supply increases, ceteris paribus.
- Of increase, decrease, or stay the same, the effect on the equilibrium interest rate when the nominal money supply decreases, ceteris paribus.
- Term for the time period before price level changes occur in the money market model.

7.10 IMPACT OF AN INCREASE IN PRICE LEVELS (INFLATION) ON INTEREST RATES

Now let's consider the effects of a price level increase in the money market. When the price level rises in an economy, the average price of all goods and services sold is increasing. Inflation is calculated as the percentage increase in a country's price level over some period, usually a year. This means that in the period during which the price level increases, inflation is occurring. Thus studying the effects of a price level increase is the same as studying the effects of inflation.

Inflation can arise for several reasons that will be discussed later in this chapter. For now, we will imagine that the price level increases for some unspecified reason and consider the consequences.

Suppose the money market is originally in equilibrium at point A in Figure 7.4 «Effects of a Price Level Increase» with real money supply $M^S/P_\$'$ and interest rate $i_\$'$. Suppose the price level increases, ceteris paribus. Again, the ceteris paribus assumption means that we assume all other exogenous variables in the model remain fixed at their original levels. In this exercise, it means that the money supply (M^S) and real GDP ($Y_\$$) remain fixed. An increase in the price level ($P_\$$) causes a decrease in the real money supply ($M^S/P_\$$) since M^S remains constant. In the adjoining diagram, this is shown as a shift from $M^S/P_\$'$ to $M^S/P_\$''$. At the original interest rate, $i_\$'$, the real money supply has fallen to level 2 along the horizontal axis, while real money demand remains at level 1. This means that money demand exceeds money supply and the actual interest rate is lower than the new equilibrium rate. Adjustment to the higher interest rate will follow the "interest rate too low" equilibrium story.

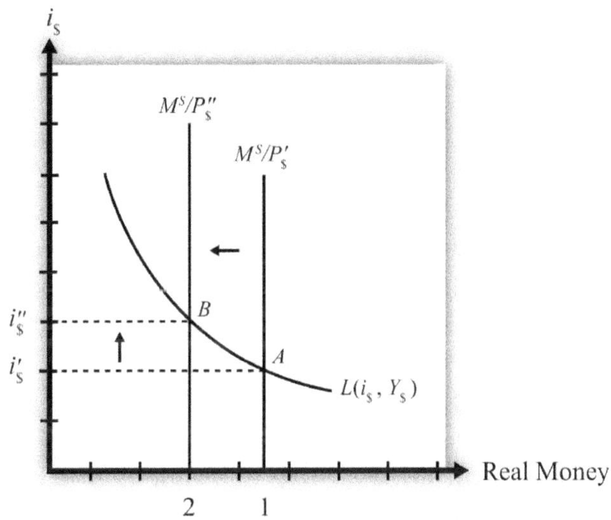

Figure 7.4 Effects of a Price Level Increase

More intuition concerning these effects arises if one recalls that price level increases will increase the transactions demand for money. In this version, nominal money demand will exceed nominal money supply and set off the same adjustment process described in the previous paragraph.

The final equilibrium will occur at point B on the diagram. The real money supply will have fallen from level 1 to level 2 while the equilibrium interest rate has risen from $i_\$'$ to $i_\$''$. Thus an increase in the price level (i.e., inflation) will cause an increase in average interest rates in an economy. In contrast, a decrease in the price level (deflation) will cause a decrease in average interest rates in an economy.

KEY TAKEAWAY

- An increase in the price level (i.e., inflation), ceteris paribus, will cause an increase in average interest rates in an economy. In contrast, a decrease in the price level (deflation), ceteris paribus, will cause a decrease in average interest rates in an economy.

EXERCISE

- Jeopardy Questions: As in the popular television game show, you are given an answer to a question and you must respond with the question. For example, if the answer is "a tax on imports," then the correct question is "What is a tariff?"
- The term used to describe a percentage increase in a country's price level over a period of time.
- Of increase, decrease, or stay the same, the effect on the equilibrium interest rate when the domestic price level decreases, ceteris paribus.
- Of increase, decrease, or stay the same, the effect on the equilibrium interest rate when the domestic price level increases, ceteris paribus.

7.11 EFFECT OF A REAL GDP INCREASE (ECONOMIC GROWTH) ON INTEREST RATES

Suppose the money market is originally in equilibrium at point A in Figure 7.5 «Effects of an Increase in Real GDP» with real money supply $M^S/P_\$$ and interest rate $i_\$'$. Suppose real GDP ($Y_\$$) increases, ceteris paribus. Again, the ceteris paribus assumption means that we assume all other exogenous variables in the model remain fixed at their original levels. In this exercise, it means that the money supply (M^S) and the price level ($P_\$$) remain fixed. An increase in GDP will raise the demand for money because people will need more money to make the transactions necessary to purchase the new GDP. In other words, real money demand rises due to the transactions demand effect. This increase is reflected in the rightward shift of the real money demand function from $L(i_\$, Y_\$')$ to $L(i_\$, Y_\$'')$.

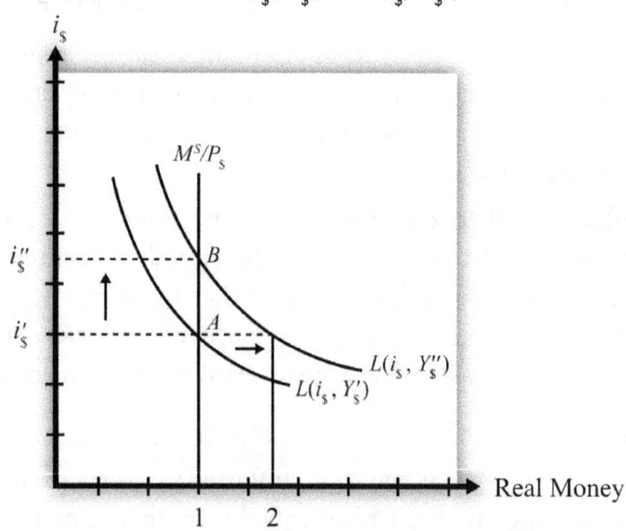

Figure 7.5 Effects of an Increase in Real GDP

At the original interest rate, $i_{\$}$', real money demand has increased to level 2 along the horizontal axis while real money supply remains at level 1. This means that real money demand exceeds real money supply and the current interest rate is lower than the equilibrium rate. Adjustment to the higher interest rate will follow the "interest rate too low" equilibrium story.

The final equilibrium will occur at point B on the diagram. As the interest rate rises from $i_{\$}'$ to $i_{\$}''$, real money demand will have fallen from level 2 to level 1. Thus an increase in real GDP (i.e., economic growth) will cause an increase in average interest rates in an economy. In contrast, a decrease in real GDP (a recession) will cause a decrease in average interest rates in an economy.

KEY TAKEAWAY

- An increase in real gross domestic product (i.e., economic growth), ceteris paribus, will cause an increase in average interest rates in an economy. In contrast, a decrease in real GDP (a recession), ceteris paribus, will cause a decrease in average interest rates in an economy.

EXERCISE

- Jeopardy Questions: As in the popular television game show, you are given an answer to a question and you must respond with the question. For example, if the answer is "a tax on imports," then the correct question is "What is a tariff?"
- The term used to describe a percentage increase in real GDP over a period of time.
- Of increase, decrease, or stay the same, the effect on the equilibrium interest rate when real GDP decreases, ceteris paribus.
- Of increase, decrease, or stay the same, the effect on the equilibrium interest rate when real GDP increases, ceteris paribus.

7.12 INTEGRATING THE MONEY MARKET AND FOREIGN EXCHANGE MARKETS

In this section, we will integrate the money market with the foreign exchange market to demonstrate the interactions that exist between the two. First, let's review.

In the money market, the endogenous variable is the interest rate ($i_{\$}$). This is the variable that is determined in equilibrium in the model. The exogenous variables are the money supply (M^S), the price level ($P_{\$}$), and the level of real gross domestic product (GDP) (Y). These variables are determined outside the money market and treated as known values. Their values determine the supply and demand for money and affect the equilibrium value of the interest rate.

In the foreign exchange (Forex) market, the endogenous variable is the exchange rate, $E_{\$/£}$. The exogenous variables are the domestic interest rate ($i_\$$), the foreign interest rate ($i_£$), and the expected exchange rate ($E_{\$/£}^e$). Their values determine the domestic and foreign rates of return and affect the equilibrium value of the exchange rate.

The linkage between the two markets arises because the domestic interest rate is the endogenous variable in the money market and an exogenous variable in the Forex market. Thus when considering the Forex, when we say the interest rate is determined outside of the Forex market, we know where it is determined: it is determined in the U.S. money market as the interest rate that satisfies real supply and demand for money.

Linking the Diagrams

We can keep track of the interactions between these two markets using a simple graphical technique. We begin with the money market diagram as developed in Chapter 7, Section 7.7 . The trick is to rotate the diagram ninety degrees in a clockwise direction. Figure 7.6 "Rotating the Money Market Diagram" shows the beginning of the rotation pivoted around the origin at zero.

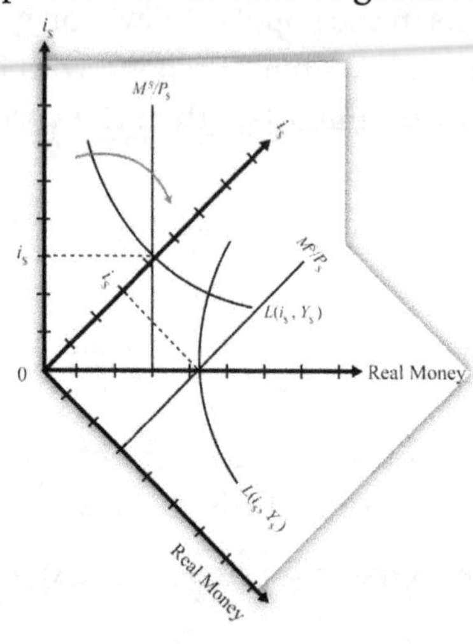

Figure 7.6 Rotating the Money Market Diagram

When rotated the full ninety degrees, it will be positioned as shown in Figure 7.7 "Ninety-Degree Rotation of the Money Market Diagram". The most important thing to remember about this new diagram is that the value of real money supply and demand increases downward away from the origin at zero along the vertical axis. Thus when the money supply "increases," this will be represented in the diagram as a "downward" shift in the real money supply line. The interest rate, in contrast, increases away from the origin to the right along the horizontal axis when rotated in this position.

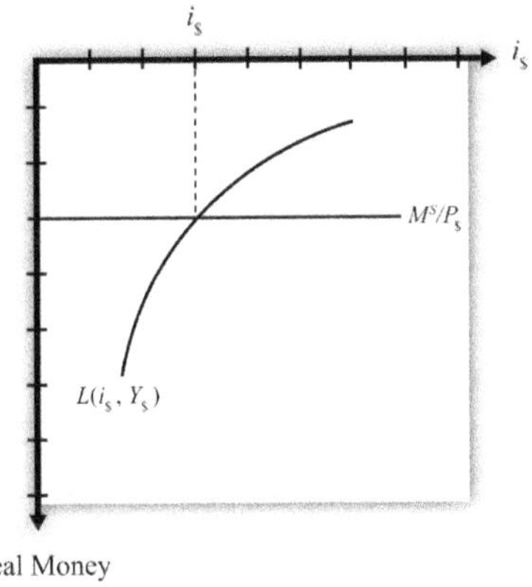

Figure 7.7 Ninety-Degree Rotation of the Money Market Diagram

Since the interest rate is identical to the rate of return on dollar assets from a U.S. dollar holder's perspective (i.e., $RoR_\$ = i_\$$), we can now place the RoR diagram directly on top of the rotated money market diagram as shown in Figure 7.8 "Money-Forex Diagram". The equilibrium interest rate ($i'_\$$), shown along the horizontal axis above the rotated money market diagram, determines the position of the $RoR_\$$ line in the Forex market above. This combined with the $RoR_£$ curve determines the equilibrium exchange rate, $E'_{\$/£}$, in the Forex market. We will call this diagram the "money-Forex diagram" and the combined model the "money-Forex model."

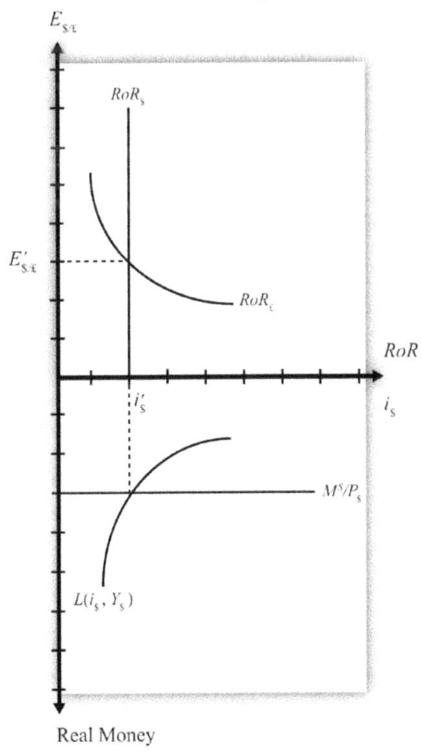

Figure 7.8 Money-Forex Diagram

KEY TAKEAWAY

- Using a two-quadrant diagram with appropriate adjustments, we can represent the equilibrium in the money market and the foreign exchange market simultaneously.

EXERCISE

- Jeopardy Questions: As in the popular television game show, you are given an answer to a question and you must respond with the question. For example, if the answer is "a tax on imports," then the correct question is "What is a tariff?"
- The value of this endogenous variable is used to determine the position of the U.S. rate of return line.
- In the money-Forex diagram, these are the two endogenous variables.
- In the money-Forex diagram, these are the five exogenous variables.

7.13 COMPARATIVE STATICS IN THE COMBINED FOREX AND MONEY MODEL

Comparative statics is any exercise examining how the endogenous variables will be affected when one of the exogenous variables is presumed to change, while holding all other exogenous variables constant. Holding other variables constant at their original values is the "ceteris paribus" assumption. We will do several such exercises here using the combined money-Forex market diagram.

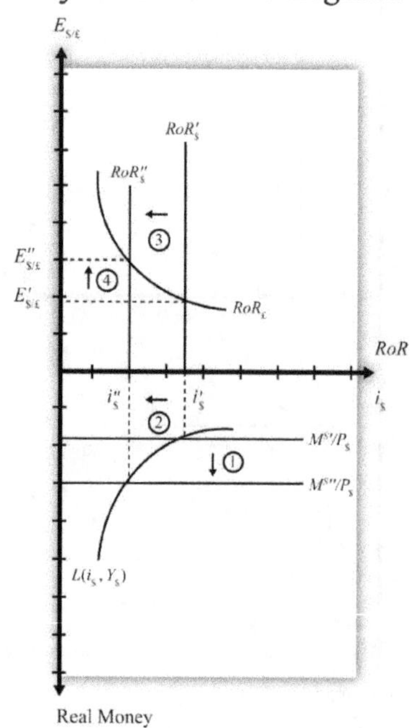

Figure 7.9 Effects of an Increase in the Money Supply

An Increase in the U.S. Money Supply

Suppose the U.S. money supply increases, ceteris paribus. The increase in M^S causes an increase in the real money supply (M^S/P\$), which causes the real money supply line to shift "down" from MS'/P\$ to MS"/P\$ (step 1) in the adjacent Money-Forex diagram, Figure 7.9 "Effects of an Increase in the Money Supply". (Be careful here: down in the diagram means an increase in the real money supply.) This causes a decrease in the equilibrium interest rate from i\$' to i\$" (step 2). The decrease in the U.S. interest rate causes a decrease in the rate of return on dollar assets: RoR\$ shifts from RoR\$' to RoR\$" (step 3). Finally, the reduction in the dollar rate of return causes an increase in the exchange rate from E'\$/£ to E"\$/£ (step 4). This exchange rate change corresponds to an appreciation of the British pound and a depreciation of the U.S. dollar. In summary, an increase in the U.S. money supply, ceteris paribus, causes a decrease in U.S. interest rates and a depreciation of the dollar.

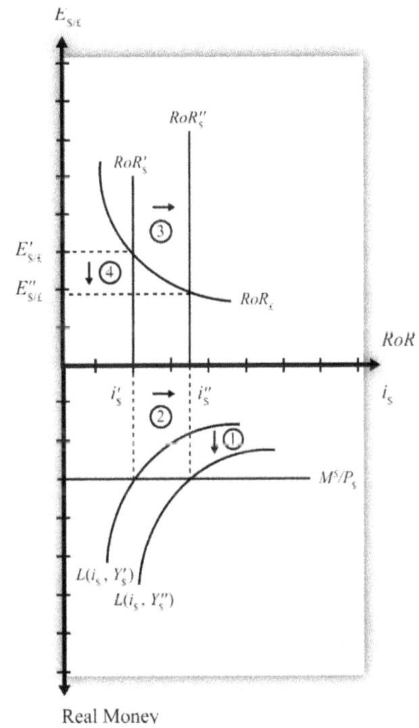

Figure 7.10 Effects of an Increase in GDP

An Increase in U.S. GDP

Suppose there is an increase in U.S. GDP, ceteris paribus. This will increase real money demand, causing a "downward" shift in the real money demand curve from $L(i_\$, Y_\$')$ to $L(i_\$, Y_\$'')$ (step 1) in the Money-Forex diagram, Figure 7.10 «Effects of an Increase in GDP». (Remember, real money increases as you move down on the rotated money diagram.) This causes an increase in the U.S. interest rate from $i_\$'$ to $i_\$''$ (step 2). The increase in the interest means that the rate of return on dollar assets increases from $RoR_\$'$ to $RoR_\$''$ (step 3). Finally, the increase in the U.S. RoR causes a decrease in the exchange rate from $E'_{\$/£}$ to $E''_{\$/£}$ (step 4). The exchange rate change corresponds to an appreciation of the U.S. dollar and a depreciation of the British pound. In summary, an increase in real U.S. GDP, ceteris paribus, causes an increase in U.S. interest rates and appreciation (depreciation) of the U.S. dollar (British pound).

KEY TAKEAWAYS

- In the money-Forex model, an increase in the U.S. money supply, ceteris paribus, causes a decrease in U.S. interest rates and a depreciation of the dollar.
- In the money-Forex model, an increase in real U.S. gross domestic product (GDP), ceteris paribus, causes an increase in U.S. interest rates and appreciation (depreciation) of the U.S. dollar (British pound).

EXERCISE

- Using the Forex market and money market models, indicate the effect of each change listed in the first row of the table, sequentially, on the variables listed in the first column. For example, "Expansionary U.S. Monetary Policy" will first cause an increase in the "Real U.S. Money Supply." Therefore, a "+" is placed in the first box of the table. In the next row, answer how "U.S. Interest Rates" will be affected. You do not need to show your work. Note $E_{\$/*}$ represents the dollar/foreign exchange rate. Use the following notation:

+ the variable increases

- the variable decreases

0 the variable does not change

A the variable change is ambiguous (i.e., it may rise, it may fall)

	Expansionary U.S. Monetary Policy	An Increase in U.S. Price Level	An Increase in U.S. Real GDP
Real U.S. Money Supply	+		
U.S. Interest Rates			
RoR on U.S. Assets			
Foreign Interest Rates			
RoR on Foreign Assets			
U.S. Dollar Value			
$E_{\$/*}$			

7.14 FINANCIAL SUPPLY AND LONG-TERM PRICES

In previous sections we assumed that price levels were given exogenously and were unaffected by changes in other variables. In this section, we will argue that money supply increases tend to have a positive effect on the price level and thus the rate of inflation in an economy. This effect is unlikely to occur quickly, instead arising over several months or years. For this reason, we will say the effect occurs in the long run. The magnitude of the price level effect is also greatly influenced by the level of unemployment in the economy. Unemployment affects the degree to which the money increase affects prices and the degree to which it affects output.

The easiest way to see the linkage between money supply and prices is to simplify the story by assuming output cannot change. We tell that in story 1. This assumption allows us to isolate the impact of money on prices alone. In the subsequent adjustment stories, we'll relax the fixed output assumption to show how money increases can also affect the level of output in an economy.

Story 1: Money Supply Increase with Extreme Full Employment

Here we'll consider the effects of a money supply increase assuming what I'll call "extreme full employment." Extreme full employment means that every person who wishes to work within the economy is employed. In addition, each working person is working the maximum number of hours that he or she is willing to work. In terms of capital usage, this too is assumed to be maximally employed. All machinery, equipment, office space, land, and so on that can be employed in production is currently being used. Extreme full employment describes a situation where it is physically impossible to produce any more output with the resources currently available.

Next, let's imagine the central bank increases the money supply by purchasing U.S. government Treasury bills (T-bills) in the open market. Suppose the transaction is made with a commercial bank that decides to sell some of its portfolio of Treasury bills to free reserves to make loans to businesses. The transaction transfers the T-bill certificate to the central bank in exchange for an accounting notation the central bank makes in the bank's reserve account. Since the transaction increases bank reserves without affecting bank deposits, the bank will now exceed its reserve requirement. Thus these new reserves are available for the bank to lend out.

Let's suppose the value of the T-bills transacted is $10 million. Suppose the bank decides to lend the $10 million to Ford Motor Corporation, which is planning to build a new corporate office building. When the loan is made, the bank will create a demand deposit account in Ford's name, which the company can use to pay its building expenses. Only after the creation of the $10 million demand deposit account is there an actual increase in the money supply.

With money in the bank, Ford will now begin the process of spending to construct the office building. This will involve hiring a construction company. However, Ford will now run into a problem given our assumption of extreme full employment. There are no construction companies available to begin construction on their building. All the construction workers and the construction equipment are already being used at their maximum capacity. There is no leeway.

Nonetheless, Ford has $10 million sitting in the bank ready to be spent and it wants its building started. So what can it do?

In this situation, the demand for construction services in the economy exceeds the supply. Profit-seeking construction companies that learn that Ford is seeking to begin building as soon as possible, can offer the following deal: "Pay us more than we are earning on our other construction projects and we'll stop working there and come over to build your building." Other construction companies may offer a similar deal. Once the companies, whose construction projects have already started, learn that their construction companies are considering abandoning them for a better offer from Ford, they will likely respond by increasing their payments to their construction crews to prevent them from fleeing to Ford. Companies that cannot afford to raise their payments will be the ones that must cease their construction, and their construction company will flee to Ford. Note that another assumption we must make for this story to work is that there are no enforceable contracts between the construction company and its client. If there were, a company that flees to Ford will find itself being sued for breach of contract. Indeed, this is one of the reasons why contracts are necessary. If all works out perfectly, the least productive construction projects will cease operations since these companies are the ones that are unwilling to raise their wages to keep the construction firm from fleeing.

Once Ford begins construction with its newly hired construction company, several effects are noteworthy. First, Ford's construction company will be working the same amount of time and producing the same amount of output, though for a different client. However, Ford's payments to the construction company are higher now. This means some workers or owners in the construction company are going home with a fatter paycheck. Other construction companies are also receiving higher payments so wages and rents will likely be higher for them as well.

Other companies that have hired the construction firms now face a dilemma, however. Higher payments have to come from somewhere. These firms may respond by increasing the prices of their products for their customers. For example, if this other firm is Coca-Cola, which must now pay higher prices to complete its construction project, it most probably will raise the price of Coke to pay for its higher overall production costs. Hence increases in wages and rents to construction companies will begin to cause increases in market prices of other products, such as Coke, televisions, computers, and so on.

At the same time, workers and owners of the construction companies with higher wages will undoubtedly spend more. Thus they will go out and demand more restaurant meals, cameras, and dance lessons and a whole host of other products. The restaurants, camera makers, and dance companies will experience a slight increase in demand for their products. However, due to the assumption of extreme full employment, they have no ability to increase their supply in response to the increase in demand. Thus these companies will do what the profit-seeking construction companies did before...they will raise their prices.

Thus price increases will begin to ripple through the economy as the extra money enters the circular flow, resulting in demand increases. As prices for final products begin to rise, workers may begin to demand higher wages to keep up with the rising cost of living. These wage increases will in turn lead firms to raise the prices of their outputs, leading to another round of increases in wages and prices. This process is known as the wage-price spiral.

Nowhere in this process can there ever be more production or output. That's because of our assumption of extreme full employment. We have assumed it is physically impossible to produce any more. For this reason, the only way for the market to reach a new equilibrium with aggregate supply equal to aggregate demand is for prices for most inputs and outputs to rise. In other words, the money supply increase must result in an increase in average prices (i.e., the price level) in the economy. Another way of saying this is that money supply increases are inflationary.

The increase in prices will not occur immediately. It will take time for the construction companies to work out their new payment scheme. It will take more time for them to receive their extra wages and rents and begin spending them. It will take more time, still, for the restaurants and camera makers and others to respond to higher demands. And it will take even more time for workers to respond to the increases in prices and to demand higher wages. The total time may be several years before an economy can get back to equilibrium. For this reason, we think about this money supply effect on the price level as a long-run effect. In other words, we say an increase in the money supply will lead to an increase in the price level in the long run.

Inflation arises whenever there is too much money chasing too few goods. This effect is easy to recognize in this example since output does not change when the money supply increases. So, in this example, there is more money chasing the same quantity of output. Inflation can also arise if there is less output given a fixed amount of money. This is an effect seen in the transition economies of the former Soviet Union. After the breakdown of the political system in the early 1990s, output dropped precipitously, while money in circulation remained much the same. The outcome was a very rapid inflation. In these cases, it was the same amount of money chasing fewer goods.

Story 2: Money Supply Increase with High Unemployment

In this story, we relax the assumption of extreme full employment and assume instead that there is a very high rate of unemployment in the economy. This example will show how money supply increases can affect national output as well as prices.

Suppose there is a money supply increase as in the previous story. When Ford Motor Company goes out looking for a construction company to hire, there is now an important new possibility. Since unemployment is very high, it is likely that most construction companies are not operating at their full capacity. Some companies may have laid off workers in the recent past due to a lack of demand. The construction company that wins the Ford contract will not have to give up other construction projects. Instead, it can simply expand output by hiring unemployed workers and capital. Because there is a ready and waiting source of inputs, even at the original wage and rental rates, there is no need for the construction company to charge Ford more than current prices for its services. Thus there is no pressure to increase wages or the prices of construction services.

It is true, there is more money being paid out in wages by this company, and the new workers will go out and spend that money, leading to an increase in demand for restaurant services, cameras, dance lessons, and other products. These companies are also likely to respond by hiring more workers and idle equipment to provide more restaurant meals, cameras, and dance lessons. Here too, with a ready and willing source of new inputs from the ranks of the unemployed, these companies will not have an incentive to raise wages, rents, or prices. Instead, they will provide more output of goods and services.

Thus as the increase in money ripples through the economy, it will stimulate demand for a wide variety of products. However, because of high unemployment, the money supply increase need not result in higher prices. Instead, national output increases and the unemployment rate falls.

A comparison of stories 1 and 2 highlights the importance of the unemployment rate in determining the extent to which a money supply increase will be inflationary. In general, we can conclude that an increase in the money supply will raise the domestic price level to a larger degree in the long run, thus lowering the unemployment rate of labor and capital.

Natural Rate of Unemployment

Economists typically say that an economy is at full employment output when the unemployment rate is at the natural rate. The natural rate is defined as the rate that does not cause inflationary pressures in the economy. It is a rate that allows for common transitions that characterize labor markets. For example, some people are currently unemployed because they have recently finished school and are looking for their first job. Some are unemployed because they have quit one job and are in search of another. Some people have decided to move to another city, and are unemployed during the transition. Finally, some people may have lost a job in a company that has closed or downsized and may spend a few weeks or months in search of their next job.

These types of transitions are always occurring in the labor market and are known as frictional (or transitional) unemployment. When employment surveys are conducted each month, they will always identify a group of people unemployed for these reasons. They count as unemployed, since they are all actively seeking work. However, they all will need some time to find a job. As one group of unemployed workers find employment, others will enter the unemployment ranks. Thus there is a constant turnover of people in this group and thus a natural unemployment rate. This type of unemployment is also called frictional, or transitional, unemployment. It is distinguished from a second type called structural unemployment. Structural unemployment occurs when there is a change in the structure of production in an economy. For example, if the textile and apparel industry closes down and moves abroad, the workers with skills specific to the industry and the capital equipment designed for use in the industry will not be employable in other sectors. These workers and capital may remain unemployed for a longer period of time, or may never find alternative employment.

There is no simple way to measure the natural rate of unemployment. It will likely vary with economic conditions and the fluidity of the labor market. Nonetheless, economists estimate the natural rate of unemployment to be around 5 percent in the United States today.

When economists talk about the inflationary effect of money supply increases, they typically refer to the natural rate of unemployment. A money supply increase will likely be inflationary when the unemployment rate is below the natural rate. In contrast, inflationary effects of money supply increases are reduced if the economy has unemployment above the natural rate. Here's how the story would work.

Story 3: Money Supply Increase above and below the Natural Unemployment Rate

Suppose there is a money supply increase as in the previous story, but now let's assume the economy is operating above full employment, meaning that unemployment is below its natural rate.

As the money supply increase ripples through the economy causing excess demand, as described above, businesses have some leeway to expand output. Since unemployment is not zero, they can look to hire unemployed workers and expand output. However, as frictional unemployment decreases, the labor market will pick up speed. Graduating students looking for their first job will find one quickly. Workers moving to another job will also find one quickly. In an effort to get the best workers, firms may begin to raise their wage offers. Workers in transition may quickly find themselves entertaining several job offers, rather than just one. These workers will begin to demand higher wages. Ultimately, higher wages and rents will result in higher output prices, which in turn will inspire demands for higher wages. Thus despite the existence of some unemployment, the money supply increase may increase output slightly but it is also likely to be inflationary.

In contrast, suppose the economy were operating with unemployment above the natural rate. In this case, the increase in demand caused by a money supply increase is likely to have a more significant effect upon output. As firms try to expand output, they will face a much larger pool of potential employees. Competition by several workers for one new job will put power back in the hands of the company, allowing it to hire the best quality worker without having to raise its wage offer to do so. Thus, in general, output will increase more and prices will increase less, if at all. Thus the money supply increase is less likely to be inflationary in the long run when the economy is operating above the natural rate of unemployment.

KEY TAKEAWAYS

- Inflation arises whenever there is too much money chasing too few goods.
- A money supply increase will lead to increases in aggregate demand for goods and services.
- A money supply increase will tend to raise the price level in the long run.
- A money supply increase may also increase national output.
- A money supply increase will raise the price level more and national output less the lower the unemployment rate of labor and capital is.
- A money supply increase will raise national output more and the price level less the higher the unemployment rate of labor and capital is.
- The natural rate of unemployment is the rate that accounts for frictional unemployment. It is also defined as the rate at which there are no aggregate inflationary pressures.
- If a money supply increase drives an economy below the natural rate of unemployment, price level increases will tend to be large while output increases will tend to be small.
- If a money supply increase occurs while an economy is above the natural rate of unemployment, price level increases will tend to be small while output increases will tend to be large.

EXERCISE

- Jeopardy Questions: As in the popular television game show, you are given an answer to a question and you must respond with the question. For example, if the answer is "a tax on imports," then the correct question is "What is a tariff?"
- The term coined in this text for the situation when everybody who wishes to work is employed.
- The term used to describe how increases in output prices lead to increases in wages, which further cause output prices to rise ad infinitum.
- The term for the unemployment rate at which there is no inflationary or deflationary pressure on average prices.
- The term for the level of GDP in an economy when the unemployment rate is at its natural level.
- The term used to describe the type of unemployment that arises because of the typical adjustments of workers into, out of, and between jobs in an economy.
- The likely larger long-run effect of a money supply increase when an economy has unemployment below the natural rate.
- The likely larger long-run effect of a money supply increase when an economy has unemployment above the natural rate.

CHAPTER

DETERMINATION OF NATIONAL OUTPUT

8

INTRODUCTION

In most introductory macroeconomics courses, the basic Keynesian model is presented as a way of showing how government spending and taxation policies can influence the size of a country's growth national product (GNP). This chapter revisits the basic Keynesian model but adds an international angle by including impacts on domestic demand for goods and services caused by changes in the exchange rate. With this relationship in place, the chapter concludes with several comparative statics exercises showing how changes in key variables may influence the level of GNP.

8.1 NATIONAL OUTPUT DETERMINATION: AN OVERVIEW

This chapter describes how the supply and demand for the national output of goods and services combine to determine the equilibrium level of national output for an economy. The model is called the goods and services market model, or just the G&S market model.

In this model, we use gross national product (GNP) as the measure of national output rather than gross domestic product (GDP). This adjustment is made because we wish to define the trade balance (EX - IM) as the current account (defined as the difference between exports and imports of goods, services incomes payments/receipts, and unilateral transfers). This adjustment is discussed in more detail in Section 8.6 .

The diagram used to display this model is commonly known as the Keynesian cross. The model assumes, for simplicity, that the amount of national output produced by an economy is determined by the total amount demanded. Thus if, for some reason, the demand for GNP were to rise, then the amount of GNP supplied would rise up to satisfy it. If demand for the GNP falls—for whatever reason—then supply of GNP would also fall. Consequently, it is useful to think of this model as "demand driven."

The model is developed by identifying the key determinants of GNP demand. The starting point is the national income identity, which states that

$$GNP = C + I + G + EX - IM,$$

that is, the gross national product is the sum of consumption expenditures (C), investment expenditures (I), government spending (G), and exports (EX) minus imports (IM).

Note that the identity uses GNP rather than GDP if we define EX and IM to include income payments, income receipts, and unilateral transfers as well as goods and services trade.

We rewrite this relationship as

$$AD = C^{D + ID + GD + EXD - IMD},$$

where AD refers to aggregate demand for the GNP and the right-side variables are now read as consumption demand, investment demand, and so on. The model further assumes that consumption demand is positively related to changes in disposable income (Y_d). Furthermore, since disposable income is in turn negatively related to taxes and positively related to transfer payments, these additional variables can also affect aggregate demand.

The model also assumes that demand on the current account ($CA^D = EX^D - IM^D$) is negatively related to changes in the domestic real currency value (i.e., the real exchange rate) and changes in disposable income. Furthermore, since the domestic real currency value is negatively related to the domestic price level (inflation) and positively related to the foreign price level, these variables will also affect current account demand.

Using the G&S market model, several important relationships between key economic variables are shown:

- When government demand (G) or investment demand (I) for G&S rises (falls), equilibrium GNP rises (falls).
- When disposable income rises (falls) due to a decrease (increase) in taxes or an increase (decrease) in transfer payments, equilibrium GNP increases (decreases).
- When the real exchange rate depreciates (appreciates), either due to a depreciation of the nominal exchange rate, an increase in the domestic price level, or a decrease in the foreign price level, equilibrium GNP rises (falls).

Connections

The G&S market model connects with the money market because the value of GNP determined in the G&S model affects money demand. If equilibrium GNP rises in the G&S model, then money demand will rise, causing an increase in the interest rate.

The G&S model also connects with the foreign exchange (Forex) market. The equilibrium exchange rate determined in the Forex affects the real exchange rate that in turn influences demand on the current account.

A thorough discussion of these interrelationships is given in Chapter 9 "The AA-DD Model".

Omissions

There is one important relationship omitted in this version of the G&S model, and that is the relationship between interest rates and investment. In most standard depictions of the Keynesian G&S model, it is assumed that increases (decreases) in interest rates will reduce (increase) demand for investment. In this version of the model, to keep things simple, investment is assumed to be exogenous (determined in an external process) and unrelated to the level of interest rates.

Some approaches further posit that interest rates affect consumption demand as well. This occurs because household borrowing, to buy new cars or other consumer items, will tend to rise as interest rates fall. However, this relationship is also not included in this model.

KEY TAKEAWAYS

- The Keynesian, or G&S, model of output determination is a demand-driven model in that the amount of national output produced by an economy is determined by the total amount demanded.
- One important relationship omitted in this version of the G&S model is the lack of a relationship between interest rates and investment.
- The main results from the G&S model are the following:
- When government demand (G) or investment demand (I) for G&S rises (falls), equilibrium GNP rises (falls).
- When disposable income rises (falls) due to a decrease (increase) in taxes or an increase (decrease) in transfer payments, equilibrium GNP increases (decreases).
- When the real exchange rate depreciates (appreciates), either due to a depreciation of the nominal exchange rate, an increase in the domestic price level, or a decrease in the foreign price level, equilibrium GNP rises (falls).

EXERCISE

- Jeopardy Questions:As in the popular television game show, you are given an answer to a question and you must respond with the question. For example, if the answer is "a tax on imports," then the correct question is "What is a tariff?"

- In the Keynesian, or G&S, model, this is the primary determinant of aggregate supply.
- Of increase, decrease, or stay the same, this is the effect on equilibrium GNP if government spending decreases in the G&S model.
- Of increase, decrease, or stay the same, this is the effect on equilibrium GNP if investment spending increases in the G&S model.
- Of increase, decrease, or stay the same, this is the effect on equilibrium GNP if tax revenue decreases in the G&S model.
- Of increase, decrease, or stay the same, this is the effect on equilibrium GNP if transfer payments increase in the G&S model.
- Of increase, decrease, or stay the same, this is the effect on equilibrium GNP if the domestic currency depreciates in the G&S model.
- Of increase, decrease, or stay the same, this is the effect on equilibrium GNP if the domestic price level decreases in the G&S model.
- Of increase, decrease, or stay the same, this is the effect on equilibrium GNP if the foreign price level decreases in the G&S model.

8.2 DEMAND FOR GOODS AND SERVICES OVERALL

The Keynesian model of aggregate demand for goods and services is developed by identifying key determinants of demand for the national output. When we talk about aggregate demand (AD), it means demand by households, businesses, and the government for anything and everything produced within the economy. The starting point is the national income identity, which states that

$$GNP = C + I + G + EX - IM,$$

that is, the gross national product is the sum of consumption expenditures, investment expenditures, government spending, and exports minus imports of goods and services.

We rewrite this relationship as

$$AD = C^{D + ID + GD + EXD - IMD,}$$

where the left side, AD, refers to aggregate demand for the GNP and the right-side variables are read as consumption demand, investment demand, and so on. Determinants of the right-side variables will be considered in turn.

It is important to remember that demand is merely what households, businesses, and the government "would like" to purchase given the conditions that exist in the economy. Sometimes demand will be realized, as when the economy is in equilibrium, but sometimes demand will not be satisfied. On the other hand, the variable Y, for real GNP, represents the aggregate supply of G&S. This will correspond to the actual GNP whether in equilibrium or not.

Next, we'll present the determinants of each demand term: consumption, investment, government, and export and import demand.

KEY TAKEAWAY

In the G&S model, aggregate demand for the GNP is the sum of consumption demand, investment demand, government demand, and current account demand.

EXERCISE

- Jeopardy Questions: As in the popular television game show, you are given an answer to a question and you must respond with the question. For example, if the answer is "a tax on imports," then the correct question is "What is a tariff?"
- In the G&S model, the variable Y stands for this.
- In the G&S model, the variable AD stands for this.
- In the G&S model, the variable I^D stands for this.
- In the G&S model, the variable EX^D stands for this.
- In the G&S model, the variable CA^D stands for this.

8.3 CONSUMPTION DEMAND

Consumption demand represents the demand for goods and services by individuals and households in the economy. This is the major category in the national income accounts for most countries, typically comprising from 50 percent to 70 percent of the gross national product (GNP) for most countries.

In this model, the main determinant of consumption demand is disposable income. Disposable income is all the income households have at their disposal to spend. It is defined as national income (GNP) minus taxes taken away by the government, plus transfer payments that the government pays out to people. More formally, this is written as

$$Y_d = Y - T + TR,$$

where Y_d refers to disposable income, Y is real GNP, T is taxes, and TR represents transfer payments.

In this relationship, disposable income is defined in the same way as in the circular flow diagram presented in Chapter 2 , Section 2.7. Recall that taxes withdrawn from GNP are assumed to be all taxes collected by the government from all sources. Thus income taxes, social insurance taxes, profit taxes, sales taxes, and property taxes are all assumed to be included in taxes (T). Also, transfer payments refer to all payments made by the government that do not result in the provision of a good or service. All social insurance payments, welfare payments, and unemployment compensation, among other things, are included in transfers (TR).

In the G&S model, demand for consumption G&S is assumed to be positively related to disposable income. This means that when disposable income rises, demand for consumption G&S will also rise, and vice versa. This makes sense since households who have more money to spend will quite likely wish to buy more G&S.

We can write consumption demand in a functional form as follows:

This expression says that consumption demand is a function C^D that depends positively (+) on disposable income (Y_d). The second term simply substitutes the variables that define disposable income in place of Y_d. It is a more complete way of writing the function. Note well that C^D here denotes a function, not a variable. The expression is the same as if we had written f(x), but instead we substitute a C^D for the f and Y_d for the x.

It is always important to keep track of which variables are exogenous and which are endogenous. In this model, real GNP (Y) is the key endogenous variable since it will be determined in the equilibrium. Taxes (T) and transfer payments (TR) are exogenous variables, determined outside the model. Since consumption demand C^D is dependent on the value of Y, which is endogenous, C^D is also endogenous. By the same logic, Y_d is endogenous as well.

Linear Consumption Function

It is common in most introductory textbooks to present the consumption function in linear form. For our purposes here, this is not absolutely necessary, but doing so will allow us to present a few important points.

In linear form, the consumption function is written as

Here C_0 represents autonomous consumption and mpc refers to the marginal propensity to consume.

Autonomous consumption (C_0) is the amount of consumption that would be demanded even if income were zero. (Autonomous simply means "independent" of income.) Graphically, it corresponds to the y-intercept of the linear function. Autonomous consumption will be positive since households will spend some money (drawing on savings if necessary) to purchase consumption goods (like food) even if income were zero.

The marginal propensity to consume (mpc) represents the additional (or marginal) demand for G&S given an additional dollar of disposable income. Graphically, it corresponds to the slope of the consumption function. This variable must be in the range of zero to one and is most likely to be between 0.5 and 0.8 for most economies. If mpc were equal to one, then households would spend every additional dollar of income. However, because most households put some of their income into savings (i.e., into the bank, or pensions), not every extra dollar of income will lead to a dollar increase in consumption demand. That fraction of the dollar not used for consumption but put into savings is called the marginal propensity to save (mps). Since each additional dollar must be spent or saved, the following relationship must hold:

mpc + mps = 1,

that is, the sum of the marginal propensity to consume and the marginal propensity to save must equal 1.

KEY TAKEAWAYS

- In the G&S model, consumption demand is determined by disposable income.
- A linear consumption function includes the marginal propensity to consume and an autonomous consumption component, besides disposable income.
- Disposable income is defined as national income (GNP) minus taxes plus transfer payments.
- An increase (decrease) in disposable income will cause an increase (decrease) in consumption demand.
- An increase (decrease) in the marginal propensity to consume will cause an increase (decrease) in consumption demand.

EXERCISE

1. Jeopardy Questions: As in the popular television game show, you are given an answer to a question and you must respond with the question. For example, if the answer is "a tax on imports," then the correct question is "What is a tariff?"
2. The term that represents the additional amount of consumption demand caused by an additional dollar of disposable income.
3. The term that represents the additional amount of saving caused by an additional dollar of disposable income.
4. The term for the amount of consumption demand that would arise even if disposable income were zero.
5. Of positive or negative, the relationship between changes in disposable income and changes in consumption demand.
6. Of positive or negative, the relationship between changes in tax revenues and changes in consumption demand.
7. Of positive or negative, the relationship between changes in real GNP and changes in consumption demand.
8. A household purchase of a refrigerator would represent demand recorded in this component of aggregate demand in the G&S model.

8.4 INVESTMENT DEMAND

Investment demand refers to the demand by businesses for physical capital goods and services used to maintain or expand its operations. Think of it as the office and factory space, machinery, computers, desks, and so on that are used to operate a business. It is important to remember that investment demand here does not refer to financial investment. Financial investment is a form of saving, typically by households that wish to maintain or increase their wealth by deferring consumption till a later time.

In this model, investment demand will be assumed to be exogenous. This means that its value is determined outside of the model and is not dependent on any variable within the model. This assumption is made primarily to simplify the analysis and to allow the focus to be on exchange rate changes later. The simple equation for investment demand can be written as

$$I^D = I_0,$$

where the "0," or naught, subscript on the right side indicates that the variable is exogenous or autonomous. In words, the equation says that investment demand is given exogenously as I_0.

Admittedly, this is not a realistic assumption. In many other macro models, investment demand is assumed to depend on two other aggregate variables: GNP and interest rates. GNP may affect investment demand since the total demand for business expansion is more likely the higher the total size of the economy. The growth rate of GNP may also be an associated determinant since the faster GNP is growing, the more likely companies will predict better business in the future, inspiring more investment.

Interest rates can affect investment demand because many businesses must borrow money to finance expansions. The interest rate is the cost of borrowing money; thus, the higher the interest rates are, the lower the investment demand should be, and vice versa.

If we included the GNP and interest rate effects into the model, the solution to the extended model later would prove to be much more difficult. Thus we simplify things by assuming that investment is exogenous. Since many students have learned about the GNP and interest rate effect in previous courses, you need to remember that these effects are not a part of this model.

KEY TAKEAWAYS

- In the G&S model, investment demand is assumed to be exogenous, meaning not dependent on any other variable within the model such as GNP or interest rates.
- The omission of an effect by GNP and interest rates on investment demand is made to simplify the model.

EXERCISE

1. Jeopardy Questions: As in the popular television game show, you are given an answer to a question and you must respond with the question. For example, if the answer is "a tax on imports," then the correct question is "What is a tariff?"
2. Term for a type of investment by households that wish to maintain or increase their wealth by deferring consumption till a later time.
3. Investment demand refers to this type of goods and services.
4. Of exogenous or endogenous, this describes investment demand in the G&S model in the text.
5. The name of two variables that are likely to influence investment demand in reality but are excluded from the G&S model as a simplification.
6. A business purchase of a company delivery van would represent demand recorded in this component of aggregate demand in the G&S model.

8.5 GOVERNMENT DEMAND

Government demand refers to the government's demand for goods and services produced in the economy. In some cases this demand is for G&S produced by private businesses, as when the government purchases a naval aircraft. Other government demand is actually produced by the government itself, as what occurs with teachers providing educational services in the public schools. All levels of government demand—federal, state, and local—are included in this demand term. Excluded are transfer payments such as social insurance, welfare assistance, and unemployment compensation.

In this model, government demand is treated the same way as investment demand: it is assumed to be exogenous. This means that its value is determined outside of the model and is not dependent on any variable within the model. A simple equation for government demand can be written as

$G^D = G_0$,

where the "0," or naught, subscript on the right side indicates that the variable is exogenous or autonomous. In words, the equation says that government demand is given exogenously as G_0.

This is a more common assumption in many other macro models, even though one could argue dependencies of government demand on GNP and interest rates. However, these linkages are not likely to be as strong as with investment, thus assuming exogeneity here is a more realistic assumption than with investment.

KEY TAKEAWAY

In the G&S model, government demand is assumed to be exogenous, meaning not dependent on any other variable within the model such as GNP or interest rates.

EXERCISE

1. Jeopardy Questions: As in the popular television game show, you are given an answer to a question and you must respond with the question. For example, if the answer is "a tax on imports," then the correct question is "What is a tariff?"
2. These three levels of government demand are included in G^D in the G&S model.
3. This type of government expenditure is not included in G^D in the G&S model.
4. Of exogenous or endogenous, this describes government demand in the G&S model in the text.
5. An expenditure by a state school system on teachers' salaries would represent demand recorded in this component of aggregate demand in the G&S model.

8.6 EXPORT AND IMPORT DEMAND

Export demand refers to the demand by foreign countries for G&S produced domestically. Ultimately, these goods are exported to foreign residents. Import demand refers to demand by domestic residents for foreign-produced G&S. Imported G&S are not a part of domestic GNP. Recall from Chapter 2 , Section 2.3 that imports are subtracted from the national income identity because they are included as a part of consumption, investment, and government expenditures as well as in exports. Likewise in this model, consumption, investment, government, and export demand are assumed to include demand for imported goods. Thus imports must be subtracted to assure that only domestically produced G&S are included.

We will define current account demand as $CA^D = EX^D - IM^D$. The key determinants of current account demand in this model are assumed to be the domestic real currency value and disposable income.

First, let's define the real currency value, then show how it relates to the demand for exports and imports. The real British pound value in terms of U.S. dollars (also called the real exchange rate between dollars and pounds), $RE_{\$/£}$, is a measure of the cost of a market basket of goods abroad relative to the cost of a similar basket domestically. It captures differences in prices, converted at the spot exchange rate, between the domestic country and the rest of the world. It is defined as

where $E_{\$/£}$ is the spot exchange rate, $CB_£$ is the cost of a market basket of goods in Britain, and $CB_\$$ is the cost of a comparable basket of goods in the United States. The top expression, $E_{\$/£} CB_£$, represents the cost of a British market basket of goods converted to U.S. dollars. Thus if $RE_{\$/£} > 1$, then a British basket of goods costs more than a comparable U.S. basket of goods. If $RE_{\$/£} < 1$, then a U.S. basket of goods costs more than a British basket. Also note that $RE_{\$/£}$ is a unitless number. If $RE_{\$/£} = 2$, for example, it means that British goods cost twice as much as U.S. goods, on average, at the current spot exchange rate.

Note that we could also have defined the reciprocal real exchange rate, $RE_{£/\$}$. This real exchange rate is the real value of the pound in terms of U.S. dollars.

Since the real exchange rate can be defined in two separate ways between any two currencies, it can be confusing to say things like "the real exchange rate rises" since the listener may not know which real exchange rate the speaker has in mind. Thus it is always preferable to say the real dollar value rises, or the real pound value falls, since this eliminates any potential confusion. In this text, I will always adhere to the convention of writing the spot exchange rate and the real exchange rate with the U.S. dollar in the numerator. Thus references to the real exchange rate in this text will always refer to that form.

Since the cost of a market basket of goods is used to create a country's price index, changes in CB will move together with changes in the country's price level P. For this reason, it is common to rewrite the real exchange rate using price levels rather than costs of market baskets and to continue to interpret the expression in the same way. For more information related to this, see Chapter 6 , Section 6.2. We will follow that convention here and rewrite $RE_{\$/£}$ as

where $P_£$ is the British price index and $P_\$$ is the U.S. price index. From this point forward, we'll mean this expression whenever we discuss the real exchange rate.

Next, we'll discuss the connection to current account demand. To understand the relationship it is best to consider a change in the real exchange rate. Suppose $RE_{\$/£}$ rises. This means that the real value of the pound rises and, simultaneously, the real U.S. dollar value falls. This also means that goods and services are becoming relatively more expensive, on average, in Britain compared to the United States.

Relatively cheaper G&S in the United States will tend to encourage U.S. exports since the British would prefer to buy some cheaper products in the United States. Similarly, relatively more expensive British G&S will tend to discourage U.S. imports from Britain. Since U.S. exports will rise and imports will fall with an increase in the real U.S. dollar value, current account demand, $CA^D = EX^D - IM^D$, will rise. Similarly, if the real U.S. dollar value falls, U.S. exports will fall and imports rise, causing a decrease in CA^D. Hence, there is a positive relationship between this real exchange rate (i.e., the real value of the pound) and U.S. current account demand.

Disposable income can also affect the current account demand. In this case, the effect is through imports. An increase in disposable income means that households have more money to spend. Some fraction of this will be consumed, the marginal propensity to consume, and some fraction of that consumption will be for imported goods. Thus an increase in disposable income should result in an increase in imports and a subsequent reduction in current account demand. Thus changes in disposable income are negatively related to current account demand.

We can write current account demand in functional form as follows:

The expression indicates that current account demand is a function of $RE_{\$/£}$ and Y_d. The "+" sign above $RE_{\$/£}$ indicates the positive relationship between the real exchange rate (as defined) and current account demand. The "-" sign above the disposable income term indicates a negative relationship with current account demand.

KEY TAKEAWAYS

- The key determinants of current account demand in the G&S model are assumed to be the domestic real currency value and disposable income.
- The real exchange rate captures differences in prices, converted at the spot exchange rate, between the domestic country and the rest of the world.
- In the G&S model, there is a positive relationship between the real exchange rate (as defined) and current account demand and a negative relationship between disposable income and current account demand.

EXERCISE

- Jeopardy Questions: As in the popular television game show, you are given an answer to a question and you must respond with the question. For example, if the answer is "a tax on imports," then the correct question is "What is a tariff?"
- Of positive or negative, the relationship between changes in the domestic price level and the real value of the domestic currency.
- Of positive or negative, the relationship between changes in the foreign price level and the real value of the domestic currency.
- Of positive or negative, the relationship between changes in the nominal value of the domestic currency and the real value of the domestic currency.
- Of increase, decrease, or stay the same, the effect of a real appreciation of the domestic currency on current account demand in the G&S model.
- Of increase, decrease, or stay the same, the effect of a depreciation of the domestic currency on current account demand in the G&S model.
- Of increase, decrease, or stay the same, the effect of an increase in the domestic price level on current account demand in the G&S model.
- Of increase, decrease, or stay the same, the effect of an increase in the foreign price level on current account demand in the G&S model.
- Of increase, decrease, or stay the same, the effect of a decrease in real GNP on current account demand in the G&S model.

1. An expenditure by a domestic business for a microscope sold by a Swiss firm would represent demand recorded in this component of aggregate demand in the G&S model.
2. An expenditure by a foreign business for a microscope sold by a U.S. firm would represent demand recorded in this component of aggregate demand in the G&S model.

8.7 THE COMBINED DEMAND FUNCTION

Notice that the right side indicates that if disposable income were to rise, consumption demand would rise but current account demand, which is negatively related to disposable income, would fall. This would seem to make ambiguous the effect of a disposable income change on aggregate demand. However, by thinking carefully about the circular flow definitions, we can recall that consumption expenditures consist of the sum of expenditures on domestically produced goods and imported goods. This was the reason imports are subtracted away in the national income identity. This also means that the marginal propensity to spend on imported goods must be lower than the total marginal propensity to consume, again since imports are a fraction of total consumption spending. This implies that the negative effect on imports from a $1 increase in disposable income must be less than the positive impact on consumption demand.

We indicate the net positive effect on aggregate demand of changes in disposable income with the "+" sign above Y_d on the left-hand side. The positive impact of changes in the real exchange rate, investment demand, and government demand is obvious and is also shown.

We can write the aggregate demand function in several different ways. To be more explicit, we can include all the fundamental variables affecting aggregate demand by writing out the disposable income and real exchange rate terms as follows:

Writing the expression in this way allows us to indicate that the spot exchange rate, the price levels domestically and abroad, and domestic taxes and transfer payments also affect aggregate demand. For example, increases in autonomous transfer payments will raise aggregate demand since it raises disposable income, which in turn raises demand. Increases in taxes, however, will lower disposable income, which in turn will lower aggregate demand. Similarly, an increase in the spot exchange rate (as defined) or the foreign price level will raise aggregate demand, since both changes will increase the real exchange rate. However, an increase in the domestic price level will reduce the real exchange rate (because it is in the denominator) and thus reduce aggregate demand.

KEY TAKEAWAY

- Aggregate demand is positively related to changes in disposable income, the real exchange rate (as defined), and investment and government demands.

EXERCISE

1. Jeopardy Questions: As in the popular television game show, you are given an answer to a question and you must respond with the question. For example, if the answer is "a tax on imports," then the correct question is "What is a tariff?"
2. Of increase, decrease, or stay the same, the effect of a real appreciation of the domestic currency on aggregate demand in the G&S model.

3. Of increase, decrease, or stay the same, the effect of an increase in investment demand on aggregate demand in the G&S model.
4. Of increase, decrease, or stay the same, the effect of an increase in disposable income on aggregate demand in the G&S model.
5. Of increase, decrease, or stay the same, the effect of an increase in income taxes on aggregate demand in the G&S model.
6. Of increase, decrease, or stay the same, the effect of an increase in government demand on aggregate demand in the G&S model.
7. Of increase, decrease, or stay the same, the effect of an increase in the real currency value on aggregate demand in the G&S model.
8. Of increase, decrease, or stay the same, the effect of an increase in the domestic price level on aggregate demand in the G&S model.

8.8 THE KEYNESIAN CROSS DIAGRAM

The Keynesian cross diagram depicts the equilibrium level of national income in the G&S market model. We begin with a plot of the aggregate demand function with respect to real GNP (Y) in Figure 8.1 "Aggregate Demand Function". Real GNP (Y) is plotted along the horizontal axis, and aggregate demand is measured along the vertical axis. The aggregate demand function is shown as the upward sloping line labeled AD(Y, ...). The (...) is meant to indicate that AD is a function of many other variables not listed. There are several important assumptions about the form of the AD function that are needed to assure an equilibrium. We discuss each assumption in turn.

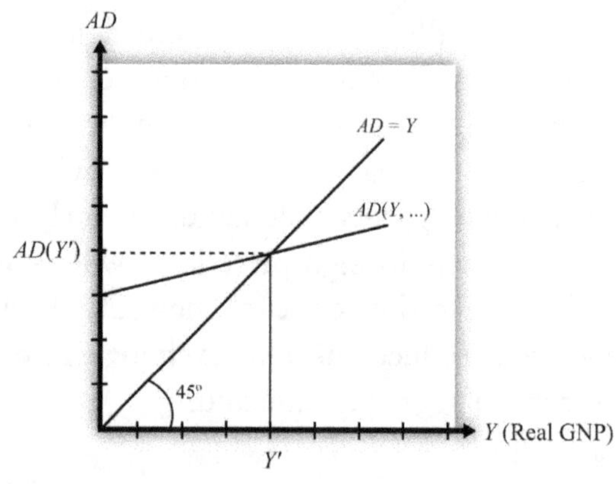

Figure 8.1 Aggregate Demand Function

First, the AD function is positively sloped with respect to changes in Y, ceteris paribus. Recall that ceteris paribus means that all other variables affecting aggregate demand are assumed to remain constant as GNP changes. The positive slope arises from the rationale given previously that an increase in disposable income should naturally lead to an increase in consumption demand and a smaller decrease in CA demand, resulting in a net increase in aggregate demand. Next, if GNP rises, ceteris paribus, it means that taxes and transfer payments remain fixed and disposable income must increase. Thus an increase in GNP leads to an increase in AD.

Second, the AD function has a positive vertical intercept term. In other words, the AD function crosses the vertical axis at a level greater than zero. For reasons that are not too important, this feature is critical for generating the equilibrium later. The reason it arises is because autonomous consumption, investment, and government demand are all assumed to be independent of income and positive in value. These assumptions guarantee a positive vertical intercept.

Third, the AD function has a slope that is less than one. This assumption means that for every $1 increase in GNP (Y), there is a less than $1 increase in aggregate demand. This arises because the marginal propensity to consume domestic GNP is less than one for two reasons. First, some of the additional income will be spent on imported goods, and second, some of the additional income will be saved. Thus the AD function will have a slope less than one.

Also plotted in the diagram is a line labeled AD = Y. This line is also sometimes called the forty-five-degree line since it sits at a forty-five-degree angle to the horizontal axis. This line represents all the points on the diagram where AD equals GNP. Since GNP can be thought of as aggregate supply, the forty-five-degree line contains all the points where AD equals aggregate supply.

Because of the assumptions about the shape and position of the AD function, AD will cross the forty-five-degree line, only once, from above. The intersection determines the equilibrium value of GNP, labeled Y′ in the diagram.

KEY TAKEAWAYS

1. The Keynesian cross diagram plots the aggregate demand function versus GNP together with a forty-five-degree line representing the set of points where AD = GNP. The intersection of these two lines represents equilibrium GNP in the economy.
2. An equilibrium exists if the AD function crosses the forty-five-degree line from above. This occurs if three conditions hold:
3. The AD function has a positive slope. (It does.)
4. The AD function has a slope less than one. (It does.)
5. The AD function intersects the vertical axis in the positive range. (It does.)

EXERCISE

- Jeopardy Questions: As in the popular television game show, you are given an answer to a question and you must respond with the question. For example, if the answer is "a tax on imports," then the correct question is "What is a tariff?"
- Of positive, negative, or zero, the slope of an aggregate demand function with respect to changes in real GNP.

- Of positive, negative, or zero, the value of the vertical intercept of an aggregate demand function.
- Of greater than one, less than one, or equal to one, the value of the slope of an aggregate demand function with respect to changes in real GNP.
- The equality that is satisfied on the forty-five-degree line in a Keynesian cross diagram.
- The value of this variable is determined at the intersection of the aggregate demand function and the forty-five-degree line in a Keynesian cross diagram.

8.9 GOODS AND SERVICES MARKET EQUILIBRIUM STORIES

Any equilibrium in economics has an associated behavioral story to explain the forces that will move the endogenous variable to the equilibrium value. In the G&S market model, the endogenous variable is Y, real GNP. This is the variable that will change to achieve the equilibrium. Variables that do not change in the adjustment to the equilibrium are the exogenous variables. In this model, the exogenous variables are I_0, G_0, T, TR, $E_{\$/£}$, $P_\$$, and $P_£$. (If one uses a linear consumption demand function, the C_0 and mpc are also exogenous.) Changes in the exogenous variables are necessary to cause an adjustment to a new equilibrium. However, in telling an equilibrium story, it is typical to simply assume that the endogenous variable is not at the equilibrium (for some unstated reason) and then to explain how and why the variable will adjust to the equilibrium value.

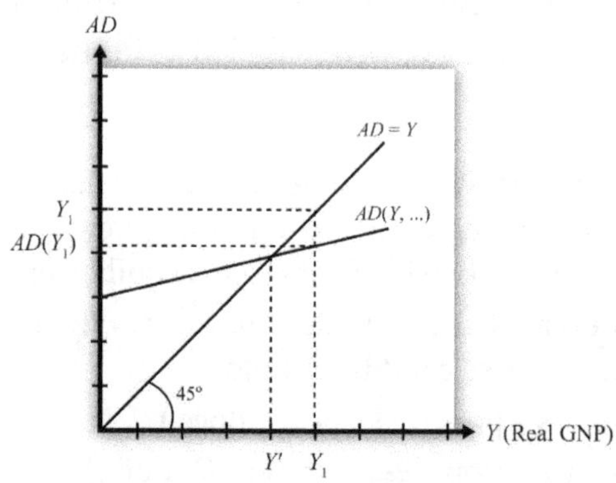

Figure 8.2 G&S Market Adjustment to Equilibrium: GNP Too High

GNP Too High

Suppose for some reason actual GNP, Y_1, is higher than the equilibrium GNP, Y', as shown in Figure 8.2 «G&S Market Adjustment to Equilibrium: GNP Too High». In this case, aggregate demand is read from the AD function as $AD(Y_1)$ along the vertical axis. We project aggregate supply, Y_1, to the vertical axis using the forty-five-degree line so that we can compare supply with demand. This helps us to see that $Y_1 > AD(Y_1)$—that is, aggregate supply is greater than aggregate demand.

We now tell what can be called the "Inventory Story." When total demand is less than supply, goods will begin to pile up on the shelves in stores. That's because at current prices (and all other fixed exogenous parameters), households, businesses, and government would prefer to buy less than what is available for sale. Thus inventories begin to rise. Merchants, faced with storerooms filling up, send orders for fewer goods to producers. Producers respond to fewer orders by producing less, and thus GNP begins to fall.

As GNP falls, disposable income also falls, which causes a drop in aggregate demand as well. In the diagram, this is seen as a movement along the AD curve from Y_1 to Y′. However, GNP falls at a faster rate, along the AD = Y line in the diagram. Eventually, the drop in aggregate supply catches up to the drop in demand when the equilibrium is reached at Y′. At this point, aggregate demand equals aggregate supply and there is no longer an accumulation of inventories.

It is important to recognize a common perception or intuition that does not hold in the equilibrium adjustment process. Many students imagine a case of rising inventories and ask, "Won't producers just lower their prices to get rid of the excess?" In real-world situations this will frequently happen; however, that response violates the ceteris paribus assumption of this model. We assume here that the U.S. price level ($P_\$$) and consequently all prices in the economy remain fixed in the adjustment to the new equilibrium. Later, with more elaborate versions of the model, some price flexibility is considered.

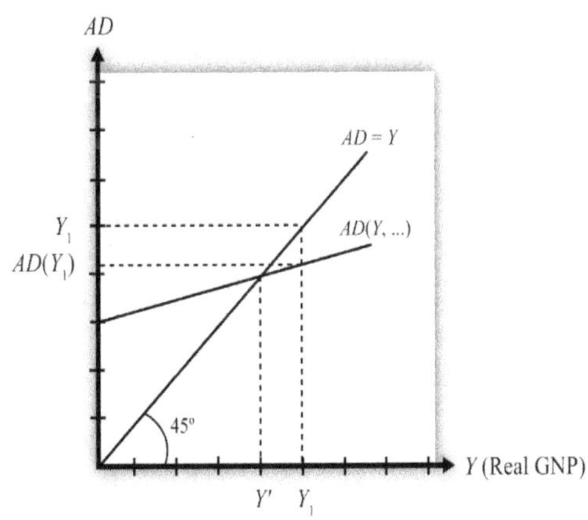

Figure 8.3 G&S Market Adjustment to Equilibrium: GNP Too Low

GNP Too Low

Suppose for some reason, actual GNP, Y2, is lower than the equilibrium GNP, Y, as shown in Figure 8.3 «G&S Market Adjustment to Equilibrium: GNP Too Low». In this case, aggregate demand is read from the AD function as AD(Y2) along the vertical axis. We project aggregate supply (Y2) to the vertical axis using the forty-five-degree line. This shows that AD(Y2) > Y2—that is, aggregate demand is greater than aggregate supply.

When total demand exceeds supply, inventories of goods that had previously been accumulated will begin to deplete in stores. That's because, at current prices (and all other fixed exogenous parameters), households, businesses, and government would prefer to buy more than is needed to keep stocks at a constant level. Merchants, faced with depleted inventories and the possibility of running out of goods to sell, send orders to producers for greater quantities of goods. Producers respond to more orders by producing more and thus GNP begins to rise.

As GNP rises, disposable income also rises, which causes an increase in aggregate demand as well. In the diagram, this is seen as a movement along the AD curve from Y_2 to Y′. However, GNP rises at a faster rate, along the AD = Y line in the diagram. Eventually, the increase in aggregate supply catches up to the increase in demand when the equilibrium is reached at Y′. At this point, aggregate demand equals aggregate supply and there is no further depletion of inventories.

KEY TAKEAWAYS

- If the actual GNP is higher than the equilibrium rate, then excess supply leads to an accumulation of inventories. Firms respond to the surplus by cutting production, causing GNP to fall until the GNP supplied is equal to aggregate demand.
- If the actual GNP is lower than the equilibrium rate, then excess demand leads to a depletion of inventories. Firms respond to the surplus by raising production, which causes GNP to rise until the GNP supplied is equal to aggregate demand.

EXERCISE

- Jeopardy Questions: As in the popular television game show, you are given an answer to a question and you must respond with the question. For example, if the answer is "a tax on imports," then the correct question is "What is a tariff?"
- Of increase, decrease, or stay the same, this will happen to store inventories when aggregate demand exceeds GNP.
- Of increase, decrease, or stay the same, this will happen to store inventories when actual GNP is greater than equilibrium GNP.
- Of increase, decrease, or stay the same, this is the direction of GNP change when inventories are accumulating in the Keynesian model.
- Of increase, decrease, or stay the same, this is the direction of GNP change when inventories are depleting in the Keynesian model.

- Of faster, slower, or the same rate, the rate of increase of aggregate demand compared to the increase in GNP as GNP rises to an equilibrium value in the Keynesian model.

8.10 REAL GNP AND THE IMPACT OF INCREASING GOVERNMENT DEMAND

Suppose the economy is initially in equilibrium in the G&S market with government demand at level G_1 and real GNP at Y_1, shown in Figure 8.4 "Effect of an Increase in Government Demand in the G&S Market". The initial AD function is written as AD(..., G_1, ...) to signify the level of government demand and to denote that other variables affect AD and are at some initial and unspecified values.

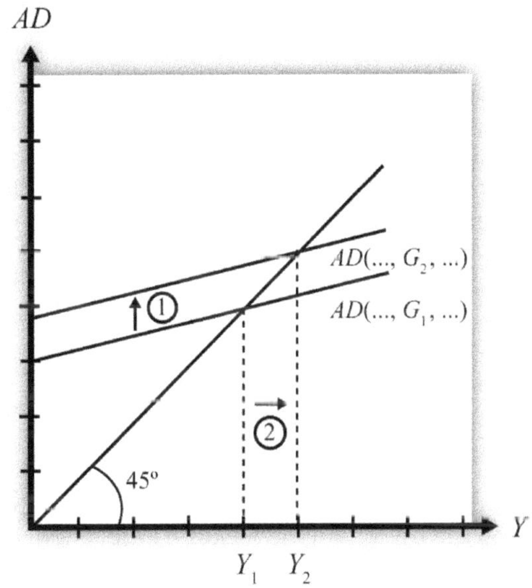

Figure 8.4 Effect of an Increase in Government Demand in the G&S Market

Next, suppose the government raises demand for G&S from G_1 to G_2, ceteris paribus. The increase might arise because a new budget is passed by the legislature with new spending initiatives. The ceteris paribus assumption means that all other exogenous variables are assumed to remain fixed. Most importantly in this context, this means that the increase in government demand is not paid for with increases in taxes or decreases in transfer payments.

Since higher government demand raises aggregate demand, the AD function shifts up from AD(..., G_1, ...) to AD(..., G_2, ...) (step 1). The equilibrium GNP in turn rises to Y_2 (step 2). Thus the increase in government demand causes an increase in real GNP.

The adjustment process follows the "GNP too low" story. When government demand increases, but before GNP rises to adjust, AD is greater than Y_1. The excess demand for G&S depletes inventories, in this case for firms that supply the government, causing merchants to increase order size. This leads firms to increase output, thus raising GNP.

KEY TAKEAWAY

- In the G&S model, an increase (decrease) in government demand causes an increase (decrease) in real GNP.

EXERCISES

- Jeopardy Questions: As in the popular television game show, you are given an answer to a question and you must respond with the question. For example, if the answer is "a tax on imports," then the correct question is "What is a tariff?"
- Of increase, decrease, or stay the same, the effect on equilibrium real GNP from a decrease in government demand in the G&S model.
- Of increase, decrease, or stay the same, the effect on equilibrium real GNP caused by an increase in government demand in the G&S model.
- Of GNP too low or GNP too high, the equilibrium story that must be told following an increase in government demand in the G&S model.
- Of GNP too low or GNP too high, the equilibrium story that must be told following a decrease in government demand in the G&S model.
- In the text, the effect of a change in government demand is analyzed. Use the G&S model (diagram) to individually assess the effect on equilibrium GNP caused by the following changes. Assume ceteris paribus.
- An increase in investment demand.
- An increase in transfer payments.
- An increase in tax revenues.
- Consider an economy in equilibrium in the G&S market.
- Suppose investment demand decreases, ceteris paribus. What is the effect on equilibrium GNP?
- Now suppose investment demand decreases, but ceteris paribus does not apply because at the same time government demand rises. What is the effect on equilibrium GNP?
- In general, which of these two assumptions, ceteris paribus or no ceteris paribus, is more realistic? Explain why.
- If ceteris paribus is less realistic, why do economic models so frequently apply the assumption?

8.11 REAL GNP AND THE IMPACT OF US DOLLAR APPRECIATION

Suppose the economy is initially in equilibrium in the G&S market with the exchange rate at level $E_{\$/£}^{1}$ and real GNP at Y_1 as shown in Figure 8.5 «Effect of an Increase in the U.S. Dollar Value in the G&S Market». The initial AD function is written as AD(..., $E_{\$/£}^{1}$, ...) to signify the level of the exchange rate and to denote that other variables affect AD and are at some initial and unspecified values.

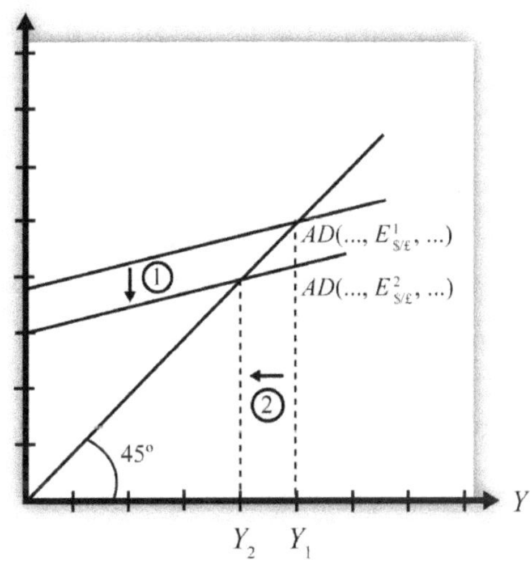

Figure 8.5 Effect of an Increase in the U.S. Dollar Value in the G&S Market

Next, suppose the U.S. dollar value rises, corresponding to a decrease in the exchange rate from $E_{\$/£}^{1}$ to $E_{\$/£}^{2}$, ceteris paribus. As explained in Chapter 8, Section 8.6 , the increase in the spot dollar value also increases the real dollar value, causing foreign G&S to become relatively cheaper and U.S. G&S to become more expensive. This change reduces demand for U.S. exports and increases import demand, resulting in a reduction in aggregate demand. The ceteris paribus assumption means that all other exogenous variables are assumed to remain fixed.

Since the higher dollar value lowers aggregate demand, the AD function shifts down from AD(..., $E_{\$/£}^{1}$, ...) to AD(..., $E_{\$/£}^{2}$, ...) (step 1), and equilibrium GNP in turn falls to Y_2 (step 2). Thus the increase in the U.S. dollar value causes a decrease in real GNP.

The adjustment process follows the "GNP too high" story. When the dollar value rises but before GNP falls to adjust, Y_1 > AD. The excess supply of G&S raises inventories, causing merchants to decrease order size. This leads firms to decrease output, lowering GNP.

KEY TAKEAWAY

- In the G&S model, an increase (decrease) in the U.S. dollar value causes a decrease (increase) in real GNP.

EXERCISES

- Jeopardy Questions: As in the popular television game show, you are given an answer to a question and you must respond with the question. For example, if the answer is "a tax on imports," then the correct question is "What is a tariff?"
- Of increase, decrease, or stay the same, the effect on equilibrium real U.S. GNP from a decrease in the value of the U.S. dollar in the G&S model.
- Of increase, decrease, or stay the same, the effect on equilibrium real GNP caused by an increase in the value of the U.S. dollar in the G&S model.
- Of GNP too low or GNP too high, the equilibrium story that must be told following an increase in the value of the U.S. dollar in the G&S model.
- Of GNP too low or GNP too high, the equilibrium story that must be told following a decrease in the value of the U.S. dollar in the G&S model.
- In the text, the effect of a change in the currency value is analyzed. Use the G&S model (diagram) to individually assess the effect on equilibrium GNP caused by the following changes. Assume ceteris paribus.
- A decrease in the real currency value.
- An increase in the domestic price level.
- An increase in the foreign price level.

8.12 J-CURVE IMPACT

In the goods market model, it is assumed that the exchange rate ($E_{\$/£}$) is directly related to current account demand in the United States. The logic of the relationship goes as follows. If the dollar depreciates, meaning $E_{\$/£}$ rises, then foreign goods will become more expensive to U.S. residents, causing a decrease in import demand. At the same time U.S. goods will appear relatively cheaper to foreign residents, causing an increase in demand for U.S. exports. The increase in export demand and decrease in import demand both contribute to an increase in the current account demand. Since in the goods market model, any increase in demand results in an increase in supply to satisfy that demand, the dollar depreciation should also lead to an increase in the actual current account balance.

In real-world economies, however, analysis of the data suggests that in many instances a depreciating currency tends to cause, at least, a temporary increase in the deficit rather than the predicted decrease. The explanation for this temporary reversal of the cause-and-effect relationship is called the J-curve theory. In terms of future use of the AA-DD model, we will always assume the J-curve effect is not operating, unless otherwise specified. One should think of this effect as a possible short-term exception to the standard theory.

The theory of the J-curve is an explanation for the J-like temporal pattern of change in a country's trade balance in response to a sudden or substantial depreciation (or devaluation) of the currency.

Consider Figure 8.6 "J-Curve Effect", depicting two variables measured, hypothetically, over some period: the U.S. dollar / British pound ($E_{\$/£}$) and the U.S. current account balance (CA = EX - IM). The exchange rate is meant to represent the average value of the dollar against all other trading country currencies and would correspond to a dollar value index that is often constructed and reported. Since the units of these two data series would be in very different scales, we imagine the exchange rate is measured along the left axis, while the CA balance is measured in different units on the right-hand axis. With appropriately chosen scales, we can line up the two series next to each other to see whether changes in the exchange rate seem to correlate with positive or negative changes in the CA balance.

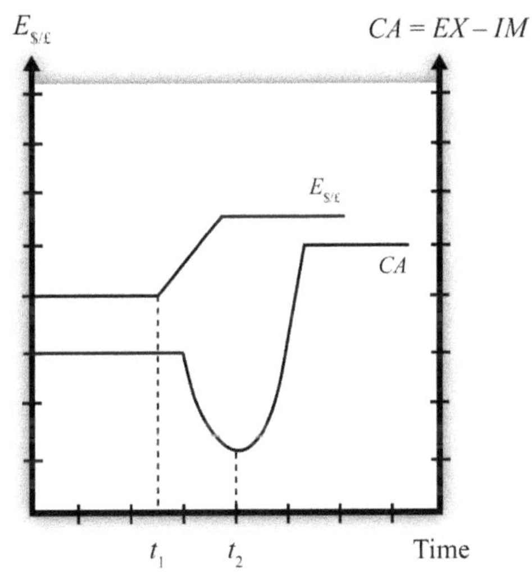

Figure 8.6 J-Curve Effect

As previously mentioned, the standard theory suggests a positive relationship between $E_{\$/£}$ and the U.S. current account, implying that, ceteris paribus, any dollar depreciation (an increase in $E_{\$/£}$) should cause an increase in the CA balance.

However, what sometimes happens instead, is immediately following the dollar depreciation at time t_1, the CA balance falls for a period of time, until time t_2 is reached. In this phase, a CA deficit would become larger, not smaller.

Eventually, after period t_2, the CA balance reverses direction and begins to increase—in other words, a trade deficit falls. The diagram demonstrates clearly how the CA balance follows the pattern of a "J" in the transition following a dollar depreciation, hence the name J-curve theory.

In the real world, the period of time thought necessary for the CA balance to traverse the J pattern is between one and two years. However, this estimate is merely a rough rule of thumb as the actual paths will be influenced by many other variable changes also occurring at the same time. Indeed, in some cases the J-curve effect may not even arise, so there is nothing automatic about it.

The reasons for the J-curve effect can be better understood by decomposing the current account balance. The basic definition of the current account is the difference between the value of exports and the value of imports. That is,

$CA = EX - IM.$

The current account also includes income payments and receipts and unilateral transfers, but these categories are usually small and will not play a big role in this discussion—so we'll ignore them. The main thing to take note about this definition is that the CA is measured in "value" terms, which means in terms of dollars. The way these values are determined is by multiplying the quantity of imports by the price of each imported item. We expand the CA definition by using the summation symbol and imagining summing up across all exported goods and all imported goods:

$CA = \Sigma P_{EX} Q_{EX} - \Sigma_{PIM} Q_{IM}.$

Here $\Sigma P_{EX} Q_{EX}$ represents the summation of the price times quantities of all goods exported from the country, while $\Sigma P_{EX} Q_{EX}$ is the summation of the price times quantities of all goods imported from the country.

However, for imported goods we could also take note that foreign products are denominated in foreign currency terms. To convert them to U.S. dollars we need to multiply by the current spot exchange rate. Thus we can expand the CA definition further by incorporating the exchange rate into the import term as follows:

$CA = \Sigma P_{EX} Q_{EX - \Sigma E\$/£P*IM} Q_{IM.}$

Here $E_{\$/£}$ represents whatever dollar/pound rate prevailed at the time of imports, and $P_{IM}{}^{*}$ represents the price of each imported good denominated in foreign (*) pound currency terms. Thus the value of imports is really the summation across all foreign imports of the exchange rate times the foreign price times quantity.

The J-curve theory recognizes that import and export quantities and prices are often arranged in advance and set into a contract. For example, an importer of watches is likely to enter into a contract with the foreign watch company to import a specific quantity over some future period. The price of the watches will also be fixed by the terms of the contract. Such a contract provides assurances to the exporter that the watches he makes will be sold. It provides assurances to the importer that the price of the watches will remain fixed. Contract lengths will vary from industry to industry and firm to firm, but may extend for as long as a year or more.

The implication of contracts is that in the short run, perhaps over six to eighteen months, both the local prices and quantities of imports and exports will remain fixed for many items. However, the contracts may stagger in time—that is, they may not all be negotiated and signed at the same date in the past. This means that during any period some fraction of the contracts will expire and be renegotiated. Renegotiated contracts can adjust prices and quantities in response to changes in market conditions, such as a change in the exchange rate. Thus in the months following a dollar depreciation, contract renegotiations will gradually occur, causing eventual, but slow, changes in the prices and quantities traded.

With these ideas in mind, consider a depreciation of the dollar. In the very short run—say, during the first few weeks—most of the contract terms will remain unchanged, meaning that the prices and quantities of exports and imports will also stayed fixed. The only change affecting the CA formula, then, is the increase in $E_{\$/*}$. Assuming all importers have not hedged their trades by entering to forward contracts, the increase in $E_{\$/*}$ will result in an immediate increase in the value of imports measured in dollar terms. Since the prices and quantities do not change immediately, the CA balance falls. This is what can account for the initial stage of the J-curve effect, between periods t_1 and t_2.

As the dollar depreciation continues, and as contracts begin to be renegotiated, traders will adjust quantities demanded. Since the dollar depreciation causes imported goods to become more expensive to U.S. residents, the quantity of imported goods demanded and purchased will fall. Similarly, exported goods will appear cheaper to foreigners, and so as their contracts are renegotiated, they will begin to increase demand for U.S. exports. The changes in these quantities will both cause an increase in the current account (decrease in a trade deficit). Thus, as several months and years pass, the effects from the changes in quantities will surpass the price effect caused by the dollar depreciation and the CA balance will rise as shown in the diagram after time t_2.

It is worth noting that the standard theory, which says that a dollar depreciation causes an increase in the current account balance, assumes that the quantity effects—that is, the effects of the depreciation on export and import demand—are the dominant effects. The J-curve theory qualifies that effect by suggesting that although the quantity or demand effects will dominate, it may take several months or years before becoming apparent.

KEY TAKEAWAYS

- The J-curve theory represents a short-term exception to the standard assumption applied in the G&S model in which a currency depreciation causes a decrease in the trade deficit.

- The theory of the J-curve is an explanation for the J-like temporal pattern of change in a country's trade balance in response to a sudden or substantial depreciation (or devaluation) of the currency.
- The J-curve effect suggests that after a currency depreciation, the current account balance will first fall for a period of time before beginning to rise as normally expected. If a country has a trade deficit initially, the deficit will first rise and then fall in response to a currency depreciation.

EXERCISE

- Jeopardy Questions: As in the popular television game show, you are given an answer to a question and you must respond with the question. For example, if the answer is "a tax on imports," then the correct question is "What is a tariff?"
- Of short run or long run, the period in which the J-curve theory predicts that a country's trade deficit will rise with a currency depreciation.
- Of short run or long run, the period in which the J-curve theory predicts that a country's trade deficit will fall with a currency depreciation.
- Of value of U.S. imports or quantity of U.S. imports, this is expected to rise in the short run after a dollar depreciation according to the J-curve theory.
- Of value of Turkish imports or quantity of Turkish imports, this is expected to fall in the long run after a Turkish lira depreciation according to the J-curve theory.
- Of increase, decrease, or stay the same, the effect on U.S. exports in the short run due to a U.S. dollar depreciation according to the J-curve theory.
- Of increase, decrease, or stay the same, the effect on U.S. imports in the short run due to a U.S. dollar depreciation according to the J-curve theory.

CHAPTER

9 THE AA-DD MODEL

INTRODUCTION

Ideally, it would be nice to develop a way to keep track of all the cause-and-effect relationships that are presumed to exist at the same time. From the previous chapters it is clear, for example, that the money supply affects the interest rates in the money market, which in turn affects the exchange rates in the foreign exchange (Forex) market, which in turn affects demand on the current account in the goods and services (G&S) market, which in turn affects the level of GNP, which in turn affects the money market, and so on. The same type of string of repercussions can be expected after many other changes that might occur. Keeping track of these effects and establishing the final equilibrium values would be a difficult task if not for a construction like the AA-DD model. This model merges the money market, the Forex market, and the G&S market into one supermodel. The construction of the AA-DD model is presented in this chapter.

9.1 AA-DD MODEL: AN OVERVIEW

This chapter describes the derivation and the mechanics of the AA-DD model. The AA-DD model represents a synthesis of the three previous market models: the foreign exchange (Forex) market, the money market, and the goods and services market. In a sense, there is really very little new information presented here. Instead, the chapter provides a graphical approach to integrate the results from the three models and to show their interconnectedness. However, because so much is going on simultaneously, working with the AA-DD model can be quite challenging.

The AA-DD model is described with a diagram consisting of two curves (or lines): an AA curve representing asset market equilibriums derived from the money market and foreign exchange markets and a DD curve representing goods market (or demand) equilibriums. The intersection of the two curves identifies a market equilibrium in which each of the three markets is simultaneously in equilibrium. Thus we refer to this equilibrium as a superequilibrium.

Results

The main results of this section are descriptive and purely mechanical. The chapter describes the derivation of the AA and DD curves, explains how changes in exogenous variables will cause shifts in the curves, and explains adjustment from one equilibrium to another.

- The DD curve is the set of exchange rate and GNP combinations that maintain equilibrium in the goods and services market, given fixed values for all other exogenous variables.
- The DD curve shifts rightward whenever government demand (G), investment demand (I), transfer payments (TR), or foreign prices ($P_£$) increase or when taxes (T) or domestic prices ($P_\$$) decrease. Changes in the opposite direction cause a leftward shift.
- The AA curve is the set of exchange rate and GNP combinations that maintain equilibrium in the asset markets, given fixed values for all other exogenous variables.
- The AA curve shifts upward whenever money supply (M^S), foreign interest rates ($i_£$), or the expected exchange rate ($E_{\$/£}{}^e$) increase or when domestic prices ($P_\$$) decrease. Changes in the opposite direction cause a downward shift.
- The intersection of the AA and DD curves depicts a superequilibrium in an economy since at that point the goods and services market, the domestic money market, and the foreign exchange market are all in equilibrium simultaneously.
- Changes in any exogenous variable that is not plotted on the axes (anything but Y and $E_{\$/£}$) will cause a shift of the AA or DD curves and move the economy out of equilibrium, temporarily. Adjustment to a new equilibrium follows the principle that adjustment in the asset markets occurs much more rapidly than adjustment in the goods and services market. Thus adjustment to the AA curve will always occur before adjustment to the DD curve.

Connections

The AA-DD model will allow us to understand how changes in macroeconomic policy—both monetary and fiscal—can affect key aggregate economic variables when a country is open to international trade and financial flows while accounting for the interaction of the variables among themselves. Specifically, the model is used to identify potential effects of fiscal and monetary policy on exchange rates, trade balances, GDP levels, interest rates, and price levels both domestically and abroad. In subsequent chapters, analyses will be done under both floating and fixed exchange rate regimes.

KEY TAKEAWAYS

- The AA-DD model integrates the workings of the money-Forex market and the G&S model into one supermodel.
- The AA curve is derived from the money-Forex model. The DD curve is derived from the G&S model.
- The intersection of the AA and DD curves determines the equilibrium values for real GNP and the exchange rate.
- Comparative statics exercises using the AA-DD model allow one to identify the effects of changes in exogenous variables on the level of GDP and the exchange rate, while assuring that the Forex, the money market, and the G&S market all achieve simultaneous equilibrium.

EXERCISE

- Jeopardy Questions: As in the popular television game show, you are given an answer to a question and you must respond with the question. For example, if the answer is "a tax on imports," then the correct question is "What is a tariff?"
- At the intersection of the AA and DD curves, the goods and services market, the money market, and this market are simultaneously in equilibrium.
- The term used to describe the type of equilibrium at the intersection of the AA curve and the DD curve.

9.2 THE DD CURVE'S DERIVATION

The DD curve is derived by transferring information described in the goods and services (G&S) market model onto a new diagram to show the relationship between the exchange rate and equilibrium gross national product (GNP). The original G&S market, depicted in the top part of Figure 9.1 "Derivation of the DD Curve", plots the aggregate demand (AD) function with respect to changes in U.S. GNP ($Y_\$$). Aggregate demand is measured along the vertical axis and aggregate supply (or the GNP) is measured on the horizontal axis. As discussed in Chapter 8 , Section 8.7 , the AD function is dependent upon several different exogenous variables, most notably the exchange rate between domestic and foreign currency ($E_{\$/£}$). However, AD is also affected by investment demand (I), government demand (G), government tax revenues (T), government transfer payments (TR), and the price level in the domestic ($P_\$$) and foreign ($P_£$) countries. The endogenous variable in the model is U.S. GNP ($Y_\$$). (See Table 9.1 "G&S Market" for a quick reference.) In this exercise, since our focus is on the exchange rate, we label the AD function in Figure 9.1 «Derivation of the DD Curve» as AD($E_{\$/£}$, ...), where the ellipsis (...) is meant to indicate there are other unspecified variables that also influence AD.

Table 9.1 G&S Market

Exogenous Variables	$E_{\$/£}, I, G, T, TR, P_{\$}, P_{£}$
Endogenous Variable	$Y_{\$}$

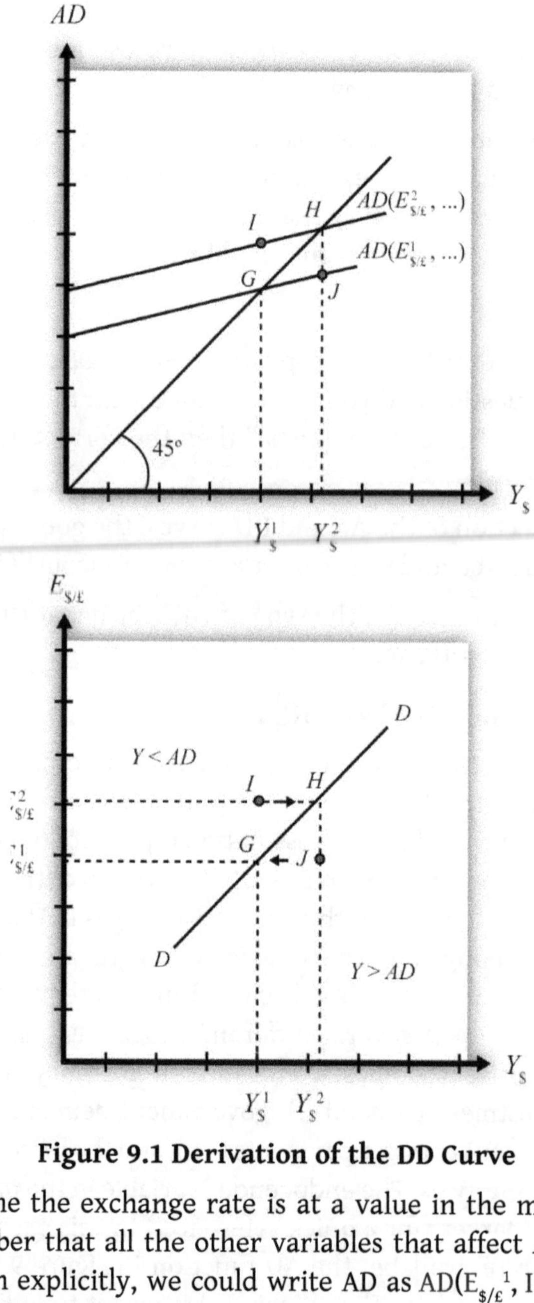

Figure 9.1 Derivation of the DD Curve

Initially, let's assume the exchange rate is at a value in the market given by $E_{\$/*}^{1}$. We need to remember that all the other variables that affect AD are also at some initial level. Written explicitly, we could write AD as $AD(E_{\$/£}^{1}, I^{1}, G^{1}, T^{1}, TR^{1}, P_{\$}^{1}, P_{£}^{1})$. The AD function with exchange rate $E_{\$/£}^{1}$ intersects the forty-five-degree line at point G which determines the equilibrium level of GNP given by $Y_{\$}^{1}$. These two values are transferred to the lower diagram at point G determining one point on the DD curve ($Y_\$^1$, $E_{\$/£}^1$).

Next, suppose $E_{\$/£}$ rises from $E_{\$/£}^1$ to $E_{\$/£}^2$, ceteris paribus. This corresponds to a depreciation of the U.S. dollar with respect to the British pound. The ceteris paribus assumption means that investment, government, taxes, and so on stay fixed at levels I^1, G^1, T^1, and so on. Since a dollar depreciation makes foreign G&S relatively more expensive and domestic goods relatively cheaper, AD shifts up to AD($E_{\$/£}^2$, ...). The equilibrium shifts to point H at a GNP level $Y_\$^2$. These two values are transferred to the lower diagram at point H, determining a second point on the DD curve ($Y_\$^2$, $E_{\$/£}^2$).

The line drawn through points G and H on the lower diagram is called the DD curve. The DD curve plots an equilibrium GNP level for every possible exchange rate that may prevail, ceteris paribus. Stated differently, the DD curve is the combination of exchange rates and GNP levels that maintain equilibrium in the G&S market, ceteris paribus. We can think of it as the set of aggregate demand equilibriums.

A Note about Equilibriums

An equilibrium in an economic model typically corresponds to a point toward which the endogenous variable values will converge based on some behavioral assumption about the participants in the model. In this case, equilibrium is not represented by a single point. Instead every point along the DD curve is an equilibrium value.

If the economy were at a point above the DD curve, say, at I in the lower diagram, the exchange rate would be $E_{\$/£}^2$ and the GNP level at $Y_\$^1$. This corresponds to point I in the upper diagram where AD > Y, read off the vertical axis. In the G&S model, whenever aggregate demand exceeds aggregate supply, producers respond by increasing supply, causing GNP to rise. This continues until AD = Y at point H. For all points to the left of the DD curve, AD > Y, therefore the behavior of producers would cause a shift to the right from any point like I to a point like H on the DD curve.

Similarly, at a point such as J, to the right of the DD curve, the exchange rate is $E_{\$/£}^1$ and the GNP level is at $Y_\$^2$. This corresponds to point J in the upper diagram above where aggregate demand is less than supply (AD < Y). In the G&S model, whenever supply exceeds demand, producers respond by reducing supply, thus GNP falls. This continues until AD = Y at point G. For all points to the right of the DD curve, AD < Y, therefore the behavior of producers would cause a shift to the left from any point like J to a point like G on the DD curve.

A useful analogy is to think of the DD curve as a river flowing through a valley. (See the 3-D diagram in Figure 9.2 "A 3-D DD Curve".) The hills rise up to the right and left along the upward-sloping DD curve. Just as gravity will move a drop of water downhill onto the river valley, firm behavior will move GNP much in the same way: right or left to the lowest point along the DD curve.

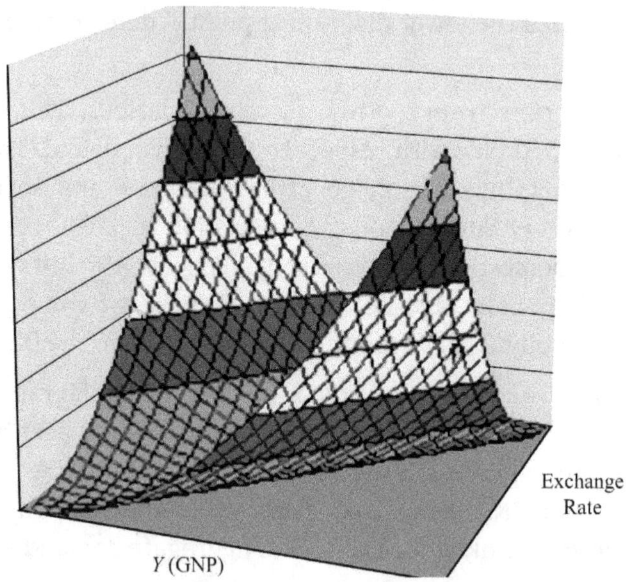

Figure 9.2 A 3-D DD Curve

KEY TAKEAWAYS

- The DD curve plots an equilibrium GNP level for every possible exchange rate that may prevail, ceteris paribus.
- Every point on a DD curve represents an equilibrium value in the G&S market.
- The DD curve is positively sloped because an increase in the exchange rate (meaning a decrease in the U.S. dollar value) raises equilibrium GNP in the G&S model.

EXERCISE

- Jeopardy Questions: As in the popular television game show, you are given an answer to a question and you must respond with the question. For example, if the answer is "a tax on imports," then the correct question is "What is a tariff?"
- This is what has happened to its currency value if an economy's exchange rate and GNP combination moves upward along an upward-sloping DD curve.
- Of greater than, less than, or equal to, this is how aggregate demand compares to GNP when the economy has an exchange rate and GNP combination that places it to the left of the DD curve.
- Of greater than, less than, or equal to, this is how aggregate demand compares to GNP when the economy has an exchange rate and GNP combination that places it on the DD curve.
- The equilibriums along a DD curve satisfy this condition.

9.3 DD CURVE SHIFTING

The DD curve depicts the relationship between changes in one exogenous variable and one endogenous variable within the goods and services (G&S) market model. The exogenous variable assumed to change is the exchange rate. The endogenous variable affected is the gross national product (GNP). At all points along the DD curve, it is assumed that all other exogenous variables remain fixed at their original values.

The DD curve will shift, however, if there is a change in any of the other exogenous variables. We illustrate how this works in Figure 9.3 "DD Curve Effects from a Decrease in Investment Demand". Here, we assume that the level of investment demand in the economy falls from its initial level I_1 to a lower level I_2.

At the initial investment level (I_1) and initial exchange rate ($E_{\$/£}^1$) the AD curve is given by AD(..., $E_{\$/£}^1$, I_1, ...). The AD curve intersects the forty-five-degree line at point G, which is transferred to point G on the DD curve below. If the investment level and all other exogenous variables remain fixed while the exchange rate increases to $E_{\$/£}^2$, then the AD curve shifts up to AD(..., $E_{\$/£}^2$, I_1, ...), generating the equilibrium points H in both diagrams. This exercise plots out the initial DD curve labeled $DD|_{I1}$ in the lower diagram connecting points G and H. $DD|_{I1}$ is read as "the DD curve given that $I = I_1$."

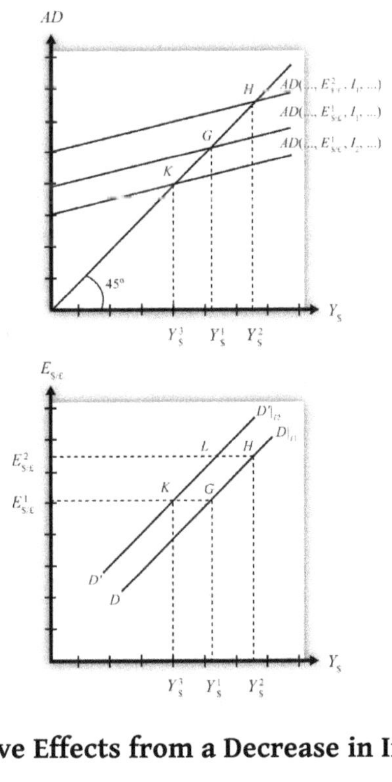

Figure 9.3 DD Curve Effects from a Decrease in Investment Demand

Now, suppose I falls to I_2. The reduction in I leads to a reduction in AD, ceteris paribus. At the exchange rate $E_{\$/£}^1$, the AD curve will shift down to AD(..., $E_{\$/£}^1$, I_2, ...), intersecting the forty-five-degree line at point K. Point K above, which corresponds to the combination ($E_{\$/£}^1$, I_2), is transferred to point K on the lower diagram. This point lies on a new DD curve because a second exogenous variable, namely I, has changed. If we maintain the investment level at I_2 and change the exchange rate up to $E_{\$/£}^2$, the equilibrium will shift to point L (shown only on the lower diagram), plotting out a whole new DD curve. This DD curve is labeled $D'D'|_{I2}$, which means "the DD curve given is $I = I_2$."

The effect of a decrease in investment demand is to lower aggregate demand and shift the DD curve to the left. Indeed, a change in any exogenous variable that reduces aggregate demand, except the exchange rate, will cause the DD curve to shift to the left. Likewise, any change in an exogenous variable that causes an increase in aggregate demand will cause the DD curve to shift right. An exchange rate change will not shift DD because its effect is accounted for by the DD curve itself. Note that curves or lines can shift only when a variable that is not plotted on the axis changes.

The following table presents a list of all variables that can shift the DD curve right and left. The up arrow indicates an increase in the variable, and the down arrow indicates a decrease.

DD right-shifters	↑G↑I↓T↑TR↓$P_\$$↑$P_£$
DD left-shifters	↓G↓I↓T↑TR↓$P_\$$↑$P_£$

Refer to Chapter 8 for a complete description of how and why each variable affects aggregate demand. For easy reference, recall that G is government demand, I is investment demand, T refers to tax revenues, TR is government transfer payments, $P_\$$ is the U.S. price level, and $P_£$ is the foreign British price level.

KEY TAKEAWAYS

- The effect of an increase in investment demand (an increase in government demand, a decrease in taxes, an increase in transfer payments, a decrease in U.S. prices, or an increase in foreign prices) is to raise aggregate demand and shift the DD curve to the right.
- The effect of a decrease in investment demand (a decrease in government demand, an increase in taxes, a decrease in transfer payments, an increase in U.S. prices, or a decrease in foreign prices) is to lower aggregate demand and shift the DD curve to the left.

EXERCISE

- Identify whether the DD curve shifts in response to each of the following changes. Indicate whether the curve shifts up, down, left, or right. Possible answers are DD right, DD left, or neither.

- Decrease in government transfer payments.
- Decrease in the foreign price level.
- Increase in foreign interest rates.
- Decrease in the expected exchange rate $E_{\$/£}^{e}$.
- Decrease in U.S. GNP.
- Decrease in the U.S. money supply.

9.4 THE AA CURVE'S DERIVATION

The AA curve is derived by transferring information described in the money market and foreign exchange market models onto a new diagram to show the relationship between the exchange rate and equilibrium GNP. (At this point we will substitute GNP for its virtually equivalent measure, GDP, as a determinant of real money demand.) Since both models describe supply and demand for money, which is an asset, I'll refer to the two markets together as the asset market.

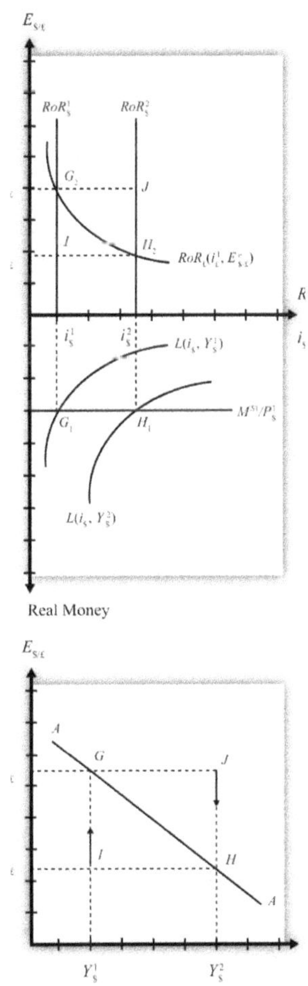

Figure 9.4 Derivation of the AA Curve

The foreign exchange market, depicted in the top part of Figure 9.4 "Derivation of the AA Curve", plots the rates of return on domestic U.S. assets (RoR\$) and foreign British assets (RoR£). (See Chapter 5 "Interest Rate Parity", Section 5.3 "Forex Equilibrium with the Rate of Return Diagram" for a complete description.) The domestic U.S. money market, in the lower quadrant, plots the real U.S. money supply (M\$S/P\$) and real money demand (L(i\$, Y\$)). The asset market equilibriums have several exogenous variables that determine the positions of the curves and the outcome of the model. These exogenous variables are the foreign British interest rate (i£) and the expected future exchange rate (E\$/£e), which influence the foreign British rate of return (RoR£); the U.S. money supply (M\$S) and domestic U.S. price level (P\$), which influence real money supply; and U.S. GNP (Y\$), which influences real money demand. The endogenous variables in the asset model are the domestic interest rates (i\$) and the exchange rate (E\$/£). See Table 9.2 "Asset Market (Money + Forex)" for easy reference.

Table 9.2 Asset Market (Money + Forex)

Exogenous Variables	$i_£$, $E_{\$/£}{}^{e}$, $M_\$^S$, $P_\$$, $Y_\$$
Endogenous Variables	$i_\$$, $E_{\$/£}$

Initially, let's assume GNP is at a value in the market given by $Y_\$^1$. We need to remember that all the other exogenous variables that affect the asset market are also at some initial level such as $i_£^1$, $E_{\$/£}{}^{e1}$, $M_\$^{S1}$, and $P_\$^1$. The real money demand function with GNP level $Y_\$^1$ intersects with real money supply at point G_1 in the money market diagram determining the interest rate $i_\$^1$. The interest rate in turn determines $RoR_\$^1$, which intersects with $RoR_£$ at point G_2, determining the equilibrium exchange rate $E_{\$/£}{}^1$. These two values are transferred to the lowest diagram at point G, establishing one point on the AA curve ($Y_\$^1$, $E_{\$/£}{}^1$).

Next, suppose GNP rises, for some unstated reason, from $Y_\$^1$ to $Y_\$$, ceteris paribus. The ceteris paribus assumption means that all exogenous variables in the model remain fixed. Since the increase in GNP raises real money demand, $L(i_\$, Y_\$)$, it shifts out to $L(i_\$, Y_\$^2)$. The equilibrium shifts to point H_1, raising the equilibrium interest rate to $i_\$^2$. The $RoR_\$$ line shifts right with the interest rate, determining a new equilibrium in the Forex at point H_2 with equilibrium exchange rate $E_{\$/£}{}^2$. These two values are then transferred to the diagram below at point H, establishing a second point on the AA curve ($Y_\$^2$, $E_{\$/£}{}^2$).

The line drawn through points G and H on the lower diagram in Figure 9.4 «Derivation of the AA Curve» is called the AA curve. The AA curve plots an equilibrium exchange rate for every possible GNP level that may prevail, ceteris paribus. Stated differently, the AA curve is the combination of exchange rates and GNP levels that maintain equilibrium in the asset market, ceteris paribus. We can think of it as the set of aggregate asset equilibriums.

A Note about Equilibriums

If the economy were at a point off the AA curve, like at I in the lower diagram, the GNP level is at $Y_{\$}^{1}$ and the exchange rate is $E_{\$/\pounds}^{2}$. This corresponds to point I in the upper diagram where $RoR_{\pounds} > RoR_{\$}$. In the Forex model, when foreign assets have a higher rate of return than domestic assets, investors respond by buying pounds in exchange for dollars in the foreign exchange market. This leads to a depreciation of the dollar and an increase in $E_{\$/\pounds}$. This continues until $RoR_{\pounds} = RoR_{\$}$ at point G. For all points below the AA curve, $RoR_{\pounds} > RoR_{\$}$; therefore, the behavior of investors would cause an upward adjustment toward the AA curve from any point like I to a point like G.

Similarly, at a point such as J, above the DD curve, the GNP level is at Y_{2} and the exchange rate is $E_{\$/\pounds}^{1}$. This corresponds to point J in the upper diagram where $RoR_{\$} > RoR_{\pounds}$ and the rate of return on dollar assets is greater than the rate of return abroad. In the Forex model, when U.S. assets have a higher rate of return than foreign assets, investors respond by buying dollars in exchange for pounds in the foreign exchange market. This leads to an appreciation of the dollar and a decrease in $E_{\$/\pounds}$. This continues until $RoR_{\pounds} = RoR_{\$}$ at point H. For all points above the AA curve, $RoR_{\$} > RoR_{\pounds}$; therefore, the behavior of investors would cause a downward adjustment to the AA curve from a point like J to a point like H.

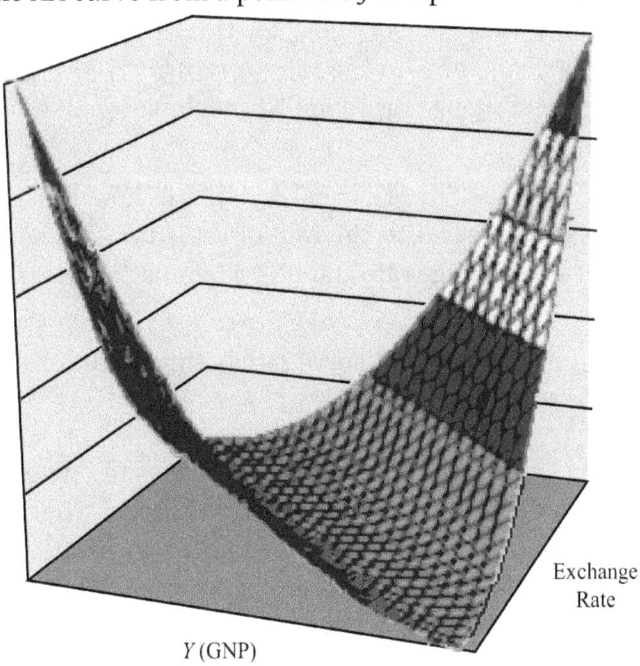

Figure 9.5 A 3-D AA Curve

As with the DD curve, it is useful to think of the AA curve as a river flowing through a valley. (See the 3-D diagram in Figure 9.5 "A 3-D AA Curve".) The hills rise up both above and below. Just as gravity will move a drop of water down the hill to the river valley, in much the same way, investor behavior will move the exchange rate up or down to the lowest point lying on the AA curve.

KEY TAKEAWAYS

- The AA curve plots an equilibrium exchange rate level for every possible GNP value that may prevail, ceteris paribus.
- Every point on an AA curve represents an equilibrium value in the money-Forex market.
- The AA curve is negatively sloped because an increase in the real GNP lowers the equilibrium exchange rate in the money-Forex model.

EXERCISE

- Jeopardy Questions: As in the popular television game show, you are given an answer to a question and you must respond with the question. For example, if the answer is "a tax on imports," then the correct question is "What is a tariff?"
- This is what has happened to its GNP if an economy's exchange rate and GNP combination move downward along a downward-sloping AA curve.
- Of greater than, less than, or equal to, this is how the rate of return on domestic assets compares to the rate of return on foreign assets when the economy has an exchange rate and GNP combination that places it above the AA curve.
- Of greater than, less than, or equal to, this is how the rate of return on domestic assets compares to the rate of return on foreign assets when the economy has an exchange rate and GNP combination that places it on the AA curve.
- The equilibriums along an AA curve satisfy this condition.

9.5 SHIFTING THE AA CURVE

The AA curve depicts the relationship between changes in one exogenous variable and one endogenous variable within the asset market model. The exogenous variable changed is gross national product (GNP). The endogenous variable affected is the exchange rate. At all points along the AA curve, it is assumed that all other exogenous variables remain fixed at their original values.

The AA curve will shift if there is a change in any of the other exogenous variables. We illustrate how this works in Figure 9.6 "AA Curve Effects from a Decrease in the Money Supply", where we assume that the money supply in the economy falls from its initial level M^{S1} to a lower level M^{S2}.

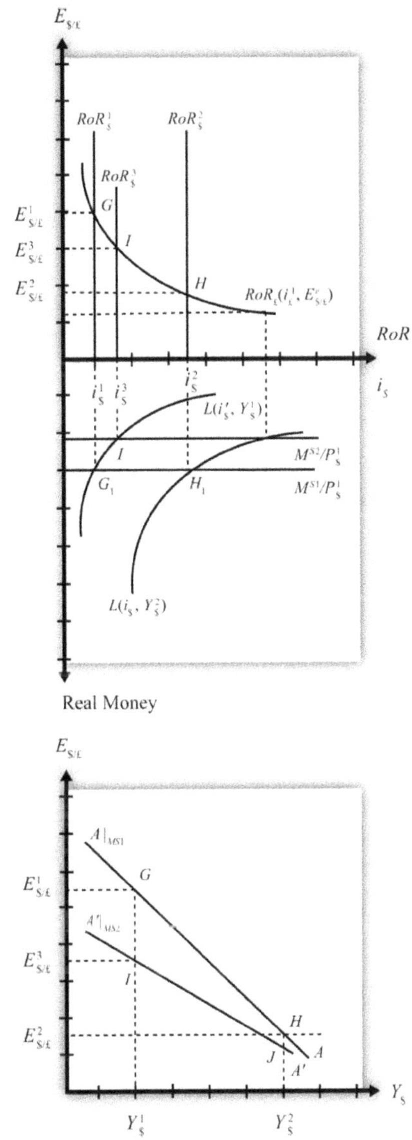

Figure 9.6 AA Curve Effects from a Decrease in the Money Supply

At the initial money supply (M^{S1}) and initial GNP level $Y_{\$}^{1}$, real money demand intersects real money supply at point G, determining the interest rate $i_{\$}^{1}$. This in turn determines the rate of return on U.S. assets, $RoR_{\$}^{1}$, which intersects the foreign British $RoR_{£}$ at G in the upper diagram, determining the equilibrium exchange rate $E_{\$/£}^{1}$. If the money supply and all other exogenous variables remain fixed, while GNP increases to $Y_{\$}^{2}$, the equilibriums shift to points H in the lower and upper diagrams, determining exchange rate $E_{\$/£}^{2}$. This exercise plots out the initial AA curve labeled $AA|_{MS1}$ in the lower diagram connecting points G and H. Note, $AA|_{MS1}$ is read as "the AA curve given that $M^{S} = M^{S1}$."

Now, suppose the money supply M^S falls to M^{S2}. The reduction in M^S leads to a reduction in the real money supply, which, at GNP level $Y_\$^1$, shifts the money market equilibrium to point I, determining a new interest rate, $i_\$^3$. In the Forex market, the rate of return rises to $RoR_\$^3$, which determines the equilibrium exchange rate $E_{\$/£}^3$. The equilibriums at points I corresponding to the combination ($Y_\$^1$, $E_{\$/£}^3$) are transferred to point I on the lower diagram. This point lies on a new AA curve because a second exogenous variable, namely, M^S, has changed. If we maintain the money supply at M^{S2} and change the GNP up to $Y_\$^2$, the equilibrium will shift to point J (shown only on the lower diagram), plotting out a whole new AA curve. This AA curve is labeled $A'A'|_{MS2}$, which means "the AA curve given that $M^S = M^{S2}$."

The effect of a decrease in the money supply is to shift the AA curve downward. Indeed, a change in any exogenous variable in the asset markets that reduces the equilibrium exchange rate, except a change in GNP, will cause the AA curve to shift down. Likewise, any change in an exogenous variable that causes an increase in the exchange rate will cause the AA curve to shift up. A change in GNP will not shift AA because its effect is accounted for by the AA curve itself. Note that curves or lines can shift only when a variable not plotted on the axis changes.

The following table presents a list of all variables that can shift the AA curve up and down. The up arrow indicates an increase in the variable, and a down arrow indicates a decrease.

AA up-shifters	$\uparrow M^S \downarrow P_\$ \uparrow i_£ \uparrow E_{\$/£}^e$
AA down-shifters	$\downarrow M^S \uparrow P_\$ \downarrow i_£ \downarrow E_{\$/£}^e$

Refer to Chapter 5 "Interest Rate Parity" and Chapter 7 «Interest Rate Determination» for a complete description of how and why each variable affects the exchange rate. For easy reference though, recall that M^S is the U.S. money supply, $P_\$$ is the U.S. price level, $i_£$ is the foreign British interest rate, and $E_{\$/£}^e$ is the expected future exchange rate.

KEY TAKEAWAYS

- The effect of an increase in the money supply (or a decrease in the price level, an increase in foreign interest rates, or an increase in the expected exchange rate [as defined]) is to shift the AA curve upward.
- The effect of a decrease in the money supply (or an increase in the price level, a decrease in foreign interest rates, or a decrease in the expected exchange rate [as defined]) is to shift the AA curve downward.

EXERCISE

Identify whether the AA curve shifts in response to each of the following changes. Indicate whether the curve shifts up, down, left, or right. Possible answers are AA right, AA left, or neither.

- Decrease in government transfer payments.
- Decrease in the foreign price level.
- Increase in foreign interest rates.
- Decrease in the expected exchange rate $E_{\$/£}^{e}$.
- Decrease in U.S. GNP.
- Decrease in the U.S. money supply.

9.6 SUPEREQUILIBRIUM: COMBINING DD AND AA

The DD curve represents the set of equilibriums in the goods and services (G&S) market. It describes an equilibrium gross national product (GNP) level for each and every exchange rate that may prevail. Due to the assumption that firms respond to excess demand by increasing supply (and to excess supply by decreasing supply), GNP rises or falls until the economy is in equilibrium on the DD curve.

The AA curve represents the set of equilibriums in the asset market. It indicates an equilibrium exchange rate for each and every GNP level that might prevail. Due to the assumption that investors will demand foreign currency when the foreign rate of return exceeds the domestic return and that they will supply foreign currency when the domestic rate of return exceeds the foreign return, the exchange rate will rise or fall until the economy is in equilibrium on the AA curve.

Since both the G&S market and the asset markets are operating concurrently, equilibriums in both markets can only occur where the DD curve intersects the AA curve. This is shown in Figure 9.7 "AA-DD Superequilibrium" at point F, with equilibrium GNP ($\_{\$}$) and exchange rate ($\hat{E}_{\$/£}$). It is worth emphasizing that at point F, the three markets—that is, the G&S market, the money market, and the foreign exchange market—are in equilibrium simultaneously. For this reason, point F is more than a plain old equilibrium; instead it is a superequilibrium.

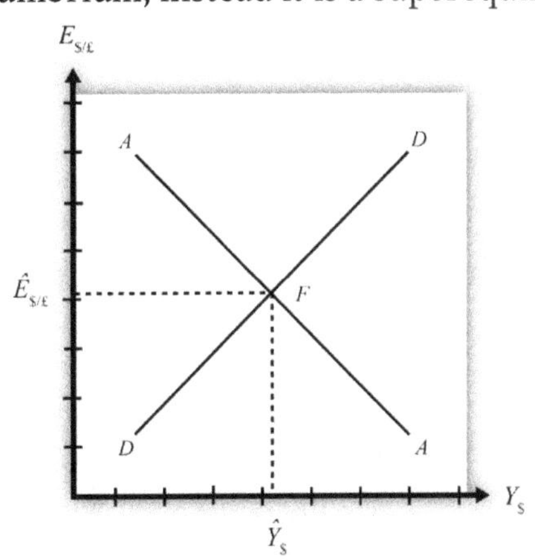

Figure 9.7 AA-DD Superequilibrium

The superequilibrium point is where we would expect behavioral responses by firms, households, and investors to move the exchange rate and GNP level, assuming the exogenous variables remain fixed at their original levels and assuming sufficient time is allowed for adjustment to the equilibrium to take place.

The equilibrium at F is like the lowest point of two intersecting valleys that reach their combined lowest point at a pool where the two valleys meet. A -3D rendition of this is shown in Figure 9.8 «A -3D AA-DD Depiction». The steepness of the valleys is meant to represent the speed of adjustment. Thus the AA valley is drawn much steeper than the DD valley to reflect the much more rapid adjustment in the asset markets in comparison to goods market adjustment. Anytime the economy is away from the equilibrium, forces will act to move it to the pool in the center. However, as will be shown later, adjustment to the AA curve will occur much faster than adjustment to the DD curve.

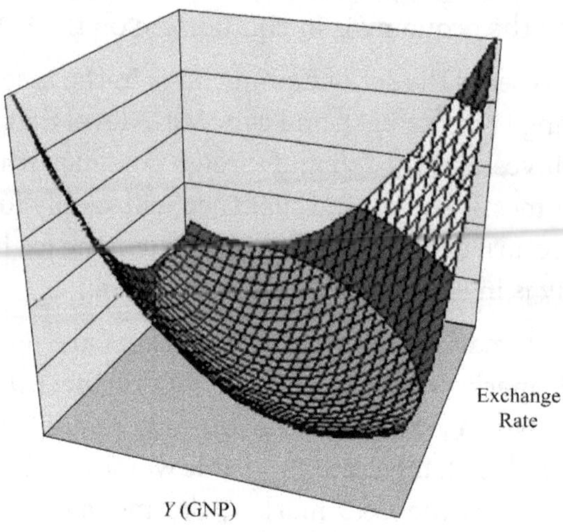

Figure 9.8 A 3-D AA-DD Depiction

KEY TAKEAWAY

- A superequilibrium describes the GNP level and exchange rate value at the intersection of the AA and DD curves. It represents the values that provide for equilibriums in the money market, the Forex market, and the G&S market simultaneously.

EXERCISE

- Jeopardy Questions: As in the popular television game show, you are given an answer to a question and you must respond with the question. For example, if the answer is "a tax on imports," then the correct question is "What is a tariff?"

- This market is in equilibrium when an economy is on an AA curve.
- This market is in equilibrium when an economy is on a DD curve.
- The term used to describe the equilibrium at the intersection of a DD curve and an AA curve.

9.7 ADJUSTMENT TO THE SUPEREQUILIBRIUM

In order to discuss adjustment to the superequilibrium, we must first talk about how an economy can end up out of equilibrium. This will occur anytime there is a change in one or more of the exogenous variables that cause the AA or DD curves to shift. In a real economy, we should expect these variables to be changing frequently. Variables such as interest rates will certainly change every day. A variable such as the average expected future exchange rate held by investors probably changes every minute. Each time an exogenous variable changes, the superequilibrium point will shift, setting off behavioral responses by households, businesses, and investors that will affect the exchange rate and gross national product (GNP) in the direction of the new superequilibrium. However, as we will indicate below, the adjustment process will take time, perhaps several months or more, depending on the size of the change. Since we should expect that as adjustment to one variable change is in process, other exogenous variables will also change, we must recognize that the superequilibrium is really like a moving target. Each day, maybe each hour, the target moves, resulting in a continual adjustment process.

Although an equilibrium may never be reached in the real-world economy, the model remains very useful in understanding how changes in some variables will affect the behavior of agents and influence other variables. The model in essence offers us the opportunity to conduct experiments in simplified settings. Changing one exogenous variable and inferring its effect is a comparative statics experiment because of the ceteris paribus assumption. Ceteris paribus allows us to isolate one change and work through its impact with certainty that nothing else could influence the result.

Below, we'll consider adjustment to two changes: a reduction in investment demand, which shifts the DD curve, and an increase in foreign interest rates, which shifts the AA curve.

Reduction in Investment

Consider adjustment to a decrease in investment demand. Begin with an original superequilibrium, where DD crosses AA at point F with GNP at $Y_{\$}^{1}$ and exchange rate at $E_{\$/£}^{1}$. When investment decreases, ceteris paribus, the DD curve shifts to the left, as was shown in Chapter 9, Section 9.3 . This shift is shown in Figure 9.9 "Effects of an Investment Demand Decrease in the AA-DD Model" as a shift from DD to D'D'.

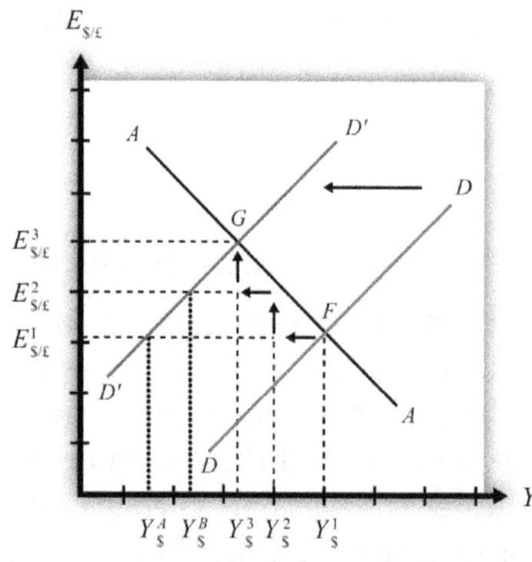

Figure 9.9 Effects of an Investment Demand Decrease in the AA-DD Model

The quick result is that the equilibrium shifts to point G, GNP falls to $Y_\$^3$, and the exchange rate rises to $E_{\$/£}^3$. The increase in the exchange rate represents a depreciation of the U.S. dollar value. However, this result does not explain the adjustment process, so let's take a more careful look at how the economy gets from point F to G.

Step 1: When investment demand falls, aggregate demand falls short of aggregate supply, leading to a buildup of inventories. Firms respond by cutting back supply, and GNP slowly begins to fall. Initially, there is no change in the exchange rate. On the graph, this is represented by a leftward shift from the initial equilibrium at point F ($Y_\$^1$ to $Y_\$^2$). Adjustment to changes in aggregate demand will be gradual, perhaps taking several months or more to be fully implemented.

Step 2: As GNP falls, it causes a decrease in U.S. interest rates. With lower interest rates, the rate of return on U.S. assets falls below that in the United Kingdom and international investors shift funds abroad, leading to a dollar depreciation (pound appreciation)—that is, an increase in the exchange rate $E_{\$/£}$. This moves the economy upward, back to the AA curve. The adjustment in the asset market will occur quickly after the change in interest rates, so the leftward shift from point F in the diagram results in adjustment upward to regain equilibrium in the asset market on the AA curve.

Step 3: Continuing reductions in GNP caused by excess aggregate demand, results in continuing decreases in interest rates and rates of return, repeating the stepwise process above until the new equilibrium is reached at point G in the diagram.

During the adjustment process, there are several other noteworthy changes taking place. At the initial equilibrium, when investment demand first falls, aggregate supply exceeds demand by the difference of $Y_\$^2$ - $Y_\$^A$. Adjustment in the goods market will be trying to reachieve equilibrium by getting back to the DD curve. However, the economy will never get to $Y_\$^A$. That's because the asset market will adjust in the meantime. As GNP falls, the exchange rate is pushed up to get back onto the AA curve. Remember, that asset market adjustment takes place quickly after an interest rate change (perhaps in several hours or days), while goods market adjustment can take months. When the exchange rate rises, the dollar depreciation makes foreign goods more expensive and reduces imports. It also makes U.S. goods cheaper to foreigners and stimulates exports, both of which cause an increase in current account demand. This change in demand is represented as a movement along the new D'D' curve. Thus when the exchange rate rises up to $E_{\$/£}^2$ during the adjustment process, aggregate demand will have risen from $Y_\$^A$ to $Y_\$^B$ along the new D'D' curve. In other words, the "target" for GNP adjustment moves closer as the exchange rate rises. In the end, the target for GNP reaches $Y_\$^3$ just as the exchange rate rises to $E_{\$/£}^3$.

Increase in Foreign Interest Rates

Consider adjustment to an increase in the foreign interest rate, $i_£$. Begin with an original superequilibrium where DD crosses AA at point F with GNP at Y^1 and exchange rate at $E_{\$/£}^1$. When the foreign interest rate increases, ceteris paribus, the AA curve shifts upward, as was shown in Chapter 9 Section 9.5 . This shift is shown in Figure 9.10 "Effects of an Increase in Foreign Interest Rates in the AA-DD Model" as a shift from AA to A'A'.

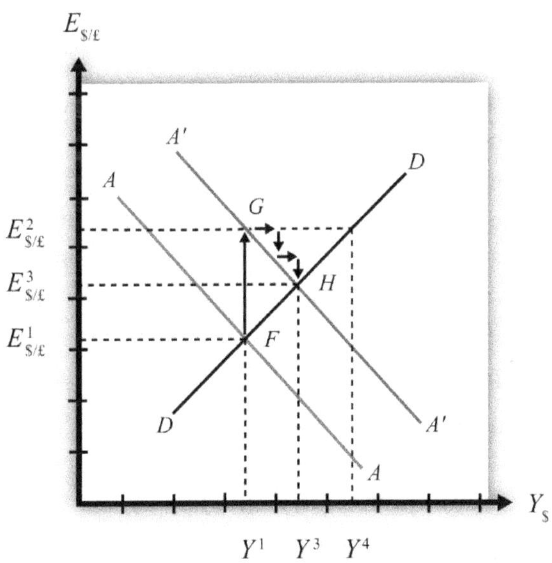

Figure 9.10 Effects of an Increase in Foreign Interest Rates in the AA-DD Model

The quick result is that the equilibrium shifts to point H, GNP rises to Y^3, and the exchange rate rises to E^3. The increase in the exchange rate represents a depreciation of the U.S. dollar value.

The convenience of the graphical approach is that it allows us to quickly identify the final outcome using only our knowledge about the mechanics of the AA-DD diagram. However, this quick result does not explain the adjustment process, so let's take a more careful look at how the economy gets from point F to H.

Step 1: When the foreign interest rate ($i_£$) rises, the rate of return on foreign British assets rises above the rate of return on domestic U.S. assets in the foreign exchange market. This causes an immediate increase in the demand for foreign British currency, causing an appreciation of the pound and a depreciation of the U.S. dollar. Thus the exchange rate ($E_{\$/£}$) rises. This change is represented by the movement from point F to G on the AA-DD diagram. The AA curve shifts up to reflect the new set of asset market equilibriums corresponding to the now-higher foreign interest rate. Since the foreign exchange market adjusts very swiftly to changes in interest rates, the economy will not remain off the new A'A' curve for very long.

Step 2: Now that the exchange rate has risen to $E_{\$/£}^2$, the real exchange has also increased. This implies foreign goods and services are relatively more expensive while U.S. G&S are relatively cheaper. This will raise demand for U.S. exports, curtail demand for U.S. imports, and result in an increase in current account and thereby aggregate demand. Note that the new equilibrium demand at exchange rate is temporarily at GNP level Y^4, which is on the DD curve given the exchange rate $E_{\$/£}^2$. Because aggregate demand exceeds aggregate supply, inventories will begin to fall, stimulating an increase in production and thus GNP. This is represented by a rightward shift from point G (small arrow).

Step 3: As GNP rises, so does real money demand, causing an increase in U.S. interest rates. With higher interest rates, the rate of return on U.S. assets rises above that in the United Kingdom and international investors shift funds back to the United States, leading to a dollar appreciation (pound depreciation), or the decrease in the exchange rate ($E_{\$/£}$). This moves the economy downward, back to the A'A' curve. The adjustment in the asset market will occur quickly after the change in interest rates. Thus the rightward shift from point G in the diagram results in quick downward adjustment to regain equilibrium in the asset market on the A'A' curve, as shown.

Step 4: Continuing increases in GNP caused by excess aggregate demand, results in continuing increases in U.S. interest rates and rates of return, repeating the stepwise process above until the new equilibrium is reached at point H in the diagram.

During the adjustment process, there are several other noteworthy changes taking place. At point G, aggregate demand exceeds supply by the difference $Y^4 - Y^1$. Adjustment in the goods market will be trying to reachieve equilibrium by getting back to the DD curve. However, the economy will never get to Y^4. That's because the asset market will adjust during the transition. As GNP rises, the exchange rate is gradually pushed down to get back onto the A'A' curve. When the exchange rate falls, the dollar appreciation makes foreign goods cheaper, raising imports. It also makes U.S. goods more expensive to foreigners, reducing exports—both of which cause a decrease in current account demand. This change in demand is represented as a movement along the DD curve. Thus when the exchange rate falls during the adjustment process, aggregate demand falls from Y^4 along the DD curve. In other words, the "target" for GNP adjustment moves closer as the exchange rate falls. In the end, the target for GNP reaches Y^3 just as the exchange rate falls to $E_{\$/£}^3$.

KEY TAKEAWAYS

- Adjustment in the asset market occurs quickly, whereas adjustment in the G&S market occurs much more slowly.
- In the AA-DD model, a decrease in investment demand ultimately reduces GNP and raises the exchange rate, which, as defined, means a depreciation of the dollar.
- In the AA-DD model, an increase in foreign interest rates ultimately raises GNP and raises the exchange rate, which, as defined, means a depreciation of the dollar.

EXERCISE

- Jeopardy Questions: As in the popular television game show, you are given an answer to a question and you must respond with the question. For example, if the answer is "a tax on imports," then the correct question is "What is a tariff?"
- Of increase, decrease, or stay the same, the final effect on equilibrium GNP following an increase in investment demand in the AA-DD model.
- Of increase, decrease or stay the same, the immediate effect on $E_{\$/£}$ following an increase in investment demand in the AA-DD model.
- Of increase, decrease, or stay the same, the final effect on equilibrium GNP following a decrease in foreign interest rates in the AA-DD model.
- Of increase, decrease, or stay the same, the immediate effect on $E_{\$/£}$ following a decrease in British interest rates in the AA-DD model.
- Of faster, slower, or the same rate, this describes the speed of adjustment to a DD curve relative to an AA curve.

9.8 THE CURRENT ACCOUNT BALANCE AND AA-DD

In later chapters we will use the AA-DD model to describe the effects of policy changes on macroeconomic variables in an open economy. The two most important macro variables are the exchange rate and the current account (trade) balance. The effects of changes on the exchange rate are vividly portrayed in the AA-DD diagram since this variable is plotted along the vertical axis and its value is determined as an element of the equilibrium. The current account (CA) variable is not displayed in the AA-DD diagram, but with some further thought we can devise a method to identify the current account balance at different positions in the AA-DD diagram.

First, note that there is no "equilibrium" current account balance in a floating exchange rate system. Any balance on the current account is possible because any balance can correspond to balance on the balance of payments. The balance of payments is made up of two broad subaccounts: the current account and the financial account, the sum of whose balances must equal zero. When the balances sum to zero, the foreign demand for domestic goods, services, income, and assets is equal to domestic supply of goods, services, income, and assets. Thus there must always be "balance" on the balance of payments regardless of the balances on the individual subaccounts.

Iso-CAB Line

An iso-CAB line is a line drawn on an AA-DD diagram, Figure 9.11 «Iso-CAB Lines in an AA-DD Diagram», representing a set of points along which the current account balance (CAB) is the same. Note that "iso" is a prefix that means the same. In the adjoining diagram, we have superimposed three-dotted iso-CAB lines labeled CC, C'C', and C"C". Each line represents a set of GNP and exchange rate combinations that generate the same balance on the current account. The higher the CAB line, the larger is the balance on the current account. Thus the CAB balance on C"C" is greater than the balance along CC. Also note that each CAB line is positively sloped with a slope less than the slope of the DD curve. Next, we'll continue with a justification for this description.

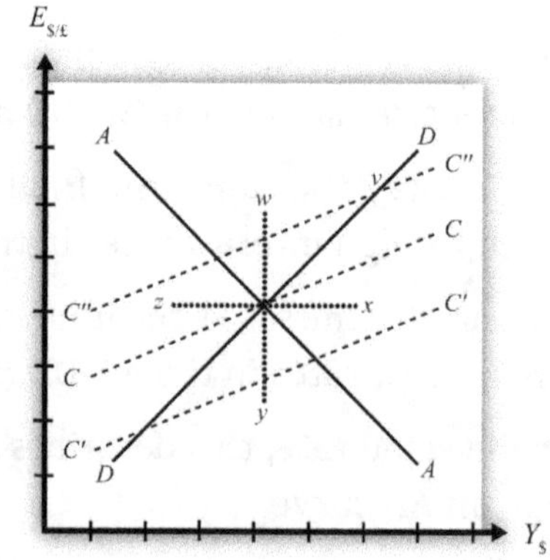

Figure 9.11 Iso-CAB Lines in an AA-DD Diagram

Justifying the Shape of the Iso-CAB Line

Consider the superequilibrium point at the intersection of AA and DD. The positions of these two curves are determined by the values of the exogenous variables in the model, including the domestic price level ($P_{\$}$), the foreign price level ($P_{£}$), tax revenues (T), and transfer payments (TR), among others. The intersection of the two curves determines the equilibrium GNP level ($Y_{\$}$) and the exchange rate ($E_{\$/£}$) (not labeled in diagram). Recall from Chapter 9 ,Section 9.2 that the DD curve is derived from the aggregate demand function, one component of which is the current account function. The current account function, as shown below, is a function of all the variables listed immediately above:

Thus at the intersection of AA and DD there are presumed known values for the exogenous variables and determined values for the endogenous variables, $E_{\$/£}$ and $Y_{\$}$.

All these values could, in principle, be plugged into the current account demand function (CA^D) to determine the CA balance at the equilibrium. Let's assume that value is given by K, as shown in the above expression.

Now let's consider movements in the superequilibrium to other points on the diagram. Let's suppose that the equilibrium moved to point x directly to the right. That could arise from a rightward shift of DD and an upward shift of AA. We will also assume that this shift did not arise due to changes in $P_{\$}$, $P_{£}$, T, or TR, the other exogenous variables that affect the current account. (More on this issue below.) One possibility is an increase in the money supply and an increase in investment demand. Note that these shifts are not depicted.

At point x, GNP is higher while the exchange rate and the other exogenous variables are the same as before. Since an increase in $Y_{\$}$ raises disposable income, which reduces current account demand, the current account balance must be at a lower level at point x compared to the initial equilibrium.

If the equilibrium had shifted to point z instead, then GNP is lower while the exchange rate and the other exogenous variables are the same as before. Since a decrease in $Y_{\$}$ lowers disposable income, which raises current account demand, the current account balance must be at a higher level at point z compared to the initial equilibrium.

Next, suppose the equilibrium had shifted to point y instead. In this case, the exchange rate ($E_{\$/£}$) is lower while GNP and the other exogenous variables are the same as before. Since a decrease in $E_{\$/£}$ reduces the real exchange rate, which reduces current account demand, the current account balance must be at a lower level at point y compared to the initial equilibrium.

Finally, suppose the equilibrium had shifted to point w. In this case, the exchange rate, $E_{\$/£}$, is higher while GNP and the other exogenous variables are the same as before. Since an increase in $E_{\$/£}$ raises the real exchange rate, which increases current account demand, the current account balance must be at a higher level at point y compared to the initial equilibrium.

Since a movement to w and z results in an increase in the current account balance, while a shift to x or y causes a reduction in the balance, the line representing a constant CAB must be positively sloped.

Another way to see this is to use the CA^D function above. Suppose the CAB is originally at the value K. If the exchange rate ($E_{\$/£}$) rises, ceteris paribus, then CA will rise. We can now ask how GNP would have to change to get back to a CA balance of K. Clearly, if Y rises, disposable income rises and the current account balance falls. Raise GNP by precisely the right amount, and we can get the CAB back to K. Thus an increase in $E_{\$/£}$ must accompany an increase in GNP to maintain a fixed current account balance and therefore an iso-CAB line must be positively sloped.

The last thing we need to show is that the iso-CAB line is less steeply sloped than the DD line. Suppose the economy moved to a point such as v, which is on the same DD curve as the original superequilibrium. Recall from Chapter 9 , Section 9.2 , the DD curve is derived from a change in the exchange rate and its effect on equilibrium GNP in the G&S market alone. The increase in the exchange rate causes an increase in current account demand through its effect on the real exchange rate. This causes an increase in aggregate demand, which inspires the increase in GNP. When equilibrium is reached in the G&S market, at point v, aggregate supply, Y, will equal aggregate demand and the following expression must hold:

The left side is aggregate supply given by the equilibrium value at point v and the right side is aggregate demand. Since GNP is higher at v, consumption demand (C^D) must also be higher. However, because the marginal propensity to consume is less than one, not all the extra GNP will be spent on consumption goods; some will be saved. Nevertheless, aggregate demand (on the right side) must rise up to match the increase in supply on the left side. Since all the increase in demand cannot come from consumption, the remainder must come from the current account. This implies that a movement along the DD curve to v results in an increase in the current account balance. It also implies that the iso-CAB line must be less steeply sloped than the DD curve.

Using the Iso-CAB Line

The iso-CAB line can be used to assess the change in the country's current account balance from any exogenous variable change except changes in $P_\$$, $P_£$, T, and TR. The reason we must exclude these variables is because the current account demand function is also dependent on these exogenous variables. If tax revenues increased, for example, all the iso-CAB lines would shift, making it much more difficult to pinpoint the final effect on the current account balance.

However, for monetary policy changes and government spending fiscal policy changes, the iso-CAB line will work. Anytime the superequilibrium shifts above the original iso-CAB line, the economy will move onto another iso-CAB line with a higher balance. (This is like the shift to point v in Figure 9.11 «Iso-CAB Lines in an AA-DD Diagram».) Recall that the CA = EX - IM, which can be positive or negative. If CAB were in surplus originally, an increase in the CAB (as with a movement to v) would imply an increase in the CA surplus. However, if the CAB were in deficit originally, then an increase in CAB implies a reduction in the deficit. If the increase in the CAB were sufficiently large, the CAB could move from deficit to surplus.

In a similar way, anytime the superequilibrium shifts below an initial iso-CAB line, the CAB surplus will fall, or the CAB deficit will rise.

Remember that the iso-CAB line is only used a reference to track the current account balance. The iso-CAB line is not used to determine the superequilibrium. For this reason, the iso-CAB line is plotted as a dashed line rather than a solid line.

KEY TAKEAWAYS

- An iso-CAB line is a line drawn on an AA-DD diagram, representing a set of points along which the current account balance (CAB) is the same.
- An iso-CAB line is positively sloped and with a slope that is less than the slope of the DD curve.
- The iso-CAB line can be used to assess the change in the country's current account balance from any exogenous variable change except changes in $P_\$$, $P_£$, T, and TR.

EXERCISE

- Jeopardy Questions: As in the popular television game show, you are given an answer to a question and you must respond with the question. For example, if the answer is "a tax on imports," then the correct question is "What is a tariff?"
- Of greater than, less than, or equal, the current account balance for an exchange rate and GNP combination that lies above an iso-CAB line relative to a combination that lies on the line.
- Of greater than, less than, or equal, the current account surplus for an exchange rate and GNP combination that lies below an iso-CAB line relative to the surplus for a combination that lies on the line.
- Of greater than, less than, or equal, the current account deficit for an exchange rate and GNP combination that lies below an iso-CAB line relative to the deficit for a combination that lies on the line.
- Of higher, ower, or equal, the position of an iso-CAB line for a country with a current account deficit relative to an iso-CAB line when the country runs a surplus.
- Of positive, negative, or zero, this describes the slope of an iso-CAB line.
- Of steeper, flatter, or the same, this describes an iso-CAB line relative to a DD curve.

[illegible]

[illegible]

1. [illegible]

CHAPTER

IMPACTS OF POLICY ON FLOATING EXCHANGE RATES 10

INTRODUCTION

The effects of government policies on key macroeconomic variables are an important issue in international finance. The AA-DD model constructed in Chapter 9 is used in this chapter to analyze the effects of fiscal and monetary policy under a regime of floating exchange rates. The results are more comprehensive than the previous analyses of the same policies because they take into account all the between-market effects across the money market, the foreign exchange (Forex) market, and the goods and services (G&S) market.

10.1 POLICY WITH FLOATING EXCHANGE RATES: AN OVERVIEW

This chapter uses the AA-DD model to describe the effects of fiscal and monetary policy under a system of floating exchange rates. Fiscal and monetary policies are the primary tools governments use to guide the macroeconomy. In introductory macroeconomics courses, students learn how fiscal and monetary policy levers can be used to influence the level of gross national product (GNP), the inflation rate, the unemployment rate, and interest rates. In this chapter, that analysis is expanded to an open economy (i.e., one open to trade) and to the effects on exchange rates and current account balances.

Results

Using the AA-DD model, several important relationships between key economic variables are shown:

Expansionary monetary policy (↑MS) causes an increase in GNP and a depreciation of the domestic currency in a floating exchange rate system in the short run.

- Contractionary monetary policy (↓MS) causes a decrease in GNP and an appreciation of the domestic currency in a floating exchange rate system in the short run.

- Expansionary fiscal policy (↑G, ↑TR, or ↓T) causes an increase in GNP and an appreciation of the domestic currency in a floating exchange rate system.
- Contractionary fiscal policy (↓G, ↓TR, or ↑T) causes a decrease in GNP and a depreciation of the domestic currency in a floating exchange rate system.
- In the long run, once inflation effects are included, expansionary monetary policy (↑M^S) in a full employment economy causes no long-term change in GNP and a depreciation of the domestic currency in a floating exchange rate system. In the transition, the exchange rate overshoots its long-run target and GNP rises then falls.
- A sterilized foreign exchange intervention will have no effect on GNP or the exchange rate in the AA-DD model, unless international investors adjust their expected future exchange rate in response.
- A central bank can influence the exchange rate with direct Forex interventions (buying or selling domestic currency in exchange for foreign currency). To sell foreign currency and buy domestic currency, the central bank must have a stockpile of foreign currency reserves.
- A central bank can also influence the exchange rate with indirect open market operations (buying or selling domestic treasury bonds). These transactions work through money supply changes and their effect on interest rates.
- Purchases (sales) of foreign currency on the Forex will raise (lower) the domestic money supply and cause a secondary indirect effect upon the exchange rate.

Connections

The AA-DD model was developed to describe the interrelationships of macroeconomic variables within an open economy. Since some of these macroeconomic variables are controlled by the government, we can use the model to understand the likely effects of government policy changes. The two main levers the government controls are monetary policy (changes in the money supply) and fiscal policy (changes in the government budget). In this chapter, the AA-DD model is applied to understand government policy effects in the context of a floating exchange rate system. In Chapter 12 , we'll revisit these same government policies in the context of a fixed exchange rate system.

It is important to recognize that these results are what "would" happen under the full set of assumptions that describe the AA-DD model. These effects may or may not happen in reality. Despite this problem, the model surely captures some of the simple cause-and-effect relationships and therefore helps us to understand the broader implications of policy changes. Thus even if in reality many more elements not described in the model may act to influence the key endogenous variables, the AA-DD model at least gives a more complete picture of some of the expected tendencies.

KEY TAKEAWAYS

- The main objective of the AA-DD model is to assess the effects of monetary and fiscal policy changes.
- It is important to recognize that these results are what "would" happen under the full set of assumptions that describes the AA-DD model; they may or may not accurately describe actual outcomes in actual economies.

EXERCISE

- Jeopardy Questions: As in the popular television game show, you are given an answer to a question and you must respond with the question. For example, if the answer is "a tax on imports," then the correct question is "What is a tariff?"
- Of increase, decrease, or stay the same, this is the effect on equilibrium GNP in the short run if government spending decreases in the AA-DD model with floating exchange rates.
- Of increase, decrease, or stay the same, this is the effect on the domestic currency value in the short run if government spending decreases in the AA-DD model with floating exchange rates.
- Of increase, decrease, or stay the same, this is the effect on the foreign currency value (vis-à-vis the domestic) in the short run if domestic government spending decreases in the AA-DD model with floating exchange rates.
- Of increase, decrease, or stay the same, this is the effect on equilibrium GNP in the short run if the nominal money supply decreases in the AA-DD model with floating exchange rates.
- Of increase, decrease, or stay the same, this is the effect on the domestic currency value in the short run if the nominal money supply decreases in the AA-DD model with floating exchange rates.
- Of increase, decrease, or stay the same, this is the effect on equilibrium GNP in the long run if the nominal money supply increases in the AA-DD model with floating exchange rates.
- Of increase, decrease, or stay the same, this is the effect on the domestic currency value in the long run if the nominal money supply increases in the AA-DD model with floating exchange rates.

10.2 MONETARY POLICY WITH FLOATING EXCHANGE RATES

In this section, we use the AA-DD model to assess the effects of monetary policy in a floating exchange rate system. Recall from Chapter 7 that the money supply is effectively controlled by a country's central bank. In the case of the United States, this is the Federal Reserve Board, or the Fed for short. When the money supply increases due to action taken by the central bank, we refer to it as expansionary monetary policy. If the central bank acts to reduce the money supply, it is referred to as contractionary monetary policy. Methods that can be used to change the money supply are discussed in Chapter 7, Section 7.5

Expansionary Monetary Policy

Suppose the economy is originally at a superequilibrium shown as point F in Figure 10.1 «Expansionary Monetary Policy in the AA-DD Model with Floating Exchange Rates». The original GNP level is Y^1 and the exchange rate is $E_{\$/£}^{1}$. Next, suppose the U.S. central bank (or the Fed) decides to expand the money supply. As shown in Chapter 9 , Section 9.5 , money supply changes cause a shift in the AA curve. More specifically, an increase in the money supply will cause AA to shift upward (i.e., ↓M^S is an AA up-shifter). This is depicted in the diagram as a shift from the red AA to the blue A'A' line.

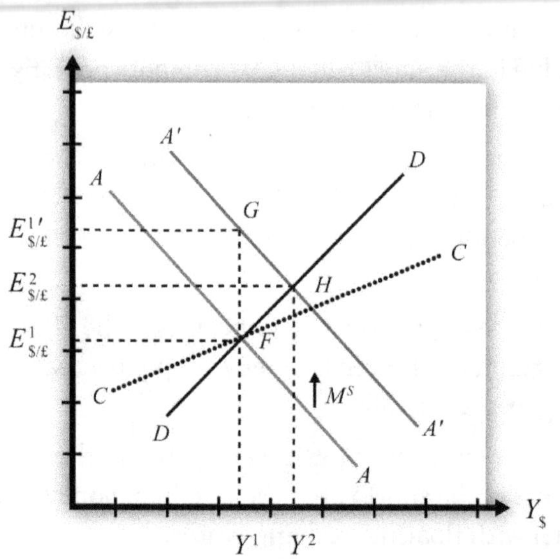

Figure 10.1 Expansionary Monetary Policy in the AA-DD Model with Floating Exchange Rates

There are several different levels of detail that can be provided to describe the effects of this policy. Below, we present three descriptions with increasing degrees of completeness. First the quick result, then the quick result with the transition process described, and finally the complete adjustment story.

Quick Result

The increase in AA causes a shift in the superequilibrium point from F to H. In adjusting to the new equilibrium at H, GNP rises from Y^1 to Y^2 and the exchange rate increases from $E_{\$/£}^{1}$ to $E_{\$/£}^{2}$. The increase in the exchange rate represents an increase in the British pound value and a decrease in the U.S. dollar value. In other words, it is an appreciation of the pound and a depreciation of the dollar. Since the final equilibrium point H is above the initial iso-CAB line CC, the current account balance increases. If the CAB were in surplus at F, then the surplus increases; if the CAB were in deficit, then the deficit falls. Thus U.S. expansionary monetary policy causes an increase in GNP, a depreciation of the U.S. dollar, and an increase in the current account balance in a floating exchange rate system according to the AA-DD model.

Transition Description

Consider the upward shift of the AA curve due to the increase in the money supply. Since exchange rates adjust much more rapidly than GNP, the economy will initially adjust back to the new A'A' curve before any change in GNP occurs. That means the first adjustment will be from point F to point G directly above. The exchange rate will increase from $E_{\$/£}^{1}$ to $E_{\$/£}^{1'}$, representing a depreciation of the U.S. dollar.

Now at point G, the economy lies to the left of the DD curve. Thus GNP will begin to rise to get back to goods and services (G&S) market equilibrium on the DD curve. However, as GNP rises, the economy moves to the right above the A'A' curve, which forces a downward readjustment of the exchange rate to get back to A'A'. In the end, the economy will adjust in a stepwise fashion from point G to point H, with each rightward movement in GNP followed by a quick reduction in the exchange rate to remain on the A'A' curve. This process will continue until the economy reaches the superequilibrium at point H.

Notice that in the transition the exchange rate first rises to $E_{\$/£}^{1'}$. Above the rate it will ultimately reach $E_{\$/£}^{2}$ before settling back to superequilibrium value. This is an example of exchange rate overshooting. In the transition, the exchange rate overshoots its ultimate long-run value.

Exchange rate overshooting is used as one explanation for the volatility of exchange rates in floating markets. If many small changes occur frequently in an economy, the economy may always be in transition moving to a superequilibrium. Because of the more rapid adjustment of exchange rates, it is possible that many episodes of overshooting—both upward and downward—can occur in a relatively short period.

Complete Adjustment Story

Step 1: When the money supply increases, real money supply will exceed real money demand in the economy. Since households and businesses hold more money than they would like, at current interest rates, they begin to convert liquid money assets into less-liquid nonmoney assets. This raises the supply of long-term deposits and the amount of funds available for banks to loan. More money to lend will lower average U.S. interest rates, which in turn will result in a lower U.S. rate of return in the Forex market. Since $RoR_{\$} < ROR_{£}$ now, there will be an immediate increase in the demand for foreign British currency, thus causing an appreciation of the pound and a depreciation of the U.S. dollar. Thus the exchange rate ($E_{\$/£}$) rises. This change is represented by the movement from point F to G on the AA-DD diagram. The AA curve has shifted up to reflect the new set of asset market equilbria corresponding to the higher U.S. money supply. Since the money market and foreign exchange (Forex) markets adjust very swiftly to the money supply change, the economy will not remain off the new A'A' curve for very long.

Step 2: Now that the exchange rate has risen to $E_{\$/£}^{1'}$, the real exchange has also increased. This implies foreign goods and services are relatively more expensive while U.S. G&S are relatively cheaper. This will raise demand for U.S. exports, curtail demand for U.S. imports, and result in an increase in current account and, thereby, aggregate demand. Because aggregate demand exceeds aggregate supply, inventories will begin to fall, stimulating an increase in production and thus GNP. This is represented by a rightward shift from point G.

Step 3: As GNP rises, so does real money demand, causing an increase in U.S. interest rates. With higher interest rates, the rate of return on U.S. assets rises above that in the United Kingdom, and international investors shift funds back to the United States, resulting in a dollar appreciation (pound depreciation)—that is, a decrease in the exchange rate ($E_{\$/£}$). This moves the economy downward, back to the A'A' curve. The adjustment in the asset market will occur quickly after the change in interest rates. Thus the rightward shift from point G in the diagram results in quick downward adjustment to regain equilibrium in the asset market on the A'A' curve, as shown in the figure.

Step 4: Continuing increases in GNP caused by excess aggregate demand, results in continuing increases in U.S. interest rates and rates of return, repeating the stepwise process above until the new equilibrium is reached at point H in the diagram.

Step 5: The equilibrium at H lies to the northeast of F along the original DD curve. As shown in Chapter 9 , Section 9.8 ", the equilibrium at H lies above the original iso-CAB line. Therefore, the current account balance will rise.

Contractionary Monetary Policy

Contractionary monetary policy corresponds to a decrease in the money supply. In the AA-DD model, a decrease in the money supply shifts the AA curve downward. The effects will be the opposite of those described above for expansionary monetary policy. A complete description is left for the reader as an exercise.

The quick effects, however, are as follows. U.S. contractionary monetary policy will cause a reduction in GNP and a reduction in the exchange rate, $E_{\$/£}$, implying an appreciation of the U.S. dollar and a decrease in the current account balance.

KEY TAKEAWAYS

- The U.S. expansionary monetary policy causes an increase in GNP, a depreciation of the U.S. dollar, and an increase in the current account balance in a floating exchange rate system according to the AA-DD model.
- Contractionary monetary policy will cause a reduction in GNP and a reduction in the exchange rate ($E_{\$/£}$), implying an appreciation of the U.S. dollar and a decrease in the current account balance.

EXERCISES

- Use the AA-DD model (not necessarily the diagram) to explain the sequential short-run adjustment process of an increase in the money supply on the following economic variables under floating exchange rates. (In other words, first answer how the money supply increase immediately affects the interest rate. Next, answer how the previous economic variable—i.e., the interest rate—affects the nominal exchange rate. Continue this process through investment.)
- The interest rate
- The nominal exchange rate
- The real exchange rate
- The current account balance
- GNP
- Disposable income
- Consumption
- Saving
- Investment
- Repeat the exercise above assuming a decrease in the money supply.
- Suppose a country with floating exchange rates has a current account deficit that its government considers too large. Use an AA-DD diagram to show how monetary policy could be used to reduce the current account deficit. Does this action help or hinder its goal of maintaining low unemployment? Explain.

10.3 FISCAL POLICY WITH FLOATING EXCHANGE RATES

In this section, we use the AA-DD model to assess the effects of fiscal policy in a floating exchange rate system. Recall that fiscal policy refers to any change in expenditures or revenues within any branch of the government. This means any change in government spending—transfer payments, or taxes, by either federal, state, or local governments—represents a fiscal policy change. Since changes in expenditures or revenues will often affect a government budget balance, we can also say that a change in the government surplus or deficit represents a change in fiscal policy.

When government spending or transfer payments increase, or tax revenues decrease, we refer to it as expansionary fiscal policy. These actions would also be associated with an increase in the government budget deficit or a decrease in its budget surplus. If the government acts to reduce government spending or transfer payments, or increase tax revenues, it is referred to as contractionary fiscal policy. These actions would also be associated with a decrease in the government budget deficit, or an increase in its budget surplus.

Expansionary Fiscal Policy

Suppose the economy is originally at a superequilibrium shown as point J in Figure 10.2 «Expansionary Fiscal Policy in the AA-DD Model with Floating Exchange Rates». The original gross national product (GNP) level is Y^1 and the exchange rate is $E_{\$/£}^1$. Next, suppose the government decides to increase government spending (or increase transfer payments or decrease taxes). As shown in Chapter 9 , Section 9.3 , fiscal policy changes cause a shift in the DD curve. More specifically, an increase in government spending (or an increase in transfer payments or a decrease in taxes) will cause DD to shift rightward (i.e., ↑G, ↑TR, and ↓T all are DD right-shifters). This is depicted in the diagram as a shift from the red DD to the blue D'D' line.

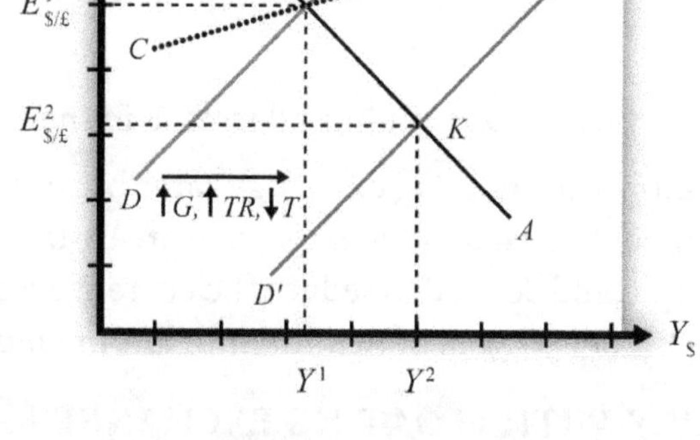

Figure 10.2 Expansionary Fiscal Policy in the AA-DD Model with Floating Exchange Rates

There are several different levels of detail that can be provided to describe the effects of this policy. Below, we present three descriptions with increasing degrees of completeness: first the quick result, then the quick result with the transition process described, and finally the complete adjustment story.

Quick Result

The increase in DD causes a shift in the superequilibrium point from J to K. In adjusting to the new equilibrium at K, GNP rises from Y^1 to Y^2 and the exchange rate decreases from $E_{\$/£}{}^1$ to $E_{\$/£}{}^2$. The decrease in the exchange represents a decrease in the British pound value and an increase in the U.S. dollar value. In other words, it is a depreciation of the pound and an appreciation of the dollar. Since the final equilibrium point K is below the initial iso-CAB line CC, the current account balance decreases. (Caveat: this will be true for all fiscal expansions, but the iso-CAB line can only be used with an increase in G for an explanation.) If the CAB were in surplus at J, then the surplus decreases; if the CAB were in deficit, then the deficit rises. Thus the U.S. expansionary fiscal policy causes an increase in the U.S. GNP, an appreciation of the U.S. dollar, and a decrease in the current account balance in a floating exchange rate system according to the AA-DD model.

Transition Description

If the expansionary fiscal policy occurs because of an increase in government spending, then government demand for goods and services (G&S) will increase. If the expansionary fiscal policy occurs due to an increase in transfer payments or a decrease in taxes, then disposable income will increase, leading to an increase in consumption demand. In either case aggregate demand increases, and this causes the rightward shift in the DD curve. Immediately after aggregate demand increases, but before any adjustment has occurred at point J, the economy lies to the left of the new D′D′ curve. Thus GNP will begin to rise to get back to G&S market equilibrium on the D′D′ curve. However, as GNP rises, the economy will move above the AA curve, forcing a downward readjustment of the exchange rate to get back to asset market equilibrium on the AA curve. In the end, the economy will adjust in a stepwise fashion from point J to point K, with each rightward movement in GNP followed by a quick reduction in the exchange rate to remain on the AA curve. This process will continue until the economy reaches the superequilibrium at point K.

Complete Adjustment Story

Step 1: If the expansionary fiscal policy occurs because of an increase in government spending, then government demand for G&S will increase. If the expansionary fiscal policy occurs due to an increase in transfer payments or a decrease in taxes, then disposable income will increase, leading to an increase in consumption demand. In either case aggregate demand increases. Before any adjustment occurs, the increase in aggregate demand implies aggregate demand exceeds aggregate supply, which will lead to a decline in inventories. To prevent this decline, retailers (or government suppliers) will signal firms to produce more. As supply increases so does the GNP, and the economy moves to the right of point J.

Step 2: As GNP rises, so does real money demand, causing an increase in U.S. interest rates. With higher interest rates, the rate of return on U.S. assets rises above that in the United Kingdom and international investors shift funds back to the United States, resulting in a dollar appreciation (pound depreciation)—that is, a decrease in the exchange rate $E_{\$/£}$. This moves the economy downward, back to the AA curve. The adjustment in the asset market will occur quickly after the change in interest rates. Thus the rightward shift from point J in the diagram results in quick downward adjustment to regain equilibrium in the asset market on the AA curve, as shown.

Step 3: Continuing increases in GNP caused by excess aggregate demand, results in continuing increases in U.S. interest rates and rates of return, repeating the stepwise process above until the new equilibrium is reached at point K in the diagram.

Step 4: The equilibrium at K lies to the southeast of J along the original AA curve. As shown in Chapter 9 Section 9.8 , the current account balance must be lower at K since both an increase in GNP and a dollar appreciation cause decreases in current account demand. Thus the equilibrium at K lies below the original iso-CAB line. However, this is only assured if the fiscal expansion occurred due to an increase in G.

If transfer payments increased or taxes were reduced, these would both increase disposable income and lead to a further decline in the current account balance. Thus also with these types of fiscal expansions, the current account balance is reduced; however, one cannot use the iso-CAB line to show it.

Contractionary Fiscal Policy

Contractionary fiscal policy corresponds to a decrease in government spending, a decrease in transfer payments, or an increase in taxes. It would also be represented by a decrease in the government budget deficit or an increase in the budget surplus. In the AA-DD model, a contractionary fiscal policy shifts the DD curve leftward. The effects will be the opposite of those described above for expansionary fiscal policy. A complete description is left for the reader as an exercise.

The quick effects, however, are as follows. U.S. contractionary fiscal policy will cause a reduction in GNP and an increase in the exchange rate ($E_{\$/£}$), implying a depreciation of the U.S. dollar.

KEY TAKEAWAYS

- Expansionary fiscal policy causes an increase in GNP, an appreciation of the currency, and a decrease in the current account balance in a floating exchange rate system according to the AA-DD model.

- Contractionary fiscal policy will cause a reduction in GNP, a depreciation of the currency, and an increase in the current account balance in a floating exchange rate system according to the AA-DD model.

EXERCISES

- Suppose a country with floating exchange rates has a current account deficit that its government considers too large. Use an AA-DD diagram to show how fiscal policy could be used to reduce the current account deficit. Does this action help or hinder its goal of maintaining low unemployment?
- The United States maintains a floating exchange rate. In the past few years, its government budget deficit has risen to a very high level. At the same time, its trade deficit has also become much larger.
- Suppose the government reduces government spending to reduce the budget deficit. Assume the U.S. economy can be described with the AA-DD model. In the adjustment to the new equilibrium, the following variables will be affected in the order listed. Indicate whether each variable rises (+) or falls (-) during the adjustment process.

	Indicate + or -
Government Demand (G)	
Aggregate Demand (AD)	
Aggregate Supply ($Y_\$$)	
Real Money Demand ($L[i_\$,Y_\$]$)	
U.S. Interest Rates ($i_\$$)	
U.S. Rate of Return ($RoR_\$$)	
Exchange Rate ($E_{\$/£}$)	
Foreign Rate of Return ($RoR_£$)	
Real Exchange Rate ($q_{\$/£}$)	
Current Account Demand (CA^D)	
Aggregate Demand (AD)	

- Once the final short-run equilibrium is reached, indicate the effect of the decrease in government spending on the following variables:

	Indicate + or -
U.S. Government Budget Deficit	
U.S. Dollar Value	
U.S. Current Account Deficit	
U.S. GNP	

Consider the following actions/occurrences listed in the first column. For each one, use the AA-DD model to determine the impact on the variables from the twin-deficit identity listed along the top row. Consider the final equilibrium short-run effects. Use the following notation:

- + the variable increases
- the variable decreases
- 0 the variable does not change
- A the variable change is ambiguous (i.e., it may rise, it may fall)

	Impact on			
	S_p	I	$IM - EX$	$G + TR - T$
a. A decrease in investment demand with floating ERs				
b. A decrease in investment demand under floating ERs				
c. An increase in foreign interest rates under floating ERs				
d. An increase in government demand under floating ERs				

10.4 LONG-TERM EXPANSIONARY MONETARY POLICY WITH FLOATING EXCHANGE RATES

If expansionary monetary policy occurs when the economy is operating at full employment output, then the money supply increase will eventually put upward pressure on prices. Thus we say that eventually, or in the long run, the aggregate price level will rise and the economy will experience an episode of inflation in the transition. See Chapter 7 , Section 7.14 for a complete description of this process.

- Here, we will describe the long-run effects of an increase in the money supply using the AA-DD model. We break up the effects into short-run and long-run components. In the short run, the initial money supply effects are felt and investor anticipations about future effects are implemented. In the long run, we allow the price level to rise.

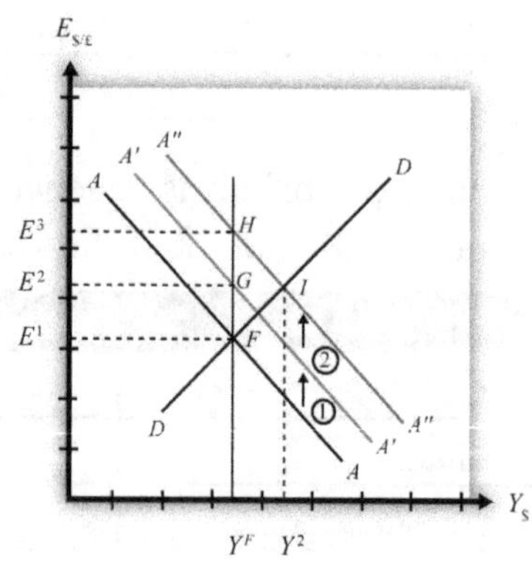

Figure 10.3 Expansionary Monetary Policy in the Long Run

- Suppose the economy is originally at a superequilibrium, shown as point F in Figure 10.3 «Expansionary Monetary Policy in the Long Run». The original GNP level is Y^F, and the exchange rate is E^1. Y^F represents the full-employment level of output, which also implies that the natural rate of unemployment prevails. Any movement of the economy to the right of Y^F will cause an eventual increase in the aggregate price level. Any movement to the left of Y^F causes an eventual decrease in the price level.

Next, suppose the U.S. central bank (or the Fed) decides to expand the money supply. As shown in Chapter 9 , Section 9.5 , money supply changes cause a shift in the AA curve. More specifically, an increase in the money supply will cause AA to shift upward (i.e., $\uparrow M^S$ is an AA up-shifter). This is depicted in the diagram as a shift from the AA line to the red A'A' line.

In the long-run adjustment story, several different changes in exogenous variables will occur sequentially, thus it is difficult to describe the quick final result, so we will only describe the transition process in partial detail.

Partial Detail

The increase in the money supply causes the first upward shift of the AA curve, shown as step 1 in the diagram. Since exchange rates adjust much more rapidly than gross national product (GNP), the economy will quickly adjust to the new A'A' curve before any change in GNP occurs. That means the first adjustment will be from point F to point G directly above. The exchange rate will increase from E^1 to E^2, representing a depreciation of the U.S. dollar.

The second effect is caused by changes in investor expectations. Investors generally track important changes in the economy, including money supply changes, because these changes can have important implications for the returns on their investments. Investors who see an increase in money supply in an economy at full employment are likely to expect inflation to occur in the future. When investors expect future U.S. inflation, and when they consider both domestic and foreign investments, they will respond today with an increase in their expected future exchange rate ($E_{\$/£}^e$). There are two reasons to expect this immediate effect:

- Investors are very likely to understand the story we are in the process of explaining now. As we will see below, the long-run effect of a money supply increase for an economy (initially, at full employment) is an increase in the exchange rate ($E_{\$/£}$)—that is, a depreciation of the dollar. If investors believe the exchange rate will be higher next year due to today's action by the Fed, then it makes sense for them to raise their expected future exchange rate in anticipation of that effect. Thus the average $E_{\$/£}^e$ will rise among investors who participate in the foreign exchange (Forex) markets.

6. Investors may look to the purchasing power parity (PPP) theory for guidance. PPP is generally interpreted as a long-run theory of exchange rate trends. If PPP holds in the long run, then $E_{\$/£} = P_{\$}/P_{£}$. In other words, the exchange rate will equal the ratio of the two countries' price levels. If $P_{\$}$ is expected to rise due to inflation, then PPP predicts that the exchange rate ($E_{\$/£}$) will also rise and the dollar will depreciate.

The timing of the change in $E_{\$/£}^{e}$ will depend on how quickly investors recognize the money supply change, compute its likely effect, and incorporate it into their investment plans. Since investors are typically very quick to adapt to market changes, the expectations effect should take place in the short run, perhaps long before the inflation ever occurs. In some cases, the expectations change may even occur before the Fed increases the money supply, if investors anticipate the Fed's action.

The increase in the expected exchange rate (this means a decrease in the expected future dollar value) causes a second upward shift of the AA curve, shown as step 2 in the diagram. Again, rapid exchange rate adjustment implies the economy will quickly adjust to the new A"A" curve at point H directly above. The exchange rate will now increase from E^2 to E^3, representing a further depreciation of the U.S. dollar.

Once at point H, aggregate demand, which is on the DD curve to the right of H, exceeds aggregate supply, which is still at Y^F. Thus GNP will begin to rise to get back to G&S market equilibrium on the DD curve. However, as GNP rises, the economy moves above the A"A" curve that forces a downward readjustment of the exchange rate to get back to asset market equilibrium on A"A". In the end, the economy will adjust in a stepwise fashion from point H to point I, with each rightward movement in GNP followed by a quick reduction in the exchange rate to remain on the A"A" curve. This process will continue until the economy reaches the temporary superequilibrium at point I.

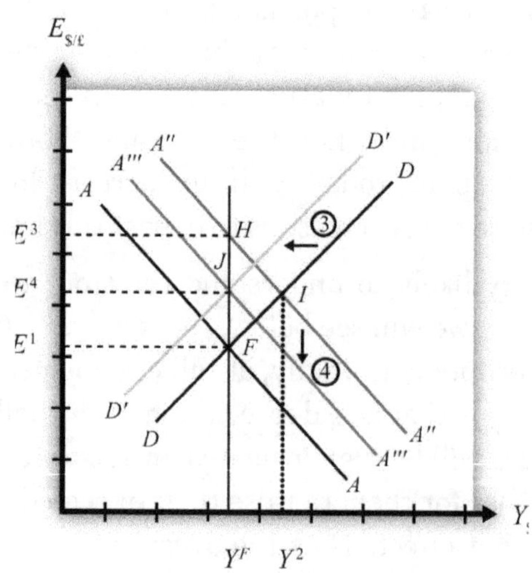

Figure 10.4 Expansionary Monetary Policy in the Long Run, Continued

The next effect occurs because GNP, now at Y^2 at point I, has risen above the full employment level at Y^F. This causes an increase in U.S. prices, meaning that $P_\$$ (the U.S. price level) begins to rise. The increase in U.S. prices has two effects as shown in Figure 10.4 "Expansionary Monetary Policy in the Long Run, Continued". An increase in $P_\$$ is both a DD left-shifter and an AA down-shifter.

In step 3, we depict a leftward shift of DD to D'D'. DD shifts left because higher U.S. prices will reduce the real exchange rate. This makes U.S. G&S relatively more expensive compared with foreign G&S, thus reducing export demand, increasing import demand, and thereby reducing aggregate demand.

In step 4, we depict a downward shift of A"A" to A'"A'". AA shifts down because a higher U.S. price level reduces real money supply. As the real money supply falls, U.S. interest rates rise, leading to an increase in the rate of return for U.S. assets as considered by international investors. This in turn raises the demand for U.S. dollars on the Forex, leading to a dollar appreciation. Since this effect occurs for any GNP level, the entire AA curve shifts downward.

Steps 3 and 4 will both occur simultaneously, and since both are affected by the increase in the price level, it is impossible to know which curve will shift faster or precisely how far each curve will shift. However, we do know two things. First, the AA and DD shifting will continue as long as GNP remains above the full employment level. Once GNP falls to Y_F, there is no longer upward pressure on the price level and the shifting will cease. Second, the final equilibrium exchange rate must lie above the original exchange rate. This occurs because output will revert back to its original level, the price level will be higher, and according to PPP, eventually the exchange rate will have to be higher as well.

The final equilibrium will be at a point like J, which lies to the left of I. In this transition, the exchange rate will occasionally rise when DD shifts left and will occasionally fall when AA shifts down. Thus the economy will wiggle its way up and down, from point I to J. Once at point J, there is no reason for prices to rise further and no reason for a change in investor expectations. The economy will have reached its long-run equilibrium.

Note that one cannot use the iso-CAB line to assess the long-run effect on the current account balance. In the final adjustment, although the final equilibrium lies above the original iso-CAB line, in the long run the $P_\$$ changes will raise the iso-CAB lines, making it impossible to use these to identify the final effect.

However, in adjusting to the long-run equilibrium, the only two variables affecting the current account that will ultimately change are the exchange rate and the price level. If these two rise proportionally to each other, as they would if purchasing power parity held, then there will be no long-run effect on the current account balance.

The final long-run effect of an increase in the U.S. money supply in a floating exchange rate system is a depreciation of the U.S. dollar and no change in real GNP. Along the way, GNP temporarily rises and unemployment falls below the natural rate. However, this spurs an increase in the price level, which reduces GNP to its full employment level and raises unemployment back to its natural rate. U.S. inflation occurs in the transition while the price level is increasing.

KEY TAKEAWAY

- The final long-run effect of an increase in the money supply in a floating exchange rate system is a depreciation of the currency and no change in real GNP. In the transition process, there is an inflationary effect.

EXERCISES

- Jeopardy Questions: As in the popular television game show, you are given an answer to a question and you must respond with the question. For example, if the answer is "a tax on imports," then the correct question is "What is a tariff?"
- Of increase, decrease, or stay the same, this is the effect on equilibrium GNP in the long run if the nominal money supply increases in the AA-DD model with floating exchange rates.
- Of increase, decrease, or stay the same, this is the effect on the domestic currency value in the long run if the nominal money supply increases in the AA-DD model with floating exchange rates.
- Of increase, decrease, or stay the same, this is the effect on equilibrium GNP in the long run if the nominal money supply decreases in the AA-DD model with floating exchange rates.
- Of increase, decrease, or stay the same, this is the effect on the domestic currency value in the long run if the nominal money supply decreases in the AA-DD model with floating exchange rates.
- Repeat the analysis in the text for contractionary monetary policy. Explain each of the four adjustment steps and depict them on an AA-DD diagram.

10.5 FOREIGN EXCHANGE INTERVENTIONS WITH FLOATING EXCHANGE RATES

In a pure floating exchange rate system, the exchange rate is determined as the rate that equalizes private market demand for a currency with private market supply. The central bank has no necessary role to play in the determination of a pure floating exchange rate. Nonetheless, sometimes central banks desire or are pressured by external groups to take actions (i.e., intervene) to either raise or lower the exchange rate in a floating exchange system. When central banks do intervene on a semiregular basis, the system is sometimes referred to as a "dirty float." There are several reasons such interventions occur.

The first reason central banks intervene is to stabilize fluctuations in the exchange rate. International trade and investment decisions are much more difficult to make if the exchange rate value is changing rapidly. Whether a trade deal or international investment is good or bad often depends on the value of the exchange rate that will prevail at some point in the future. (See Chapter 4 , for a discussion of how future exchange rates affect returns on international investments.) If the exchange rate changes rapidly, up or down, traders and investors will become more uncertain about the profitability of trades and investments and will likely reduce their international activities. As a consequence, international traders and investors tend to prefer more stable exchange rates and will often pressure governments and central banks to intervene in the foreign exchange (Forex) market whenever the exchange rate changes too rapidly.

The second reason central banks intervene is to reverse the growth in the country's trade deficit. Trade deficits (or current account deficits) can rise rapidly if a country's exchange rate appreciates significantly. A higher currency value will make foreign goods and services (G&S) relatively cheaper, stimulating imports, while domestic goods will seem relatively more expensive to foreigners, thus reducing exports. This means a rising currency value can lead to a rising trade deficit. If that trade deficit is viewed as a problem for the economy, the central bank may be pressured to intervene to reduce the value of the currency in the Forex market and thereby reverse the rising trade deficit.

There are two methods central banks can use to affect the exchange rate. The indirect method is to change the domestic money supply. The direct method is to intervene directly in the foreign exchange market by buying or selling currency.

Indirect Forex Intervention

The central bank can use an indirect method to raise or lower the exchange rate through domestic money supply changes. As was shown in Chapter 10 , Section 10.2 , increases in the domestic U.S. money supply will cause an increase in $E_{\$/£}$, or a dollar depreciation. Similarly, a decrease in the money supply will cause a dollar appreciation.

Despite relatively quick adjustments in assets markets, this type of intervention must traverse from open market operations to changes in domestic money supply, domestic interest rates, and exchange rates due to new rates of returns. Thus this method may take several weeks or more for the effect on exchange rates to be realized.

A second problem with this method is that to affect the exchange rate the central bank must change the domestic interest rate. Most of the time, central banks use interest rates to maintain stability in domestic markets. If the domestic economy is growing rapidly and inflation is beginning to rise, the central bank may lower the money supply to raise interest rates and help slow down the economy. If the economy is growing too slowly, the central bank may raise the money supply to lower interest rates and help spur domestic expansion. Thus to change the exchange rate using the indirect method, the central bank may need to change interest rates away from what it views as appropriate for domestic concerns at the moment. (Below we'll discuss the method central banks use to avoid this dilemma.)

Direct Forex Intervention

The most obvious and direct way for central banks to intervene and affect the exchange rate is to enter the private Forex market directly by buying or selling domestic currency. There are two possible transactions.

First, the central bank can sell domestic currency (let's use dollars) in exchange for a foreign currency (say, pounds). This transaction will raise the supply of dollars on the Forex (also raising the demand for pounds), causing a reduction in the value of the dollar and thus a dollar depreciation. Of course, when the dollar depreciates in value, the pound appreciates in value with respect to the dollar. Since the central bank is the ultimate source of all dollars (it can effectively print an unlimited amount), it can flood the Forex market with as many dollars as it desires. Thus the central bank's power to reduce the dollar value by direct intervention in the Forex is virtually unlimited.

If instead, the central bank wishes to raise the value of the dollar, it will have to reverse the transaction described above. Instead of selling dollars, it will need to buy dollars in exchange for pounds. The increased demand for dollars on the Forex by the central bank will raise the value of the dollar, thus causing a dollar appreciation. At the same time, the increased supply of pounds on the Forex explains why the pound will depreciate with respect to the dollar.

The ability of a central bank to raise the value of its currency through direct Forex interventions is limited, however. In order for the U.S. Federal Reserve Bank (or the Fed) to buy dollars in exchange for pounds, it must have a stockpile of pound currency (or other pound assets) available to exchange. Such holdings of foreign assets by a central bank are called foreign exchange reserves. Foreign exchange reserves are typically accumulated over time and held in case an intervention is desired. In the end, the degree to which the Fed can raise the dollar value with respect to the pound through direct Forex intervention will depend on the size of its pound denominated foreign exchange reserves.

Indirect Effect of Direct Forex Intervention

There is a secondary indirect effect that occurs when a central bank intervenes in the Forex market. Suppose the Fed sells dollars in exchange for pounds in the private

Forex. This transaction involves a purchase of foreign assets (pounds) in exchange for U.S. currency. Since the Fed is the ultimate source of dollar currency, these dollars used in the transaction will enter into circulation in the economy in precisely the same way as new dollars enter when the Fed buys a Treasury bill on the open market. The only difference is that with an open market operation, the Fed purchases a domestic asset, while in the Forex intervention it buys a foreign asset. But both are assets all the same and both are paid for with newly created money. Thus when the Fed buys pounds and sells dollars on the Forex, there will be an increase in the U.S. money supply.

The higher U.S. money supply will lower U.S. interest rates, reduce the rate of return on U.S. assets as viewed by international investors, and result in a depreciation of the dollar. The direction of this indirect effect is the same as the direct effect.

In contrast, if the Fed were to buy dollars and sell pounds on the Forex, there will be a decrease in the U.S. money supply. The lower U.S. money supply will raise U.S. interest rates, increase the rate of return on U.S. assets as viewed by international investors, and result in an appreciation of the dollar.

The only difference between the direct and indirect effects is the timing and sustainability. The direct effect will occur immediately with central bank intervention since the Fed will be affecting today's supply of dollars or pounds on the Forex. The indirect effect, working through money supply and interest rates, may take several days or weeks. The sustainability of the direct versus indirect effects is discussed next when we introduce the idea of a sterilized Forex intervention.

Sterilized Forex Interventions

There are many times in which a central bank either wants or is pressured to affect the exchange rate value by intervening directly in the foreign exchange market. However, as shown above, direct Forex interventions will change the domestic money supply. A change in the money supply will affect the average interest rate in the short run and the price level, and hence the inflation rate, in the long run. Because central banks are generally entrusted to maintain domestic price stability or to assist in maintaining appropriate interest rates, a low unemployment rate, and GDP growth, Forex intervention will often interfere with one or more of their other goals.

For example, if the central bank believes that current interest rates should be raised slowly during the next several months to slow the growth of the economy and prevent a resurgence of inflation, then a Forex intervention to lower the value of the domestic currency would result in increases in the money supply and a decrease in interest rates, precisely the opposite of what the central bank wants to achieve. Conflicts such as this one are typical and usually result in a central bank choosing to sterilize its Forex interventions.

The intended purpose of a sterilized intervention is to cause a change in the exchange rate while at the same time leaving the money supply and hence interest rates unaffected. As we will see, the intended purpose is unlikely to be realized in practice.

A sterilized foreign exchange intervention occurs when a central bank counters direct intervention in the Forex with a simultaneous offsetting transaction in the domestic bond market. For example, suppose the U.S. Fed decides to intervene to lower the value of the U.S. dollar. This would require the Fed to sell dollars and buy foreign currency on the Forex. Sterilization, in this case, involves a Fed open market operation in which it sells Treasury bonds (T-bonds) at the same time and in the same value as the dollar sale in the Forex market. For example, if the Fed intervenes and sells \$10 million on the Forex, sterilization means it will also sell \$10 million of Treasury bonds on the domestic open market at the same time.

Consider the effects of a sterilized Forex intervention by the U.S. Fed shown in the adjoining AA-DD diagram, Figure 10.5 "Sterilization in the AA-DD Model". Suppose the economy is initially in equilibrium at point F with GDP (Y^1) and exchange rate ($E_{\$/£}{}^1$). Now, suppose the Fed intervenes in the Forex by selling dollars and buying British pounds. The direct effect on the exchange rate is not represented in the AA-DD diagram. The only way it can have an effect is through the increase in the money supply, which will shift the AA curve up from AA to A'A'. However, sterilization means the Fed will simultaneously conduct an offsetting open market operation, in this case selling Treasury bonds equal in value to the Forex sales. The sale of T-bonds will lower the U.S. money supply, causing an immediate shift of the AA curve back from A'A' to AA. In fact, because the two actions take place on the same day or within the same week at least, the AA curve does not really shift out at all. Instead, a sterilized Forex intervention maintains the U.S. money supply and thus achieves the Fed's objective of maintaining interest rates.

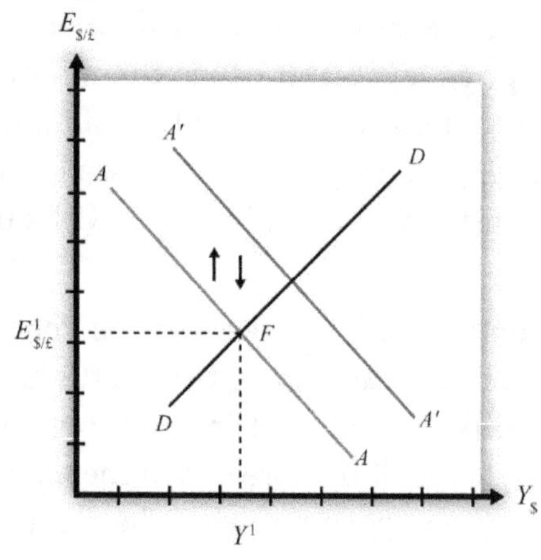

Figure 10.5 Sterilization in the AA-DD Model

However, because there is no shift in the AA or DD curves, the equilibrium in the economy will never move away from point F. This implies that a sterilized Forex intervention not only will not affect GNP, but also will not affect the exchange rate. This suggests the impossibility of the Fed's overall objective to lower the dollar value while maintaining interest rates.

Empirical studies of the effects of sterilized Forex interventions tend to support the results of this simple model. In other words, real-world sterilizations have generally been ineffective in achieving any lasting effect upon a country's currency value.

However, there are several reasons why sterilized interventions may be somewhat effective nonetheless. Temporary effects are certainly possible. If a central bank makes a substantial intervention in the Forex over a short period, this will certainly change the supply or demand of currency and have an immediate effect on the exchange rate on those days.

A more lasting impact can occur if the intervention leads investors to change their expectations about the future. This could happen if investors are not sure whether the central bank is sterilizing its interventions. Knowing that sterilization is occurring would require a careful observation of several markets unless the Fed announces its policy. However, rather than announcing a sterilized intervention, a central bank that wants to affect expectations should announce the Forex intervention while hiding its offsetting open market operation. In this way, investors may be fooled into thinking that the Forex intervention will lower the future dollar value and thus may adjust their expectations.

If investors are fooled, they will raise $E_{\$/£}^e$ in anticipation of the future dollar depreciation. The increase in $E_{\$/£}^e$ will shift the AA curve upward, resulting in an increase in GNP and a depreciation of the dollar. In this way, sterilized interventions may have a more lasting effect on the exchange rate. However, the magnitude of the exchange rate change in this case—if it occurs—will certainly be less than that achieved with a nonsterilized intervention.

KEY TAKEAWAYS

- If the central bank sells domestic currency in exchange for a foreign currency on the Forex, it will cause a direct reduction in the value of the domestic currency, or a currency depreciation.
- If the Fed were to sell dollars on the Forex, there will be an increase in the U.S.1 money supply that will reduce U.S. interest rates, decrease the rate of return on U.S. assets, and lead to a depreciation of the dollar.
- A sterilized foreign exchange intervention occurs when a central bank counters direct intervention in the Forex with a simultaneous offsetting transaction in the domestic bond market.

- The intended purpose of a sterilized intervention is to cause a change in the exchange rate while at the same time leaving interest rates unaffected.

EXERCISE

- Jeopardy Questions: As in the popular television game show, you are given an answer to a question and you must respond with the question. For example, if the answer is "a tax on imports," then the correct question is "What is a tariff?"
- Of buy domestic currency or sell domestic currency on the foreign exchange market, this is one thing a central bank can do to cause a domestic currency depreciation.
- Of buy foreign currency or sell foreign currency on the foreign exchange market, this is one thing a central bank can do to cause a domestic currency appreciation.
- Of increase, decrease, or keep the same, this is one thing a central bank can do to the domestic money supply to induce a domestic currency appreciation.
- Of increase, decrease, or keep the same, this is one thing a central bank can do to the domestic money supply to induce a domestic currency depreciation.
- The term used to describe a central bank transaction on the domestic bond market intended to offset the central bank's intervention on the foreign exchange market.
- Of increase, decrease, or stay the same, this is the effect on equilibrium GNP in the short run if the central bank sterilizes a sale of foreign reserves on the foreign exchange market in the AA-DD model with floating exchange rates.
- Of increase, decrease, or stay the same, this is the effect on the domestic currency value in the short run if the central bank sterilizes a purchase of foreign reserves on the foreign exchange market in the AA-DD model with floating exchange rates.

CHAPTER

FIXED EXCHANGE RATES 11

INTRODUCTION

Fixed exchange rates around the world were once the only game in town; however, since the collapse of the Bretton Woods system in 1973, floating exchange rates predominate for the world's most-traded currencies. Nonetheless, many countries continue to use some variant of fixed exchange rates even today. This chapter addresses both the historical fixed exchange rate systems like the gold standard as well as the more modern variants like crawling pegs and currency boards.

11.1 FIXED EXCHANGE RATES: AN OVERVIEW

This chapter begins by defining several types of fixed exchange rate systems, including the gold standard, the reserve currency standard, and the gold exchange standard. The price-specie flow mechanism is described for the gold standard. It continues with other modern fixed exchange variations such as fixing a currency to a basket of several other currencies, crawling pegs, fixing within a band or range of exchange rates, currency boards, and finally the most extreme way to fix a currency: adopting another country's currency as your own, as is done with dollarization or euroization.

The chapter proceeds with the basic mechanics of a reserve currency standard in which a country fixes its currency to another's. In general, a country's central bank must intervene in the foreign exchange (Forex) markets, buying foreign currency whenever there is excess supply (resulting in a balance of payments surplus) and selling foreign currency whenever there is excess demand (resulting in a balance of payments deficit). These actions will achieve the fixed exchange rate version of the interest parity condition in which interest rates are equalized across countries. However, to make central bank actions possible, a country will need to hold a stock of foreign exchange reserves. If a country's central bank does not intervene in the Forex in a fixed exchange system, black markets are shown to be a likely consequence.

Results

- Gold standard rules: (1) fix currency to a weight of gold; (2) central bank freely exchanges gold for currency with public.

- Adjustment under a gold standard involves the flow of gold between countries, resulting in equalization of prices satisfying purchasing power parity (PPP) and/or equalization of rates of return on assets satisfying interest rate parity (IRP) at the current fixed exchange rate.
- Reserve currency rules: (1) fix currency to another currency, known as the reserve currency; (2) central bank must hold a stock of foreign exchange reserves to facilitate Forex interventions.
- Gold-exchange standard rules: (1) reserve country fixes its currency to a weight of gold, (2) all other countries fix their currencies to the reserve, (3) reserve central bank freely exchanges gold for currency with other central banks, (4) nonreserve countries hold a stock of the reserve currency to facilitate intervention in the Forex.
- The post–World War II fixed exchange rate system, known as the Bretton Woods system, was a gold exchange standard.
- Some countries fix their currencies to a weighted average of several other currencies, called a "basket of currencies."
- Some countries implement a crawling peg in which the fixed exchange rate is adjusted regularly.
- Some countries set a central exchange rate and allow free floating within a predefined range or band.
- Some countries implement currency boards to legally mandate Forex interventions.
- Some countries simply adopt another country's currency, as with dollarization, or choose a brand-new currency, as with the euro.
- The interest rate parity condition becomes the equalization of interest rates between two countries in a fixed exchange rate system.
- A balance of payments surplus (deficit) arises when the central bank buys (sells) foreign reserves on the Forex in exchange for its own currency.
- A black market in currency trade arises when there is unsatisfied excess demand or supply of foreign currency in exchange for domestic currency on the Forex.

KEY TAKEAWAY

- See the main results previewed above.

EXERCISE

- Jeopardy Questions: As in the popular television game show, you are given an answer to a question and you must respond with the question. For example, if the answer is "a tax on imports," then the correct question is "What is a tariff?"

- The term for the currency standard that fixes its circulating currency to a quantity of gold.
- The term for the currency standard in which a reserve currency is fixed to a quantity of gold while all other currencies are fixed to the reserve currency.
- The currency standard used during the post–World War II Bretton Woods era.
- The term describing the deficits and surpluses run by a country to maintain a fixed exchange rate.
- The term used to describe a decision by another country to adopt the U.S. dollar as its currency.
- The nonintervention in the Forex market by a country's central bank is likely to lead to the development of these kinds of market activities.

11.2 SYSTEMS WITH FIXED EXCHANGE RATES

There are two basic systems that can be used to determine the exchange rate between one country's currency and another's: a floating exchange rate system and a fixed exchange rate system.

Under a floating exchange rate system, the value of a country's currency is determined by the supply and demand for that currency in exchange for another in a private market operated by major international banks.

In contrast, in a fixed exchange rate system, a country's government announces (or decrees) what its currency will be worth in terms of something else and also sets up the rules of exchange. The "something else" to which a currency value is set and the "rules of exchange" determine the type of fixed exchange rate system, of which there are many. For example, if the government sets its currency value in terms of a fixed weight of gold, then we have a gold standard. If the currency value is set to a fixed amount of another country's currency, then it is a reserve currency standard.

As we review several ways in which a fixed exchange rate system can work, we will highlight some of the advantages and disadvantages of the system. In anticipation, it is worth noting that one key advantage of fixed exchange rates is the intention to eliminate exchange rate risk, which can greatly enhance international trade and investment. A second key advantage is the discipline a fixed exchange rate system imposes on a country's monetary authority, with the intention of inducing a much lower inflation rate.

The Gold Standard

Most people are aware that at one time the world operated under something called a gold standard. Some people today, reflecting back on the periods of rapid growth and prosperity that occurred when the world was on a gold standard, have suggested that the world abandon its current mixture of fixed and floating exchange rate systems and return to this system. (For a discussion of some pros and cons see Alan Greenspan's remarks on this from the early 1980s.See Alan Greenspan's remarks in "Can the US Return to a Gold Standard," Wall Street Journal, September 1981 ,1; reprinted online at http://www.gold-eagle.com/greenspan011098.html[0]. See Murray Rothbard's article for an argument in favor of a return to the gold standard. See Murray Rothbard, "The Case for a Genuine Gold Dollar," in The Gold Standard: An Austrian Perspective (Lexington, MA: D. C. Heath, 1985), 1–17; also available online at http://www.mises.org/rothbard/genuine.asp.) Whether or not countries seriously consider this in the future, it is instructive to understand the workings of a gold standard, especially since, historically, it is the first major international system of fixed exchange rates.

Most of the world maintained a pure gold standard during the late 1800s and early 1900s, with a major interruption during World War I. Before the enactment of a gold standard, countries were generally using a Bimetallic standard consisting of both gold and silver.See Angela Radish, "Bimetallism," Economic History Online at http://www.eh.net/encyclopedia/?article=redish.bimetallism The earliest establishment of a gold standard was in Great Britain in 1821, followed by Australia in 1852 and Canada in 1853. The United States established its gold standard system with the Coinage Act of 1873, sometimes known as "The Crime of '73."For more info see Wikipedia, "Coinage Act of 1873," http://en.wikipedia.org/wiki/Coinage_Act_of_1873. The gold standard was abandoned in the early days of the Great Depression. Britain dropped the standard in 1931, the United States in 1933.

The rules of a gold standard are quite simple. First, a country's government declares that its issued currency (it may be coin or paper currency) will exchange for a weight in gold. For example, in the United States during the late 1800s and early 1900s, the government set the dollar exchange rate to gold at the rate $20.67 per troy ounce. During the same period, Great Britain set its currency at the rate £4.24 per troy ounce. Second, in a pure gold standard, a country's government declares that it will freely exchange currency for actual gold at the designated exchange rate. This "rule of exchange" means that anyone can go to the central bank with coin or currency and walk out with pure gold. Conversely, one could also walk in with pure gold and walk out with the equivalent in coin or currency.

Because the government bank must always be prepared to give out gold in exchange for coin and currency on demand, it must maintain a storehouse of gold. That store of gold is referred to as "gold reserves." That is, the central bank maintains a reserve of gold so that it can always fulfill its promise of exchange. As discussed in Chapter 11 , Section 11.4, a well-functioning system will require that the central bank always have an adequate amount of reserves.

The two simple rules, when maintained, guarantee that the exchange rate between dollars and pounds remains constant. Here's why.

First, the dollar/pound exchange rate is defined as the ratio of the two-currency-gold exchange rates. Thus

Next, suppose an individual wants to exchange \$4.875 for one pound. Following the exchange rules, this person can enter the central bank in the United States and exchange dollars for gold to get

This person can then take the gold into the central bank in the United Kingdom, and assuming no costs of transportation, can exchange the gold into pounds as follows:

Hence, the \$4.875 converts to precisely £1 and this will remain the fixed exchange rate between the two currencies, as long as the simple exchange rules are followed. If many countries define the value of their own currency in terms of a weight of gold and agree to exchange gold freely at that rate with all who desire to exchange, then all these countries will have fixed currency exchange rates with respect to each other.

Price-Specie Flow Mechanism

The price-specie flow mechanism is a description about how adjustments to shocks or changes are handled within a pure gold standard system. Although there is some disagreement whether the gold standard functioned as described by this mechanism, the mechanism does fix the basic principles of how a gold standard is supposed to work.

Consider the United States and United Kingdom operating under a pure gold standard. Suppose there is a gold discovery in the United States. This will represent a shock to the system. Under a gold standard, a gold discovery is like digging up money, which is precisely what inspired so many people to rush to California after 1848 to strike it rich.

Once the gold is unearthed, the prospectors bring it into town and proceed to the national bank where it can be exchanged for coin and currency at the prevailing dollar/gold exchange rate. The new currency in circulation represents an increase in the domestic money supply.

Indeed, it is this very transaction that explains the origins of the gold and silver standards in the first place. The original purpose of banks was to store individuals' precious metal wealth and to provide exchangeable notes that were backed by the gold holdings in the vault. Thus rather than carrying around heavy gold, one could carry lightweight paper money. Before national or central banks were founded, individual commercial banks issued their own currencies, which circulated together with many other bank currencies. However, it was also common for governments to issue coins that were made directly from gold or silver.

Now, once the money supply increases following the gold discovery, it can have two effects: operating through the goods market and financial market. The price-specie flow mechanism describes the adjustment through goods markets.

First, let's assume that the money increase occurs in an economy that is not growing—that is, with a fixed level of GDP. Also assume that both purchasing power parity (PPP) and interest rate parity (IRP) holds. PPP implies an equalization of the cost of a market basket of goods between the United States and the United Kingdom at the current fixed exchange rate. IRP implies an equalization of the rates of return on comparable assets in the two countries.

As discussed in Chapter 7 "Interest Rate Determination", Section 7.14 "Money Supply and Long-Run Prices", when the U.S. money supply increases, and when there is no subsequent increase in output, the prices of goods and services will begin to rise. This inflationary effect occurs because more money is chasing (i.e., demanding) the same amount of goods and services. As the price level rises in an economy open to international trade, domestic goods become more expensive relative to foreign goods. This will induce domestic residents to increase demand for foreign goods; hence import demand will rise. Foreign consumers will also find domestic goods more expensive, so export supply will fall. The result is a demand for a current account deficit. To make these transactions possible in a gold standard, currency exchange will take place as follows.

U.S. residents wishing to buy cheaper British goods will first exchange dollars for gold at the U.S. central bank. Then they will ship that gold to the United Kingdom to exchange for the pounds that can be used to buy UK goods. As gold moves from the United States to the United Kingdom, the money supply in the United States falls while the money supply in the United Kingdom rises. Less money in the United States will eventually reduce prices, while more money in the United Kingdom will raise prices. This means that the prices of goods will move together until purchasing power parity holds again. Once PPP holds, there is no further incentive for money to move between countries. There will continue to be demand for UK goods by U.S. residents, but this will balance with the United Kingdom demands for similarly priced U.S. goods. Hence, the trade balance reverts to zero.

The adjustment process in the financial market under a gold standard will work through changes in interest rates. When the U.S. money supply rises after the gold discovery, average interest rates will begin to fall. Lower U.S. interest rates will make British assets temporarily more attractive, and U.S. investors will seek to move investments to the United Kingdom. The adjustment under a gold standard is the same as with goods. Investors trade dollars for gold in the United States and move that gold to the United Kingdom where it is exchanged for pounds and used to purchase UK assets. Thus the U.S. money supply will begin to fall, causing an increase in U.S. interest rates, while the UK money supply rises, leading to a decrease in UK interest rates. The interest rates will move together until interest rate parity again holds.

In summary, adjustment under a gold standard involves the flow of gold between countries, resulting in equalization of prices satisfying purchasing power parity (PPP) and/or equalization of rates of return on assets satisfying interest rate parity (IRP) at the current fixed exchange rate. The only requirement for the government to maintain this type of fixed exchange rate system is to maintain the fixed price of its currency in terms of gold and to freely and readily exchange currency for gold on demand.

Reserve Currency Standard

In a reserve currency system, another country's currency takes the role that gold played in a gold standard. In other words a country fixes its own currency value to a unit of another country's currency. For example, suppose Britain decided to fix its currency to the dollar at the exchange rate $E_{\$/£} = 1.50$. To maintain this fixed exchange rate, the Bank of England would stand ready to exchange pounds for dollars (or dollars for pounds) on demand at the specified exchange rate. To accomplish this, the Bank of England would need to hold dollars on reserve in case there was ever any excess demand for dollars in exchange for pounds on the Forex. In the gold standard, the central bank held gold to exchange for its own currency; with a reserve currency standard, it must hold a stock of the reserve currency. Always, the reserve currency is the currency to which the country fixes.

A reserve currency standard is the typical method for fixing a currency today. Most countries that fix its exchange rate will fix to a currency that either is prominently used in international transactions or is the currency of a major trading partner. Thus many countries fixing their exchange rate today fix to the U.S. dollar because it is the most widely traded currency internationally. Alternatively, fourteen African countries that were former French colonies had established the CFA franc zone and fixed the CFA franc (current currency used by these African countries) to the French franc. Since 1999, the CFA franc has been fixed to the euro. Namibia, Lesotho, and Swaziland are all a part of the common monetary area (CMA) and fix their currency to the South African rand.

Gold Exchange Standard

A gold exchange standard is a mixed system consisting of a cross between a reserve currency standard and a gold standard. In general, it includes the following two rules:

7. A reserve currency is chosen. All nonreserve countries agree to fix their exchange rates to the reserve at some announced rate. To maintain the fixity, these nonreserve countries will hold a stockpile of reserve currency assets.

8. The reserve currency country agrees to fix its currency value to a weight in gold. Finally, the reserve country agrees to exchange gold for its own currency with other central banks within the system on demand.

One key difference in this system from a gold standard is that the reserve country does not agree to exchange gold for currency with the general public, only with other central banks.

The system works exactly like a reserve currency system from the perspective of the nonreserve countries. However, if over time the nonreserve countries accumulate the reserve currency, they can demand exchange for gold from the reserve country central bank. In this case, gold reserves will flow away from the reserve currency country.

The fixed exchange rate system set up after World War II was a gold exchange standard, as was the system that prevailed between 1920 and the early 1930s. The post–World War II system was agreed to by the allied countries at a conference in Bretton Woods, New Hampshire, in the United States in June 1944. As a result, the exchange rate system after the war also became known as the Bretton Woods system.

Also proposed at Bretton Woods was the establishment of an international institution to help regulate the fixed exchange rate system. This institution was the International Monetary Fund (IMF). The IMF's main mission was to help maintain the stability of the Bretton Woods fixed exchange rate system.

Other Fixed Exchange Rate Variations

Basket of Currencies

Countries that have several important trading partners, or who fear that one currency may be too volatile over an extended period, have chosen to fix their currency to a basket of several other currencies. This means fixing to a weighted average of several currencies. This method is best understood by considering the creation of a composite currency. Consider the following hypothetical example: a new unit of money consisting of 1 euro, 100 Japanese yen, and one U.S. dollar. Call this new unit a Eur-yen-dol. A country could now fix its currency to one Eur-yen-dol. The country would then need to maintain reserves in one or more of the three currencies to satisfy excess demand or supply of its currency on the Forex.

A better example of a composite currency is found in the SDR. SDR stands for special drawing rights. It is a composite currency created by the International Monetary Fund (IMF). One SDR now consists of a fixed quantity of U.S. dollars, euros, Japanese yen, and British pounds. For more info on the SDR see the IMF factsheet. International Monetary Fund, About the IMF, Factsheet, "Special Drawing Rights (SDRs)," http://www.imf.org/external/np/exr/facts/sdr.htm[0]. Now Saudi Arabia officially fixes its currency to the SDR. Botswana fixes to a basket consisting of the SDR and the South African rand.

Crawling Pegs

A crawling peg refers to a system in which a country fixes its exchange rate but also changes the fixed rate at periodic or regular intervals. Central bank interventions in the Forex may occur to maintain the temporary fixed rate. However, central banks can avoid interventions and save reserves by adjusting the fixed rate instead. Since crawling pegs are adjusted gradually, they can help eliminate some exchange rate volatility without fully constraining the central bank with a fixed rate. In 2010 Bolivia, China, Ethiopia, and Nicaragua were among several countries maintaining a crawling peg.

Pegged within a Band

In this system, a country specifies a central exchange rate together with a percentage allowable deviation, expressed as plus or minus some percentage. For example, Denmark, an EU member country, does not yet use the euro but participates in the Exchange Rate Mechanism (ERM2). Under this system, Denmark sets its central exchange rate to 7.46038 krona per euro and allows fluctuations of the exchange rate within a 2.25 percent band. This means the krona can fluctuate from a low of 7.63 kr/€ to a high of 7.29 kr/€. (Recall that the krona is at a high with the smaller exchange rate value since the kr/euro rate represents the euro value.) If the market determined floating exchange rate rises above or falls below the bands, the Danish central bank must intervene in the Forex. Otherwise, the exchange rate is allowed to fluctuate freely.

As of 2010, Slovenia, Syria, and Tonga were fixing their currencies within a band.

Currency Boards

A currency board is a legislated method to provide greater assurances that an exchange rate fixed to a reserve currency will indeed remain fixed. In this system, the government requires that domestic currency is always exchangeable for the specific reserve at the fixed exchange rate. The central bank authorities are stripped of all discretion in the Forex interventions in this system. As a result, they must maintain sufficient foreign reserves to keep the system intact.

In 2010 Bulgaria, Hong Kong, Estonia, and Lithuania were among the countries using a currency board arrangement. Argentina used a currency board system from 1991 until 2002. The currency board was very effective in reducing inflation in Argentina during the 1990s. However, the collapse of the exchange rate system and the economy in 2002 demonstrated that currency boards are not a panacea.

Dollarization/Euroization

The most extreme and convincing method for a country to fix its exchange rate is to give up one's national currency and adopt the currency of another country. In creating the euro-zone among twelve of the European Union (EU) countries, these

European nations have given up their own national currencies and have adopted the currency issued by the European Central Bank. This is a case of euroization. Since all twelve countries now share the euro as a common currency, their exchange rates are effectively fixed to each other at a 1:1 ratio. As other countries in the EU join the common currency, they too will be forever fixing their exchange rate to the euro. (Note, however, that although all countries that use the euro are fixed to each other, the euro itself floats with respect to external currencies such as the U.S. dollar.)

Other examples of adopting another currency as one's own are the countries of Panama, Ecuador, and El Salvador. These countries have all chosen to adopt the U.S. dollar as their national currency of circulation. Thus they have chosen the most extreme method of assuring a fixed exchange rate. These are examples of dollarization.

KEY TAKEAWAYS

- In a gold standard, a country's government declares that its issued currency will exchange for a weight in gold and that it will freely exchange currency for actual gold at the designated exchange rate.
- Adjustment under a gold standard involves the flow of gold between countries, resulting in equalization of prices satisfying purchasing power parity (PPP) and/or equalization of rates of return on assets satisfying interest rate parity (IRP) at the current fixed exchange rate.
- In a reserve currency system, a country fixes its own currency value to a unit of another country's currency. The other country is called the reserve currency country.
- A gold exchange standard is a mixed system consisting of a cross between a reserve currency standard and a gold standard. First, a reserve currency is chosen. Second, the reserve currency country agrees to fix its currency value to a weight in gold. Finally, the reserve country agrees to exchange gold for its own currency with other central banks within the system on demand.
- The post–World War II Bretton Woods system was a gold exchange currency standard.
- Other fixed exchange rate choices include fixing to a market basket, fixing in a nonrigid way by implementing a crawling peg or an exchange rate band, implementing a currency board, or adopting another country's currency.

EXERCISES

- Jeopardy Questions: As in the popular television game show, you are given an answer to a question and you must respond with the question. For example, if the answer is "a tax on imports," then the correct question is "What is a tariff?"

- The term used to describe the adjustment mechanism within a gold standard.
- The term given to the currency standard using both gold and silver.
- The term given to the currency standard in which all countries fix to one central currency, while the central currency is not fixed to anything.
- The name of the international organization created after World War II to oversee the fixed exchange rate system.
- In the late nineteenth century, the U.S. dollar was fixed to gold at this exchange rate.
- In the late nineteenth century, the British pound was fixed to gold at this exchange rate.
- In the late nineteenth century, one U.S. dollar was worth approximately this many shillings (note: a shilling is one-tenth of a pound).
- Of gold inflow or gold outflow, this is likely to occur for a country whose interest rates rise under a gold standard with free capital mobility.
- The term used to describe a currency system in which a country fixes its exchange rate but also changes the fixed rate at periodic or regular intervals.
- As of 2004, Estonia and Hong Kong implemented this type of currency system.
- Use the IMF's "De Facto Classification of Exchange Rate Regimes and Monetary Policy Frameworks" at http://www.imf.org/external/np/mfd/er/2008/eng/0408.htm to answer the following questions:
- What are four countries that maintained currency board arrangements?
- What are four countries that maintained a conventional fixed peg?
- What are four countries that maintained a crawling peg?
- What are four countries whose currencies were independently floating?

11.3 COMPARING INTEREST RATES TO FIXED EXCHANGE RATES

One of the main differences between a fixed exchange rate system and a floating system is that under fixed exchange rates the central bank will have to "do something" periodically. In contrast, in a floating system, the central bank can just sit back and watch since it has no responsibility for the value of the exchange rate. In a pure float, the exchange rate is determined entirely by private transactions.

However, in a fixed exchange rate system, the central bank will need to intervene in the foreign exchange market, perhaps daily, if it wishes to maintain the credibility of the exchange rate.

We'll use the AA-DD model to explain why. Although the AA-DD model was created under the assumption of a floating exchange rate, we can reinterpret the model in light of a fixed exchange rate assumption. This means we must look closely at the interest rate parity condition, which represents the equilibrium condition in the foreign exchange market.

Recall that the AA-DD model assumes the exchange rate is determined as a result of investor incentives to maximize their rate of return on investments. The model ignores the potential effect of importers and exporters on the exchange rate value. That is, the model does not presume that purchasing power parity holds. As such, the model describes a world economy that is very open to international capital flows and international borrowing and lending. This is a reasonable representation of the world in the early twenty-first century, but would not be the best characterization of the world in the mid-1900s when capital restrictions were more common. Nonetheless, the requisite behavior of central banks under fixed exchange rates would not differ substantially under either assumption.

When investors seek the greatest rate of return on their investments internationally, we saw that the exchange rate will adjust until interest rate parity holds. Consider interest rate parity (IRP) for a particular investment comparison between the United States and the United Kingdom. IRP means that $RoR_\$ = RoR_£$. We can write this equality out in its complete form to get

where the left-hand side is the U.S. interest rate and the right side is the more complicated rate of return formula for a UK deposit with interest rate $i_£$. (See Chapter 4 and Chapter 5 for the derivation of the interest rate parity condition.) The last term on the right represents the expected appreciation (if positive) or depreciation (if negative) of the pound value with respect to the U.S. dollar.

In a floating exchange rate system, the value of this term is based on investor expectations about the future exchange rate as embodied in the term $E_{\$/£}^e$, which determines the degree to which investors believe the exchange rate will change over their investment period.

If these same investors were operating in a fixed exchange rate system, however, and if they believed the fixed exchange rate would indeed remain fixed, then the investors' expected exchange rate should be set equal to the current fixed spot exchange rate. In other words, under credible fixed exchange rates, $E_{\$/£}^e = E_{\$/£}$. Investors should not expect the exchange rate to change from its current fixed value. (We will consider a case in which the investors' expected exchange rate does not equal the fixed spot rate in Chapter 12 , Section 12.6)

With $E_{\$/£}^e = E_{\$/£}$, the right side of the above expression becomes zero, and the interest rate parity condition under fixed exchange rates becomes

$i_\$ = i_£$.

Thus for interest rate parity to hold in a fixed exchange rate system, the interest rates between two countries must be equal.

Indeed, the reason this condition in a floating system is called "interest rate parity" rather than "rate of return parity" is because of our history with fixed exchange rates. Before 1973, most of the world had maintained fixed exchange rates for most of the time. We can see now that under fixed exchange rates, rates of return in each country are simply the interest rates on individual deposits. In other words, in a fixed system, which is what most countries had through much of their histories, interest rate parity means the equality of interest rates. When the fixed exchange rate system collapsed, economists and others continued to use the now-outdated terminology: interest rate parity. Inertia in language usage is why the traditional term continues to be applied (somewhat inappropriately) even today.

KEY TAKEAWAY

- For interest rate parity to hold in a fixed exchange rate system, the interest rates between two countries must be equal.

EXERCISE

- Jeopardy Questions: As in the popular television game show, you are given an answer to a question and you must respond with the question. For example, if the answer is "a tax on imports," then the correct question is "What is a tariff?"
- These must be equalized between countries for interest rate parity to hold under fixed exchange.
- If the fixed exchange rates are credible, then the expected exchange rate should be equal to this exchange rate.
- Of intervene or do not intervene, this is what a central bank should do in the Forex market if it intends to maintain credible fixed exchange rates.

11.4 CENTRAL BANK INTERVENTION WITH FIXED EXCHANGE RATES

In a fixed exchange rate system, most of the transactions of one currency for another will take place in the private market among individuals, businesses, and international banks. However, by fixing the exchange rate the government would have declared illegal any transactions that do not occur at the announced rate. However, it is very unlikely that the announced fixed exchange rate will at all times equalize private demand for foreign currency with private supply. In a floating exchange rate system, the exchange rate adjusts to maintain the supply and demand balance. In a fixed exchange rate system, it becomes the responsibility of the central bank to maintain this balance.

The central bank can intervene in the private foreign exchange (Forex) market whenever needed by acting as a buyer and seller of currency of last resort. To see how this works, consider the following example.

Suppose the United States establishes a fixed exchange rate to the British pound at the rate $\bar{E}_{\$/£}$. In Figure 11.1 "Central Bank Intervention to Maintain a Fixed Exchange Rate", we depict an initial private market Forex equilibrium in which the supply of pounds ($S_£$) equals demand ($D_£$) at the fixed exchange rate ($\bar{E}_{\$/£}$). But suppose, for some unspecified reason, the demand for pounds on the private Forex rises one day to $D'_£$.

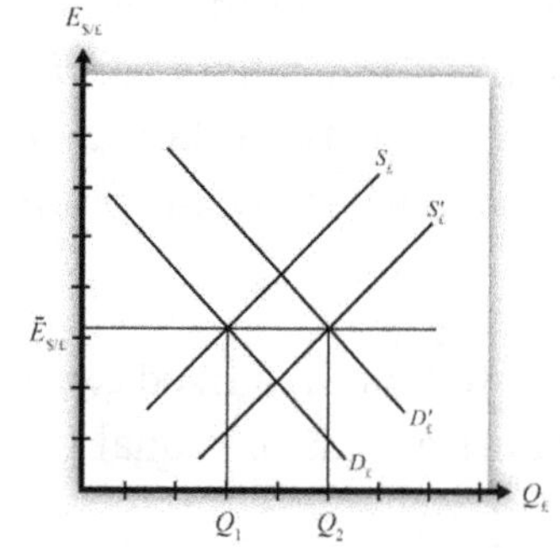

Figure 11.1 Central Bank Intervention to Maintain a Fixed Exchange Rate

At the fixed exchange rate ($\bar{E}_{\$/£}$), private market demand for pounds is now Q_2, whereas supply of pounds is Q_1. This means there is excess demand for pounds in exchange for U.S. dollars on the private Forex.

To maintain a credible fixed exchange rate, the U.S. central bank would immediately satisfy the excess demand by supplying additional pounds to the Forex market. That is, it sells pounds and buys dollars on the private Forex. This would cause a shift of the pound supply curve from $S_£$ to $S'_£$. In this way, the equilibrium exchange rate is automatically maintained at the fixed level.

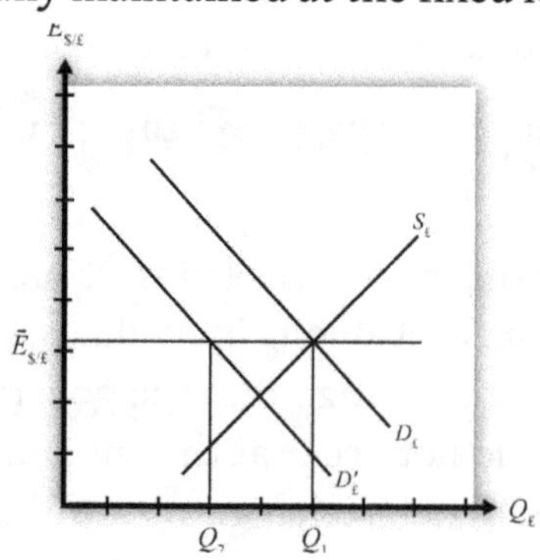

Figure 11.2 Another Central Bank Intervention to Maintain a Fixed Exchange Rate

In this case, an excess supply of pounds also means an excess demand for dollars in exchange for pounds. The U.S. central bank can satisfy the extra dollar demand by entering the Forex and selling dollars in exchange for pounds. This means it is supplying more dollars and demanding more pounds. This would cause a shift of the pound demand curve from $D'_£$ back to $D_£$. Since this intervention occurs immediately, the equilibrium exchange rate is automatically and always maintained at the fixed level.

KEY TAKEAWAYS

- If, for example, the United States fixes its currency to the British pound (the reserve), when there is excess demand for pounds in exchange for U.S. dollars on the private Forex, the U.S. central bank would immediately satisfy the excess demand by supplying additional pounds to the Forex market. By doing so, it can maintain a credible fixed exchange rate.
- If, for example, the United States fixes its currency to the British pound (the reserve), when there is excess demand for dollars in exchange for British pounds on the private Forex, the U.S. central bank would immediately satisfy the excess demand by supplying dollars to the Forex market. By doing so, it can maintain a credible fixed exchange rate.

EXERCISE

- Jeopardy Questions: As in the popular television game show, you are given an answer to a question and you must respond with the question. For example, if the answer is "a tax on imports," then the correct question is "What is a tariff?"
- Of buy, sell, or do nothing, this is what a central bank must do with its reserve currency if there is excess demand for its own currency in the private Forex market while maintaining a fixed exchange rate.
- Of buy, sell, or do nothing, this is what a central bank must do with its reserve currency if there is excess demand for the reserve currency in the private Forex market while maintaining a fixed exchange rate.
- Of buy dollars, sell dollars, or do nothing, this is what China's central bank must do if there is excess demand for Chinese yuan in the private Forex market if China fixes its currency to the U.S. dollar.
- Of buy yuan, sell yuan, or do nothing, this is what China's central bank must do if there is excess demand for U.S. dollars in the private Forex market if China fixes its currency to the U.S. dollar.

11.5 BALANCE OF PAYMENTS SURPLUSES AND DEFICITS

To maintain a fixed exchange rate, the central bank will need to automatically intervene in the private foreign exchange (Forex) by buying or selling domestic currency in exchange for the foreign reserve currency. Clearly, in order for these transactions to be possible, a country's central bank will need a stock of the foreign reserve currency at the time the fixed exchange rate system begins. Subsequently, if excess demand for foreign currency in some periods is balanced with excess supply in other periods, then falling reserves in some periods (when dollars are bought on the Forex) will be offset with rising reserves in other periods (when dollars are sold in the Forex) and a central bank will be able to maintain the fixed exchange rate. Problems arise, though, if a country begins to run out of foreign reserves. But before discussing that situation, we need to explain some terminology.

When the central bank buys domestic currency and sells the foreign reserve currency in the private Forex, the transaction indicates a balance of payments deficit. Alternatively, when the central bank sells domestic currency and buys foreign currency in the Forex, the transaction indicates a balance of payments surplus.

Central bank transactions are recorded in an account titled official reserve transactions. It is found in the financial account of the balance of payments. If this account indicates an addition to official reserves over some period, then the country is running a balance of payments surplus. If over some period the official reserve balance is falling, then the country is running a balance of payments deficit. The deficit or surplus terminology arises from the following circumstances.

Suppose a country runs a trade deficit in a fixed exchange rate system. A trade deficit means that demand for imports exceeds foreign demand for our exports. This implies that domestic demand for foreign currency (to buy imports) exceeds foreign demand for domestic currency (to buy our exports). Assuming no additional foreign demands for domestic currency on the financial account (to keep the exchange rate fixed), the central bank would need to intervene by selling foreign currency in exchange for domestic currency. This would lead to a reduction of foreign reserves and hence a balance of payments deficit. In the absence of transactions on the financial account, to have a trade deficit and a fixed exchange rate implies a balance of payments deficit as well.

More generally, a balance of payments deficit (surplus) arises whenever there is excess demand for (supply of) foreign currency on the private Forex at the official fixed exchange rate. To satisfy the excess demand (excess supply), the central bank will automatically intervene on the Forex and sell (buy) foreign reserves. Thus by tracking sales or purchases of foreign reserves in the official reserve account, we can determine if the country has a balance of payments deficit or surplus.

- Note that in a floating exchange rate system, a central bank can intervene in the private Forex to push the exchange rate up or down. Thus official reserve transactions can show rising or falling foreign reserves and hence suggest a balance of payments deficit or surplus in a floating exchange system. However, it is not strictly proper to describe a country with floating exchange rates as having a balance of payment deficit or surplus. The reason is that interventions are not necessary in a floating exchange rate. In a floating system, an imbalance between supply and demand in the private Forex is relieved by a change in the exchange rate. Thus there need never be an imbalance in the balance of payments in a floating system.

KEY TAKEAWAYS

- When the central bank buys domestic currency and sells the foreign reserve currency in the private Forex, the transaction indicates a balance of payments deficit.
- When the central bank sells domestic currency and buys foreign currency in the Forex, the transaction indicates a balance of payments surplus.
- A balance of payments deficit (surplus) arises whenever there is excess demand for (supply of) foreign currency on the private Forex at the official fixed exchange rate.

EXERCISE

- Jeopardy Questions: As in the popular television game show, you are given an answer to a question and you must respond with the question. For example, if the answer is "a tax on imports," then the correct question is "What is a tariff?"
- The account on the balance of payments (BoP) used to record all central bank transactions.
- The balance on the BoP when the central bank sells foreign reserves.
- Of BoP deficit, BoP surplus, or BoP balance, this is what a central bank will run if there is excess demand for its own currency in the private Forex market while maintaining a fixed exchange rate.
- Of BoP deficit, BoP surplus, or BoP balance, this is what a central bank will run if there is excess demand for the reserve currency in the private Forex market while maintaining a fixed exchange rate.
- Of BoP deficit, BoP surplus, or BoP balance, this is what China's central bank will run if there is excess demand for Chinese yuan in the private Forex market if China fixes its currency to the U.S. dollar.
- Of BoP deficit, BoP surplus, or BoP balance, this is what China's central bank will run if there is excess demand for U.S. dollars in the private Forex market if China fixes its currency to the U.S. dollar.

11.6 BLACK MARKETS

Till now we have said that a central bank must intervene in the foreign exchange (Forex) market whenever there is excess demand or supply of foreign currency. However, we might consider what would happen if the central bank did not intervene.

Surely the government could simply mandate that all Forex transactions take place at the official fixed rate and implement severe penalties if anyone is caught trading at a different rate. A black market arises, however, when exchanges for foreign currency take place at an unofficial (or illegal) exchange rate.

Let's consider why a black market may arise. Suppose the United States fixes its exchange rate to the British pound at the rate $\bar{E}_{\$/£}$. This is indicated in Figure 11.3 "Conditions for a Black Market" as a horizontal line drawn at $\bar{E}_{\$/£}$. Suppose further that demand for pounds (Q_1) on the private Forex exceeds supply (Q_2) at the official fixed exchange rate, but the central bank does not intervene to correct the imbalance. In this case, suppliers of pounds will come to the market with Q_2 quantity of pounds, but many people who would like to buy pounds will not find a willing supplier. Those individuals and businesses demanding the excess ($Q_1 - Q_2$) will leave the market empty-handed. Now if this were a one-time occurrence, the unsatisfied demand might be fulfilled in later days when excess supply of pounds comes to the market. However, a more likely scenario is that this unsatisfied demand persists for a long period. With each passing day of unsatisfied demand, total unsatisfied demand grows insidiously.

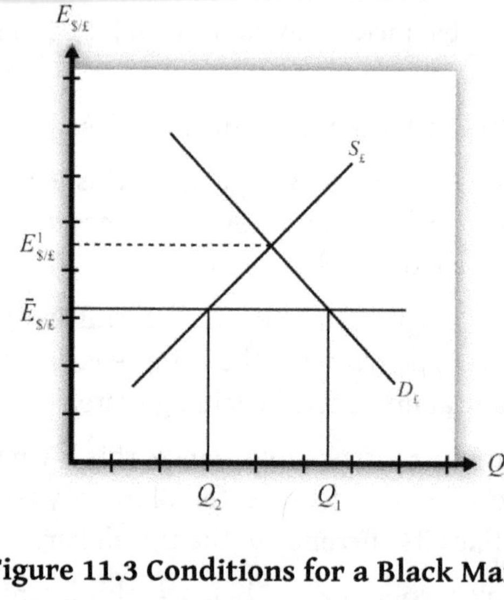

Figure 11.3 Conditions for a Black Market

Together with the excess demand is a willingness to pay more than the official rate to obtain currency. Since the market equilibrium rate is at $E_{\$/£}^{1}$, excess demanders would be willing to pay more dollars to obtain a pound than is required in the official market. The willingness to pay more creates a profit-making possibility. Suppose an individual or business obtains pounds, perhaps by selling goods in Britain and being paid in foreign currency. This person could convert the pounds for dollars at the official rate or, if he or she wants to make more money, could trade the currency "unofficially" at a higher exchange rate. The only problem is finding someone willing to buy the pounds at the unofficial rate. This turns out rarely to be a problem. Wherever black markets develop, unofficial traders find each other on street corners, at hotels, and even within banks.

Thus a central bank doesn't absolutely need to intervene in the Forex market in a fixed exchange rate system. However, if it does not, a black market will very likely arise and the central bank will lose control of the exchange rate. One main purpose of fixed exchange rates, namely the certainty of knowing what the currency will exchange for, is also lost since traders will have to decide whether to trade officially or unofficially. Furthermore, the black market exchange rate typically rises and falls with changes in supply and demand, thus one is never sure what that rate will be.

In light of the potential for black markets to arise, if a government wishes to maintain a credible fixed exchange rate, regular intervention to eliminate excess demand or supply of foreign currency is indeed required.

KEY TAKEAWAYS

- A black market arises when exchanges for foreign currency take place at an unofficial (or illegal) exchange rate.
- If a central bank does not intervene regularly in the Forex market, a black market will very likely arise and the central bank will lose control of the exchange rate.

EXERCISE

- Jeopardy Questions: As in the popular television game show, you are given an answer to a question and you must respond with the question. For example, if the answer is "a tax on imports," then the correct question is "What is a tariff?"
- The term used to describe currency transactions that occur at unofficial exchange rates in a fixed exchange rate system.
- Of buy, sell, or do nothing, a central bank will likely do this with its reserve currency if excess demand for its own currency leads to illegal trades at a higher value.
- Of credible or not credible, this describes a fixed exchange rate system that coexists with a black market.

CHAPTER

POLICY IMPLICATIONS OF FIXED EXCHANGE RATES 12

INTRODUCTION

Government policies work differently under a system of fixed exchange rates rather than floating rates. Monetary policy can lose its effectiveness whereas fiscal policy can become supereffective. In addition, fixed exchange rates offer another policy option, namely, exchange rate policy. Even though a fixed exchange rate should mean the country keeps the rate fixed, sometimes countries periodically change their fixed rate.

This chapter considers these policies under the assumptions of the AA-DD model. It concludes with a case study about the decline of the Bretton Woods fixed exchange rate system that was in place after World War II.

12.1 POLICY WITH FIXED EXCHANGE RATES: AN OVERVIEW

This chapter uses the AA-DD model to describe the effects of fiscal, monetary, and exchange rate policy under a system of fixed exchange rates. Fiscal and monetary policies are the primary tools governments use to guide the macroeconomy. With fixed exchange rates, a third policy option becomes available—that is, exchange rate policy. Thus we also examine the effects of changes in the fixed exchange rate. These exchange rate changes are called devaluations (sometimes competitive devaluations) and revaluations.

In introductory macroeconomics courses, students learn how government policy levers can be used to influence the level of the gross national product (GNP), inflation rate, unemployment rate, and interest rates. In this chapter, that analysis is expanded to an open economy (i.e., one open to trade) and to the effects on exchange rates and current account balances.

Results

Using the AA-DD model, several important relationships between key economic variables are shown:

- A monetary policy (change in M^S) has no effect on GNP or the exchange rate in a fixed exchange system. As such, the trade balance, unemployment, and interest rates all remain the same as well. Monetary policy becomes ineffective as a policy tool in a fixed exchange rate system.
- Expansionary fiscal policy (↑G, ↑TR, or ↓T) causes an increase in GNP while maintaining the fixed exchange rate and constant interest rates. The trade balance and unemployment are both reduced.
- Contractionary fiscal policy (↓G, ↓TR, or ↑T) reduces GNP while maintaining the fixed exchange rate and constant interest rates. The trade balance and unemployment both rise.
- A competitive devaluation lowers the currency value and causes an increase in GNP. Unemployment falls, interest rates remain the same, and the trade balance rises.
- A currency revaluation raises the currency value and causes a decrease in GNP. Unemployment rises, interest rates remain the same, and the trade balance falls.
- Monetary expansion by the reserve currency country forces the domestic country to run a balance of payments surplus to maintain its fixed exchange rate. The resulting money supply increase causes domestic interest rates to fall to maintain equality with the falling foreign interest rates. Domestic GNP remains fixed, as do unemployment and the trade balance.
- A currency crisis arises when a country runs persistent balance of payments deficits while attempting to maintain its fixed exchange rate and is about to deplete its foreign exchange reserves. A crisis can force a country to devalue its currency or move to a floating exchange rate. To postpone the crisis, countries can sometimes borrow money from organizations like the International Monetary Fund (IMF).
- Anticipation of a balance of payments crisis can induce investors to sell domestic assets in favor of foreign assets. This is called capital flight. Capital flight will worsen a balance of payments problem and can induce a crisis to occur.

Connections

The AA-DD model was developed to describe the interrelationships of macroeconomic variables within an open economy. Since some of these macroeconomic variables are controlled by the government, we can use the model to understand the likely effects of government policy changes. The main levers the government controls are monetary policy (changes in the money supply), fiscal policy (changes in the government budget), and exchange rate policy (setting the fixed exchange rate value). In this chapter, the AA-DD model is applied to understand government policy effects in the context of a fixed exchange rate system. In Chapter 10 , we considered these same government policies in the context of a floating exchange rate system. In Chapter 13 , we'll compare fixed and floating exchange rate systems and discuss the pros and cons of each system.

It is important to recognize that these results are what "would" happen under the full set of assumptions that describe the AA-DD model. These effects may or may not happen in reality. Nevertheless, the model surely captures some of the simple cause-and-effect relationships and therefore helps us to understand the broader implications of policy changes. Thus even if in reality many more elements (not described in the model) may act to influence the key endogenous variables, the AA-DD model at least gives a more complete picture of some of the expected tendencies.

KEY TAKEAWAYS

- The main objective of the AA-DD model is to assess the effects of monetary, fiscal, and exchange rate policy changes.
- It is important to recognize that these results are what "would" happen under the full set of assumptions that describes the AA-DD model; they may or may not accurately describe actual outcomes in actual economies.

EXERCISE

- Jeopardy Questions: As in the popular television game show, you are given an answer to a question and you must respond with the question. For example, if the answer is "a tax on imports," then the correct question is "What is a tariff?"
- Of appreciation, depreciation, or no change, the effect of expansionary monetary policy on the domestic currency value under fixed exchange rates in the AA-DD model.
- Of increase, decrease, or no change, the effect of contractionary monetary policy on GNP under fixed exchange rates in the AA-DD model.
- Of increase, decrease, or no change, the effect of expansionary monetary policy on the current account deficit under fixed exchange rates in the AA-DD model.
- Of increase, decrease, or no change, the effect of contractionary monetary policy on the current account surplus under fixed exchange rates in the AA-DD model.
- Of appreciation, depreciation, or no change, the effect of expansionary fiscal policy on the domestic currency value under fixed exchange rates in the AA-DD model.

- Of increase, decrease, or no change, the effect of contractionary fiscal policy on GNP under fixed exchange rates in the AA-DD model.
- Of increase, decrease, or no change, the effect of expansionary fiscal policy on the current account deficit under fixed exchange rates in the AA-DD model.
- Of increase, decrease, or no change, the effect of a devaluation on GNP under fixed exchange rates in the AA-DD model.
- Of increase, decrease, or no change, the effect of a revaluation on the current account deficit under fixed exchange rates in the AA-DD model.
- The term used to describe a rapid purchase of foreign investments often spurred by the expectation of an imminent currency devaluation.
- The term used to describe the situation when a central bank runs persistent balance of payments deficits and is about to run out of foreign exchange reserves.

12.2 MONETARY POLICY WITH FIXED EXCHANGE RATES

In this section, we use the AA-DD model to assess the effects of monetary policy in a fixed exchange rate system. Recall from Chapter 7 that the money supply is effectively controlled by a country's central bank. In the case of the United States, this is the Federal Reserve Board, or the Fed. When the money supply increases due to action taken by the central bank, we refer to it as expansionary monetary policy. If the central bank acts to reduce the money supply, it is referred to as contractionary monetary policy. Methods that can be used to change the money supply are discussed in Chapter 7 , Section 7.5 .

Expansionary Monetary Policy

Suppose the United States fixes its exchange rate to the British pound at the rate $\bar{E}_{\$/£}$. This is indicated in Figure 12.1 "Expansionary Monetary Policy with a Fixed Exchange Rate" as a horizontal line drawn at $\bar{E}_{\$/£}$. Suppose also that the economy is originally at a superequilibrium shown as point F with original gross national product (GNP) level Y1. Next, suppose the U.S. central bank (the Fed) decides to expand the money supply by conducting an open market operation, ceteris paribus. Ceteris paribus means that all other exogenous variables are assumed to remain at their original values. A purchase of Treasury bonds by the Fed will lead to an increase in the dollar money supply. As shown in Chapter 9 "The AA-DD Model", Section 9.5 "Shifting the AA Curve", money supply changes cause a shift in the AA curve. More specifically, an increase in the money supply will cause AA to shift upward (i.e., $\uparrow M^S$ is an AA up-shifter). This is depicted in the diagram as a shift from the red AA to the blue A'A' line.

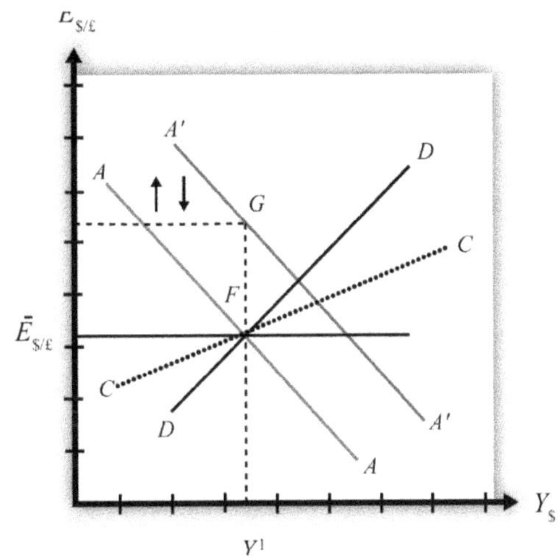

Figure 12.1 Expansionary Monetary Policy with a Fixed Exchange Rate

The money supply increase puts upward pressure on the exchange rate in the following way. First, a money supply increase causes a reduction in U.S. interest rates. This in turn reduces the rate of return on U.S. assets below the rate of return on similar assets in Britain. Thus international investors will begin to demand more pounds in exchange for dollars on the private Forex to take advantage of the relatively higher RoR of British assets. In a floating exchange system, excess demand for pounds would cause the pound to appreciate and the dollar to depreciate. In other words, the exchange rate $E_{\$/£}$ would rise. In the diagram, this would correspond to a movement to the new A'A' curve at point G.

However, because the country maintains a fixed exchange rate, excess demand for pounds on the private Forex will automatically be relieved by Fed intervention. The Fed will supply the excess pounds demanded by selling reserves of pounds in exchange for dollars at the fixed exchange rate. As we showed in Chapter 10 , Section 10.5 , Fed sales of foreign currency result in a reduction in the U.S. money supply. This is because when the Fed buys dollars in the private Forex, it is taking those dollars out of circulation and thus out of the money supply. Since a reduction of the money supply causes AA to shift back down, the final effect will be that the AA curve returns to its original position. This is shown as the up and down movement of the AA curve in the diagram. The final equilibrium is the same as the original at point F.

The AA curve must return to the same original position because the exchange rate must remain fixed at $\bar{E}$\$/£. This implies that the money supply reduction due to Forex intervention will exactly offset the money supply expansion induced by the original open market operation. Thus the money supply will temporarily rise but then will fall back to its original level. Maintaining the money supply at the same level also assures that interest rate parity is maintained. Recall that in a fixed exchange rate system, interest rate parity requires equalization of interest rates between countries (i.e., i$ = i£). If the money supply did not return to the same level, interest rates would not be equalized.

Thus after final adjustment occurs, there are no effects from expansionary monetary policy in a fixed exchange rate system. The exchange rate will not change and there will be no effect on equilibrium GNP. Also, since the economy returns to the original equilibrium, there is also no effect on the current account balance.

Contractionary Monetary Policy

Contractionary monetary policy corresponds to a decrease in the money supply or a Fed sale of Treasury bonds on the open bond market. In the AA-DD model, a decrease in the money supply shifts the AA curve downward. The effects will be the opposite of those described above for expansionary monetary policy. A complete description is left for the reader as an exercise.

The quick effects, howev1er, are as follows. U.S. contractionary monetary policy with a fixed exchange rate will have no effects within the economy. $E_{\$/£}$, $Y_{\$}$ and the current account balance will all be maintained or return to their initial levels.

Discussion

This result indicates that monetary policy is ineffective in influencing the economy in a fixed exchange rate system. In contrast, in a floating exchange rate system, monetary policy can either raise or lower GNP, at least in the short run. Thus monetary policy has some effectiveness in a floating system, and central bank authorities can adjust policy to affect macroeconomic conditions within their economy. For example, if the economy is growing only sluggishly, or perhaps is contracting, the central bank can raise the money supply to help spur an expansion of GNP, if the economy has a floating exchange rate. However, with a fixed exchange rate, the central bank no longer has this ability. This explains why countries lose monetary autonomy (or independence) with a fixed exchange rate. The central bank can no longer have any influence over the interest rate, exchange rate, or the level of GNP.

One other important comparison worth making is between expansionary monetary policy in a fixed exchange rate system with sterilized foreign exchange (Forex) interventions in a floating system. In the first case, expansionary monetary policy is offset later with a contraction of the money supply caused by automatic Forex intervention. In the second case, Forex intervention leading to an expansion of the money supply is countered with contractionary open market operations. In the first case, the interest rate is maintained to satisfy interest rate parity. In the second case, the interest rate remains fixed by design. Clearly, these two situations represent exactly the same set of actions, though in a different order. Thus it makes sense that the two policies would have the same implications—that is, "no impact" on any of the economic variables.

KEY TAKEAWAYS

- There are no effects from expansionary or contractionary monetary policy in a fixed exchange rate system. The exchange rate will not change, there will be no effect on equilibrium GNP, and there will be no effect on the current account balance.
- Monetary policy in a fixed exchange rate system is equivalent in its effects to sterilized Forex interventions in a floating exchange rate system.

EXERCISE

Suppose that Latvia can be described with the AA-DD model and that Latvia fixes its currency, the lats (Ls), to the euro. Consider the changes in the exogenous variable in the left column. Indicate the short-run effects on the equilibrium levels of Latvian GNP, the Latvian interest rate (i_{Ls}) , the Latvian trade balance, and the exchange rate ($E_{Ls/€}$). Use the following notation:

+ the variable increases

- the variable decreases

0 the variable does not change

A the variable change is ambiguous (i.e., it may rise, it may fall)

	GNP	i_{Ls}	Trade Balance	$E_{Ls/€}$
An increase in the Latvian money supply				
A decrease in the Latvian money supply				

12.3 FISCAL POLICY WITH FIXED EXCHANGE RATES

In this section, we use the AA-DD model to assess the effects of fiscal policy in a fixed exchange rate system. Recall from Chapter 8 that fiscal policy refers to any change in expenditures or revenues within any branch of the government. This means any change in government spending (e.g., transfer payments or taxes) by federal, state, or local governments represents a fiscal policy change. Since changes in expenditures or revenues will often affect a government budget balance, we can also say that a change in the government surplus or deficit represents a change in fiscal policy.

When government spending or transfer payments increase, or tax revenues decrease, we refer to it as expansionary fiscal policy. These actions would also be associated with an increase in the government budget deficit, or a decrease in its budget surplus. If the government acts to reduce government spending or transfer payments, or increase tax revenues, it is referred to as contractionary fiscal policy. These actions would also be associated with a decrease in the government budget deficit, or an increase in its budget surplus.

Expansionary Fiscal Policy

Suppose the United States fixes its exchange rate to the British pound at the rate $\bar{E}_{\$/£}$. This is indicated in Figure 12.2 "Expansionary Fiscal Policy with a Fixed Exchange Rate" as a horizontal line drawn at $\bar{E}_{\$/£}$. Suppose also that the economy is originally at a superequilibrium shown as point J with GNP at level Y1. Next, suppose the government decides to increase government spending (or increase transfer payments or decrease taxes). As shown in Chapter 9 "The AA-DD Model", Section 9.3 "Shifting the DD Curve", fiscal policy changes cause a shift in the DD curve. More specifically, an increase in government spending (or an increase in transfer payments or a decrease in taxes) will cause DD to shift rightward (i.e., ↑G, ↑TR, and ↓T all are DD right-shifters). This is depicted in the diagram as a shift from the red DD to the blue D'D' line (step 1).

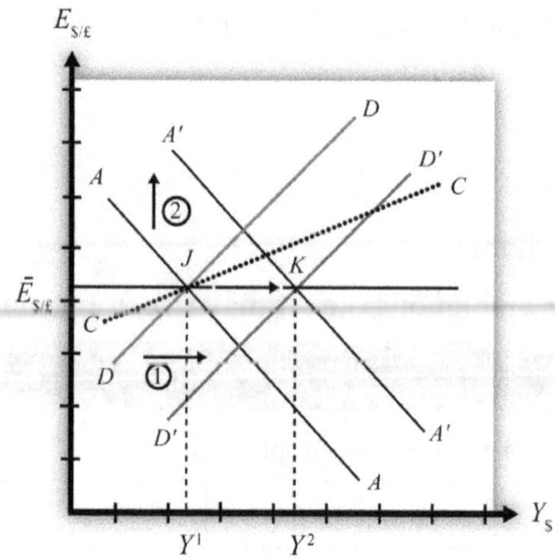

Figure 12.2 Expansionary Fiscal Policy with a Fixed Exchange Rate

If the expansionary fiscal policy occurs because of an increase in government spending, then government demand for goods and services (G&S) will increase. If the expansionary fiscal policy occurs due to an increase in transfer payments or a decrease in taxes, then disposable income will increase, leading to an increase in consumption demand. In either case, aggregate demand increases. Before any adjustment occurs, the increase in aggregate demand causes aggregate demand to exceed aggregate supply, which will lead to an expansion of GNP. Thus the economy will begin to move rightward from point J.

As GNP rises, so does real money demand, causing an increase in U.S. interest rates. With higher interest rates, the rate of return on U.S. assets rises above that in the United Kingdom and international investors increase demand for dollars (in exchange for pounds) on the private Forex. In a floating exchange rate system this would lead to a U.S. dollar appreciation (and pound depreciation)—that is, a decrease in the exchange rate $E_{\$/£}$.

However, because the country maintains a fixed exchange rate, excess demand for dollars on the private Forex will automatically be relieved by the U.S. Federal Reserve (or the Fed) intervention. The Fed will supply the excess dollars demanded by buying pounds in exchange for dollars at the fixed exchange rate. As we showed in Chapter 10, Section 10.5, the foreign currency purchases by the Fed result in an increase in the U.S. money supply. This is because when the Fed sells dollars in the private Forex, these dollars are entering into circulation and thus become a part of the money supply. The increase in the money supply causes the AA curve to shift up (step 2). The final equilibrium will be reached when the new A'A' curve intersects the D'D' curve at the fixed exchange rate ($\bar{E}_{\$/£}$) shown at point K.

Note that in the transition, the Fed intervention in the Forex occurred because investors responded to rising U.S. interest rates by increasing demand for dollars on the Forex. The Fed's response causes an increase in the money supply, which in turn will lower interest rates back to their original level. This result is necessary to maintain the fixed exchange rate interest rate parity (IRP) condition of $i_{\$} = i_{£}$.

Note also that as GNP increases in the transition, causing interest rates to rise, this rise is immediately countered with automatic Fed intervention in the Forex. Thus the exchange rate will never fall below the fixed rate. There will be pressure for the exchange rate to fall, but the Fed will always be there to relieve the pressure with its intervention. Thus the adjustment path from the original equilibrium at J to the final equilibrium at K will follow the rightward arrow between the two points along the fixed exchange rate.

The final result is that expansionary fiscal policy in a fixed exchange rate system will cause an increase in GNP (from Y^1 to $Y^{2)}$ and no change in the exchange rate in the short run. Since the new equilibrium at K lies below the original CC curve representing a fixed current account balance, expansionary fiscal policy, consisting of an increase in G, will cause the current account balance to fall. This corresponds to a decrease in a trade surplus or an increase in a trade deficit.

Contractionary Fiscal Policy

Contractionary fiscal policy corresponds to a decrease in government spending, a decrease in transfer payments, or an increase in taxes. It would also be represented by a decrease in the government budget deficit or an increase in the budget surplus. In the AA-DD model, a contractionary fiscal policy shifts the DD curve leftward. The effects will be the opposite of those described above for expansionary fiscal policy. A complete description is left for the reader as an exercise.

The quick effects, however, are as follows. Contractionary fiscal policy in a fixed exchange rate system will cause a decrease in GNP and no change in the exchange rate in the short run. Contractionary fiscal policy, consisting of a decrease in G, will also cause the current account balance to rise. This corresponds to an increase in a trade surplus or a decrease in a trade deficit.

KEY TAKEAWAYS

- Expansionary fiscal policy in a fixed exchange rate system will cause an increase in GNP, no change in the exchange rate (of course), and a decrease in the current account balance.
- Contractionary fiscal policy in a fixed exchange rate system will cause a decrease in GNP, no change in the exchange rate (of course), and an increase in the current account balance.

EXERCISES

- Sri Lanka fixes its currency, the Sri Lankan rupee (LKR), to the U.S. dollar. Suppose Sri Lanka can be described using the AA-DD model. Consider changes in the exogenous variables in Sri Lanka in the left column. Suppose each change occurs ceteris paribus. Indicate the short-run effects on the equilibrium values of Sri Lankan GNP, the Sri Lankan interest rate (i_{LKR}), the Sri Lankan trade deficit, and the exchange rate ($E_{LKR/\$}$). Use the following notation:
- + the variable increases
- the variable decreases
- 0 the variable does not change
- A the variable change is ambiguous (i.e., it may rise, it may fall)

	GNP	*i*LKR	Sri Lankan Trade Deficit	*E*LKR/$
A decrease in domestic taxes				
An increase in government demand				
An increase in transfer payments				

Consider the following occurrences. Use the AA-DD model to determine the impact on the variables (+, -, 0, or A) from the twin-deficit identity listed along the top row. Consider only short-run effects (i.e., before inflationary effects occur) and assume ceteris paribus for all other exogenous variables.

	Impact on			
	Sp	*I*	*IM* - *EX*	*G* + *TR* - *T*
A reduction in government spending with a fixed exchange rate				
An increase in transfer payments with fixed exchange rates				
A decrease in taxes with fixed exchange rates				

12.4 EXCHANGE RATE REGIME WITH FIXED RATES

In this section, we use the AA-DD model to assess the effects of exchange rate policy in a fixed exchange rate system. In a sense we can say that the government's decision to maintain a fixed exchange is the country's exchange rate policy. However, over time, the government does have some discretion concerning the value of the exchange rate. In this section, we will use "exchange rate policy" to mean changes in the value of the fixed exchange rate.

If the government lowers the value of its currency with respect to the reserve currency or to gold, we call the change a devaluation. If the government raises the value of its currency with respect to the reserve currency or to gold, we call the change a revaluation. The terms devaluation and revaluation should properly be used only in reference to a government change in the fixed exchange rate since each term suggests an action being taken. In contrast, natural market changes in supply and demand will result in changes in the exchange rate in a floating system, but it is not quite right to call these changes devaluations or revaluations since no concerted action was taken by anyone. Nonetheless, some writers will sometimes use the terms this way.

In most cases, devaluations and revaluations occur because of persistent balance of payments disequilibria. We will consider these situations in Chapter 12 , Section 12.6 on balance of payments crises and capital flight. In this section, we will consider the basic effects of devaluations and revaluations without assuming any notable prior events caused these actions to occur.

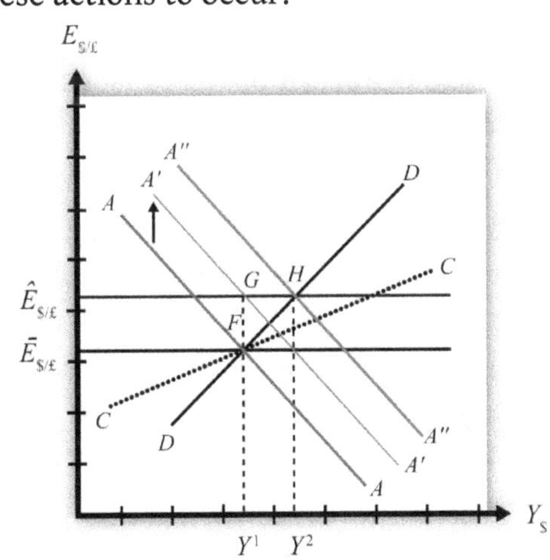

Figure 12.3 Effects of a Devaluation

Devaluation

Suppose the United States fixes its exchange rate to the British pound at the rate $\bar{E}_{\$/£}$. This is indicated in Figure 12.3 "Effects of a Devaluation" as a horizontal line drawn at $\bar{E}_{\$/£}$. Suppose also that the economy is originally at a superequilibrium shown as point F with gross national product (GNP) at level Y^1. Next, suppose the U.S. central bank (or the Fed) decides to devalue the U.S. dollar with respect to the British pound corresponding to an increase in the fixed rate from $\bar{E}_{\$/£}$ to $\hat{E}_{\$/£}$. Recall that a devaluation corresponds to an increase in the \$/£ exchange rate. Assume that there was no anticipation of the devaluation and that it comes about as a complete surprise to all market participants. The first effect of the devaluation, of course, is that the exchange rate rises. Immediately the economy moves from F to G on the diagram. It may seem that this would move the economy off the AA curve, but instead the AA curve shifts up with the devaluation to A'A'. This occurs because the AA curve is a function of the expected exchange rate. As long as investors believe that the new exchange rate will now remain fixed at its new rate ($\hat{E}_{\$/£}$), the expected future exchange rate will immediately rise to this new level as well. It is this increase in $E_{\$/£}^e$ that causes AA to shift up.

When at point G, however, the economy is not at a superequilibrium. Because of the dollar devaluation, the real exchange rate has increased, making foreign goods relatively more expensive and U.S. goods relatively cheaper. This raises aggregate demand, which at the new exchange rate ($\hat{E}_{\$/£}$) is now at the level where the exchange rate line crosses the DD curve at point H.

Since the economy, for now, lies at G to the left of point H on the DD curve, aggregate demand exceeds supply. Producers will respond by increasing supply to satisfy the demand, and GNP will begin to rise.

As GNP rises, real money demand will rise, causing an increase in U.S. interest rates, which will raise the rate of return on U.S. assets. Investors will respond by increasing their demand for U.S. dollars on the foreign exchange (Forex) market, and there will be pressure for a dollar appreciation.

To maintain the fixed exchange rate, however, the U.S. Fed will have to automatically intervene on the Forex and sell dollars to satisfy the excess demand in exchange for pounds. This represents a balance of payments surplus since by buying pounds on the Forex the United States is adding to its stock of foreign reserves. A balance of payments surplus in turn causes an increase in the U.S. money supply, which will shift the AA curve to the right.

As GNP rises toward Y^2 at point H, the AA curve will shift right with the Fed intervention to maintain the equilibrium exchange rate at the new fixed value, which is $\hat{E}_{\$/£}$. The final superequilibrium occurs at point H where excess aggregate demand is finally satisfied.

The final result is that a devaluation in a fixed exchange rate system will cause an increase in GNP (from Y^1 to Y^2) and an increase in the exchange rate to the new fixed value in the short run. Since the new equilibrium at H lies above the original

CC curve representing a fixed current account balance, a devaluation will cause the current account balance to rise. This corresponds to an increase in a trade surplus or a decrease in a trade deficit.

Revaluation

A revaluation corresponds to change in the fixed exchange rate such that the country's currency value is increased with respect to the reserve currency. In the AA-DD model, a U.S. dollar revaluation would be represented as a decrease in the fixed $/£ exchange rate. The effects will be the opposite of those described above for a devaluation. A complete description is left for the reader as an exercise.

The quick effects, however, are as follows. A revaluation in a fixed exchange rate system will cause a decrease in GNP and a decrease in the fixed exchange rate in the short run. A revaluation will also cause the current account balance to fall. This corresponds to a decrease in a trade surplus or an increase in a trade deficit.

KEY TAKEAWAYS

- If the government lowers (raises) the value of its currency with respect to the reserve currency, or to gold, we call the change a devaluation (revaluation).
- A devaluation in a fixed exchange rate system will cause an increase in GNP, an increase in the exchange rate to the new fixed value in the short run, and an increase in the current account balance.
- A revaluation in a fixed exchange rate system will cause a decrease in GNP, an increase in the currency value to the new fixed rate, and a decrease in the current account balance.

EXERCISES

- Vietnam fixes its currency, the Vietnamese dong (VND), to the US dollar. Suppose Vietnam can be described using the AA-DD model. Consider changes in the exogenous variables in Vietnam in the left column. Suppose each change occurs ceteris paribus. Indicate the short-run effects on the equilibrium values of Vietnamese GNP, the Vietnamese interest rate (i_{VND}), the Vietnamese trade deficit, and the exchange rate ($E_{VND//\$}$). Use the following notation:

+ the variable increases

- the variable decreases

0 the variable does not change

A the variable change is ambiguous (i.e., it may rise, it may fall)

	GNP	iVND	EVND/$
A devaluation of the Vietnamese dong			
A revaluation of the Vietnamese dong			

Consider the following occurrences. Use the AA-DD model to determine the impact on the variables (+, –, 0, or A) from the twin-deficit identity listed along the top row. Consider only short-run effects (i.e., before inflationary effects occur) and assume ceteris paribus for all other exogenous variables.

	Impact on			
	Sp	*I*	*IM* – *EX*	*G* + *TR* – *T*
A currency devaluation under fixed exchange rates				
A currency revaluation under fixed exchange rates				

China maintains an exchange rate fixed to the U.S. dollar at the rate E_1. Use the following AA-DD diagram for China to depict answers to the questions below. Suppose China's current account is in surplus originally. Suppose Y_F indicates the full employment level of output.

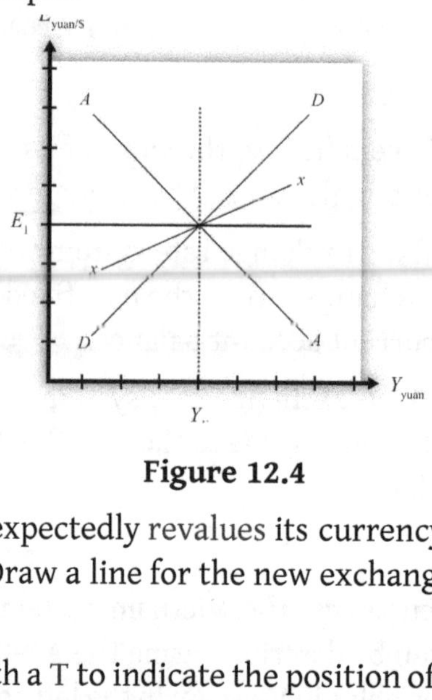

Figure 12.4

- Suppose China unexpectedly revalues its currency under pressure from the U.S. government. Draw a line for the new exchange rate and mark the graph with an E_2.
- Mark the graph with a T to indicate the position of the economy immediately after the revaluation when investor expectations adjust to the new exchange rate.
- What effect does the revaluation have for the prices of Chinese goods to Americans?
- Mark the graph with a W to indicate the position of the economy once a new short-run equilibrium is achieved. Mark the graph with Y_2 to indicate the new level of GDP.
- Does China's stock of foreign reserves rise or fall after the revaluation?
- Does China's current account surplus rise or fall?
- In the adjustment to a long-run equilibrium, would the Chinese price level rise or fall?

12.5 RESERVE COUNTRY MONETARY REGULATIONS WITH FIXED EXCHANGE RATES

Suppose the United States fixes its exchange rate to the British pound. In this circumstance, the exchange rate system is a reserve currency standard in which the British pound is the reserve currency. The U.S. government is the one that fixes its exchange rate and will hold some quantity of British pounds on reserve so it is able to intervene on the Forex to maintain the credible fixed exchange rate.

It is worth noting that since the United States fixes its exchange rate to the pound, the British pound is, of course, fixed to the U.S. dollar as well. Since the pound is the reserve currency, however, it has a special place in the monetary system. The Bank of England, Britain's central bank, will never need to intervene in the Forex market. It does not need to hold dollars. Instead, all market pressures for the exchange rate to change will be resolved by U.S. intervention, that is, by the nonreserve currency country.

Expansionary Monetary Policy by the Reserve Country

Now let's suppose that the reserve currency country, Britain, undertakes expansionary monetary policy. We will consider the impact of this change from the vantage point of the United States, the nonreserve currency country. Suppose the United States is originally in a superequilibrium at point F in the adjoining diagram with the exchange rate fixed at $\bar{E}_{\$/£}$. An increase in the British money supply will cause a decrease in British interest rates, $i_£$.

As shown in Chapter 9 , Section 9.5 , foreign interest rate changes cause a shift in the AA curve. More specifically, a decrease in the foreign interest rate will cause the AA curve to shift downward (i.e., $\downarrow i_£$ is an AA down-shifter). This is depicted in Figure 12.5 «Expansionary Monetary Policy by a Reserve Country» as a shift from the red AA to the blue A'A' line.

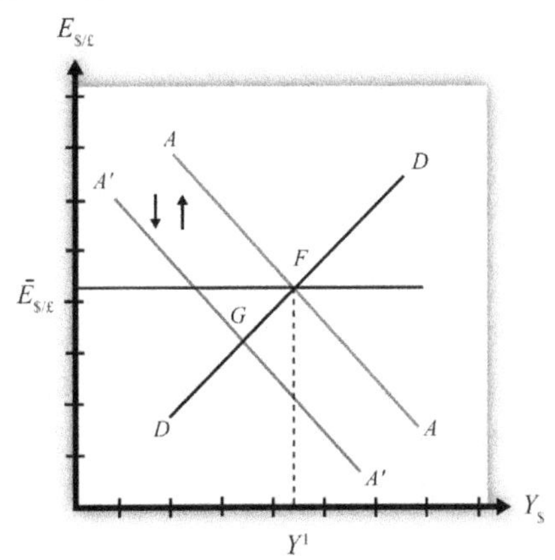

Figure 12.5 Expansionary Monetary Policy by a Reserve Country

The money supply decrease puts downward pressure on the exchange rate in the following way. When British interest rates fall, it will cause $i_£ < i_\$$ and interest rate parity (IRP) will be violated. Thus international investors will begin to demand more dollars in exchange for pounds on the private Forex to take advantage of the relatively higher rate of return on U.S. assets. In a floating exchange system, excess demand for dollars would cause the dollar to appreciate and the pound to depreciate. In other words, the exchange rate ($E_{\$/£}$) would fall. In the diagram, this would correspond to a movement to the new A'A' curve at point G.

Because the country maintains a fixed exchange rate, however, excess demand for dollars on the private Forex will automatically be relieved by the U.S. Federal Reserve (or the Fed) intervention. The Fed will supply the excess dollars demanded by buying pounds in exchange for dollars at the fixed exchange rate. As we showed in Chapter 10 , Section 10.5 , the foreign currency purchases by the Fed result in an increase in the U.S. money supply. This is because when the Fed sells dollars in the private Forex, these dollars are entering into circulation and thus become a part of the money supply. Since an increase in the money supply causes AA to shift up, the AA curve will return to its original position to maintain the fixed exchange rate. This is shown as the up-and-down movement of the AA curve in the diagram. Thus the final equilibrium is the same as the original equilibrium at point F.

Remember that in a fixed exchange rate system, IRP requires equalization of interest rates between countries. When the British interest rates fell, they fell below the rates in the United States. When the U.S. Fed intervenes on the Forex, however, the U.S. money supply rises and U.S. interest rates are pushed down. Pressure for the exchange rate to change will cease only when U.S. interest rates become equal to British interest rates and IRP ($i_£ = i_\$$) is again satisfied.

Thus after final adjustment occurs, expansionary monetary policy by the foreign reserve currency country in a fixed exchange rate system causes no effects on U.S. GNP or the exchange rate. Since the economy also returns to the original equilibrium, there is also no effect on the current account balance. Fed intervention in the Forex to maintain the fixed exchange rate, however, will cause U.S. interest rates to fall to maintain IRP with the lower reserve country interest rates.

Contractionary Monetary Policy by the Reserve Country

Contractionary monetary policy corresponds to a decrease in the British money supply that would lead to an increase in British interest rates. In the AA-DD model, an increase in foreign interest rates shifts the AA curve upward. The effects will be the opposite of those described above for expansionary monetary policy. A complete description is left for the reader as an exercise.

KEY TAKEAWAYS

- Expansionary monetary policy by the foreign reserve currency country in a fixed exchange rate system causes no effects on domestic GNP, the exchange rate, or the current account balance in the AA-DD model. However, it will cause domestic interest rates to fall.
- Contractionary monetary policy by the foreign reserve currency country in a fixed exchange rate system causes no effects on domestic GNP, the exchange rate, or the current account balance in the AA-DD model. However, it will cause domestic interest rates to rise.

EXERCISES

- Honduras fixes its currency, the Honduran lempira (HNL), to the U.S. dollar. Suppose Honduras can be described using the AA-DD model. Consider changes in the exogenous variables in the left column. Suppose each change occurs ceteris paribus. Indicate the short-run effects on the equilibrium values of Honduran GNP, the Honduran interest rate (i_{HNL}), the Honduran trade deficit, and the exchange rate ($E_{HNL/\$}$). Use the following notation:

\+ the variable increases

\- the variable decreases

0 the variable does not change

A the variable change is ambiguous (i.e., it may rise, it may fall)

	GNP	iHNL	EHNL/$
An increase in U.S. interest rates			
A decrease in U.S. interest rates			

Consider the following occurrences. Use the AA-DD model to determine the impact on the variables (+, –, 0, or A) from the twin-deficit identity listed along the top row. Consider only short-run effects (i.e., before inflationary effects occur) and assume ceteris paribus for all other exogenous variables.

	Impact on			
	Sp	*I*	*IM* – *EX*	*G* + *TR* – *T*
An increase in foreign interest rates under fixed exchange rates				
A decrease in foreign interest rates under fixed exchange rates				

12.6 CURRENCY CRISES AND CAPITAL FLIGHT

To maintain a credible fixed exchange rate system, a country will need to buy and sell the reserve currency whenever there is excess demand or supply in the private foreign exchange (Forex). To make sales of foreign currency possible, a country will need to maintain a foreign exchange reserve. The reserve is a stockpile of assets denominated in the reserve currency. For example, if the United States fixes the dollar to the British pound, then it would need to have a reserve of pound assets in case it needs to intervene on the Forex with a sale of pounds.

Generally, a central bank holds these reserves in the form of Treasury bonds issued by the reserve country government. In this way, the reserve holdings earn interest for the central bank and thus the reserves will grow in value over time. Holding reserves in the form of currency would not earn interest and thus are less desirable. Nonetheless, a central bank will likely keep some of its reserves liquid in the form of currency to make anticipated daily Forex transactions. If larger sales of reserves become necessary, the U.S. central bank can always sell the foreign Treasury bonds on the bond market and convert those holdings to currency.

A fixed exchange rate is sustainable if the country's central bank can maintain that rate over time with only modest interventions in the Forex. Ideally, one would expect that during some periods of time, there would be excess demand for domestic currency on the Forex, putting pressure on the currency to appreciate. In this case, the central bank would relieve the pressure by selling domestic currency and buying the reserve on the Forex, thus running a balance of payments (BoP) surplus. During these periods, the country's reserve holdings would rise. At other periods, there may be excess demand for the reserve currency, putting pressure on the domestic currency to depreciate. Here, the central bank would relieve the pressure by selling the reserve currency in exchange for domestic currency, thus running a balance of payments deficit. During these periods, the country's reserve holdings would fall. As long as the country's reserve holdings stay sufficiently high during its ups and downs, the fixed exchange rate could be maintained indefinitely. In this way, the central bank's interventions "smooth-out" the fluctuations that would have occurred in a floating system.

Problems arise if the reserves cannot be maintained if, for example, there is a persistent excess demand for the foreign currency over time with very few episodes of excess supply. In this case, the central bank's persistent BoP deficits will move reserve holdings closer and closer to zero. A balance of payments crisis occurs when the country is about to run out of foreign exchange reserves.

Borrowing Reserves

Several things may happen leading up to a balance of payments crisis. One option open to the central bank is to borrow additional quantities of the reserve currency from the reserve country central bank, government, or an international institution like the International Monetary Fund (IMF). The IMF was originally created to help countries with balance of payments problems within the Bretton Woods fixed exchange rate system (1945–1973). When a country was near to depleting its reserves, it could borrow reserve currency from the IMF. As long as the balance of payments deficits leading to reserve depletion would soon be reversed with balance of payments surpluses, the country would be able to repay the loans to the IMF in the near future. As such, the IMF "window" was intended to provide a safety valve in case volatility in supply and demand in the Forex was greater than a country's reserve holdings could handle.

Devaluation

If a country cannot acquire additional reserves and if it does not change domestic policies in a way that causes excess demand for foreign currency to cease or reverse, then the country will run out of foreign reserves and will no longer be able to maintain a credible fixed exchange rate. The country could keep the fixed exchange rate at the same level and simply cease intervening in the Forex; however, this would not relieve the pressure for the currency to depreciate and would quickly create conditions for a thriving black market.

If the country remains committed to a fixed exchange rate system, its only choice is to devalue its currency with respect to the reserve. A lower currency value will achieve two things. First, it will reduce the prices of all domestic goods from the viewpoint of foreigners. In essence, a devaluation is like having a sale in which all the country's goods are marked down by some percentage. At the same time, the devaluation will raise the price of foreign goods to domestic residents. Thus foreign goods have all been marked up in price by some percentage. These changes should result in an increase in demand for domestic currency to take advantage of the lower domestic prices and a decrease in demand for foreign currency due to the higher foreign prices.

The second effect occurs for investors. When the currency is devalued, the rate of return on foreign assets may fall, especially if investors had anticipated a devaluation and had adjusted their expectations accordingly. (See the next section on capital flight for further discussion.) When the rate of return on foreign assets falls, the demand for foreign currency will also fall.

If the devaluation is large enough to reverse the currency demand in the Forex, generating excess demand for the domestic currency, the central bank will have to buy foreign reserves to maintain the new devalued exchange rate and can begin to accumulate a stockpile of reserves once again.

Capital Flight

Balance of payments crises are often anticipated by investors in the marketplace. When this occurs it will result in capital flight, which in turn is likely to aggravate the balance of payments crisis. Here's why.

The interest rate parity condition holds when rates of return on domestic and foreign assets are equalized. Recall from Chapter 11 "Fixed Exchange Rates", Section 11.3 "Interest Rate Parity with Fixed Exchange Rates" that in a fixed exchange rate system the IRP condition simplifies to equalization of interest rates between two countries. However, this result assumed that investors expected the currency to remain fixed indefinitely. If investors believe instead that a country is about to suffer a balance of payments crisis and run out of foreign reserves, they will also anticipate that a devaluation will occur soon.

Assume as before that the United States fixes its currency to the British pound. The interest rate parity condition can be written as

where the left side is the rate of return on U.S. assets, equal to the average U.S. interest rate, and the right side is the rate of return on British assets. When there is no imminent balance of payments crisis, investors should expect the future exchange rate ($E_{\$/£}^{e}$) to equal the current fixed exchange rate ($E_{\$/£}$) and the interest parity condition simplifies to $i_{\$} = i_{£}$. However, if investors recognize that the central bank is selling large quantities of its foreign reserves in the Forex regularly, then they are likely also to recognize that the balance of payments deficits are unsustainable. Once the reserves run out, the central bank will be forced to devalue its currency. Thus forward-looking investors should plan for that event today. The result is an increase in the expected exchange rate, above the current fixed rate, reflecting the expectation that the dollar will be devalued soon.

This, in turn, will increase the expected rate of return of British assets, raising the right side of the above expression. Now, $RoR_{£} > RoR_{\$}$, and investors will increase demand for British pounds on the Forex. In this instance, investors are "fleeing" their own domestic assets to purchase foreign assets (or capital) that now have a greater expected return. Thus the action is called capital flight.

The intuition for capital flight is simple. If an investor expects the domestic currency (and assets denominated in that currency) will soon fall in value, it is better to sell now before the value actually does fall. Also, as the domestic currency falls in value, the British pound is expected to rise in value. Thus it is wise to buy British pounds and assets while their prices are lower and profit on the increase in the pound value when the dollar devaluation occurs.

The broader effect of capital flight, which occurs in anticipation of a balance of payments crisis, is that it can actually force a crisis to occur much sooner. Suppose the United States was indeed running low on foreign reserves after running successive balance of payments deficits. Once investors surmise that a crisis may be possible soon and react with a change in their expected exchange rate, there will be a resulting increase in demand for pounds on the Forex. This will force the central bank to intervene even further in the Forex by selling foreign pound reserves to satisfy investor demand and to keep the exchange rate fixed. However, additional interventions imply an even faster depletion of foreign reserve holdings, bringing the date of crisis closer in time.

It is even possible for investor behavior to create a balance of payments crisis when one might not have occurred otherwise. Suppose the U.S. central bank (or the Fed) depletes reserves by running balance of payments deficits. However, suppose the Fed believes the reserve holdings remain adequate to defend the currency value, whereas investors believe the reserve holdings are inadequate. In this case, capital flight will likely occur that would deplete reserves much faster than before. If the capital flight is large enough, even if it is completely unwarranted based on market conditions, it could nonetheless deplete the remaining reserves and force the central bank to devalue the currency.

Return to Float

There is one other possible response for a country suffering from a balance of payments crisis. The country could always give up on the fixed exchange rate system and allow its currency to float freely. This means the central bank no longer needs to intervene on the Forex and the exchange rate value will be determined by daily supply and demand conditions on the private Forex. Since the reason for the BoP crisis was continual pressure for the currency to depreciate, moving to a floating system would undoubtedly result in a rapidly depreciating currency.

The main advantage of returning to a floating exchange rate is that the private Forex market will quickly move the exchange rate to the level that equalizes supply and demand. In contrast, many times countries that devalue their fixed exchange rate do not devalue sufficiently and a second devaluation becomes necessary shortly thereafter. When the countries in the Bretton Woods system switched to floating rates in 1973, the original intention was to allow markets to adjust to the equilibrium exchange rates reflecting market conditions and then to refix the exchange rates at the sustainable equilibrium level. However, an agreement to reestablish fixed rates was never implemented. The U.S. dollar and many other currencies have been floating ever since.

A second advantage of switching to a floating system is that it relieves the central bank from the necessity of maintaining a stockpile of reserves. Thus the whole problem of balance of payments crises disappears completely once a country lets its currency float.

KEY TAKEAWAYS

- A fixed exchange rate is sustainable if the country's central bank can maintain that rate over time with only modest interventions in the Forex.
- A balance of payments crisis occurs when persistent balance of payments deficits bring a country close to running out of foreign exchange reserves.

- BoP crises can be resolved by (a) borrowing foreign reserves, (b) devaluation of the currency, or (c) moving to a floating exchange rate.
- In the midst of a BoP crisis, investors often purchase assets abroad in anticipation of an imminent currency devaluation or depreciation. This is known as capital flight.
- Capital flight works to exacerbate the BoP crisis because it results in a more rapid depletion of foreign exchange reserves and makes the crisis more likely to occur.

EXERCISES

- List the three ways in which a balance of payments crisis can be resolved either temporarily or permanently. Which of these methods will be most effective, especially if the country continues to pursue the policies that led to the crisis?
- Explain why capital flight, spurred by the expectation of a currency devaluation, can be a self-fulfilling prophecy.
- If an expected currency devaluation inspires capital flight, explain what might happen if investors expect a currency revaluation.

12.7 CASE STUDY: THE BREAKUP OF THE BRETTON WOODS SYSTEM, 1973

In July 1944, delegates from forty-five of the allied powers engaged in World War II met in Bretton Woods, New Hampshire, in the United States to plan for the economic institutions believed necessary to assist in the reconstruction, development, and growth of the postwar economy. Foremost on the delegates' minds was the instability of the international economic system after World War I, including the experiences of hyperinflation as in Germany in 1922–1923 and the worldwide depression of the 1930s. One element believed necessary to avoid repeating the mistakes of the past was to implement a system of fixed exchange rates. Not only could fixed exchange rates help prevent inflation, but they could also eliminate uncertainties in international transactions and thus serve to promote the expansion of international trade and investment. It was further hoped that economic interconnectedness would make it more difficult for nationalism to reassert itself.

The Bretton Woods system of exchange rates was set up as a gold exchange standard, a cross between a pure gold standard and a reserve currency standard. In a gold exchange standard, one country is singled out to be the reserve currency. In the Bretton Woods case, the currency was the U.S. dollar. The U.S. dollar was fixed to a weight in gold, originally set at 35$ per ounce. The U.S. central bank agreed to exchange dollars for gold on demand, but only with foreign central banks. In a pure gold standard, the central bank would exchange gold for dollars with the general public as well.

The nonreserve countries agreed to fix their currencies to the U.S. dollar or to gold.More accurately, countries agreed to establish a "par value" exchange rate to the dollar and to maintain the exchange to within a 1 percent band around that par value. However, this detail is not an essential part of the story that follows. However, there was no obligation on the part of the nonreserve countries to exchange their currencies for gold. Only the reserve country had that obligation. Instead, the nonreserve-currency countries were obliged to maintain the fixed exchange rate to the U.S. dollar by intervening on the foreign exchange (Forex) market and buying or selling dollars as necessary. In other words, when there was excess demand on the Forex for the home currency in exchange for dollars, the nonreserve central bank would supply their currency and buy dollars, thus running a balance of payments surplus, to maintain the fixity of their exchange rate. Alternatively, when there was excess supply of the home currency, in exchange for dollars, the nonreserve central bank would supply dollars and buy its own currency on the Forex, resulting in a balance of payments deficit. Thus for all nonreserve countries the Bretton Woods system functioned like a reserve currency standard.

One of the problems that typically arises with a reserve currency standard is the persistence of balance of payments (BoP) deficits. BoP deficits require a country to sell its dollar reserves on the Forex market. When these deficits are recurring and large, a country will eventually run out of reserves. When that happens, it will no longer be able to defend its fixed currency value. The likely outcome would be a devaluation, an action that runs counter to the goals of the system, namely to maintain exchange rate stability and to ward off inflationary tendencies.

To provide a safety valve for countries that may face this predicament, the International Monetary Fund (IMF) was established to provide temporary loans to countries to help maintain their fixed exchange rates. Each member country was required to maintain a quota of reserves with the IMF that would then be available to lend to those countries experiencing balance of payments difficulties.

Today the IMF maintains the same quota system and member countries enjoy the same privilege to borrow even though many are no longer maintaining a fixed exchange rate. Instead, many countries borrow from the IMF when they become unable to maintain payments on international debts. Go to the IMF Factsheet for more information about the current quota system.International Monetary Fund, Factsheet, "IMF Quotas," http://www.imf.org/external/np/exr/facts/quotas.htm

The Bretton Woods exchange rate system was an imperfect system that suffered under many strains during its history. Nonetheless, it did achieve fixed exchange rates among its members for almost thirty years. For a more detailed, though brief, account of the history of the system, see Benjamin Cohen's article.Benjamin Cohen, "Bretton Woods System," http://www.polsci.ucsb.edu/faculty/cohen/recent/bretton.html.

We can learn much about the intended workings of the system by studying the system's collapse. The collapse occurred mostly because the United States would not allow its internal domestic policies to be compromised for the sake of the fixed exchange rate system. Here's a brief account of what happened. For a more detailed account, see Barry Eichengreen's Globalizing CapitalBarry Eichengreen, Globalizing Capital: A History of the International Monetary System (Princeton, NJ: Princeton University Press, 1996). and Alfred Eckes's A Search for Solvency.Alfred E. Eckes Jr., A Search for Solvency (Austin, TX: University of Texas Press, 1975).

Throughout the 1960s and early 1970s, there was excessive supply of U.S. dollars on Forex markets in exchange for other currencies. This put pressure on the U.S. dollar to depreciate and nonreserve currencies to appreciate. To maintain the fixed exchange rate, nonreserve countries were required to intervene on the private Forex. For example, the British central bank was required to run a balance of payments surplus, buy the excess dollars, and sell pounds on the private Forex market.

As was shown in Chapter 12, Section 12.6 , persistent balance of payments surpluses do not pose a long-term problem in the same way as BoP deficits. The British central bank had an unlimited capacity to "print" as many pounds as necessary to buy the oversupplied dollars on the Forex. However, persistently large BoP surpluses will result in an ever-increasing British money supply that will lead to inflationary effects eventually.

Indeed, U.S. inflation was rising, especially in the late 1960s. Federal government spending was rising quickly—first, to finance the Vietnam War, and second, to finance new social spending arising out of President Johnson's Great Society initiatives. Rather than increasing taxes to finance the added expenses, the United States resorted to expansionary monetary policy, effectively printing money to finance growing government budget deficits. This is also called "monetizing the debt."

The immediate financial impact of a rising U.S. money supply was lower U.S. interest rates, leading to extra demand for foreign currency by investors to take advantage of the higher relative rates of return outside the United States. The longer-term impact of a rising U.S. money supply was inflation. As U.S. prices rose, U.S. goods became relatively more expensive relative to foreign goods, also leading to extra demand for foreign currency.

A look at the statistics of the 1960s belies this story of excessive monetary expansion and fiscal imprudence. Between 1959 and 1970, U.S. money supply growth and U.S. inflation were lower than in every other G-7 country. U.S. government budget deficits were also not excessively large. Nonetheless, as Eichengreen suggests, the G-7 countries could support a much higher inflation rate than the United States since they were starting from such low levels of GDP in the wake of post–World War II reconstruction.Barry Eichengreen, Globalizing Capital: A History of the International Monetary System (Princeton, NJ: Princeton University Press, 1996), 131. Thus the U.S. policy required to maintain a stable exchange rate without intervention would correspond to an inflation rate that was considerably lower vis-à-vis the other G7-countries.

In any case, to maintain the fixed exchange rate, non-U.S. countries' central banks needed to run balance of payments surpluses. BoP surpluses involved a nonreserve central bank purchase of dollars and sale of their own domestic currency. Thus the German, British, French, Japanese, et al., central banks bought up dollars in great quantities and at the same time continually increased their own domestic money supplies.

One effect of the continual balance of payments surpluses was a subsequent increase in inflation caused by rising money supplies in the nonreserve countries. In effect, expansionary monetary policy in the United States, and its inflationary consequences, are exported to the nonreserve countries by virtue of the fixed exchange rate system. This effect was not welcomed by the nonreserve countries like Britain, France, and Germany.

A second effect of the continual balance of payments surpluses was a rising stock of dollar reserves. Nonreserve central banks held those reserves in the form of U.S. Treasury bills; thus, increasingly, U.S. government debt was held by foreign countries.

Although such BoP surpluses could technically continue indefinitely, the inflationary consequences in Europe and Japan and the rising dollar holdings abroad put the sustainability of the system into question. Ideally in a fixed exchange system, BoP surpluses will be offset with comparable BoP deficits over time, if the exchange rate is fixed at an appropriate (i.e., sustainable) level. Continual BoP surpluses, however, indicate that the sustainable exchange rate should be at a much lower U.S. dollar value if the surpluses are to be eliminated. Recognition of this leads observers to begin to expect a dollar devaluation.

If (or when) a dollar devaluation occurred, dollar asset holdings by foreigners—including the U.S. government Treasury bills comprising the reserves held by foreign central banks—would suddenly fall in value. In other words, foreign asset holders would lose a substantial amount of money if the dollar were devalued.

For private dollar investors there was an obvious response to this potential scenario: divest of dollar assets—that is, sell dollars and convert to pounds, deutschmarks, or francs. This response in the late 1960s and early 1970s contributed to the capital flight from the U.S. dollar, put added downward pressure on the U.S. dollar value, and led to even greater BoP surpluses by nonreserve central banks.

The nonreserve central banks, on the other hand, could not simply convert dollars to pounds or francs, as this would add to the pressure for a depreciating dollar. Further, it was their dollar purchases that were preventing the dollar depreciation from happening in the first place.

During the 1960 and early 1970s the amount of U.S. dollar reserves held by nonreserve central banks grew significantly, which led to what became known as the Triffin dilemma (dollar overhang). Robert Triffin was a Belgian economist and Yale University professor who highlighted the problems related to dollar overhang. Dollar overhang occurred when the amount of U.S. dollar assets held by nonreserve central banks exceeded the total supply of gold in the U.S. Treasury at the exchange rate of $35 per ounce. Dollar overhang occurred in the system by 1960 and continued to worsen throughout the decade of the 1960s. By 1971 foreign holdings of U.S. dollars stood at $50 billion while U.S. gold reserves were valued at only $15 billion. Déclaration de Valéry Giscard d'Estaing à l'Assemblée nationale (12 mai 1971), dans La politique étrangère de la France. 1er semestre, octobre 1971, pp. 162–67. Translated by le CVCE [Declaration by Valerie Giscargd'Estaing to the National Assembly (May 12, 1971)].

Under the Bretton Woods system, foreign central banks were allowed to exchange their dollars for gold at the rate of $35 per ounce. Once the dollar overhang problem arose, it became conceivable that the United States could run out of its reserve asset—gold. Thus the potential for this type of BoP deficit could lead to speculation that the U.S. dollar would have to be devalued at some point in the future.

Now, if one expects the dollar will fall in value at some future date, then it would make sense to convert those dollars to something that may hold its value better; gold was the alternative asset. Throughout the 1950s and 1960s, foreign central banks did convert some of their dollar holdings to gold, but not all. In 1948, the United States held over 67 percent of the world's monetary gold reserves. By 1970, however, the U.S. gold holdings had fallen to just 16 percent of the world total.Alfred E. Eckes Jr., A Search for Solvency (Austin, TX: University of Texas Press, 1975), 238. In a gold exchange standard, the linkage between gold and the reserve currency is supposed to provide the constraint that prevents the reserve currency country from excessive monetary expansion and its subsequent inflationary effects. However, in the face of BoP deficits leading to a severe depletion of gold reserves, the United States had several adjustment options open.

One option was a devaluation of the dollar. However, this option was not easy to implement. The U.S. dollar could not be devalued with respect to the pound, the franc, or the yen since the United States did not fix its currency to them. (Recall that the other countries were fixed to the dollar.) Thus the only way to realize this type of dollar devaluation was for the other countries to "revalue" their currencies with respect to the dollar. The other "devaluation" option open to the United States was devaluation with respect to gold. In other words, the United States could raise the price of gold to $40 or $50 per ounce or more. However, this change would not change the fundamental conditions that led to the excess supply of dollars. At most, this devaluation would only reduce the rate at which gold flowed out to foreign central banks. Also, since U.S. gold holdings had fallen to very low levels by the early 1970s and since the dollar overhang was substantial, the devaluation would have had to be extremely large to prevent the depletion of U.S. gold reserves.

The other option open to the United States was a change in domestic monetary policy to reduce the excess supply of dollars on the Forex. Recall that money supply increases were high to help finance rising federal deficit spending. A reversal of this policy would mean a substantial reduction in the growth of the money supply. If money supply increases were not available to finance the budget deficit, the government would have to resort to a much more unpopular method of financing—that is, raising taxes or reducing spending.

The unpopularity and internal difficulty of such fiscal and monetary prudence led the United States to resort to other options. One suggestion made repeatedly by the United States was that the nonreserve countries should "revalue" their currencies to the dollar. However, their response was that the fundamental problem was not their fault; therefore, they shouldn't be the ones to implement a solution. Instead, it was the United States that needed to change.

By the spring of 1971, the imbalances in the system reached crisis proportions. In April 1971, the Bundesbank (Germany's central bank) purchased over $3 billion to maintain the fixed exchange rate. In early May, it bought over $2 billion in just two days to maintain the rate. Fearing inflation after such huge purchases, Germany decided to let its currency float to a new value, 8 percent higher than its previous fixed rate. Austria, Holland, and Switzerland quickly followed suit.Alfred E. Eckes Jr., A Search for Solvency (Austin, TX: University of Texas Press, 1975), 261. Despite these revaluations, they were insufficient to stem the excess supply of dollars on the Forex. By August 1971, another major realignment seemed inevitable that substantially increased the pace of dollar capital flight. On August 1971 ,15, President Nixon announced a bold plan for readjustment. The plan had three main aspects:

- A 10 percent import surcharge on all imports was implemented. This tariff would remain in effect until a new international monetary order was negotiated.

- Suspension of dollar convertibility into gold. Foreign central banks would no longer have the option to exchange dollars for gold with the U.S. central bank.
- Wage and price controls were implemented to stem the rising U.S. inflation

The import surcharge meant that an extra 10 percent would be assessed over the existing import tariff. This was implemented to force other countries to the bargaining table where, presumably, they would agree to a multilateral revaluation of their currencies to the dollar. The tax was especially targeted to pressure Japan, which had not revalued its currency as others had done during the previous years, to agree to a revaluation. The 10 percent import tax effectively raised the prices of foreign goods in U.S. markets and would have a similar effect as a 10 percent currency revaluation. The expectation was that the average revaluation necessary to bring the system into balance would be somewhat less than 10 percent, thus an 8 percent revaluation, say, would be less painful to exporters than a 10 percent import tax.

The suspension of dollar-gold convertibility was really the more significant change as it effectively ended the gold exchange standard and marked the death of the Bretton Woods system. With no obligation to exchange gold for dollars, the system essentially was changed to a reserve currency system. Previous constraints on the United States, caused when it runs a BoP deficit and loses gold reserves, were thus eliminated. There was no longer a possibility that the United States could run out of gold.

The wage and price controls, implemented for a ninety-day period, put added pressure on foreign exporters. Being forced to pay a 10 percent surcharge but not being allowed to raise prices meant they would not be allowed to push the tax increase onto consumers.

These three measures together resulted in a rapid renegotiation of the Bretton Woods system, culminating in the Smithsonian Agreement in December 1971. In this agreement, the nonreserve countries accepted an average 8 percent revaluation of their currencies to the dollar in return for the elimination of the import surcharge. They also enlarged the currency bands around the par values from 1 percent to 2.25 percent. By virtue of the revaluations, the dollar naturally became "devalued." The United States also devalued dollars with respect to gold, raising the price to $38 per ounce. However, since the United States did not agree to reopen the gold window, the change in the price of gold was meaningless.

More important, since the United States no longer needed to be concerned about a complete loss of gold reserves, the dollar overhang problem was "solved," and it was free to continue its monetary growth and inflationary policies. During the following year, the United States did just that; within a short time, there arose renewed pressure for the dollar to depreciate from its new par values.

In the end, the Smithsonian Agreement extended the life of Bretton Woods for just over a year. By March 1973, a repeat of the severe dollar outflows in 1971 led to a suspension of Forex trading for almost three weeks. Upon reopening, the major currencies were floating with respect to each other. The Bretton Woods system was dead.

The hope at the time was that floating rates could be allowed for a time to let exchange rates move to their market equilibrium rates. Once stability to the exchange rates was restored, a new fixed exchange rate system could be implemented. However, despite negotiations, an agreement was never reached, and a unified international system of fixed exchange rates has never since been tried.

How Bretton Woods Was Supposed to Work

In theory, a gold-exchange standard can work to provide exchange rate stability and reduce inflationary tendencies. However, it will only work if the reserve currency country maintains prudent monetary policies and if countries follow the rules of the system.

For the nonreserve countries, their task was to avoid balance of payments deficits. These deficits would arise if they pursued excessive expansionary monetary policy. The lower interest rates and eventual inflation would lead to capital flight, creating pressure for the currency to depreciate. To avoid a devaluation, and hence to follow the fixity rule, the nonreserve country would have to contract its money supply to take pressure off its currency and to reverse the BoP deficits.

The problem that usually arises here is that contractionary monetary policies will raise interest rates and eliminate an important source of government budget financing, namely debt monetization (printing money). These changes are likely to result in an increase in taxes, a decrease in government spending, a contraction of the economy, and a loss of jobs. Thus following the rules of the system will sometimes be painful.

However, this was not the source of the Bretton Woods collapse. Instead, it was excessive monetary expansion by the reserve country, the United States. In this case, when the United States expanded its money supply, to finance budget deficits, it caused lower U.S. interest rates and had inflationary consequences. This led to increased demand for foreign currency by investors and traders. However, the United States was not obligated to intervene to maintain the fixed exchange rates since the United States was not fixing to anyone. Rather, it was the obligation of the nonreserve countries to intervene, buy dollars, sell their own currencies, and consequently run BoP surpluses. These surpluses resulted in the growing stock of dollar reserves abroad.

However, if the system had worked properly, foreign central banks would have cashed in their dollar assets for gold reserves long before the dollar overhang problem arose. With diminishing gold reserves, the United States would have been forced (i.e., if it followed the rules of the system) to reverse its expansionary monetary practices. However, as mentioned above, contractionary monetary policies will likely result in higher taxes, lower government spending, a contraction of the economy, and a loss of jobs.

Most countries faced with a choice between a policy that violates international monetary system rules and policies that maintain domestic vitality, even if only temporarily, will usually choose in favor of domestic interests. Of course, this choice will likely have negative longer-term consequences. Price and exchange rate stability will be compromised through these actions, and it will eliminate the benefits that would have come from expanded trade and international investments.

The gold exchange standard might have worked effectively if the United States and the others had committed themselves more intently on following the rules of the system. In the final analysis, what matters is the importance placed on maintaining the integrity of the cooperative fixed exchange rate system relative to the importance placed on domestic economic and political concerns. In the Bretton Woods case, domestic interests clearly dominated international interests.

The Bretton Woods experience should cast a shadow of doubt on fixed exchange rate systems more generally too. Every fixed exchange rate system requires countries to give up the independence of their monetary policy regardless of domestic economic circumstances. That this is difficult, or impossible, to do is demonstrated by the collapse of the Bretton Woods system.

KEY TAKEAWAYS

- The Bretton Woods system of exchange rates was set up as a gold exchange standard. The U.S. dollar was the reserve currency, and the dollar was fixed to gold at $35 per ounce.
- The International Monetary Fund (IMF) was established to provide temporary loans to countries to help maintain their fixed exchange rates.
- U.S. expansionary monetary policy and its inflationary consequences were exported to the nonreserve countries by virtue of the fixed exchange rate system.
- The suspension of dollar-gold convertibility in 1971 effectively ended the gold exchange standard and marked the death of the Bretton Woods system.
- The Bretton Woods system collapsed in 1973 when all the currencies were allowed to float.

- A fixed exchange rate system requires nonreserve countries to give up the independence of their monetary policy regardless of domestic economic circumstances.

EXERCISE

- Jeopardy Questions:As in the popular television game show, you are given an answer to a question and you must respond with the question. For example, if the answer is "a tax on imports," then the correct question is "What is a tariff?"
- The Bretton Woods exchange system was this type of exchange rate standard.
- The price of gold in terms of dollars when the Bretton Woods system began.
- This international organization was created to help countries with balance of payments problems in the Bretton Woods system.
- The percentage of world monetary gold held by the United States in 1948.
- The percentage of world monetary gold held by the United States in 1970.
- The name given to the problem of excessive U.S. dollar holdings by foreign central banks.
- This country's suspension of dollar convertibility to gold eliminated an important constraint that allowed the system to function properly.
- The name of the agreement meant to salvage the Bretton Woods system in the early 1970s.
- The month and year in which the Bretton Woods system finally collapsed.

CHAPTER 13

FLOATING AS COMPARED TO FIXED EXCHANGE RATES

INTRODUCTION

One of the big issues in international finance is the appropriate choice of a monetary system. Countries can choose between a floating exchange rate system and a variety of fixed exchange rate systems. Which system is better is explored in this chapter. However, rather than suggesting a definitive answer, the chapter highlights the pros and cons of each type of system, arguing in the end that both systems can and have worked in some circumstances and failed in others.

13.1 FIXED VERSUS FLOATING EXCHANGE RATES: AN OVERVIEW

This chapter addresses what is perhaps the most important policy issue in international finance: to have fixed or floating exchange rates. The chapter focuses on three main features that affect the choice of system: volatility and risk, inflationary consequences, and monetary autonomy.

Volatility and risk refers to the tendency for exchange rates to change and the effect these changes have on the risk faced by traders and investors. Although in floating exchange systems volatility is a natural day-to-day occurrence, even in fixed exchange systems, devaluations or revaluations make volatility an issue. This chapter compares the two systems in light of this issue.

Inflationary consequences are shown to be a major potential problem for countries with floating exchange rates. For many countries facing this problem, fixed exchange rate systems can provide relief. The section shows that the relationship between inflation and the exchange rate system is an important element in the choice of system.

Finally, monetary autonomy, and the ability to control the economy, is lost with the choice of fixed exchange rates. We discuss why this loss of autonomy can be problematic in some circumstances but not in others.

The chapter concludes by providing some answers to the policy question, "fixed or floating?"

KEY TAKEAWAYS

- Three main features affect the choice of the exchange rate system: volatility and risk, inflationary consequences, and monetary autonomy.
- The choice between fixed and floating exchange rates is one of the most important policy decisions in international finance.

EXERCISE

- Jeopardy Questions: As in the popular television game show, you are given an answer to a question and you must respond with the question. For example, if the answer is "a tax on imports," then the correct question is "What is a tariff?"
- The choice between these two types of exchange rate systems is an important policy debate in international finance.
- This term describing the extent to which an exchange rate may vary over time is an important consideration in the choice of exchange rate systems.
- This term describing the likelihood of losing money is an important consideration in the choice of exchange rate systems.
- Fixed exchange rates are sometimes chosen to mitigate this kind of general price problem.
- This term describing the ability to influence the economy through monetary policy is an important consideration in the choice of exchange rate systems.

13.2 EXCHANGE RATE RISK AND

Probably the most important characteristic of alternative exchange rate systems is the feature used to describe them, namely fixed or floating. Fixed exchange rates, by definition, are not supposed to change. They are meant to remain fixed, preferably permanently. Floating rates float up and down and down and up from year to year, week to week, and minute by minute. What a floating exchange rate will be a year from now, or even a week from now, is often very difficult to predict.

Volatility represents the degree to which a variable changes over time. The larger the magnitude of a variable change, or the more quickly it changes ov1er time, the more volatile it is.

Since fixed exchange rates are not supposed to change—by definition—they have no volatility. Please note the cautious wording because fixed exchange rates are quite frequently devalued or revalued, implying that they can and do indeed change. However, we will explore this issue in more detail later. A floating exchange rate may or may not be volatile depending on how much it changes over time. However, since floating exchange rates are free to change, they are usually expected to be more volatile.

Volatile exchange rates make international trade and investment decisions more difficult because volatility increases exchange rate risk. Exchange rate risk refers to the potential to lose money because of a change in the exchange rate. Below are two quick examples of how traders and investors may lose money when the exchange rate changes.

Exchange Rate Risk for Traders

First consider a business that imports soccer balls into the United States. Suppose one thousand soccer balls purchased from a supplier in Pakistan costs 300,000 Pakistani rupees. At the current exchange rate of 60 Rs/$, it will cost the importer $5,000 dollars or $5 per soccer ball. The importer determines that transportation, insurance, advertising, and retail costs will run about $5 per soccer ball. If the competitive market price for this type of soccer ball is $12, he will make a $2 profit per ball if all balls are sold.

Suppose the shipment is scheduled to occur in three months and that payment for the shipment need not be made until that time. Let's assume the importer waits to convert currency until the payment is made and that in three months' time the Pakistani rupee has appreciated to a new value of 55 Rs/$. The shipment cost in rupees remains the same at Rs 300,000, but the dollar value of the shipment rises to $5,454 or $5.45 per soccer ball. Assuming the same $5 of extra costs and a $12 final sale price, the importer will now make only $1.45 profit per soccer ball, if all balls are sold. While this is still a profit, it is about 25 percent less than expected when the decision to purchase was made three months before.

This is an example of the risk an importer faces because of a change in the currency value. Of course, it is true that the currency value could have changed in the opposite direction. Had the rupee value risen to 65 Rs/$, the shipment value would have cost just $4,615, or $4.62 per ball, generating a profit of $2.38 per soccer ball. In this case, the currency moves in the importer's favor. Thus a volatile exchange rate will sometimes lead to greater losses than expected, and at other times, to greater gains.

There are several methods to protect oneself from this type of currency risk. The importer could have exchanged currency at the time the deal was struck and held his 300,000 rupees in a Pakistani bank until payment is made. However, this involves a substantial additional opportunity cost since the funds must be available beforehand and become unusable while they are held in a Pakistani bank account. Alternatively, the importer may be able to find a bank willing to write a forward exchange contract, fixing an exchange rate today for an exchange to be made three months from now.

In any case, it should be clear that exchange rate fluctuations either increase the risk of losses relative to plans or increase the costs to protect against those risks.

Exchange Rate Risk for Investors

Volatile exchange rates also create exchange rate risk for international investors. Consider the following example. Suppose in October 2004, a U.S. resident decides to invest (i.e., save) $10,000 for the next year. Given that the U.S. dollar had been weakening with respect to the Danish krone for several years and since the interest rate on a money market deposit was slightly higher in Denmark at 2.25 percent compared to the 1.90 percent return in the United States, the investor decides to put the $10,000 into the Danish account. At the time of the deposit, the exchange rate sits at 5.90 kr/$. In October 2005, the depositor cashes in and converts the money back to U.S. dollars. The exchange rate in October 2005 was 6.23 kr/$. To determine the return on then apply the rate of return formula derived in Chapter 4 , Section 4.3 and Chapter 4 , Section 4.4 .

The rate of return works out to be negative, which means that instead of making money on the foreign deposit, this investor actually loses $317. Had he deposited the $10,000 in a U.S. account, he would have had a guaranteed return of 1.90 percent, earning him $190 instead.

By depositing in a foreign account, the depositor subjected himself to exchange rate risk. The dollar unexpectedly appreciated during the year, resulting in a loss. Had the dollar remain fixed in value during that same time, the foreign return would have been 2.25 percent, which is larger than that obtained in the United States.

Thus fluctuating exchange rates make it more difficult for investors to know the best place to invest. One cannot merely look at what the interest rate is across countries but must also speculate about the exchange rate change. Make the wrong guess about the exchange rate movement and one could lose a substantial amount of money.

There are some ways to hedge against exchange rate risk. For example, with short-term deposits, an investor can purchase a forward contract or enter a futures market. In these cases, the investor would arrange to sell Danish krone in the future when the deposit is expected to be converted back to dollars. Since the future exchange rate is predetermined on such a contract, the rate of return is guaranteed as well. Thus the risk of floating exchange rates can be reduced. However, for long-term investment such as foreign direct investment, these types of arrangements are more difficult and costly to implement.

Volatility and the Choice of Exchange Rate System

On the face of it, floating exchange rates would appear to be riskier than fixed rates since they are free to change regularly. For this reason, countries may choose fixed exchange rates to reduce volatility and thus to encourage international trade and investment.

The problem with this perception is that it has not worked out this way in practice. A 2004 International Monetary Fund (IMF) studyPeter Clark, Natalia Tamirisa, and Shang-Jin Wei, "Exchange Rate Volatility and Trade Flows—Some New Evidence," International Monetary Fund, May 2004[0], http://www.imf.org/external/np/res/exrate/2004/eng/051904.pdf. notes that on average, during the 1970s, 1980s, and 1990s, the volatility of fixed exchange rates was approximately the same as that of floating rates. There are two reasons this can occur. First, a currency fixed to another reserve currency will continue to float against other currencies. Thus when China pegged its currency to the U.S. dollar, it continued to float with the dollar vis-à-vis the euro. Second, it is common for fixed currencies to be devalued or revalued periodically, sometimes dramatically. When this happens, the effects of volatility are concentrated in a very short time frame and can have much larger economic impacts.

The second thing noted by this study is that volatility had only a small effect on bilateral international trade flows, suggesting that the choice of exchange rate system on trade flows may be insignificant. However, the study does not consider the effects of volatility on international investment decisions. Other studies do show a negative relationship between exchange rate volatility and foreign direct investment. But if these results were true and fixed exchange rates are just as volatile as floating rates, then there is no obvious exchange system "winner" in terms of the effects on volatility. Nevertheless, volatility of exchange rate systems remains something to worry about and consider in the choice of exchange rate systems.

KEY TAKEAWAYS

- Volatile exchange rates make international trade and investment decisions more difficult because volatility increases exchange rate risk.
- Volatile exchange rates can quickly and significantly change the expected rates of return on international investments.
- Volatile exchange rates can quickly and significantly change the profitability of importing and exporting.
- Despite the expectation that fixed exchange rates are less volatile, a 2004 IMF study notes that on average, during the 1970s, 1980s, and 1990s, the volatility of fixed exchange rates was approximately the same as that of floating rates.

EXERCISES

- Jeopardy Questions: As in the popular television game show, you are given an answer to a question and you must respond with the question. For example, if the answer is "a tax on imports," then the correct question is "What is a tariff?"

- This term describes the unpredictable movement of an exchange rate.
- Of increase, decrease, or no change, the effect on an importer's profits if he waits to exchange currency and the foreign currency rises in value vis-à-vis the domestic currency in the meantime.
- Of increase, decrease, or no change, the effect on an importer's profits if he waits to exchange currency and the domestic currency falls in value vis-à-vis the foreign currency in the meantime.
- Of increase, decrease, or no change, the effect on an investor's rate of return on foreign assets if the foreign currency rises in value more than expected vis-à-vis the domestic currency after purchasing a foreign asset.
- Of increase, decrease, or no change, the effect on an investor's rate of return on foreign assets if the foreign currency falls in value less than expected vis-à-vis the domestic currency after purchasing a foreign asset.
- Between 2007 and 2008, the U.S. dollar depreciated significantly against the euro. Answer the following questions. Do not use graphs to explain. A one- or two-sentence verbal explanation is sufficient.
- Explain whether European businesses that compete against U.S. imports gain or lose because of the currency change.
- Explain whether European businesses that export their products to the United States gain or lose because of the currency change.
- Explain whether European investors who purchased U.S. assets one year ago gain or lose because of the currency change.

13.3 EXCHANGE RATE SYSTEMS' INFLATIONARY EFFECTS

One important reason to choose a system of fixed exchange rates is to try to dampen inflationary tendencies. Many countries have (over time) experienced the following kind of situation. The government faces pressure from constituents to increase spending and raise transfer payments, which it does. However, it does not finance these expenditure increases with higher taxes since this is very unpopular. This leads to a sizeable budget deficit that can grow over time. When the deficits grow sufficiently large, the government may become unable to borrow additional money without raising the interest rate on bonds to unacceptably high levels. An easy way out of this fiscal dilemma is to finance the public deficits with purchases of bonds by the country's central bank. In this instance, a country will be financing the budget deficit by monetizing the debt, also known as printing money. New money means an increase in the domestic money supply, which will have two effects.

The short-term effect will be to lower interest rates. With free capital mobility, a reduction in interest rates will make foreign deposits relatively more attractive to investors and there is likely to be an increase in supply of domestic currency on the foreign exchange market. If floating exchange rates are in place, the domestic currency will depreciate with respect to other currencies. The long-term effect of the money supply increase will be inflation, if the gross domestic product (GDP) growth does not rise fast enough to keep up with the increase in money. Thus we often see countries experiencing a rapidly depreciating currency together with a rapid inflation rate. A good example of this trend was seen in Turkey during the 1980s and 1990s.

One effective way to reduce or eliminate this inflationary tendency is to fix one's currency. A fixed exchange rate acts as a constraint that prevents the domestic money supply from rising too rapidly. Here's how it works.

Suppose a country fixes its currency to another country—a reserve country. Next, imagine that the same circumstances from the story above begin to occur. Rising budget deficits lead to central bank financing, which increases the money supply of the country. As the money supply rises, interest rates decrease and investors begin to move savings abroad, and so there is an increase in supply of the domestic currency on the foreign exchange market. However, now the country must prevent the depreciation of the currency since it has a fixed exchange rate. This means that the increase in supply of domestic currency by private investors will be purchased by the central bank to balance supply and demand at the fixed exchange rate. The central bank will be running a balance of payments deficit in this case, which will result in a reduction in the domestic money supply.

This means that as the central bank prints money to finance the budget deficit, it will simultaneously need to run a balance of payments deficit, which will soak up domestic money. The net effect on the money supply should be such as to maintain the fixed exchange rate with the money supply rising proportionate to the rate of growth in the economy. If the latter is true, there will be little to no inflation occurring. Thus a fixed exchange rate system can eliminate inflationary tendencies.

Of course, for the fixed exchange rate to be effective in reducing inflation over a long period, it will be necessary that the country avoid devaluations. Devaluations occur because the central bank runs persistent balance of payments deficits and is about to run out of foreign exchange reserves. Once the devaluation occurs, the country will be able to support a much higher level of money supply that in turn will have a positive influence on the inflation rate. If devaluations occur frequently, then it is almost as if the country is on a floating exchange rate system in which case there is no effective constraint on the money supply and inflation can again get out of control.

To make the fixed exchange rate system more credible and to prevent regular devaluation, countries will sometime use a currency board arrangement. With a currency board, there is no central bank with discretion over policy. Instead, the country legislates an automatic exchange rate intervention mechanism that forces the fixed exchange rate to be maintained.

For even more credibility, countries such as Ecuador and El Salvador have dollarized their currencies. In these cases, the country simply uses the other country's currency as its legal tender and there is no longer any ability to print money or let one's money supply get out of control.

However, in other circumstances fixed exchange rates have resulted in more, rather than less, inflation. In the late 1960s and early 1970s, much of the developed world was under the Bretton Woods system of fixed exchange rates. The reserve currency was the U.S. dollar, meaning that all other countries fixed their currency value to the U.S. dollar. When rapid increases in the U.S. money supply led to a surge of inflation in the United States, the other nonreserve countries like Britain, Germany, France, and Japan were forced to run balance of payments surpluses to maintain their fixed exchange rates. These BoP surpluses raised these countries' money supplies, which in turn led to an increase in inflation. Thus, in essence, U.S. inflation was exported to many other countries because of the fixed exchange rate system.

The lesson from these stories is that sometimes fixed exchange rates tend to lower inflation while at other times they tend to increase it. The key is to fix your currency to something that is not likely to rise in value (inflate) too quickly. In the 1980 and 1990s, when the European Exchange Rate Mechanism (ERM) was in place, countries were in practice fixed to the German deutschmark. Since the German central bank was probably the least prone to inflationary tendencies, all other European countries were able to bring their inflation rates down substantially due to the ERM system. However, had the countries fixed to the Italian lira, inflation may have been much more rapid throughout Europe over the two decades.

Many people propose a return to the gold standard precisely because it fixes a currency to something that is presumed to be steadier in value over time. Under a gold standard, inflation would be tied to the increase in monetary gold stocks. Because gold is strictly limited in physical quantity, only a limited amount can be discovered and added to gold stocks each year, Thus inflation may be adequately constrained. But because of other problems with a return to gold as the monetary support, a return to this type of system seems unlikely.

KEY TAKEAWAYS

- A fixed exchange rate can act as a constraint to prevent the domestic money supply from rising too rapidly (i.e., if the reserve currency country has noninflationary monetary policies).

- Adoption of a foreign country's currency as your own is perhaps the most credible method of fixing the exchange rate.
- Sometimes, as in the Bretton Woods system, a fixed exchange rate system leads to more inflation. This occurs if the reserve currency country engages in excessively expansionary monetary policy.
- A gold standard is sometimes advocated precisely because it fixes a currency to something (i.e., gold) that is presumed to be more steady in value over time.

EXERCISE

- Jeopardy Questions: As in the popular television game show, you are given an answer to a question and you must respond with the question. For example, if the answer is "a tax on imports," then the correct question is "What is a tariff?"
- Hyperactivity in this aggregate variable is often a reason countries turn to fixed exchange rates.
- If a country fixes its exchange rate, it effectively imports this policy from the reserve country.
- A country fixing its exchange rate can experience high inflation if this country also experiences high inflation.
- Of relatively low or relatively high, to limit inflation a country should choose to fix its currency to a country whose money supply growth is this.
- The name for the post–World War II exchange rate system that demonstrated how countries fixing their currency could experience high inflation.

13.4 EXCHANGE RATE AND MONETARY AUTONOMY

Monetary autonomy refers to the independence of a country's central bank to affect its own money supply and conditions in its domestic economy. In a floating exchange rate system, a central bank is free to control the money supply. It can raise the money supply when it wishes to lower domestic interest rates to spur investment and economic growth. By doing so it may also be able to reduce a rising unemployment rate. Alternatively, it can lower the money supply, to raise interest rates and to try to choke off excessive growth and a rising inflation rate. With monetary autonomy, monetary policy is an available tool the government can use to control the performance of the domestic economy. This offers a second lever of control, beyond fiscal policy.

In a fixed exchange rate system, monetary policy becomes ineffective because the fixity of the exchange rate acts as a constraint. As shown in Chapter 12 , Section 12.2, when the money supply is raised, it will lower domestic interest rates and make foreign assets temporarily more attractive. This will lead domestic investors to raise demand for foreign currency that would result in a depreciation of the domestic currency, if a floating exchange rate were allowed. However, with a fixed exchange rate in place, the extra demand for foreign currency will need to be supplied by the central bank, which will run a balance of payments deficit and buy up its own domestic currency. The purchases of domestic currency in the second stage will perfectly offset the increase in money in the first stage, so that no increase in money supply will take place.

Thus the requirement to keep the exchange rate fixed constrains the central bank from using monetary policy to control the economy. In other words, the central bank loses its autonomy or independence.

In substitution, however, the government does have a new policy lever available in a fixed system that is not available in a floating system, namely exchange rate policy. Using devaluations and revaluations, a country can effectively raise or lower the money supply level and affect domestic outcomes in much the same way as it might with monetary policy. However, regular exchange rate changes in a fixed system can destroy the credibility in the government to maintain a truly "fixed" exchange rate. This in turn could damage the effect fixed exchange rates might have on trade and investment decisions and on the prospects for future inflation.

Nonetheless, some countries do apply a semifixed or semifloating exchange rate system. A crawling peg, in which exchange rates are adjusted regularly, is one example. Another is to fix the exchange rate within a band. In this case, the central bank will have the ability to control the money supply, up or down, within a small range, but will not be free to make large adjustments without breaching the band limits on the exchange rate. These types of systems provide an intermediate degree of autonomy for the central bank.

If we ask which is better, monetary autonomy or a lack of autonomy, the answer is mixed. In some situations, countries need, or prefer, to have monetary autonomy. In other cases, it is downright dangerous for a central bank to have autonomy. The determining factor is whether the central bank can maintain prudent monetary policies. If the central bank can control money supply growth such that it has only moderate inflationary tendencies, then monetary autonomy can work well for a country. However, if the central bank cannot control money supply growth, and if high inflation is a regular occurrence, then monetary autonomy is not a blessing.

One of the reasons Britain has decided not to join the eurozone is because it wants to maintain its monetary autonomy. By joining the eurozone, Britain would give up its central bank's ability to control its domestic money supply since euros would circulate instead of British pounds. The amount of euros in circulation is determined by the European Central Bank (ECB). Although Britain would have some input into money supply determinations, it would clearly have much less influence than it would for its own currency. The decisions of the ECB would also reflect the more general concerns of the entire eurozone rather than simply what might be best for Britain. For example, if there are regional disparities in economic growth (e.g., Germany, France, etc., are growing rapidly, while Britain is growing much more slowly), the ECB may decide to maintain a slower money growth policy to satisfy the larger demands to slow growth and subsequent inflation in the continental countries. The best policy for Britain alone, however, might be a more rapid increase in money supply to help stimulate its growth. If Britain remains outside the eurozone, it remains free to determine the monetary policies it deems best for itself. If it joins the eurozone, it loses its monetary autonomy.

In contrast, Argentina suffered severe hyperinflations during the 1970s and 1980s. Argentina's central bank at the time was not independent of the rest of the national government. To finance large government budget deficits, Argentina resorted to running the monetary printing presses, which led to the severe hyperinflations. In this case, monetary autonomy was a curse, not a blessing.

In an attempt to restrain the growth of the money supply, Argentina imposed a currency board in 1992. A currency board is a method of fixing one's exchange rate with a higher degree of credibility. By legislating mandatory automatic currency interventions, a currency board operates in place of a central bank and effectively eliminates the autonomy that previously existed. Although Argentina's currency board experiment collapsed in 2002, for a decade Argentina experienced the low inflation that had been so elusive during previous decades.

KEY TAKEAWAYS

- Monetary autonomy refers to the independence of a country's central bank to affect its own money supply and, through that, conditions in its domestic economy.
- In a fixed exchange rate system, a country maintains the same interest rate as the reserve country. As a result, it loses the ability to use monetary policy to control outcomes in its domestic economy.
- In a floating exchange rate system, a country can adjust its money supply and interest rates freely and thus can use monetary policy to control outcomes in its domestic economy.
- If the central bank can control money supply growth such that it has only moderate inflationary tendencies, then monetary autonomy (floating) can work well for a country. However, if the central bank cannot control money supply growth, and if high inflation is a regular occurrence, then monetary autonomy (floating) will not help the country.

EXERCISE

- Jeopardy Questions: As in the popular television game show, you are given an answer to a question and you must respond with the question. For example, if the answer is "a tax on imports," then the correct question is "What is a tariff?"
- The term describing the relationship between the U.S. Federal Reserve Board and the U.S. government that has quite likely contributed to the low U.S. inflation rate in the past two decades.
- In part to achieve this, the United Kingdom has refused to adopt the euro as its currency.
- Of fixed or floating, in this system a country can effectively set its money supply at any level desired.
- Of fixed or floating, in this system a country's interest rate will always be the same as the reserve country's.
- Of fixed or floating, in this system a country can control inflation by maintaining moderate money supply growth.

13.5 WHICH IS PREFERABLE, FLOATING OR FIXED EXCHANGE RATES?

The exchange rate is one of the key international aggregate variables studied in an international finance course. It follows that the choice of exchange rate system is one of the key policy questions.

Countries have been experimenting with different international payment and exchange systems for a very long time. In early history, all trade was barter exchange, meaning goods were traded for other goods. Eventually, especially scarce or precious commodities, for example gold and silver, were used as a medium of exchange and a method for storing value. This practice evolved into the metal standards that prevailed in the nineteenth and early twentieth centuries. By default, since gold and silver standards imply fixed exchange rates between countries, early experience with international monetary systems was exclusively with fixed systems. Fifty years ago, international textbooks dealt almost entirely with international adjustments under a fixed exchange rate system since the world had had few experiences with floating rates.

That experience changed dramatically in 1973 with the collapse of the Bretton Woods fixed exchange rate system. At that time, most of the major developed economies allowed their currencies to float freely, with exchange values being determined in a private market based on supply and demand, rather than by government decree. Although when Bretton Woods collapsed, the participating countries intended to resurrect a new improved system of fixed exchange rates, this never materialized. Instead, countries embarked on a series of experiments with different types of fixed and floating systems.

For example, the European Economic Community (now the EU) implemented the exchange rate mechanism in 1979, which fixed each other's currencies within an agreed band. These currencies continued to float with non-EU countries. By 2000, some of these countries in the EU created a single currency, the euro, which replaced the national currencies and effectively fixed the currencies to each other immutably.

Some countries have fixed their currencies to a major trading partner, and others fix theirs to a basket of currencies comprising several major trading partners. Some have implemented a crawling peg, adjusting the exchange values regularly. Others have implemented a dirty float where the currency value is mostly determined by the market but periodically the central bank intervenes to push the currency value up or down depending on the circumstances. Lastly, some countries, like the United States, have allowed an almost pure float with central bank interventions only on rare occasions.

Unfortunately, the results of these many experiments are mixed. Sometimes floating exchange rate systems have operated flawlessly. At other times, floating rates have changed at breakneck speed, leaving traders, investors, and governments scrambling to adjust to the volatility. Similarly, fixed rates have at times been a salvation to a country, helping to reduce persistent inflation. At other times, countries with fixed exchange rates have been forced to import excessive inflation from the reserve country.

No one system has operated flawlessly in all circumstances. Hence, the best we can do is to highlight the pros and cons of each system and recommend that countries adopt that system that best suits its circumstances.

Probably the best reason to adopt a fixed exchange rate system is to commit to a loss in monetary autonomy. This is necessary whenever a central bank has been independently unable to maintain prudent monetary policy, leading to a reasonably low inflation rate. In other words, when inflation cannot be controlled, adopting a fixed exchange rate system will tie the hands of the central bank and help force a reduction in inflation. Of course, in order for this to work, the country must credibly commit to that fixed rate and avoid pressures that lead to devaluations. Several methods to increase the credibility include the use of currency boards and complete adoption of the other country's currency (i.e., dollarization or euroization). For many countries, for at least a period, fixed exchange rates have helped enormously to reduce inflationary pressures.

Nonetheless, even when countries commit with credible systems in place, pressures on the system sometimes can lead to collapse. Argentina, for example, dismantled its currency board after ten years of operation and reverted to floating rates. In Europe, economic pressures have led to some "talk" about giving up the euro and returning to national currencies. The Bretton Woods system lasted for almost thirty years but eventually collapsed. Thus it has been difficult to maintain a credible fixed exchange rate system for a long period.

Floating exchange rate systems have had a similar colored past. Usually, floating rates are adopted when a fixed system collapses. At the time of a collapse, no one really knows what the market equilibrium exchange rate should be, and it makes some sense to let market forces (i.e., supply and demand) determine the equilibrium rate. One of the key advantages of floating rates is the autonomy over monetary policy that it affords a country's central bank. When used wisely, monetary policy discretion can provide a useful mechanism for guiding a national economy. A central bank can inject money into the system when the economic growth slows or falls, or it can reduce money when excessively rapid growth leads to inflationary tendencies. Since monetary policy acts much more rapidly than fiscal policy, it is a much quicker policy lever to use to help control the economy.

Prudent Monetary and Fiscal Policies

Interestingly, monetary autonomy is both a negative trait for countries choosing fixed rates to rid themselves of inflation and a positive trait for countries wishing have more control over their domestic economies. It turns out that the key to success in both fixed and floating rates hinges on prudent monetary and fiscal policies. Fixed rates are chosen to force a more prudent monetary policy, while floating rates are a blessing for those countries that already have a prudent monetary policy.

A prudent monetary policy is most likely to arise when two conditions are satisfied. First, the central bank, and the decisions it makes, must be independent of the national government that makes government-spending decisions. If it is not, governments have always been inclined to print money to finance government-spending projects. This has been the primary source of high inflation in most countries. The second condition is a clear guideline for the central bank's objective. Ideally, that guideline should broadly convey a sense that monetary policy will satisfy the demands of a growing economy while maintaining sufficiently low inflation. When these conditions are satisfied, autonomy for a central bank and floating exchange rates will function well. Mandating fixed exchange rates can also work well, but only if the system can be maintained and if the country to which the other country fixes its currency has a prudent monetary policy.

Both systems can experience great difficulties if prudent fiscal policies are not maintained. This requires governments to maintain a balanced budget over time. Balance over time does not mean balance in every period but rather that periodic budget deficits should be offset with periodic budget surpluses. In this way, government debt is managed and does not become excessive. It is also critical that governments do not overextend themselves in terms of international borrowing. International debt problems have become the bane of many countries.

Unfortunately, most countries have been unable to accomplish this objective. Excessive government deficits and borrowing are the norm for both developing and developed countries. When excessive borrowing needs are coupled with a lack of central bank independence, tendencies to hyperinflations and exchange rate volatility are common. When excessive borrowing is coupled with an independent central bank and a floating exchange rate, exchange rate volatility is also common.

Stability of the international payments system then is less related to the type of exchange rate system chosen than it is to the internal policies of the individual countries. Prudent fiscal and monetary policies are the keys.

With prudent domestic policies in place, a floating exchange rate system will operate flawlessly. Fixed exchange systems are most appropriate when a country needs to force itself to a more prudent monetary policy course.

KEY TAKEAWAYS

- Historically, no one system has operated flawlessly in all circumstances.
- Probably the best reason to adopt a fixed exchange rate system is whenever a central bank has been independently unable to maintain prudent monetary policy, leading to a reasonably low inflation rate.
- Probably the best reason to adopt a floating exchange rate system is whenever a country has more faith in the ability of its own central bank to maintain prudent monetary policy than any other country's ability.
- The key to success in both fixed and floating rates hinges on prudent monetary and fiscal policies. Fixed rates are chosen to force a more prudent monetary policy; floating rates are a blessing for those countries that already have a prudent monetary policy.

EXERCISE

- Jeopardy Questions: As in the popular television game show, you are given an answer to a question and you must respond with the question. For example, if the answer is "a tax on imports," then the correct question is "What is a tariff?"
- Of fixed or floating, this system is often chosen by countries that in their recent history experienced very high inflation.
- Of fixed or floating, this system is typically chosen when a country has confidence in its own ability to conduct monetary policy effectively.

- Of fixed or floating, this system is typically chosen when a country has little confidence in its own ability to conduct monetary policy effectively.
- Of fixed or floating, this system is sometimes rejected because it involves the loss of national monetary autonomy.
- Of fixed or floating, this system is sometimes chosen because it involves the loss of national monetary autonomy.

INDEX

www.ingramcontent.com/pod-product-compliance
Lightning Source LLC
LaVergne TN
LVHW062112200926
848484LV00007B/1644